AMERICA
IN
SPACE

THE
MAGILL
BIBLIOGRAPHIES

Other Magill Bibliographies:

The American Constitution—Robert J. Janosik
Black American Women Novelists—Craig Werner
Classical Greek and Roman Drama—Robert J. Forman
English Romantic Poetry—Bryan Aubrey
Environmental Studies—Diane McCourt Brown
The Immigrant Experience—Paul D. Mageli
The Modern American Novel—Steven G. Kellman
Twentieth Century European Short Story—Charles E. May
The Victorian Novel—Laurence W. Mazzeno

AMERICA
IN
SPACE

An Annotated Bibliography

Russell R. Tobias

SpaceFlight Editor
Ærospace Educator

SALEM PRESS
Pasadena, California   Englewood Cliffs, New Jersey

Library of Congress Cataloging-in-Publication Data

Tobias, Russell R.
    America in space / Russell R. Tobias.
        p. cm.—(Magill bibliographies)
    Includes index.
    ISBN 0-89356-669-1 (alk. paper)
    1. Astronautics—United   States—Bibliography.   I.
Title. II. Series.
Z5065.U5T6   1991
[TL789.8.U5]   91-13579
016.6294'0973—dc20   CIP

To my wife, Bobbi;
my daughters, Tina, Meghan, and Mollye;
and to the memory of my nephew, Craig.

CONTENTS

EDITORIAL STAFF

ACKNOWLEDGMENTS

It would have been impossible to find and obtain all the works listed in this bibliography without the support and assistance of a large number of persons within the National Aeronautics and Space Administration, the California State Library, the National Technical Information Service, the U.S. Geological Survey, the Library of Congress, and the Government Printing Office. I am most indebted to them.

Special thanks go to Mr. B. Michael Donahoe and Mr. Garth Hull, NASA Ames Research Center; Dr. Richard P. Hallion, U.S. Air Force; Ms. Nancy Lovato and Mr. Don Haley, NASA Ames/Dryden Research Facility; Ms. Lois Lovisolo, Grumman Aerospace Corporation; Mr. Joel K. Harris, Jet Propulsion Laboratory; Mr. Charles A. Biggs and Ms. Bunda L. Dean, NASA Johnson Space Center; Mr. Karl Kristofferson and Ms. Mary Jo Tippett, NASA Kennedy Space Center; Ms. Sharon Hansen, Martin Marietta Michoud Aerospace; Mr. Jeffrey L. Fister, McDonnell Douglas Astronautics Company; Mr. David W. Garrett, Mr. Mark S. Hess, Mr. Chester M. Lee, Ms. Patricia Riep, and Mr. Lee Saegesser, NASA Headquarters; Mr. Thomas L. Hanson, NASA Scientific and Technical Information Facility; Ms. Joyce Lincoln, Rockwell International Rocketdyne Division; Ms. Sue Cometa, Rockwell International Space Systems Group; and Ms. Tina Thompson, TRW, Inc.—Space and Technology Group.

I would like to thank the staff of the Reference Department of the Sonoma County Central Library, Santa Rosa, California, for tolerating my numerous inquiries and for being so cheerful.

Thanks to all of the staff at Salem Press for their contributions to this work and, especially, to Mr. John Wilson for his guidance and his enthusiasm.

Finally, I would like to thank my wife, Bobbi, for her proofreading of the many versions of the manuscript, for giving me the time and space to write, and for the encouragement necessary to complete such an endeavor.

AMERICA
IN
SPACE

INTRODUCTION

For more than thirty years, the United States has been engaged in the exploration of space by manned and unmanned vessels. Each time an advance is made or a temporary setback slows progress, someone will publish a book on the event. Most of these documents were produced by the agency in charge of this exploration, the National Aeronautics and Space Administration (NASA).

NASA was created in 1958, by the National Aeronautics and Space Act, with the provision that "the aeronautical and space activities of the United States shall be conducted so as to contribute . . . to the expansion of human knowledge of phenomena in the atmosphere and in space. The Administration shall provide for the widest practicable and appropriate dissemination of information concerning its activities and the results thereof."

During its first thirty-two years of operation, NASA accomplished more than a hundred aeronautical and astronomical feats thought impossible thirty-two years earlier. The fact that it was not always first to do something does not diminish the fact that it was done. Within a week of its creation on October 1, 1958, NASA was given the task of orbiting a manned spacecraft around Earth. Less than four years later, John Glenn circled the globe three times. Within two weeks of putting the first American into space, NASA was given the task of sending a man to the Moon and returning him safely to Earth. A little more than eight years later, Neil Armstrong and Edwin Aldrin strolled the lunar surface.

Americans have lived and worked in space, off and on, for three decades. During that time they have flown in tiny capsules and a giant Skylab, walked in space and walked (and even driven) on the Moon, deployed satellites and retrieved them. They have spent as little as five minutes in space and as much as eighty-four days. They have conducted experiments, taken photographs, returned lunar soil samples, and hit the longest tee-shot at the Fra Mauro Country Club.

These achievements were not without a price. Fourteen astronauts made the ultimate sacrifice in America's quest for space: Charlie Bassett, Roger Chaffee, Ted Freeman, Gus Grissom, Greg Jarvis, Christa McAuliffe, Ron McNair, Ellison Onizuka, Judy Resnik, Dick Scobee, Elliot See, Mike Smith, Ed White, and C. C. Williams. Though their deaths made the journey a little sadder, they did not deter our ambition. If the progress of manned air flight were comparable to that of manned spaceflight, the Wright brothers would have beaten Charles Lindbergh across the Atlantic by twenty years, and Lucky Lindy would have made the trip in a 747.

Not to be outdone, the unmanned sector of NASA has proven its capability to do the "impossible." Thousands of lives and homes have been saved from storms by the early warning of weather satellites observing from above. We watch live television broadcasts from the other side of the globe and can telephone our friends there, too, thanks to communications satellites. We study natural resources from our lofty observation point and try to figure ways to conserve them. The mysteries of the solar system and the universe have been revealed by robotic probes. By studying our fellow orbiters of the Sun, we are learning more about our own fragile ecosphere. We have also discovered new worlds and, perhaps, an answer to our overcrowded home. NASA has also had its triumphs in aeronautics, developing technology for commercial, private, and military aircraft. Although this technology usually takes a back seat to its extraterrestrial cousins, it helps to provide safer aircraft, more fuel-efficient automobiles, and faster ships.

It is understandable, then, that NASA's publications would play a significant part in a bibliography such as this. Most of the information presented in these documents can be considered to be accurate, since NASA is the primary source of the raw data. It would behoove the researcher to take the word of a NASA document over that of another source. However, if serious doubt exists as to the credibility of a NASA fact, a diligent researcher would be inclined to contact the NASA office responsible for the data for confirmation.

Every attempt has been made to create a comprehensive bibliography of the American space program, but the inclusion of one entry over another has to be a judgment call. A set of criteria was established, based upon content, readability, author bias, and availability.

Since this bibliographer could not possibly be aware of every text available on every aspect of the space program, it is important for any researcher to check the bibliography of every book he or she encounters. Many of the works included here were discovered in the bibliography of another text. The many books in the NASA History Series have outstanding reference listings and source notes relating to each page of the book. In addition to other books, they refer the reader to newspaper and magazine articles, as well as unpublished papers.

Before beginning a project in the study of the space program, the researcher is hereby warned of the dangers involved in the undertaking. It takes a lot of digging to track down one elusive bit of information. Verification is sometimes next to impossible. Where does one start? Well, if you are reading this introduction you have picked an excellent starting point. Decide into which general category your topic fits best—manned or unmanned. Whether you are studying a historical event or the forecasts of some soothsayer, the subject will still fit into one of these categories.

This bibliography is divided into seven sections, each dealing with a specific area or group of related subjects. Since several manned missions have launched unmanned probes and satellites, rendezvoused with them, or interacted with them in some other way, the subject you are investigating may overlap into several categories. For example, the Galileo probe to Jupiter was deployed by the Space Shuttle *Atlantis* during the STS-34 mission in October, 1989. Books about the Galileo mission will be listed under "Interplanetary Probes," while the Shuttle flight will be under "Space Transportation System."

A short list of sources that deal with the space program in general is included at the end of this introduction, followed by an equally short list of sources that deal with space pioneers. For the most part, biographies of these pioneers are included in works about other aspects of the space program. The biography section of the library can provide the researcher with a list of the individual biographies or autobiographies.

The next section, "Propulsion," takes a look at the power necessary to get the spacecraft into their proper orbit or interplanetary trajectory. The launch vehicles and engines of a particular program are usually included in the studies of that program. This section touches upon those vehicles and propulsion units which overlap. An example is the Atlas missile. In addition to being an intercontinental ballistic missile, designed to loft atomic warheads, the Atlas was drafted into peaceful uses: It has launched the *Mercury* spacecraft into orbit and sent the Mariner probes to Mercury, Venus, and Mars.

"Unmanned Vehicles" are covered in the third section and are subdivided into "Lunar Probes," "Interplanetary Probes," and "Applications Satellites." The major lunar exploratory programs—Pioneer, Ranger, Lunar Orbiter, and Surveyor—are given their own subsections, as are the well-known interplanetary probes Pioneer, Mariner, Viking, Voyager, Magellan, Galileo, and Ulysses. Since Earth satellites come in several flavors, they have been categorized by their general mission in space. These categories include astronomical observatories, biosatellites, communications, the Explorer series, military, and remote sensing.

Because of the popularity of the subject, the "Manned Spacecraft" section is the largest. In this section, the reader will find sources of information about astronauts, spacesuits, and space medicine, as well as the experimental disciplines studied by the astronauts, under "Earth Observation," "Astronomy from Space," and "Science in Orbit." One large unit of this section is devoted to "Manned Programs." The programs are presented chronologically and include Project Mercury, the Gemini program, the Apollo program, Skylab, Apollo Soyuz, and the Space Transportation System. Naturally, since the technology spills over into several programs, many works cover several programs.

"The Future" covers a broad spectrum of topics, most of which are included in the "General Studies" section. Projects in the planning stages merit their own categories. They include "Manned Planetary Exploration," the "National Aero-Space Plane," "Space Stations," and "Unmanned Planetary Exploration." The Skylab manned orbiting laboratory has been considered by many to have been the United States' first space station. Although technically Skylab was not a space station (since it was not launched with the capability of being permanently manned or resupplied), some of the works dealing with it have been included in the "Space Stations" section.

Few people realize that their personal computers, Teflon pans, impact-resistant sunglasses, lightweight automobiles, and instant coffee are all byproducts of these programs. The "Impact of Space Exploration" is covered in a separate section, divided into three subsections—"Military Technology," "Private Enterprise in Space," and "Spin-offs." Each year, NASA publishes a book of "Spin-offs."

Although they are not specifically mentioned in this bibliography, a great deal of information arguing in favor of space exploration can be derived from them. Finally, space law and politics play a big role in most programs, since it is politicians who decide which programs get money and which do not. The politics of space exploration are discussed in books about a particular program, but there are several good general studies which needed to be placed in their own subcategory.

The final section of this bibliography deals with the unsung heroes of the space program, the people behind the scenes, the "Earthbound support." They do most of the work and get the least amount of glory. There are two types of facilities under NASA's control: space centers and tracking stations. Most of these space centers are well known, such as the Kennedy Space Center, the Marshall Space Flight Center, the Johnson Space Center, the Ames Research Center, the Goddard Space Flight Center, and the Jet Propulsion Laboratory, to name a few. With the advent of the Tracking and Data Relay Satellite System (TDRSS, pronounced "tea dress"), ground tracking stations are becoming extinct. During the heyday of manned spaceflight, they were the astronauts' and space vehicles' only contact with Earth.

This bibliography is intended for high school and college students, and every effort has been made to include those works that can be found in any good public or college library. Most public libraries also participate in an interlibrary loan program, permitting the reader access to many books not immediately available on the local library's shelves. However, many of the best works are NASA publications and may not be found on the shelves of even the best public libraries. State libraries, usually located in the capital city, are depositories for government publications, as are many state colleges and universities. Congress established the Federal Depository Library Program under the Government Printing Office (GPO), with fifty regional depositories responsible for permanent retention of material, interlibrary loan, and reference services. At least one copy of nearly every NASA publication, in printed or microfiche format, is received and retained by the fifty regional depositories. A list of these depositories is available from the Government Printing Office. A researcher can have access to the publications through the interlibrary loan program.

Most larger public libraries can borrow copies of NASA publications from the regional NASA facility. Some of the documents available are NASA Technical Notes (they have a document number beginning with TN D-), Technical Memorandums (TM-), Special Publications (SP-), Reference Publications (RP-), Conference Publications (CP-), and Technical Papers (TP-). NASA publications are also available to the public for reference purposes at the library maintained by the American Institute of Aeronautics and Astronautics, Technical Information Service, 555 West 57th Street, 12th Floor, New York, NY 10019.

An extensive collection of NASA publications is maintained by the British Library Lending Division, Boston Spa, Wetherby, Yorkshire, England, for public access. European requesters may purchase facsimile copy of microfiche of many NASA documents from the European Space Agency, Information Retrieval Service, 8-10 rue Mario-Nikis, 75738 Paris CEDEX 15, France.

For those who wish to purchase copies of NASA documents, they are available from two main sources. Recent publications can be obtained from the Superintendent of Documents, U.S. Government Printing Office, Washington, DC 20402. Publications are available from the Government Printing Office in hardcopy for a limited time after publication and initial distribution. Photocopies from the original or from microfiche copies are available for older documents from the National Technical Information Service, 5285 Port Royal Road, Springfield, VA 22161.

Some of NASA's documents were not meant for direct public access. This does not mean that the researcher cannot obtain a copy, simply that it may be more difficult to get. These documents include press kits and mission reports. Press kits for individual manned and unmanned spaceflights are published by NASA Headquarters in cooperation with the NASA facility responsible for the mission. Specifications, time lines, and other technical information are provided to the members of the press in order for them to write accurate accounts of the flight. Once a mission has been completed, successfully or otherwise, a Mission Evaluation Team at the responsible facility compiles data into a mission report. These reports detail nearly every aspect of the flight and are an invaluable source of information. Copies of these press kits and mission reports can be obtained from the appropriate NASA facility through the Freedom of Information Act (FOIA).

The Freedom of Information Act of 1966 permits access to any identifiable records of the administrative agencies in the executive branch of the federal government. These records must be released upon written request, unless they fall into one or more of nine exemption categories. NASA regulations specifically state what can and cannot be obtained under the FOIA, but generally speaking, any document can be released. The major exemption encountered is with documents available through some other source, such as the Government Printing Office. The only requirement made of the requester is that the publication be clearly identified. One can request, for example, the STS-29 mission report or the press kit for the Voyager 2 encounter with Uranus. This is usually sufficient for the document to be identified. If a document number is available, it makes the work of the responding office easier. The written request does not have to state the reason for the request. It should be sent to the FOIA Officer at the facility most likely to own a copy of the publication. Press kits can be obtained from NASA Headquarters, while mission reports for manned programs can be obtained from the Johnson Space Center. If the office to which you make the request does not have a copy of the document, you will be informed of its nonexistence or of the office that does have a copy. There is a fee for all of this work. As of December, 1990, the fee is ten cents per letter-size page and $4.50 per quarter hour of research time. If you indicate that you are a private, noncommercial requester and wish to be considered in the category of "all other requesters," there is no charge for the first hundred pages and the first two hours of research time. Specific details of the FOIA can be obtained by contacting NASA.

As with any bibliographic work, this one is by no means an exhaustive list of the titles or topics available. The author does not wish to imply that any books or essays included constitute the entire list of available work on any one subject. The main object of this book is to steer the researcher onto the right path. Many of the works included were being updated as this bibliography was written. Be sure to check a copy of *Books in Print* or any similar reference in your library or bookstore, before settling for an older version of a publication.

Research can be very boring and very tedious. It can also be very rewarding. If the book or essay you have written has been published but was overlooked in this bibliography, please forgive the omission. If you are currently researching a work on the space program, perhaps it will be included in a future edition. It is my sincerest wish that this bibliography will be of some help to you.

General Studies

Benford, Timothy B., and Brian Wilkes. *The Space Program Quiz and Fact Book.* New York: Harper & Row, 1985.
According to astronaut Gus Grissom, what was the most critical part of a mission? "The part between liftoff and splashdown." When asked how well they knew the space program, the authors took the time to find out by collecting some of the most interesting facts about the U.S. space program and putting them in the form of questions and answers. The book is divided into five sections covering manned spaceflights, nicknames and code names, messages and quotes, dreamers and pioneers, and unmanned probes. There are appendices giving brief biographies of the astronauts, details on all manned and unmanned missions, characteristics of the manned spacecraft, and details of some Soviet missions and spacecraft. Provides a glossary of terms, a brief bibliography, and an index.

Bilstein, Roger E. *Orders of Magnitude: A History of the NACA and NASA, 1915-1990.* Washington, D.C.: Government Printing Office, 1989.
This is the third edition of the concise history of the National Advisory Committee for Aeronautics (NACA) and its successor agency, the National Aeronautics and Space Administration (NASA). This edition was published to coincide with the twentieth-anniversary celebration of the flight of Apollo 11. The author traces the history of the NACA and NASA in concise chapters divided into chronological eras. This is an interesting look at these aerospace pioneers and some of the programs they developed to study air and space phenomena. There are dozens of black-and-white photographs and an index.

Curtis, Anthony R. *Space Almanac.* Woodsboro, Md.: Arcsoft, 1989.
Written like many other almanacs, this book is filled with data on the U.S. and
Soviet manned and unmanned space programs and missions. The book is
divided into sections which discuss astronauts and cosmonauts, space stations,
space shuttles, rockets, satellites, the solar system, and deep space. Each
section is subdivided into pockets of information in an easy-to-find format.
There is a calendar of space exploration, which lists historical dates of significance to the space program in calendar order. There are several black-and-
white photographs and an index.

Gatland, Kenneth, et al. *The Illustrated Encyclopedia of Space Technology: A
Comprehensive History of Space Exploration.* New York: Harmony Books,
1981.
"Illustrated" should be underscored in the title of this work, because it is the
color and black-and-white photographs, drawings, paintings, and charts which
are the highlight of this work. Every launch vehicle of the major space powers
is discussed in an appropriate chapter. There are two four-page, full-color
drawings of the major launch vehicles. Each is drawn to scale for comparison.
Contains a chronology of the major space events since Sputnik 1, a glossary
of terms, and an index. The substantial amount of text does not bog down the
work but, rather, enhances the illustrations. Each chapter has its own list of
references.

Goldstein, Norm, ed. *Moments in Space.* New York: Gallery Books, 1986.
Newspaper photographs from the Associated Press are the highlight of this
book, which offers little text to accompany them. The space programs of the
United States and the Soviet Union are featured, with the emphasis on U.S.
manned programs. Much of the monograph is not to be relied on for accuracy,
especially because the information included with the photographs has not been
updated from what was known at the time of the event. Many of the photographs are grainy, but it is for their historical context that they should be
viewed, not for their clarity.

Harrison, Harry, and Malcolm Edwards. *Spacecraft in Fact and Fantasy.* New
York: Exeter Books, 1979.
This is an interesting work which compares some modern launch vehicles and
spacecraft with those created in the minds of science-fiction writers. The work
covers the history of spacecraft, primarily American, from the early pioneers
through the pre-Shuttle era. There are numerous color and black-and-white
photographs, as well as artwork from some of the science-fiction publications.
The authors show how some of the predictions of early writers have paralleled
fact and take a look at the future with an eye on the science fiction of today.
Contains a brief bibliography and an index.

Lewis, Richard S. *Appointment on the Moon*. New York: Ballantine Books, 1969. A complete account of the United States' quest to land a man on the Moon through the flight of Apollo 11. Beginning with the introduction of the German V-2 during World War II, Lewis takes the reader through each step of rocket development leading to the Apollo program. He chronicles every manned flight and adds a considerable amount of information about the unmanned programs which were necessary to accomplish the lunar landing. In the final chapter, Lewis looks into his crystal ball to forecast what the 1970's will hold and what must be done to ensure that the United States remains a leader in space. There are several pages of black-and-white photographs and an excellent listing of reference material.

Magill, Frank N., ed. *Magill's Survey of Science: Space Exploration Series*. 5 vols. Pasadena, Calif.: Salem Press, 1989.
One of the finest collections of essays on the history of space exploration, this five-volume set covers every aspect of U.S. and Soviet manned and unmanned space programs, as well as those of nations newer to the space race. Each entry averages seven printed pages and contains a brief summary of the subject, the knowledge gained, the historical context, an annotated bibliography, and cross-references to other articles in the set. Aside from a few technical inaccuracies, the work is an excellent starting point for the researcher. The essayists have written each article in simple, nontechnical language.

Thompson, Tina D., et al., eds. *TRW Space Log*. 23 vols. Redondo Beach, Calif.: TRW Space & Technology Group, 1957-1987.
Each year, TRW publishes a log of worldwide space activities. Any new spacecraft, launch vehicle, engine, or program, or one which made a significant contribution to the exploration of space during the year, is detailed. Tables include a "box score" of U.S. launches, worldwide successful space launches, Space Transportation System payload deployment records, payloads in orbit, and manned spaceflight records. The highlight of each volume is the summary of space launches, which details (in a table) the name, international designation, program direction, launch data, weight, orbital data, and status. This particular volume was published in conjunction with the thirtieth anniversary of the space age (generally considered to have begun with the launching of Sputnik 1) and contains data for the entire era. Most major libraries have or can obtain copies of these logs directly from the publisher.

U.S. House of Representatives. *Exploring in Aerospace Rocketry*. Washington, D.C.: National Technical Information Service, 1971.
This work is an introduction to the fundamentals of rocketry, developed at the NASA Lewis Research Center, Cleveland, Ohio. Scientists and engineers contributed to this work, which is an excellent primer on rocket principles.

Each of the chapters takes a basic principle of physics or chemistry and applies it to spacecraft and launch vehicles. Many of the spacecraft and boosters of the 1950's and 1960's are discussed. There are numerous black-and-white photographs and a brief bibliography for each chapter. This makes an excellent textbook for a high school or college-level course.

_____. *Space Transportation System and Associated Payloads: Glossary, Acronyms, and Abbreviations.* Washington, D.C.: National Technical Information Service, 1985.
In the fast-paced world of space travel, it has become necessary to develop a large set of new words and abbreviations. At the moment that the solid rocket boosters (SRBs) expend their fuel and are jettisoned, much can happen, and it can happen rapidly. Since the Space Shuttle is traveling at about five times the speed of sound when this occurs, it is important to communicate in a swift, compact, and clearly understood manner. Instead of the flight controllers reporting, "Everything looks fine right now and your solid rocket boosters are being separated at this point in the flight," they say, "Go at SRB sep." This book, which NASA tries to update regularly (although these updates are not published often), contains an alphabetical listing of these special words. The glossary contains definitions of some of the terms commonly used in conjunction with the Shuttle and its payloads. It is a very good reference, especially in conjunction with some of the more technical documents.

_____. *United States Civilian Space Programs 1958-1978.* Vol. 1. Washington, D.C.: Government Printing Office, 1981.
In a very concise report, the Committee on Space Science and Applications has compiled data on all U.S. space activity during its first two decades. After a brief introduction and summary chapter, the volume is divided into fourteen additional sections. The second chapter deals with the space-related issues under consideration by Congress. The remaining sections cover the history of NASA and its relationship to U.S. space policy, NASA facilities and tracking systems, launch vehicles and propulsion, manned spaceflight through 1975, the Space Transportation System, space life sciences, space science programs, materials processing in space, international cooperation in space, interagency and non-NASA governmental space activities, industrial and university support for NASA, space program benefits, and selected future space programs. Appendices contain Department of Defense manned spaceflight plans, NASA funding history, international space agreements, texts of President Jimmy Carter's space directives, documents relating to the legal aspects of the Space Shuttle, major U.S. space organizations, a master log of U.S. spaceflights, and a table of U.S. space orbital payloads by mission from 1957 through 1979.

Van Nimmen, Jane, and Leonard C. Bruno, with Robert L. Rosholt. *NASA Historical Data Book 1958-1968*. Vol. 1, *NASA Resources*. Washington, D.C.: National Technical Information Service, 1976.
This is the first in what was intended to be a series of volumes providing a comprehensive statistical summary of the first decade of the National Aeronautics and Space Administration, from its post-Sputnik creation until the Apollo 8 astronauts became the first men to circle the Moon. This volume measures dollars, people, and things and is designed to provide a reference source for a variety of purposes. The summary documents the immense growth and eventual leveling off of the agency's programs. It covers NASA's budget and financial history, its scattered installations, its manpower resources, and a statistical summary of its contractual history. This work is ideal for the "number cruncher," but it is difficult for the common researcher to wade through its 547 pages. There is no table of contents or index, and one is forced to find things by the "hunt and peck" method. Nevertheless, it provides much information about how the mighty dollar influences the decisions of NASA. There are scores of tables and charts.

Von Braun, Wernher, and Frederick I. Ordway III. *History of Rocketry and Space Travel*. 3d rev. ed. New York: Thomas Y. Crowell, 1975.
This is the story of the exploration of space from the earliest experiments with rocketry to the final flight of the Skylab program. Hundreds of experts on every aspect of this broad field contributed to the work. Most of the programs of the United States, the Soviet Union, and the other nations engaged in space exploration at that time are detailed, both descriptively and with black-and-white and color photographs. It is one of the best references on the subject. The book also contains a large, chapter-by-chapter bibliography. The authors finish their discussion of the space programs with a look at the future, including the Space Transportation System.

Wells, Helen T., Susan Whiteley, and Carrie E. Karegeannes. *Origins of NASA Names*. Washington, D.C.: National Technical Information Service, 1976.
Ever wonder how a particular spacecraft, launch vehicle, or program derived its name? Although this work is dated, it provides a great number of answers regarding these names. This is one of the volumes in the NASA History Series, and it is a wonderful book for trivia buffs. It discusses the major NASA projects, launch vehicles, satellites, space probes, sounding rockets, manned spacecraft, and NASA installations. Appendices list abbreviations, acronyms, and terms; international designation of spacecraft; NASA major launch records, 1958-1974; and NASA naming committees. There are dozens of black-and-white photographs, as well as an index and an in-depth bibliography.

Zalman, Ann Marie, and Joe Zalman. *Space: The Final Exam*. Deltona, Fla.: Zanadu Productions, 1985.
This is a pocketbook of space information, presented in question-and-answer form. There are a great number of interesting answers to some equally interesting questions. Major drawbacks to this work include the lack of organization into categories, no index, and no list of references to verify the answers.

Space Pioneers

Baker, David. *The Rocket: The History and Development of Rocket and Missile Technology*. New York: Crown, 1978.
This large, "coffee-table" book covers the technological and political development of manned and unmanned missiles and rockets. It provides a complete history of solid and liquid propulsion systems, from fire-sticks to Moon rockets. Propulsion systems are examined for their advantages and faults and for how they influence the design of the overall vehicle. The ancestry of U.S. and Soviet launch vehicles is traced to the war machines from which they were derived, all the way back to their common grandparent, the German *Vergeltungswaffe Zwei*, or V-2. The author concludes the work with a forecast about future vehicles, including reusable, atomic-powered, and interplanetary launch vehicles. A compendium of launch vehicles and ballistic missiles and of rocket-powered aircraft is provided. Each vehicle is detailed with information about its origin, configuration, development, flight history, and descendants. There is a silhouette of the vehicle, scaled for comparison with the others in the compendium. Hundreds of color and black-and-white photographs and illustrations enhance the comprehensive text. There are tables of data on space launch vehicles; research rockets; strategic and tactical ballistic missiles; and antiballistic, air-to-ground, surface-to-air, air-to-air, antiship, antisubmarine, and anti-armor missiles. Contains an index and a bibliography.

Hall, Al, ed. *Petersen's Book of Man in Space*. 5 vols. Los Angeles: Petersen, 1974.
This is a very colorful presentation of the history of spaceflight, from the early pioneers through the last Apollo flight. There are hundreds of color and black-and-white photographs and drawings. The focus of this work is the U.S. manned programs, perhaps because of the abundance of available photographs. The text is concise and enhances the pictures, although they really do not need enhancement. All of the spacecraft and launch vehicles of the U.S. programs are covered, as are the contributions of the pioneers of spaceflight and the astronauts.

Ley, Willy. *Satellites, Rockets, and Outer Space.* New York: New American
Library of World Literature, 1962.
This pocketbook is a fascinating look at the U.S. space programs to put
satellites into orbit. The author discusses these early satellites and some of the
feuding that went on between the Army and the Navy over who would be the
first to launch a satellite. Some of the earliest space launch vehicles are
described. Nontechnical physics lessons are presented in a discussion of
propulsion and orbital mechanics. There is a section devoted to the solar
system, with emphasis on the third planet. In the final chapter there is a
discussion of some future plans, including Moon cars and men on Mars. This
last chapter is perhaps the most interesting, especially in the light of events that
occurred during the subsequent quarter century. There are several line drawings
and a few color photographs.

Ordway, Frederick I., III, and Mitchell R. Sharpe. *The Rocket Team.* Foreword
by Wernher von Braun. New York: Thomas Y. Crowell, 1971.
The men responsible for the launch vehicles that put humans on the Moon also
were responsible for the missiles of World War II that brought destruction from
the sky. This is the story of the group of German scientists and engineers,
headed by von Braun, who developed the science of rocketry from the early
1930's through the Saturn family of launch vehicles. Much of the information
about their days at Pennemünde was classified until this book was written. This
is fascinating reading about scientists, dedicated to the betterment of human-
kind, being forced to develop war machines. There are black-and-white photographs, a bibliography, and an index.

Sagan, Carl. *Cosmos.* New York: Random House, 1980.
In 1980, PBS aired the series *Cosmos*, which tells the story of man's discovery
of the universe. This book is based upon that series. It presents, in a very
interesting way, how we are exploring, with modern ground- and space-based
instruments, the solar system and beyond. The history of the universe, as it
was known in 1980, is chronicled. The book is filled with color and black-and-
white photographs and paintings and etchings of the universe and its examiners,
both human and mechanical. The author describes the probabilities of galactic
civilizations and our search for them, as well as plans to go calling on them.
Provides an extensive bibliography and an index.

Stoiko, Michael. *Pioneers of Rocketry.* New York: Hawthorne Books, 1974.
This is a short but fine book about the earliest pioneers in rocketry. In brief
biographical studies, the author discusses ancient rocket pioneers, William
Congreve, Konstantin Tsiolkovsky, Robert Esnault-Pelterie, Robert Goddard,
and Hermann Oberth. There are several black-and-white photographs, an index,
and a chronology of the milestones in rocketry.

Von Braun, Wernher, and Frederick I. Ordway III. *History of Rocketry and Space Travel.* 3d rev. ed. New York: Thomas Y. Crowell, 1975.
This is the story of the exploration of space from the earliest experiments with rocketry to the final flight of the Skylab program. Hundreds of experts on every aspect of this broad field contributed to the work. Most of the programs of the United States, the Soviet Union, and the rest of the nations engaged in space exploration at that time are detailed, both descriptively and with black-and-white and color photographs. It is one of the best references on the subject. The book also contains a large, chapter-by-chapter bibliography. The authors finish their discussion of the space programs with a look at the future, including the Space Transportation System.

Ward, Robinson J., Jr., comp. *A Funny Thing Happened on the Way to the Moon.* Greenwich, Conn.: Fawcett, 1969.
Although the exploration of space is a serious, often challenging business, there is still room for humor. Some of the humor presented in this book was unintentional, evolving from the frustrations and failures of the U.S. space program. The author has collected humorous events, jokes, and other tension-relieving anecdotes from the scientists, technicians, engineers, and astronauts involved in man's conquest of space. While it does not contain any pertinent data on the history of the space program, it does make these people seem a little more human.

14

PROPULSION

General Studies

Ordway, Frederick I., III, and Mitchell R. Sharpe. *The Rocket Team.* Foreword by Wernher von Braun. New York: Thomas Y. Crowell, 1979.
The men responsible for the launch vehicles that put humans on the Moon also were responsible for the missiles of World War II that brought destruction from the sky. This is the story of the group of German scientists and engineers, headed by von Braun, who developed the science of rocketry from the early 1930's through the Saturn family of launch vehicles. Much of the information about their days at Pennemünde was classified until this book was written. This is fascinating reading about scientists, dedicated to the betterment of humankind, being forced to develop war machines. There are black-and-white photographs, a bibliography, and an index.

Rosenthal, A. *Venture into Space: Early Years of Goddard Space Flight Center.* Washington, D.C.: National Technical Information Service, 1977.
This is one of the volumes in the NASA History Series, the official history of the U.S. space programs. This book covers the history of NASA's Goddard Space Flight Center through 1963. The center, named for rocket pioneer Robert H. Goddard, was established on May 1, 1959, as NASA's first major scientific laboratory devoted entirely to the exploration of space. The modern, campuslike complex is located in Greenbelt, Maryland, only thirteen miles northeast of the nation's capital. During the early days (like today), the center was responsible for collecting and housing all of the data from every U.S. spaceflight. Its scientists and engineers have developed spacecraft and launch vehicles, including the highly successful Delta. There are dozens of black-and-white photographs, line drawings, tables, and charts. There is an impressive appendix listing source notes and bibliographic references, and an index.

Shortal, Joseph A. *A New Dimension—Wallops Island Flight Test Range: The First Fifteen Years.* Washington, D.C.: National Technical Information Service, 1978.
The Wallops Station, located on Wallops Island, Virginia, was established by the National Advisory Committee for Aeronautics in 1945 to gather information about Earth's atmosphere and its near-space environment. During its first fifteen years, the facility launched more than six thousand research vehicles. Consisting of from one to seven stages, these vehicles were used to gather scientific information on the flight characteristics of airplanes, launch vehicles, and spacecraft and to increase our understanding of the upper atmosphere and space environment. This large volume details the history of the facility, including its

role in the development of wartime aircraft and missiles, ramjets, supersonic bodies, hypersonic vehicles, high-temperature research, ballistic missile nose cones, guided missiles, sounding rockets, and Project Mercury. There are numerous black-and-white photographs and drawings, and an index. Appendices detail rocket motors used at Wallops, program identification, flight operations, preflight jet operations, and rocket propulsion systems developed at Wallops.

Thompson, Tina D., ed. *Space Log: 1957-1987*. Redondo Beach, Calif.: TRW Space & Technology Group, 1988.
Each year, TRW publishes a log of worldwide space activities. Any new spacecraft, launch vehicle, engine, or program, or one which made a significant contribution to the exploration of space during the year, is detailed. Tables include a "box score" of U.S. launches, worldwide successful space launches, Space Transportation System payload deployment records, payloads in orbit, and manned spaceflight records. The highlight of each volume is the summary of space launches, which details (in a table) the name, international designation, program direction, launch data, weight, orbital data, and status. This particular volume was published in conjunction with the thirtieth anniversary of the space age and contains data for the entire era. Most major libraries have or can obtain copies of these logs directly from the publisher.

Turnill, Reginald, ed. *Jane's Spaceflight Directory*. London: Jane's, 1985-1989.
After publishing spacecraft, missile, and rocket engine data in *Jane's All the World's Aircraft* for a number of years, the publisher found the information on space exploration too great not to be included in its own book. The biennial publication, like its parent, uses only the most reliable sources of information to provide as much technical data about the vehicle, engine, or program as is possible. Each issue highlights those systems or components that were introduced or made a significant contribution during the previous two-year period. The major manned and unmanned spaceflights are also detailed. There are black-and-white photographs and drawings of each vehicle or component.

U.S. National Aeronautics and Space Administration. *Exploring in Aerospace Rocketry*. Washington, D.C.: National Technical Information Service, 1971.
This work is an introduction to the fundamentals of rocketry, developed at the NASA Lewis Research Center, Cleveland, Ohio. Scientists and engineers contributed to this work, which is an excellent primer on rocket principles. Each of the chapters takes a basic principle of physics or chemistry and applies it to spacecraft and launch vehicles. Many of the spacecraft and boosters of the 1950's and 1960's are discussed. There are numerous black-and-white photographs and a brief bibliography for each chapter. This makes an excellent textbook for a high school or college-level course.

Van Nimmen, Jane, and Leonard C. Bruno, with Robert L. Rosholt. *NASA Historical Data Book 1958-1968*. Vol. 1, *NASA Resources*. Washington, D.C.: National Technical Information Service, 1976.

This is the first in what was intended to be a series of volumes providing a comprehensive statistical summary of the first decade of the National Aeronautics and Space Administration, from its post-Sputnik creation until the Apollo 8 astronauts became the first men to circle the Moon. This volume measures dollars, people, and things and is designed to provide a reference source for a variety of purposes. The summary documents the immense growth and eventual leveling off of the agency's programs. It covers NASA's budget and financial history, its scattered installations, its manpower resources, and a statistical summary of its contractual history. This work is ideal for the "number cruncher," but it is difficult for the common researcher to wade through its 547 pages. There is no table of contents or index, and one is forced to find things by the "hunt and peck" method. However, it does provide a great deal of information about how the mighty dollar influences the decisions of NASA. There are scores of tables and charts.

Von Braun, Wernher, and Frederick I. Ordway III. *History of Rocketry and Space Travel*. 3d rev. ed. New York: Thomas Y. Crowell, 1975.

This is the story of the exploration of space from the earliest experiments with rocketry to the final flight of the Skylab program. Hundreds of experts on every aspect of this broad field contributed to the work. Most of the programs of the United States, the Soviet Union, and the rest of the nations engaged in space exploration at that time are detailed, both descriptively and with black-and-white and color photographs. It is one of the best references on the subject. The book also contains a large, chapter-by-chapter bibliography. The authors finish their discussion of the space programs with a look at the future, including the Space Transportation System.

Launch Vehicles

Akens, David S. *Saturn Illustrated Chronology: Saturn's First Eleven Years, April 1957-April 1968*. Washington, D.C.: National Technical Information Service, 1971.

This is the year-by-year accounting of the activities surrounding the Saturn family of launch vehicles. These boosters include the Saturn I, designed to define the techniques for large, clustered rockets; the Saturn IB, used to test the Apollo spacecraft in low Earth orbit; and the Saturn V, which sent astronauts to the Moon. The first stage of each of the vehicles traces its roots back to two intermediate-range ballistic missiles, the Redstone and the Jupiter. The Saturn boosters, however, were the first launch vehicles designed only for peaceful purposes. Black-and-white photographs and drawings are featured to enhance the text. A reference list and glossary of terms are included.

Anderson, Sally. *Final Report: Mercury/Atlas Launch Vehicle Program.* El Segundo, Calif.: Aerospace Corp., 1963.
A comprehensive report summarizing the management techniques employed in the development, systems test, and launching of the Mercury-Atlas launch vehicle in support of Project Mercury. The vehicle is discussed in great detail, including sections on the airframe/structures, engines, vehicle propulsion systems, flight control systems, instrumentation, abort sensing and implementation system, and propellant delivery systems. Each section contains line drawings, tables, and charts, as well as references and a glossary of definitions. Very little is presented in overly technical language. This is the most informative book available on this vehicle. The researcher will find it an invaluable reference, although it will probably have to be obtained directly from NASA.

Baker, David. *The Rocket: The History and Development of Rocket and Missile Technology.* New York: Crown, 1978.
This large, "coffee-table" book covers the technological and political development of manned and unmanned missiles and rockets. It provides a complete history of solid and liquid propulsion systems from fire-sticks to Moon rockets. Propulsion systems are examined for their advantages and faults, and how they influence the design of the overall vehicle. The ancestry of U.S. and Soviet launch vehicles is traced to the war machines from which they were derived, all the way back to their common grandparent, the German *Vergeltungswaffe Zwei*, or V-2. The author concludes the work with a forecast about future vehicles, including reusable, atomic-powered, and interplanetary launch vehicles. A compendium of launch vehicles and ballistic missiles and of rocket-powered aircraft is provided. Each vehicle is detailed with information about its origin, configuration, development and flight history, and descendants. There is a silhouette of each vehicle, scaled for comparison with the others in the compendium. Hundreds of color and black-and-white photographs and illustrations enhance the comprehensive text. There are tables of data on space launch vehicles; research rockets; strategic and tactical ballistic missiles; and antiballistic, air-to-ground, surface-to-air, air-to-air, antiship, antisubmarine, and anti-armor missiles. Contains an index and a bibliography.

Bilstein, Roger E. *Stages to Saturn: A Technological History of the Apollo/Saturn Launch Vehicles.* Washington, D.C.: Government Printing Office, 1980.
One title in the NASA History Series, this work takes an in-depth look at the power it took to put man on the Moon. Descriptions of each member of the Saturn family—Saturn I, Saturn IB, and Saturn V—are provided, along with a chronology of the Apollo and Skylab programs. Illustrated with dozens of

black-and-white photographs not presented in any other essay, the book details the fabrication of each vehicle. The author has given life to what could have been a bland technical dissertation by including a look at some of the personnel involved.

Boeing Aerospace Co. *The Inertial Upper Stage User's Guide.* Seattle: Author, 1984.

The Inertial Upper Stage (IUS) is a high-altitude booster which is used in conjunction with either the Space Shuttle or the Titan launch vehicle. It was originally designed as a temporary stand-in for a reusable space tug and was called the "Interim" Upper Stage. When it became apparent that the space tug would not be developed in the foreseeable future, the Interim Upper Stage began its gradual evolution into the Inertial Upper Stage ("inertial" refers to its guidance technique). The IUS is built by Boeing for NASA and the Air Force. This book, filled with black-and-white photographs and line drawings, details this powerful booster and its associated hardware. It covers the vehicle's systems and subsystems, including its interfaces with the Shuttle and Titan. This book is a must for the person who wants to build an accurate model of the IUS.

Caidin, Martin. *Vanguard! The Story of the First Man-Made Satellite.* New York: E. P. Dutton, 1957.

This is one of the earlier works of this fine science writer. He took what was still very much under wraps and presented a look at the forthcoming space age. Vanguard was indeed to have been the first man-made satellite, but no one told that to the Soviet Union, which launched Sputnik shortly after this book was published. While many books on the exploration of space skim over the period of development before October 4, 1957, this work details every aspect. The author writes about Project Bumper, the Aerobee, the Viking rocket from which Vanguard evolved, the X-405, which would propel the vehicle through the atmosphere, and the satellite it would orbit. There are dozens of black-and-white photographs and line drawings. It may be difficult to track down a copy of this work, but it is well worth the effort.

Chapman, John L. *Atlas: The Story of a Missile.* New York: Harper & Brothers, 1960.

This is the "biography" of the United States' premier intercontinental ballistic missile, which would soon be used to put a man into orbit. Although the information in this work is very dated and limited to what the Air Force would reveal, it does give an insight into the creation of a missile. The text is well written and not at all technical. If one compares the information about the Atlas in this book with that in later works on the missile, it is surprising how much was available to the writer. The major attraction of this publication is that it is contemporaneous with the Atlas program.

Chrysler Corporation. *Saturn IB Vehicle Handbook.* 4 vols. Washington, D.C.: National Technical Information Service, 1966.
If you ever wanted to build your own Saturn IB, this is the book for you. Hundreds of detailed drawings point out each part that went into making this launch vehicle. Volume 1 gives a general overview of the vehicle; the other volumes go into greater detail. These books were the manuals used by the technicians who worked on the Saturn IB. There is very little text, but no other work will answer as many questions about this second-generation booster.

Corliss, William R. *NASA Sounding Rockets, 1958-1968: A Historical Summary.* Washington, D.C.: National Technical Information Service, 1971.
Sounding rockets, equipment-laden missiles, have been providing data about Earth's upper atmosphere and our neighboring planets since the end of World War II. Their reign as the chief space-research vehicles seemed to come to an end with the launch of Sputnik and the dawning of the space age. However, their role in the exploration of the upper atmosphere—too high for balloons, too low for satellites—will never be challenged. This monograph looks at the sounding rockets during the first decade of the space age. It traces their development from the earliest scientific rockets of American Robert Goddard and a Russian named Tikonoravov. There are dozens of black-and-white photographs, but it is unlikely that one will find a copy with adequately reproduced illustrations. Bibliographic footnotes supplement the complete bibliography. There are appendices which detail major sounding rockets, NASA sounding rocket firings (1959-1968), trends in vehicle usage (1959-1968), trends in use by discipline (1959-1968), and finances (1958-1970).

Gatland, Kenneth W. *Missiles and Rockets: A Pocket Encyclopedia of Spaceflight in Color.* New York: Macmillan, 1975.
A compact history of the missiles and rockets of the world, more specifically, the United States and the Soviet Union. Each vehicle is described, including its configuration and use. There are color and black-and-white photographs of each vehicle, as well as cutaway drawings of the most familiar ones. The history of the missiles and rockets, from Pennemünde to the Space Shuttle, is traced in a concise discussion. The politics and technology which influenced the design of each vehicle are also presented. The work is indexed.

Gatland, Kenneth, et al. *The Illustrated Encyclopedia of Space Technology: A Comprehensive History of Space Exploration.* New York: Harmony Books, 1981.

"Illustrated" should be underscored in the title of this work, because it is the color and black-and-white photographs, drawings, paintings, and charts which are the highlight of this work. Every launch vehicle of the major space powers is discussed in an appropriate chapter. There are two four-page, full-color drawings of the major launch vehicles. Each is drawn to scale for comparison. Contains a chronology of the major space events since Sputnik 1, a glossary of terms, and an index. There is a great quantity of text, which does not bog down the work but merely enhances the illustrations. Each chapter has its own list of references.

Green, Constance McLaughlin, and Milton Lomask. *Vanguard: A History.* Washington, D.C.: Smithsonian Institution Press, 1970.
The Vanguard program was designed to place the world's first artificial satellite into orbit in 1957. What it is most remembered for is the disastrous attempt to launch the first Vanguard satellite. The flight lasted an instant, as the vehicle lifted from its launchpad and slowly settled back down in a ball of flames. The tiny satellite tucked inside its nose cone rolled along the ground, beeping laconically. Vanguard would have its successes—after the Soviet Union launched Sputnik and after the United States orbited Explorer 1. This work chronicles the Navy's satellite program and details its spacecraft and launch vehicles. It also discusses the Cold War political climate which pressured the scientists, engineers, and technicians to get a satellite up before the Soviets. There are numerous black-and-white photographs, line drawings, and an index.

Grimwood, James M., and Barton C. Hacker, with Peter J. Vorzimmer. *Project Gemini Technology and Operations: A Chronology.* Washington, D.C.: National Technical Information Service, 1969.
This is NASA's official record of the Gemini program, covering events on a day-to-day basis. Gemini was developed as an "in-between" program. What evolved was a test program that proved that the theoretical concepts of rendezvous and docking with another orbiting spacecraft could be accomplished. Included in the coverage are the development of the spacecraft and launch vehicles, astronaut training, and mission results. There are dozens of black-and-white photographs, along with line drawings of components. Appendices provide a summary of the Gemini flights: mission objectives, orbital activities, experiments, and extravehicular activity. There are tables of vehicle manufacturing and test histories; program costs; contractors, subcontractors, and vendors; and the flight record of Project Mercury and the Gemini program.

Hacker, Barton C., and James M. Grimwood. *On the Shoulders of Titans: A History of Project Gemini.* Washington, D.C.: National Technical Information Service, 1977.

One title in the NASA History Series, this book chronicles the Gemini program, from its conception during the early days of Project Mercury to its completion following the Gemini XII flight. There are dozens of black-and-white photographs of the manned, as well as unmanned, flights. Color photographs, taken from orbit, are in the back of the book. Line drawings show the inner workings of much of the equipment related to the missions. There is an impressive hundred-page appendix listing source notes and bibliographic references. Other appendices include a summary of flight data, a glossary of abbreviations and acronyms, astronaut flight assignments, in-flight experiments, and the cost of the program.

Lay, Bierne, Jr. *Earthbound Astronauts: The Builders of Apollo-Saturn.* Englewood Cliffs, N.J.: Prentice-Hall, 1971.
This is the story of the people who conceived, designed, and built the most powerful launch vehicle ever to be launched. The author looks at the difficulties in creating the vehicle that would send men to the Moon using technology which had not been invented. The biggest challenge was accomplishing the lunar landing mission before the deadline imposed by President John F. Kennedy. Of the twelve Saturn V's used during the Apollo program, none failed, an accomplishment unmatched by any other expendable launch vehicle. The story looks at the political, scientific, and economic obstacles faced by von Braun and his associates, some of which were more challenging than the engineering problems.

Ley, Willy. *Satellites, Rockets, and Outer Space.* New York: New American Library of World Literature, 1956, rev. ed. 1962.
This pocketbook provides a fascinating look at the U.S. space programs to put satellites into orbit. The author discusses these early satellites and some of the feuding that went on between the Army and the Navy over who would be the first to launch a satellite. Some of the earliest space launch vehicles are described. Nontechnical physics lessons are presented in a discussion of propulsion and orbital mechanics. There is a section devoted to the solar system, with emphasis on the third planet. In the final chapter there is a discussion of some future plans, including Moon cars and men on Mars. This last chapter is perhaps the most interesting, especially in the light of events that occurred during the subsequent quarter century. There are several line drawings and a few color photographs.

Maguire, David W. "U.S. Launch Vehicles." In *Magill's Survey of Science: Space Exploration Series*, vol. 2, edited by Frank N. Magill. Pasadena, Calif.: Salem Press, 1989.
One of the essays on the history of space exploration in this five-volume set, which covers every aspect of the U.S. and Soviet manned and unmanned space

programs, as well as those from nations newer to the space race. Although the brevity of the essay does not permit it to go into great detail about the launch vehicles, it does discuss their history from the pencil-thin Vanguard to the mighty members of the Saturn family. Contains an annotated bibliography and cross-references.

Maguire, David W., and Ellen F. Mitchum. "Delta Launch Vehicles." In *Magill's Survey of Science: Space Exploration Series*, vol. 1, edited by Frank N. Magill. Pasadena, Calif.: Salem Press, 1989.
Considered by most to be the "workhorse" in NASA's fleet of expendable boosters, the Delta is an offspring of the Thor intermediate-range ballistic missile (IRBM). It has launched probes to the moon and into interplanetary space. The launch vehicle is detailed in this essay, as are its contributions to the space program. Contains an annotated bibliography and cross-references.

Merguerian, Charles. "The Vanguard Program." In *Magill's Survey of Science: Space Exploration Series*, vol. 5, edited by Frank N. Magill. Pasadena, Calif.: Salem Press, 1989.
As its name suggests, Vanguard was meant to lead the United States into space. Instead, it became the first "goat." Vanguard was the name of the pencil-thin launch vehicle (as well as the satellite it would carry). The Navy vehicle was given the task to place the first U.S. satellite into orbit soon after Sputnik 1 beeped its taunting message from above. Instead, it crumpled into a ball of fire moments after liftoff. It was not until the fourth Vanguard launch that a success was realized—two months after an Army Juno 1 launched Explorer 1. This essay discusses the origins of Vanguard, which developed from the Viking rocket, and its contributions to the space program. Contains an annotated bibliography and cross-references.

Miller, F. E., J. L. Cassidy, J. C. Leveye, and R. I. Johnson. *The Mercury-Redstone Project*. Washington, D.C.: National Technical Information Service, 1964.
This is a concise record of the development of the Redstone intermediate-range ballistic missile for use in the Mercury project. The Redstone was the first launch vehicle used in space exploration, in its Juno 1 configuration, to launch Explorer 1. This configuration was modified and fitted with an adapter for the Mercury spacecraft. Redstone flew five missions, including two manned, during the program. The book is divided into nine sections and covers the following topics: the Mercury-Redstone mission, vehicle description, man-rating, development test program, checkout and launch operations, flight test program, and contributions to manned launch vehicles. There are numerous black-and-white photographs, line drawings, charts, and tables. A large reference list will lead

the researcher to numerous technical publications about the missile and its contribution to manned spaceflight.

Mitchum, Ellen F. "Atlas Launch Vehicles." In *Magill's Survey of Science: Space Exploration Series*, vol. 1, edited by Frank N. Magill. Pasadena, Calif.: Salem Press, 1989.
One of the essays on the history of space exploration in the five-volume set, which covers every aspect of the U.S. and Soviet manned and unmanned space programs, as well as those from nations newer to the space race. The Atlas vehicle was first built as an intercontinental ballistic missile (ICBM) for the Air Force. It was later modified to launch a variety of manned and unmanned spacecraft. Some of these include the Mercury spacecraft, the Gemini Agena Target Vehicle, Mariner, Ranger, Lunar Orbiter, Surveyor, and many other military and civilian spacecraft. This essay discusses the development of the vehicle and its contributions to space exploration. Contains an annotated bibliography and cross-references.

_____. "Saturn Launch Vehicles." In *Magill's Survey of Science: Space Exploration Series*, vol. 3, edited by Frank N. Magill. Pasadena, Calif.: Salem Press, 1989.
Before the first satellite was placed in orbit, before there was a goal to put a man on the Moon, there were the dreamers: Wernher von Braun and his fellow scientists believed that there would be a need for a very large launch vehicle in the U.S. arsenal, not to hurl warheads at the enemy but to loft large payloads into Earth orbit and beyond. What developed was the Saturn family of vehicles: Saturn I, Saturn IB, Saturn V, and a few others that never made it past the planning stage. This chapter delves into the roots of this family of giants and details their flights and their contribution to the Apollo program. Contains an annotated bibliography and cross-references.

Newell, Homer. *Beyond the Atmosphere: Early Years of Space Science*. Washington, D.C.: Government Printing Office, 1980.
This is one of the volumes in the NASA History Series, the official history of the United States' space programs. This book covers the scientific investigations made possible by sounding rockets, satellites, and space probes. The author begins with a look at the early pioneers of rocketry and some of the first space scientists. The National Aeronautics and Space Administration was created in response to the launch of Sputnik 1 and the desire to release the military from its role in space exploration. NASA's design and organization are discussed, along with NASA's interaction with other agencies, the military, and universities. Particular attention is paid to the California Institute of Technology's Jet Propulsion Laboratory. There are dozens of black-and-white

photographs, line drawings, tables, and charts. Contains an impressive appendix listing source notes and bibliographic references, and an index.

Newman, John. "Titan Launch Vehicles." In *Magill's Survey of Science: Space Exploration Series*, vol. 5, edited by Frank N. Magill. Pasadena, Calif.: Salem Press, 1989.
The first intercontinental ballistic missile (ICBM) designed to be used as such, rather than one modified from an existing research vehicle, was the mighty Titan. Titan was designed to fit into an underground silo, and it used fuels that could be stored inside the vehicle's propellant tanks for long periods of time. In addition, the fuel and oxidizer were chosen because they ignited on contact and did not need a bulky, sometimes unreliable, ignition system. This chapter discusses the many faces of Titan and the spacecraft it launched, including the Gemini two-man spacecraft, Viking, Voyager, and many military satellites. The article closes with an annotated bibliography and cross-references.

Ordway, Frederick I., III, and Mitchell R. Sharpe. *The Rocket Team*. Foreword by Wernher von Braun. New York: Thomas Y. Crowell, 1979.
The men responsible for the launch vehicles that put humans on the Moon also were responsible for the missiles of World War II that brought destruction from the sky. This is the story of the group of German scientists and engineers, headed by von Braun, who developed the science of rocketry from the early 1930's through the Saturn family of launch vehicles. Much of the information about their days at Pennemünde was classified until this book was written. This is fascinating reading about scientists, dedicated to the betterment of humankind, being forced to develop war machines. There are black-and-white photographs, a bibliography, and an index.

Shortal, Joseph A. *A New Dimension—Wallops Island Flight Test Range: The First Fifteen Years*. Washington, D.C.: National Technical Information Service, 1978.
The Wallops Station, located on Wallops Island, Virginia, was established by the National Advisory Committee for Aeronautics in 1945 to gather information about Earth's atmosphere and its near-space environment. During its first fifteen years, the facility launched more than six thousand research vehicles. Consisting of from one to seven stages, these vehicles were used to gather scientific information on the flight characteristics of airplanes, launch vehicles, and spacecraft, and to increase our understanding of the upper atmosphere and space environment. This large volume details the history of the facility, including its role in the development of wartime aircraft and missiles, ramjets, supersonic bodies, hypersonic vehicles, high-temperature research, ballistic missile nose cones, guided missiles, sounding rockets, and Project Mercury. There are numerous black-and-white photographs and drawings, and an index.

Appendices detail rocket motors used at Wallops, program identification, flight operations, preflight jet operations, and rocket propulsion systems developed at Wallops.

Skinner, David, et al. "The Space Centres." In *The Illustrated Encyclopedia of Space Technology: A Comprehensive History of Space Exploration*, by Kenneth Gatland et al. New York: Harmony Books, 1981.
This section in the book discusses the facilities around the world from which satellites and probes are launched. Each is briefly discussed, accompanied by a map of the area in which the launch site is located. Most of the discussion about each center revolves around the launch vehicles that are launched there. There are two four-page, full-color drawings of the major launch vehicles. Each is drawn to scale for comparison. There are color and black-and-white photographs, drawings, and charts. Appendices offer a chronology of the major space events since Sputnik 1, a glossary of terms, and an index.

Taylor, John W. R., ed. *Jane's All the World's Aircraft.* 17 vols. London: Jane's, 1957- .
Considered by some to be the most complete reference on aircraft, the biennial publication began to include rockets, missiles, and spacecraft after the first Sputnik was orbited. The most reliable sources of information are used to provide as much technical data about the vehicle, engine, or program as possible. Each issue highlights those systems or components that were introduced or made a significant contribution during the previous two-year period. The major manned and unmanned spaceflights are also detailed. There are black-and-white photographs and drawings of each vehicle or component.

Thompson, Tina D., ed. *Space Log: 1957-1987.* Redondo Beach, Calif.: TRW Space & Technology Group, 1988.
Each year, TRW publishes a log of worldwide space activities. Any new spacecraft, launch vehicle, engine, or program, or one which made a significant contribution to the exploration of space during the year, is detailed. Tables include a "box score" of U.S. launches, worldwide successful space launches, Space Transportation System payload deployment records, payloads in orbit, and manned spaceflight records. The highlight of each volume is the summary of space launches, which details (in a table) the name, international designation, program direction, launch data, weight, orbital data, and status. This particular volume was published in conjunction with the thirtieth anniversary of the space age and contains data for the entire era. Most major libraries have or can obtain copies of these logs directly from the publisher.

U.S. House of Representatives. *United States Civilian Space Programs 1958-1978.* Vol. 1. Washington, D.C.: Government Printing Office, 1981.

In a very concise report, the Committee on Space Science and Applications has compiled data on all U.S. space activity during its first two decades. After a brief introduction and summary chapter, the volume is divided into fourteen additional sections. The second chapter deals with the space-related issues under consideration by Congress. The remaining sections cover the history of NASA and its relationship to U.S. space policy, NASA facilities and tracking systems, launch vehicles and propulsion, manned spaceflight through 1975, the Space Transportation System, space life sciences, space science programs, materials processing in space, international cooperation in space, interagency and non-NASA governmental space activities, industrial and university support for NASA, space program benefits, and selected future space programs. Appendices contain Department of Defense manned spaceflight plans, NASA funding history, international space agreements, texts of President Jimmy Carter's space directives, documents relating to the legal aspects of the Space Shuttle, major U.S. space organizations, a master log of U.S. spaceflights, and a table of U.S. space orbital payloads by mission from 1957 through 1979.

U.S. National Aeronautics and Space Administration. *Gemini Midprogram Conference, Including Experiment Results.* Washington, D.C.: National Technical Information Service, 1966.
A four-day conference was held at NASA's Manned Spacecraft Center in Houston, Texas, February 23-25, 1966. The purpose of the meeting was to have key members of the Gemini program report on the progress of the program at the midway point. This work presents the reports, divided into the following categories: spacecraft, launch vehicle, flight operations, mission results, physical science experiments, and medical science experiments. Each dissertation is accompanied by black-and-white photographs, line drawings, tables, and charts. There is a two-segment report on the planning and execution of the Gemini VII and VII-A rendezvous mission.

_____. *Saturn I Summary.* Washington, D.C.: National Technical Information Service, 1966.
This book was prepared by the engineers from NASA's George C. Marshall Space Flight Center, where the Saturn I was designed and built. It outlines each of the ten unmanned flights and gives a brief history of the origins of the Saturn I. The Saturn booster program was initiated solely to develop the technology of large-thrust vehicles. By modifying existing hardware, engineers were able to create a new rocket of the desired thrust. The Saturn I (and Saturn IB) first stage was composed of a central liquid-oxygen core tank surrounded by eight fuel and liquid oxygen tanks. The core was derived from the Jupiter missile, while the surrounding tanks came from the Redstone.

U.S. National Aeronautics and Space Administration and U.S. Air Force. *STS Inertial Upper Stage (IUS) Systems Handbook, Basic*, Rev., G. Washington, D.C.: Government Printing Office, 1988.
The Inertial Upper Stage (IUS) is a high-altitude booster which is used in conjunction with either the Space Shuttle or the Titan launch vehicle. It was originally designed as a temporary stand-in for a reusable space tug and was called the "Interim" Upper Stage. When it became apparent that the space tug would not be developed in the foreseeable future, the Interim Upper Stage began its gradual evolution into the Inertial Upper Stage ("inertial" refers to its guidance technique). This volume is the official handbook on the IUS used by everyone associated with its development, construction, deployment, and use. It contains hundreds of detailed drawings and schematics. Although much of it is highly technical, the illustrations make it easy to understand.

Wamboldt, J. F., and S. F. Anderson. *Gemini Program Launch Systems Final Report: Gemini Titan, Agena Target, Atlas SLV-3*. El Segundo, Calif.: Aerospace Corp., 1967.
A comprehensive report summarizing the management techniques employed in the development, systems test, and launching of the Gemini launch vehicle, Gemini Agena Target Vehicle, and the Atlas SLV-3 (Space Launch Vehicle-3) in support of the Gemini program. Each launch vehicle is discussed in great detail, including sections on the airframe/structures, engines, vehicle propulsion systems, flight control systems, instrumentation, and propellant delivery systems. Each section contains line drawings, tables, and charts, as well as references and a glossary of definitions. Very little is presented in overly technical language. This is the most informative book available on these vehicles. The researcher will find it an invaluable reference, although it will probably have to be obtained directly from NASA.

Wells, Helen T., Susan Whiteley, and Carrie E. Karegeannes. *Origins of NASA Names*. Washington, D.C.: National Technical Information Service, 1976.
Ever wonder how a particular spacecraft, launch vehicle, or program derived its name? Although this work is dated, it provides a great number of answers regarding these names. This is one of the volumes in the NASA History Series, and it is a wonderful book for trivia buffs. It discusses the major NASA projects, launch vehicles, satellites, space probes, sounding rockets, manned spacecraft, and NASA installations. Appendices list abbreviations, acronyms, and terms; international designation of spacecraft; NASA major launch records, 1958-1974; and NASA naming committees. There are dozens of black-and-white photographs, an index, and an in-depth bibliography.

Yenne, Bill. *The Encyclopedia of U.S. Spacecraft*. New York: Exeter Books, 1985.

A complete encyclopedia of U.S. spacecraft is presented in a book filled with color and black-and-white photographs. General information on the programs is provided in alphabetical order, with individual spacecraft, probes, or launch vehicles listed chronologically. Data on all the launch vehicles, including Atlas, Titan, Saturn, Juno, and Delta, are furnished. Includes lists of acronyms and abbreviations, and an index.

Engines

Boeing Aerospace Co. *The Inertial Upper Stage User's Guide.* Seattle: Author, 1984.
The Inertial Upper Stage (IUS) is a high-altitude booster used in conjunction with either the Space Shuttle or the Titan launch vehicle. It was originally designed as a temporary stand-in for a reusable space tug and was called the "Interim" Upper Stage. When it became apparent that the space tug would not be developed in the foreseeable future, the Interim Upper Stage began its gradual evolution into the Inertial Upper Stage ("inertial" refers to its guidance technique). The IUS is built by Boeing for NASA and the Air Force. This book, filled with black-and-white photographs and line drawings, details this powerful booster and its associated hardware. It covers the vehicle's systems and subsystems, including its interfaces with the Shuttle and Titan. This book is a must for the person who wants to build an accurate model of the IUS.

Ordway, Frederick I., III, and Mitchell R. Sharpe. *The Rocket Team.* Foreword by Wernher von Braun. New York: Thomas Y. Crowell, 1979.
The men responsible for the launch vehicles that put humans on the Moon also were responsible for the missiles of World War II that brought destruction from the sky. This is the story of the group of German scientists and engineers, headed by von Braun, who developed the science of rocketry from the early 1930's through the Saturn family of launch vehicles. Much of the information about their days at Pennemünde was classified until this book was written. This is fascinating reading about scientists, dedicated to the betterment of human-kind, being forced to develop war machines. There are black-and-white photo-graphs, a bibliography, and an index.

Shortal, Joseph A. *A New Dimension—Wallops Island Flight Test Range: The First Fifteen Years.* Washington, D.C.: National Technical Information Service, 1978.
The Wallops Station, located on Wallops Island, Virginia, was established by the National Advisory Committee for Aeronautics in 1945 to gather information about Earth's atmosphere and its near-space environment. During its first fifteen years, the facility launched more than six thousand research vehicles. Consisting

of from one to seven stages, these vehicles were used to gather scientific information on the flight characteristics of airplanes, launch vehicles, and spacecraft and to increase our understanding of the upper atmosphere and space environment. This large volume details the history of the facility, including its role in the development of wartime aircraft and missiles, ramjets, supersonic bodies, hypersonic vehicles, high-temperature research, ballistic missile nose cones, guided missiles, sounding rockets, and Project Mercury. There are numerous black-and-white photographs and drawings, and an index. Appendices detail rocket motors used at Wallops, program identification, flight operations, preflight jet operations, and rocket propulsion systems developed at Wallops.

Taylor, John W. R., ed. *Jane's All the World's Aircraft.* 17 vols. London: Jane's, 1957- .
Considered by some to be the most complete reference on aircraft, the biennial publication began to include rockets, missiles, and spacecraft after the first Sputnik was orbited. The most reliable sources of information are used to provide as much technical data about the vehicle, engine, or program as possible. Each issue highlights those systems or components that were introduced or made a significant contribution during the previous two-year period. The major manned and unmanned spaceflights are also detailed. There are black-and-white photographs and drawings of each vehicle or component.

Thompson, Tina D., ed. *Space Log: 1957-1987.* Redondo Beach, Calif.: TRW Space & Technology Group, 1988.
Each year, TRW publishes a log of worldwide space activities. Any new spacecraft, launch vehicle, engine, or program, or one which made a significant contribution to the exploration of space during the year, is detailed. Tables include a "box score" of U.S. launches, worldwide successful space launches, Space Transportation System payload deployment records, payloads in orbit, and manned spaceflight records. The highlight of each volume is the summary of space launches which details (in a table) the name, international designation, program direction, launch data, weight, orbital data, and status. This particular volume was published in conjunction with the thirtieth anniversary of the space age and contains data for the entire era. Most major libraries have or can obtain copies of these logs directly from the publisher.

U.S. National Aeronautics and Space Administration. *Gemini Midprogram Conference, Including Experiment Results.* Washington, D.C.: National Technical Information Service, 1966.
A four-day conference was held at NASA's Manned Spacecraft Center in Houston, Texas, February 23-25, 1966. The purpose of the meeting was to have key members of the Gemini program report on the progress of the program at the midway point. This work presents the reports, divided into the

following categories: spacecraft, launch vehicle, flight operations, mission results, physical science experiments, and medical science experiments. Each dissertation is accompanied by black-and-white photographs, line drawings, tables, and charts. There is a two-segment report on the planning and execution of the Gemini VII and VII-A rendezvous mission.

_____. *STS-41D (14) Launch Attempt Report*. Washington, D.C.: Government Printing Office, 1984.
The Shuttle program had flown thirteen successful missions without an incident that might have proven disastrous, until STS 41-D. The terminal countdown (which extends from the T-minus-20-minute mark through solid rocket booster ignition) for the second launch attempt of the mission on June 26, 1984, proceeded normally until it was time to fire the Shuttle's main engines. The three engines ignite sequentially (in a staggered start mode) at T minus 6.6 seconds. Engine 3 ignited, followed by number 2, but then number 3 shut down because of an indication of improper opening of the main fuel valve. Since the number 3 engine quit, *Discovery*'s onboard computers shut down engine number 2. This report details the apparent cause of the aborted launch and the sequence of events that led to it. STS 41-D was successfully launched on August 30, 1984.

_____. *STS-51F Launch Attempt Report*. Washington, D.C.: Government Printing Office, 1985.
The second aborted launch of the Space Shuttle program occurred during the first attempted launch of the Spacelab 3 mission on July 12, 1985. As with the abort on STS 41-D, this one came during the Space Shuttle main engine (SSME) ignition sequence. SSME number 3 ignited on time, followed by numbers 2 and 1. The abort was automatically executed by *Challenger*'s computers when the engine chamber coolant valve on SSME-2 was slow in closing from 100 percent open to 70 percent open, as required for startup. This report discusses the launch attempt and the causes for the malfunction. STS 51-F was successfully launched on July 29, 1985. At 5 minutes, 43 seconds after liftoff, both temperature readings for the SSME-1 high-pressure turbopump indicated above acceptable limits, resulting in a premature shutdown of SSME-1 and the declaration of an abort-to-orbit (ATO) condition.

U.S. National Aeronautics and Space Administration and U.S. Air Force. *STS Inertial Upper Stage (IUS) Systems Handbook, Basic, Rev. G.* Washington, D.C.: Government Printing Office, 1988.
The Inertial Upper Stage (IUS) is a high-altitude booster used in conjunction with either the Space Shuttle or the Titan launch vehicle. It was originally designed as a temporary stand-in for a reusable space tug and was called the "Interim" Upper Stage. When it became apparent that the space tug would not

be developed in the foreseeable future, the Interim Upper Stage began its gradual evolution into the Inertial Upper Stage ("inertial" refers to its guidance technique). This volume is the official handbook on the IUS used by everyone associated with its development, construction, deployment, and use. It contains hundreds of detailed drawings and schematics. Although much of it is highly technical, the illustrations make it easy to understand.

UNMANNED VEHICLES

General Studies

Baker, David. *The Rocket: The History and Development of Rocket and Missile Technology.* New York: Crown, 1978.
This large, "coffee-table" book covers the technological and political development of manned and unmanned missiles and rockets. It provides a complete history of solid and liquid propulsion systems from fire-sticks to moon rockets. Propulsion systems are examined for their advantages and faults and how they influence the design of the overall vehicle. The ancestry of U.S. and Soviet launch vehicles is traced to the war machines from which they were derived, all the way back to their common grandparent, the German *Vergeltungswaffe Zwei*, or V-2. The author concludes the work with a forecast about future vehicles, including reusable, atomic-powered, and interplanetary launch vehicles. A compendium of launch vehicles and ballistic missiles and of rocket-powered aircraft is provided. Each vehicle is detailed with information about its origin, its configuration, its development and flight history, and its descendants. There is a silhouette of the vehicle, scaled for comparison with the others in the compendium. Hundreds of color and black-and-white photographs and illustrations enhance the comprehensive text. There are tables of data on space launch vehicles; research rockets; strategic and tactical ballistic missiles; and antiballistic, air-to-ground, surface-to-air, air-to-air, antiship, antisubmarine, and anti-armor missiles. Provides an index and a bibliography.

Bilstein, Roger E. *Orders of Magnitude: A History of the NACA and NASA, 1915-1990.* Washington, D.C.: Government Printing Office, 1989.
This is the third edition of the concise history of the National Advisory Committee for Aeronautics (NACA) and its successor agency, the National Aeronautics and Space Administration (NASA). This edition was published to coincide with the twentieth-anniversary celebration of the flight of Apollo 11. The author traces the history of the NACA and NASA in concise chapters divided into chronological eras. This is an interesting look at these aerospace pioneers and some of the programs they developed to study air and space phenomena. There are dozens of black-and-white photographs and an index.

Bova, Ben, with Trudy E. Bell, eds. *Closeup: New Worlds.* New York: St. Martin's Press, 1977.
A collection of essays written by some of the best-known science and science-fiction writers in the world. This fact-filled book details our solar system, its planets, moons, and other phenomena. There are plenty of color and black-and-white photographs of these extraterrestrial entities and a description of the

efforts to obtain these pictures with space probes. Photographs taken from ground-based observatories are compared with those taken from the visiting spacecraft, such as Mariner, Viking, and Pioneer, as well as those originating in the Soviet Union. Descriptions of each spacecraft and the story of their travels are included.

Chapman, John L. *Atlas: The Story of a Missile.* New York: Harper & Brothers, 1960.
This is the "biography" of the United States' premier intercontinental ballistic missile, which would soon be used to put a man into orbit. Although the information in this work is very dated and limited to what the Air Force would tell about it, it does give an insight into the creation of a missile. The text is well written and not at all technical. If one compares the data about the Atlas in this book with later works on the missile, it is surprising how much was available to the writer. The major attraction of this publication is that it is contemporaneous with the Atlas program.

Corliss, William R. *NASA Sounding Rockets, 1958-1968: A Historical Summary.* Washington, D.C.: National Technical Information Service, 1971.
Sounding rockets, equipment-laden missiles, have been providing data about Earth's upper atmosphere and our neighbors in the solar system since the end of World War II. Their reign as chief space-research vehicle seemed to come to an end with the launch of Sputnik and the dawning of the space age. However, their role in the exploration of the upper atmosphere—too high for balloons, too low for satellites—will never be challenged. This monograph looks at the sounding rockets during the first decade of the space age. It traces their development from the earliest scientific rockets of American Robert Goddard and a Russian named Tikonoravov. There are dozens of black-and-white photographs, but it is unlikely that one will find a copy with adequately reproduced illustrations. Bibliographic footnotes supplement the complete bibliography. There are appendices which detail major sounding rockets, NASA sounding rocket firings (1959-1968), trends in vehicle usage (1959-1968), trends in use by discipline (1959-1968), and finances (1958-1970).

DeWaard, E. John, and Nancy DeWaard. *History of NASA: America's Voyage to the Stars.* New York: Exeter Books, 1984.
This is a brief, photo-filled look at NASA's programs more than it is a look at NASA itself. Each of the manned and unmanned programs, including Mercury, Gemini, Apollo, Skylab, the Space Shuttle, Voyager, and Viking, is discussed in general. There is very little "new" information provided. There are dozens of color and black-and-white photographs which, by themselves, make the book worthwhile. An index is included.

Gatland, Kenneth W. *Missiles and Rockets: A Pocket Encyclopedia of Spaceflight in Color.* New York: Macmillan, 1975.
A compact history of the missiles and rockets of the world, more specifically, the United States and the Soviet Union. Each vehicle is described, including its configuration and use. There are color and black-and-white photographs of each vehicle, as well as cutaway drawings of the most familiar ones. The history of the missiles and rockets, from Pennemünde to the Space Shuttle, is traced in a concise discussion. The politics and technology which influenced the design of each vehicle are also presented. The work is indexed.

Gatland, Kenneth, et al. *The Illustrated Encyclopedia of Space Technology: A Comprehensive History of Space Exploration.* New York: Harmony Books, 1981.
"Illustrated" should be underscored in the title of this work, because it is the color and black-and-white photographs, drawings, paintings, and charts that are the highlight of this work. Every launch vehicle of the major space powers is discussed in an appropriate chapter. There are two four-page, full-color drawings of the major launch vehicles. Each is drawn to scale for comparison. Contains a chronology of the major space events since Sputnik 1, a glossary of terms, and an index. There is a great deal of text, which does not bog down the work but merely enhances the illustrations. Each chapter has its own list of references.

Hall, Al, ed. *Petersen's Book of Man in Space.* 5 vols. Los Angeles: Petersen, 1974.
This is a colorful presentation of the history of spaceflight from the early pioneers through the last Apollo flight. There are hundreds of color and black-and-white photographs and drawings. The focus is on the U.S. manned programs, perhaps because of the abundance of available photographs. The text is concise and enhances the pictures, although they really do not need enhancement. All of the spacecraft and launch vehicles of the U.S. programs are covered, as are the contributions of the pioneers of spaceflight and the astronauts.

Harrison, Harry, and Malcolm Edwards. *Spacecraft in Fact and Fantasy.* New York: Exeter Books, 1979.
This is an interesting work which compares some of our modern launch vehicles and spacecraft to those created in the minds of science-fiction writers. The work covers the history of spacecraft, primarily American, from the early pioneers through the pre-Shuttle era. There are numerous color and black-and-white photographs, as well as artwork from some of the science-fiction publications. The authors show how some of the predictions of early writers have

paralleled fact and take a look at the future with an eye on the science fiction of today. Provides a brief bibliography and an index.

Kaplan, Judith, and Robert Muniz. *Space Patches from Mercury to the Space Shuttle.* New York: Sterling, 1986, rev. ed. 1988.
This work, written and published by one of the manufacturers and distributors of cloth patches and vinyl decals, discusses the emblems' design by the astronaut crews and other participants in space programs. Overall, the work has been well researched and contains many interesting facts about the origins of these patches. Few people realize how the practice of designing crew patches began. The authors discuss Gemini V's "covered wagon" patch, the first ever flown, and the story behind the hidden "8 Days or Bust." The only major error concerns the Apollo 1 patch. It is an error which did not originate with this book, but is perpetuated by reference to the story of the patch's design. The crew of Apollo 1, officially known as Apollo 204, were killed in a fire which swept through their command module during a ground test. According to the authors, the crew patch has a black overlock border "as a sign of mourning for the lost crew." The patch does have this black border, but if one looks carefully at color photographs or films of the crew, the black border can be seen on the patch. Unless someone went back and airbrushed black borders on these prints, the crew must have been wearing the black-bordered patches before the accident. The book is filled with color photographs of the patches from various manned and unmanned missions, as well as space centers and other miscellaneous events. There is an appendix listing the U.S. manned flights and an index.

Kerrod, Robin. *The Illustrated History of NASA.* New York: Gallery Books, 1986.
One of the better books about the manned and unmanned space programs undertaken by NASA, this work was written shortly after the *Challenger* accident. Although the book mainly discusses the programs of NASA, there is one chapter devoted to NASA and its facilities throughout the United States. There are hundreds of color and black-and-white photographs. An appendix lists some of the highlights of NASA's first quarter century in chronological order. Contains an index and an epilogue devoted to the STS 51-L mission.

Ley, Willy. *Satellites, Rockets, and Outer Space.* New York: New American Library of World Literature, 1956, rev. ed. 1962.
This pocketbook is a fascinating look at the U.S. space programs to put satellites into orbit. The author discusses these early satellites and some of the feuding that went on between the Army and the Navy over who would be the first to launch a satellite. Some of the earliest space launch vehicles are described. Nontechnical physics lessons are presented in a discussion of propulsion and orbital mechanics. There is a section devoted to the solar

system, with emphasis on the third planet. In the final chapter there is a discussion of some future plans, including Moon cars and men on Mars. This last chapter is perhaps the most interesting, especially in the light of events that occurred during the subsequent quarter century. There are several line drawings and a few color photographs.

Newell, Homer. *Beyond the Atmosphere: Early Years of Space Science.* Washington, D.C.: Government Printing Office, 1980.
This is one of the volumes in the NASA History Series, the official history of the United States' space programs. This book covers the scientific investigations made possible by sounding rockets, satellites, and space probes. The author begins with a look at the early pioneers of rocketry and some of the first space scientists. The National Aeronautics and Space Administration was created in response to the launch of Sputnik 1 and the desire to release the military from its role in space exploration. NASA's design and organization is discussed, along with its interaction with other agencies, the military, and universities. Particular attention is given to the California Institute of Technology's Jet Propulsion Laboratory. There are dozens of black-and-white photographs, line drawings, tables, and charts. Provides an impressive appendix listing source notes and bibliographic references, and an index.

Ordway, Frederick I., III, and Mitchell R. Sharpe. *The Rocket Team.* Foreword by Wernher von Braun. New York: Thomas Y. Crowell, 1979.
The men responsible for the launch vehicles that put humans on the moon also were responsible for the missiles of World War II that brought destruction from the sky. This is the story of the group of German scientists and engineers, headed by von Braun, who developed the science of rocketry from the early 1930's through the Saturn family of launch vehicles. Much of the information about their days at Pennemünde was classified until this book was written. This is fascinating reading about scientists, dedicated to the betterment of humankind, being forced to develop war machines. There are black-and-white photographs, a bibliography, and an index.

Powers, Robert M. *Planetary Encounters.* Harrisburg, Pa.: Stackpole Books, 1978.
Written at the time of the launch of the two Voyager spacecraft, this work discusses the unmanned exploration of the solar system. The Pioneer, Mariner, Viking, and Voyager spacecraft are detailed, along with many of the color and black-and-white photographs they snapped at Mercury, Venus, and Mars. Each of these planets is described, and predictions are made as to what the probes will find at Jupiter, Saturn, Uranus, and Neptune. Appendices list information about the planets and their moons, planetary encounters, space and astronomy

magazines, sources for obtaining space photographs, and a glossary of terms. There are a bibliography and an index.

Rosenthal, A. *Venture into Space: Early Years of Goddard Space Flight Center.* Washington, D.C.: National Technical Information Service, 1968.
This is one of the volumes in the NASA History Series, the official history of the U.S. space programs. This book covers the history of NASA's Goddard Space Flight Center through 1963. The center, named for rocket pioneer Robert H. Goddard, was established on May 1, 1959, as NASA's first major scientific laboratory devoted entirely to the exploration of space. The modern, campuslike complex is located in Greenbelt, Maryland, only thirteen miles northeast of the nation's capital. During the early days (like today), the center was responsible for collecting and housing all the data from every U.S. spaceflight. Its scientists and engineers have developed spacecraft and launch vehicles, including the highly successful Delta. There are dozens of black-and-white photographs, line drawings, tables, and charts. Contains an impressive appendix listing source notes and bibliographic references, and an index.

Sagan, Carl. *Cosmos.* New York: Random House, 1980.
In 1980, the Public Broadcasting System aired the series *Cosmos*, which tells the story of man's discovery of the universe. This book is based upon that series. It presents, in a very interesting way, how scientists are exploring, with modern ground- and space-based instruments, the solar system and beyond. The history of the universe, as understood in 1980, is chronicled. The book is filled with color and black-and-white photographs, paintings, and etchings of the universe and its examiners—both human and mechanical. The author describes the probabilities of galactic civilizations and our search for them, as well as plans to go calling on them. There is an extensive bibliography and an index.

Shortal, Joseph A. *A New Dimension—Wallops Island Flight Test Range: The First Fifteen Years.* Washington, D.C.: National Technical Information Service, 1978.
The Wallops Station, located on Wallops Island, Virginia, was established by the National Advisory Committee for Aeronautics in 1945 to gather information about Earth's atmosphere and its near-space environment. During its first fifteen years, the facility launched more than six thousand research vehicles. Consisting of from one to seven stages, these vehicles were used to gather scientific information on the flight characteristics of airplanes, launch vehicles, and spacecraft, and to increase our understanding of the upper atmosphere and space environment. This large volume details the history of the facility, including its role in the development of wartime aircraft and missiles, ramjets, supersonic bodies, hypersonic vehicles, high-temperature research, ballistic missile nose cones, guided missiles, sounding rockets, and Project Mercury.

There are numerous black-and-white photographs and drawings and an index. Appendices detail rocket motors used at Wallops, program identification, flight operations, preflight jet operations, and rocket propulsion systems developed at Wallops.

Taylor, John W. R., ed. *Jane's All the World's Aircraft.* 17 vols. London: Jane's, 1957- .

Considered by some to be the most complete reference on aircraft, the biennial publication began to include rockets, missiles, and spacecraft after the first Sputnik was orbited. The most reliable sources of information are used to provide as much technical data about the vehicle, engine, or program as possible. Each issue highlights those systems or components which were introduced or made a significant contribution during the previous two-year period. The major manned and unmanned spaceflights are also detailed. There are black-and-white photographs and drawings of each vehicle or component.

Thompson, Tina D., ed. *Space Log: 1957-1987.* Redondo Beach, Calif.: TRW Space & Technology Group, 1988.

Each year, TRW publishes a log of worldwide space activities. Any new spacecraft, launch vehicle, engine, or program, or one which made a significant contribution to the exploration of space during the year, is detailed. Tables include a "box score" of U.S. launches, worldwide successful space launches, Space Transportation System payload deployment records, payloads in orbit, and manned spaceflight records. The highlight of each volume is the summary of space launches, which details (in a table) the name, international designation, program direction, launch data, weight, orbital data, and status. This particular volume was published in conjunction with the thirtieth anniversary of the space age and contains data for the entire era. Most major libraries have or can obtain copies of these logs directly from the publisher.

Turnill, Reginald, ed. *Jane's Spaceflight Directory.* London: Jane's, 1985-1989.

After publishing spacecraft, missile, and rocket engine data in *Jane's All the World's Aircraft* for a number of years, the publisher found the information too great not to be included in its own book. The biennial publication, like its parent, uses only the most reliable sources of information to provide as much technical data about the vehicle, engine, or program as possible. Each issue highlights those systems or components which were introduced or made a significant contribution during the previous two-year period. The major manned and unmanned spaceflights are also detailed. There are black-and-white photographs and drawings of each vehicle or component.

U.S. House of Representatives. *United States Civilian Space Programs 1958-1978.*
Vol. 1. Washington, D.C.: Government Printing Office, 1981.
In a very concise report, the Committee on Space Science and Applications has
compiled data on all U.S. space activity during its first two decades. After a
brief introduction and summary chapter, the volume is divided into fourteen
additional sections. The second chapter deals with the space-related issues under
consideration by Congress. The remaining sections cover the history of NASA
and its relationship to U.S. space policy, NASA facilities and tracking systems,
launch vehicles and propulsion, manned spaceflight through 1975, the Space
Transportation System, space life sciences, space science programs, materials
processing in space, international cooperation in space, interagency and non-
NASA governmental space activities, industrial and university support for
NASA, space program benefits, and selected future space programs. Appendices
contain Department of Defense manned spaceflight plans, NASA funding
history, international space agreements, texts of President Jimmy Carter's space
directives, documents relating to the legal aspects of the Space Shuttle, major
U.S. space organizations, a master log of U.S. spaceflights, and a table of U.S.
space orbital payloads by mission from 1957 through 1979.

Van Nimmen, Jane, and Leonard C. Bruno, with Robert L. Rosholt. *NASA
Historical Data Book 1958-1968.* Vol. 1, *NASA Resources.* Washington, D.C.:
National Technical Information Service, 1976.
This is the first in what was intended to be a series of volumes providing a
comprehensive statistical summary of the first decade of the National Aeronautics and Space Administration, from its post-Sputnik creation until the Apollo
8 astronauts became the first men to circle the Moon. This volume measures
dollars, people, and things and is designed to provide a reference source for
a variety of purposes. The summary documents the immense growth and
eventual leveling off of the agency's programs. It covers NASA's budget and
financial history, its scattered installations, its manpower resources, and a
statistical summary of its contractual history. This work is ideal for the "number cruncher," but it is difficult for the common researcher to wade through
its 547 pages. There is no table of contents or index, and one is forced to find
things by the "hunt and peck" method. However, it does provide a great deal
of information about how the mighty dollar influences the decisions of the
NASA. There are scores of tables and charts.

Von Braun, Wernher, and Frederick I. Ordway III. *History of Rocketry and Space
Travel.* 3d rev. ed. New York: Thomas Y. Crowell, 1975.
This is the story of the exploration of space from the earliest experiments with
rocketry to the final flight of the Skylab program. Hundreds of experts on
every aspect of this broad field contributed to the work. Most of the programs
of the United States, the Soviet Union, and the rest of the nations engaged in

space exploration at that time are detailed, both descriptively and with black-and-white and color photographs. It is one of the best references on the subject. The book also contains a large, chapter-by-chapter bibliography. The authors finish their discussion of the space programs with a look at the future, including the Space Transportation System.

Wells, Helen T., Susan Whiteley, and Carrie E. Karegeannes. *Origins of NASA Names*. Washington, D.C.: National Technical Information Service, 1976.
Ever wonder how a particular spacecraft, launch vehicle, or program derived its name? Although this work is dated, it provides a great number of answers regarding these names. This is one of the volumes in the NASA History Series, and it is a wonderful book for trivia buffs. It discusses the major NASA projects, launch vehicles, satellites, space probes, sounding rockets, manned spacecraft, and NASA installations. Appendices list abbreviations, acronyms, and terms; international designation of spacecraft; NASA major launch records, 1958-1974; and NASA naming committees. There are dozens of black-and-white photographs, an index, and an in-depth bibliography.

Yenne, Bill. *The Encyclopedia of U.S. Spacecraft*. New York: Exeter Books, 1985.
A complete encyclopedia of U.S. spacecraft is presented in a book filled with color and black-and-white photographs. General information on the programs is provided in alphabetical order, with individual spacecraft, probes, or launch vehicles listed chronologically. Data on all of the unmanned spacecraft and probes, including Mariner, Voyager, Viking, LAGEOS, Ranger, and Intelsat, are furnished. Contains an appendix listing acronyms and abbreviations, and an index.

_____. *The Pictorial History of World Spacecraft*. New York: Exeter Books, 1988.
The history of the world's spacecraft and probes is told in chronological order, from Sputnik 1 through Cosmos 1870, and spans the first thirty years of the space age. Included are all of the manned and unmanned spacecraft, probes, and launch vehicles. Each is detailed with charts, diagrams, illustrations, and color and black-and-white photographs. Data on all of the unmanned spacecraft and probes, including Explorer, Big Bird, Pioneer, Relay, TIROS, and the Solar Maximum Mission, are provided. There is an appendix that lists all of the spacecraft in service as of July, 1987, grouped according to the countries or organizations responsible for them.

Lunar Probes

General Studies

Goldstein, Norm, ed. *Moments in Space.* New York: Gallery Books, 1986, pp. 107-141.

Newspaper photographs from the Associated Press are the highlight of this book, which offers little text to accompany them. The lunar and interplanetary probes are grouped together. The photographs of the planets and moons lose a lot of appeal in this black-and-white medium. Much of the monograph is not to be relied on for accuracy, especially because the information included with the photographs has not been updated from what was known at the time of the event. Many of the photographs are grainy, but it is for their historical context that they should be viewed, not for their clarity.

Lewis, Richard S. "Mare Nubium." In *Appointment on the Moon.* New York: Ballantine Books, 1969.

In one of the most complete references on the U.S. space program (through the Apollo 11 manned lunar landing), Lewis discusses the role that unmanned explorers played in Apollo. He focuses on Ranger, Surveyor, and Lunar Orbiter and their contributions to the selection of a manned landing site. They also played a part in determining what type of craft could safely land on the Moon and whether the lunar surface would support a strolling astronaut. Because of the broad range of subject matter covered in the book, there is no extensive coverage of any one aspect of these programs. There are several pages of black-and-white photographs and an excellent listing of reference material.

Lolich, Clarice. "The Jet Propulsion Laboratory." In *Magill's Survey of Science: Space Exploration Series,* vol. 2, edited by Frank N. Magill. Pasadena, Calif.: Salem Press, 1989.

One of the essays on the history of space exploration in the five-volume set, which covers every aspect of the U.S. and Soviet manned and unmanned space programs, as well as those from nations newer to the space race. The Jet Propulsion Laboratory (JPL), part of the California Institute of Technology, is primarily responsible for the exploration of the solar system with unmanned spacecraft. This essay details the origin of JPL and its contributions to the space program. Emphasis is placed on JPL's role in the lunar and planetary unmanned programs. Provides an annotated bibliography and cross-references.

Magill, Frank N., ed. *Magill's Survey of Science: Space Exploration Series.* 5 vols. Pasadena, Calif.: Salem Press, 1989.

This five-volume set covers every aspect of the U.S. and Soviet manned and unmanned space programs, as well as those of nations newer to the space race. The United States sent a variety of probes to the Moon in order to gather data for the planned Apollo manned landings. Spacecraft and programs covered in this work include Lunar Orbiter, Pioneer, Ranger, and Surveyor. Each essay lists the pertinent data of the mission, launch vehicle, and spacecraft. Presents a brief summary of the program, the knowledge gained by the probes, and the historical significance of each mission. Included is an annotated bibliography and cross-references to related articles in the set.

Moore, Patrick. *The Moon.* New York: Rand McNally, 1981.
Our nearest neighbor in space is explored in this photo-atlas of the Moon. The origin and status of the Moon are discussed, as are its orbit and its effect on Earth's tides. A history of lunar observation is presented, along with the unmanned and manned missions to study it up close. The highlight is the color and black-and-white photographs which show the features of the Moon, including the maria, highlands, craters, and unusual features. Maps of the near and far sides are presented. There is an index and a bibliography.

Sagan, Carl. *Cosmos.* New York: Random House, 1980.
In 1980, the Public Broadcasting Service aired the series *Cosmos*, which tells the story of man's discovery of the universe. This book is based upon that series. It presents, in a very interesting way, how man is exploring, with modern ground- and space-based instruments, our solar system and beyond. The history of the universe, as it was understood in 1980, is chronicled. The book is filled with color and black-and-white photographs, paintings, and etchings of the universe and its examiners—both human and mechanical. The author describes the probabilities of galactic civilizations and our search for them, as well as plans to go calling on them. Contains an extensive bibliography and an index.

Taylor, John W. R., ed. *Jane's All the World's Aircraft.* 17 vols. London: Jane's, 1957- .
Considered by some to be the most complete reference on aircraft, the biennial publication began to include rockets, missiles, and spacecraft after the first Sputnik was orbited. The most reliable sources of information are used to provide as much technical data about the vehicle, engine, or program as possible. Each issue highlights those systems or components that were introduced or made a significant contribution during the previous two-year period. The major manned and unmanned spaceflights are also detailed. There are black-and-white photographs and drawings of each vehicle or component.

Thompson, Tina D., ed. *Space Log: 1957-1987.* Redondo Beach, Calif.: TRW Space & Technology Group, 1988.
Each year, TRW publishes a log of worldwide space activities. Any new spacecraft, launch vehicle, engine, or program, or one which made a significant contribution to the exploration of space during the year, is detailed. Tables include a "box score" of U.S. launches, worldwide successful space launches, Space Transportation System payload deployment records, payloads in orbit, and manned spaceflight records. The highlight of each volume is the summary of space launches, which details (in a table) the name, international designation, program direction, launch data, weight, orbital data, and status. This particular volume was published in conjunction with the thirtieth anniversary of the space age and contains data for the entire era. Most major libraries have or can obtain copies of these logs directly from the publisher.

U.S. House of Representatives. *United States Civilian Space Programs 1958-1978.* Vol. 1. Washington, D.C.: Government Printing Office, 1981.
In a very concise report, the Committee on Space Science and Applications has compiled data on all U.S. space activity during its first two decades. After a brief introduction and summary chapter, the volume is divided into fourteen additional sections. The second chapter deals with the space-related issues under consideration by Congress. The remaining sections cover the history of NASA and its relationship to U.S. space policy, NASA facilities and tracking systems, launch vehicles and propulsion, manned spaceflight through 1975, the Space Transportation System, space life sciences, space science programs, materials processing in space, international cooperation in space, interagency and non-NASA governmental space activities, industrial and university support for NASA, space program benefits, and selected future space programs. Appendices contain Department of Defense manned spaceflight plans, NASA funding history, international space agreements, texts of President Jimmy Carter's space directives, documents relating to the legal aspects of the Space Shuttle, major U.S. space organizations, a master log of U.S. spaceflights, and a table of U.S. space orbital payloads by mission from 1957 through 1979.

Wilson, Andrew. *Solar System Log.* London: Jane's, 1987.
A comprehensive look at the unmanned spacecraft which explored the Moon and our neighboring planets. Each year of the first thirty years of the space age is explored. Each spacecraft is detailed, as is each mission flown. There are dozens of photographs of the extraterrestrial landscapes, the spacecraft, and their launches, as well as drawings diagraming the inner workings of each craft and its trajectory through the heavens. It is truly a comprehensive work and a reliable source for the researcher.

Woods, David. "Probes to the Moon." In *The Illustrated Encyclopedia of Space Technology: A Comprehensive History of Space Exploration*, by Kenneth Gatland et al. New York: Harmony Books, 1981.
This section in the book discusses the unmanned spacecraft sent to study the Moon. Some of the more exotic ones, such as the Soviet's Lunokhod 2, Luna 9, and Luna 16, are detailed with color cutaway views and diagrams of their deployment sequences. The American Ranger, Lunar Orbiter, and Surveyor spacecraft are discussed. A two-page chart lists each of the probes and its mission, weight, booster, and date of launch. There are color and black-and-white photographs of the Moon taken by several of these craft. The appendices of the book contain a chronology of the major space events since Sputnik 1, a glossary of terms, and an index.

Pioneer

Magill, Frank N., ed. *Magill's Survey of Science: Space Exploration Series*. Vol. 3. Pasadena, Calif.: Salem Press, 1989, pp. 1116-1158.
Six essays from this five-volume set on the history of space exploration, which covers every aspect of the U.S. and Soviet manned and unmanned space programs, as well as those of nations newer to the space race. The Pioneer spacecraft explored the Moon, the Sun, Venus, Jupiter, and Saturn. They helped pave the way for larger, more sophisticated probes to study these heavenly bodies. The essays discuss the development of the spacecraft and details each of the missions. Contains an annotated bibliography and cross-references.

Mitchum, Ellen F. "Atlas Launch Vehicles." In *Magill's Survey of Science: Space Exploration Series*, vol. 1, edited by Frank N. Magill. Pasadena, Calif.: Salem Press, 1989.
One of the essays on the history of space exploration in this five-volume set, which covers every aspect of the U.S. and Soviet manned and unmanned space programs, as well as those of nations newer to the space race. The Atlas vehicle was first built as an intercontinental ballistic missile (ICBM) for the Air Force. It was later modified to launch a variety of manned and unmanned spacecraft. Some of these include the Mercury spacecraft, the Gemini Agena Target Vehicle, Mariner, Pioneer, Ranger, Lunar Orbiter, Surveyor, and many other military and civilian spacecraft. This essay discusses the development of the vehicle and its contributions to space exploration. Contains an annotated bibliography and cross-references.

Ranger

Hall, R. Cargill. *Lunar Impact: A History of Project Ranger.* Washington, D.C.: National Technical Information Service, 1977.
One of the NASA History Series, this work studies the Ranger probes to the Moon. Launched to the Moon between 1961 and 1965, these nine probes (only the last three were successful) have pave the way for the unmanned lunar landing missions and the manned Apollo flights. The author looks at the origins of Ranger, as well as the campaign to get the program approved. The spacecraft are detailed, as are the cameras used to send back the television pictures. There are dozens of black-and-white photographs and line drawings. Appendices discuss lunar theory before 1964, lunar missions 1958 through 1965, spacecraft technical details, Ranger experiments, Ranger schedule history, Ranger financial history, and Ranger performance history. A comprehensive bibliography of scientific findings, as well as a complete list of sources, is provided. There is an index.

Herczeg, T. J. "The Ranger Program." In *Magill's Survey of Science: Space Exploration Series*, vol. 3, edited by Frank N. Magill. Pasadena, Calif.: Salem Press, 1989.
One of the essays on the history of space exploration in this five-volume set, which covers every aspect of the U.S. and Soviet manned and unmanned space programs, as well as those of nations newer to the space race. Ranger was the first major program developed by NASA to transmit close-up information about the surface of the Moon in preparation for the Apollo manned landings. These kamikaze probes transmitted black-and-white television pictures of some of the proposed landing sites just before crashing to the surface. This article discusses these probes, their missions, and the contributions they made to the success of Apollo. Provides an annotated bibliography and cross-references.

Mitchum, Ellen F. "Atlas Launch Vehicles." In *Magill's Survey of Science: Space Exploration Series*, vol. 1, edited by Frank N. Magill. Pasadena, Calif.: Salem Press, 1989.
One of the essays on the history of space exploration in this five-volume set, which covers every aspect of the U.S. and Soviet manned and unmanned space programs, as well as those of nations newer to the space race. The Atlas vehicle was first built as an intercontinental ballistic missile (ICBM) for the Air Force. It was later modified to launch a variety of manned and unmanned spacecraft. Some of these include the Mercury spacecraft, the Gemini Agena Target Vehicle, Mariner, Ranger, Lunar Orbiter, Surveyor, and many other military and civilian spacecraft. This essay discusses the development of the vehicle and its contributions to space exploration. Contains an annotated bibliography and cross-references.

Lunar Orbiter

Becker, Thomas W. "The Lunar Orbiter." In *Magill's Survey of Science: Space Exploration Series*, vol. 2, edited by Frank N. Magill. Pasadena, Calif.: Salem Press, 1989.
One of the essays on the history of space exploration in this five-volume set, which covers every aspect of the U.S. and Soviet manned and unmanned space programs, as well as those of nations newer to the space race. The Lunar Orbiter program was developed to provide scientists with photographic surveys of the lunar surface in preparation for the Apollo manned Moon landings. This article summarizes the program and details the spacecraft and their results. Contains an annotated bibliography and cross-references.

Hansen, Thomas P. *Guide to Lunar Orbiter Photographs*. Washington, D.C.: Government Printing Office, 1970.
This work presents a look at the photographic coverage of the Moon by five identical spacecraft, the Lunar Orbiters. The program was initiated in 1964 to obtain detailed photographs of the Moon. This document presents information on the location and coverage of all Lunar Orbiter photographs. The spacecraft's photographic system is discussed, along with details of each mission. There are dozens of black-and-white photographic maps, each of which is further detailed in tables and diagrams.

Kosofsky, L. J., and Farouk El-Baz. *The Moon as Viewed by Lunar Orbiter.* Washington, D.C.: Government Printing Office, 1970.
Hundreds of black-and-white photographs of the Moon taken by the five Lunar Orbiter spacecraft fill this volume. The surface features of the Moon are detailed with close-up views of maria, the highlands, craters, faults, rilles, and domes. There are several stereoscopic views created by overlapping medium-resolution frames of the same scene. The two shots are printed in complimentary colors (red and blue) so that when viewed through the enclosed colored spectacles, each eye sees the image of a different frame. There is an index of the photomaps and a photo reference table.

Mitchum, Ellen F. "Atlas Launch Vehicles." In *Magill's Survey of Science: Space Exploration Series*, vol. 1, edited by Frank N. Magill. Pasadena, Calif.: Salem Press, 1989.
One of the essays on the history of space exploration in this five-volume set, which covers every aspect of the U.S. and Soviet manned and unmanned space programs, as well as those of nations newer to the space race. The Atlas vehicle was first built as an intercontinental ballistic missile (ICBM) for the Air Force. It was later modified to launch a variety of manned and unmanned spacecraft. Some of these include the Mercury spacecraft, the Gemini Agena

Target Vehicle, Mariner, Ranger, Lunar Orbiter, Surveyor, and many other military and civilian spacecraft. This essay discusses the development of the vehicle and its contributions to space exploration. Contains an annotated bibliography and cross-references.

Surveyor

Flynn, George. "The Surveyor Program." In *Magill's Survey of Science: Space Exploration Series*, vol. 5, edited by Frank N. Magill. Pasadena, Calif.: Salem Press, 1989.
One of the essays on the history of space exploration in this five-volume set, which covers every aspect of the U.S. and Soviet manned and unmanned space programs, as well as those of nations newer to the space race. When the United States decided it was going to land a man on the Moon, NASA set out to find the best way to do it. It was decided that a soft landing using a retrorocket system (since parachutes will not work without air) would be best. Unlike their suicidal predecessor Ranger, the Surveyor probes soft-landed on the lunar surface. This essay briefly looks at the program and the seven flights. Contains an annotated bibliography and cross-references.

Mitchum, Ellen F. "Atlas Launch Vehicles." In *Magill's Survey of Science: Space Exploration Series*, vol. 1, edited by Frank N. Magill. Pasadena, Calif.: Salem Press, 1989.
The Atlas vehicle was first built as an intercontinental ballistic missile (ICBM) for the Air Force. It was later modified to launch a variety of manned and unmanned spacecraft. Some of these include the Mercury spacecraft, the Gemini Agena Target Vehicle, Mariner, Ranger, Lunar Orbiter, Surveyor, and many other military and civilian spacecraft. This essay discusses the development of the vehicle and its contributions to space exploration. Contains an annotated bibliography and cross-references.

U.S. National Aeronautics and Space Administration. *Analysis of Surveyor 3 Material and Photographs Returned by Apollo 12*. Washington, D.C.: National Technical Information Service, 1972.
Surveyor 3 landed on the Moon's Ocean of Storms in April, 1967, to conduct experiments, take television pictures, and sample the lunar surface to help determine whether the Moon could support a manned mission. Two years later, the Apollo 12 crew landed about six hundred feet away from Surveyor. The astronauts, in addition to photographing the spacecraft, brought back Surveyor's trenching tool, camera, and several pieces of tubing and a cable. This book provides the researcher with information about what exposure to the lunar "atmosphere" does to man-made equipment. This information was useful in

designing equipment for placement on the lunar surface by future crews. Copies of the black-and-white photographs taken by astronauts Conrad and Bean are included.

_____. *Surveyor III: A Preliminary Report*. Washington, D.C.: National Technical Information Service, 1967.
The object of the Surveyor program was to soft-land a series of spacecraft on the lunar surface to demonstrate that manned spacecraft could do the same. Surveyor 3 alighted in the Ocean of Storms on April 20, 1967. During its descent to the surface, highly reflective rocks fooled the landing radar into commanding the retrorockets to shut down early. This caused Surveyor to bounce twice. Its systems were shut down for the cold lunar night on May 3, and when it was time to revive them, Surveyor failed to respond. During its short life, its television camera transmitted more than six thousand pictures and its surface-sampling scoop dug trenches. This report details the results obtained during Surveyor's operation. Portions of the spacecraft were returned to Earth after Apollo 12 landed within six hundred feet of Surveyor.

Interplanetary Probes

General Studies

Allen, Joseph P., with Russell Martin. *Entering Space*. New York: Stewart, Tabori & Chang, 1984.
The story of an astronaut's journey in space, told in conjunction with a study of the American exploration of space. This work is filled with colorful words and spectacular photographs of space travel from the ground up, and back again. There are hundreds of color photographs taken during the manned Gemini, Apollo, Skylab, Apollo Soyuz, and Space Shuttle programs, as well as those shots of our neighbors in the solar system taken from unmanned probes. The spacecraft, launch vehicles, spacefarers, and their equipment are discussed in some detail, although this is primarily done in the perspective of a single trip into orbit and back again. There is a very real sense of "being there" as Astronaut Allen describes his feelings during the various phases of flight. Contains a brief bibliography and an index.

Batson, R. M., P. M. Bridges, and J. L. Inge. *Atlas of Mars*. Washington, D.C.: National Technical Information Service, 1979.
Images from the Mariner 9 spacecraft and the two Viking orbiters were combined to create small-scale maps and photomosaics of Mars. The Mariner 9 spacecraft was launched by an Atlas Centaur booster on May 30, 1971. It

arrived at Mars on November 13 and began ninety days of photographic mapping, taking 6,876 photographs of the Martian surface. The two Viking orbiters and their respective landing vehicles were launched in the fall of 1975 by individual Titan-3/Centaur boosters. The spacecraft went into orbit around Mars the following summer. Viking 1 returned photographs for four years, while Viking 2 lasted only two. There are dozens of black-and-white photographs, line drawings, and maps. An index of place-names details the source of each name.

Beatty, J. Kelly, Brian O'Leary, and Andrew Chaikin. *The New Solar System.* Cambridge, Mass.: Sky, 1981.
This work discusses the planets of the solar system and their moons, as observed by the unmanned probes that explored them. Using photographs and data returned by them and by the Apollo astronauts who went to the Moon, the authors detail each celestial body. Each chapter is written by an authority on the particular body or scientific discipline. There are dozens of color and black-and-white photographs, an annotated bibliography, and an index.

Bova, Ben, with Trudy E. Bell, eds. *Closeup: New Worlds.* New York: St. Martin's Press, 1977.
A collection of essays written by some of the best-known science and science-fiction writers in the world. This fact-filled book details the solar system: its planets, moons, and other phenomena. There are plenty of color and black-and-white photographs of these extraterrestrial entities and a description of the efforts to obtain these pictures with space probes. Photographs taken from ground-based observatories are compared with those from the visiting spacecraft, such as Mariner, Viking, and Pioneer, as well as those originating in the Soviet Union. Descriptions of each spacecraft and the story of their travels are included.

Briggs, Geoffrey, and Fredric Taylor. *The Cambridge Photographic Atlas of the Planets.* Cambridge, England: Cambridge University Press, 1982.
This work was completed shortly after the successful flybys of Jupiter and Saturn by the two Voyager spacecraft. Using photographic data received from them and the other unmanned explorers of the solar system, including Mariner, Viking, Lunar Orbiter, Ranger, and Pioneer, the authors have compiled photomosaic maps of the first six planets. The planets and their moons are detailed: basic physical characteristics, geology, atmosphere, and special phenomena, such as rings. There are numerous photographs, photomaps, and drawings.

Goldstein, Norm, ed. *Moments in Space.* New York: Gallery Books, 1986, pp. 107-141.

Newspaper photographs from the Associated Press are the highlight of this book, which offers little text to accompany them. The lunar and interplanetary probes are grouped together. The photographs of the planets and moons lose a lot of appeal in this black-and-white medium. Much of the book is not to be relied on for accuracy, especially because the information included with the photographs has not been updated from what was known at the time of the event. Many of the photographs are grainy, but it is for their historical context that they should be viewed, not for their clarity.

Hunt, Garry, and Patrick Moore. *Atlas of Uranus.* Cambridge, England: Cambridge University Press, 1989.
The next-to-last stop on Voyager 2's celestial journey was Uranus. This volume details Uranus and several of its moons. There are maps of the atmosphere of Uranus, as well as the surfaces of Oberon, Titania, Umbriel, Ariel, Miranda, and several smaller moons. The book also discusses the ring system of Uranus, describes the Voyager spacecraft, and makes comparisons with Earth-based observations. For some reason, the authors did not include a glossary, bibliography, or data tables on the planets of the solar system. It can be expected that there will be an Atlas of Neptune forthcoming.

_____. *Jupiter.* New York: Rand McNally, 1981.
Photographs taken by the two Voyager spacecraft are the focus of this study of giant Jupiter and several of its moons. Basic physical characteristics of Jupiter and its moons are given and compared with Earth-based observations. The structure of Jupiter and its ring system are detailed. Maps of Jupiter's cloud cover and its moons, Io, Europa, Ganymede, Callisto, and several of the outer moons, are presented. There are tables of solar system data and the positions of Jupiter, as seen from Earth, during 1981-1989. Contains a glossary of terms, an index, and a brief bibliography.

_____. *Saturn.* New York: Rand McNally, 1982.
After Jupiter, the next planet observed by the Voyager spacecraft was Saturn. This book presents details of the Saturnian system, its rings and moons. The Voyager spacecraft are discussed, as well as the technology necessary to transmit the photographs over great distances. There are maps of Saturn's atmosphere and the surfaces of some its moons, Mimas, Enceladus, Tethys, Dione, Rhea, Titan, Hyperion, Iapetus, Phoebe, and some of the smaller moons. There are tables of solar system data and the positions of Saturn, as seen from Earth, during 1982-1992. Contains a glossary of terms, an index, and a brief bibliography.

Lewis, Richard S. "No Hiding Place." In *Appointment on the Moon.* New York: Ballantine Books, 1969.

This work is a comprehensive account of the U.S. space program from its roots in Germany's V-2 of World War II through the first lunar landing of Apollo 11. The Mariner and Pioneer interplanetary probes had very little direct impact on Apollo, but their contribution to the development of space hardware is significant. One area of importance is in the field of radioisotope thermoelectric generators. They are necessary for the exploration of the outer planets, where solar power is impractical. Their use in the Apollo Lunar Surface Experiments Packages permitted the operation of the scientific stations during the long lunar night. There are several pages of black-and-white photographs and an excellent listing of reference material.

Lolich, Clarice. "The Jet Propulsion Laboratory." In *Magill's Survey of Science: Space Exploration Series*, vol. 2, edited by Frank N. Magill. Pasadena, Calif.: Salem Press, 1989.
One of the essays on the history of space exploration in this five-volume set, which covers every aspect of the U.S. and Soviet manned and unmanned space programs, as well as those of nations newer to the space race. The Jet Propulsion Laboratory (JPL), part of the California Institute of Technology, is primarily responsible for the exploration of the solar system with unmanned spacecraft. This essay details the origin of JPL and its contributions to the space program. Emphasis is placed on JPL's role in the lunar and planetary unmanned programs. Contains an annotated bibliography and cross-references.

Magill, Frank N., ed. *Magill's Survey of Science: Space Exploration Series*. 5 vols. Pasadena, Calif.: Salem Press, 1989.
This five-volume set covers every aspect of the U.S. and Soviet manned and unmanned space programs, as well as those of nations newer to the space race. The United States sent a variety of probes to study our neighbors in the solar system. They have sent back hundreds of close-up photographs, which have raised as many new questions as they have answered old ones. Spacecraft and programs covered in this work include Halley's Comet probes, Mariner, Pioneer, Viking, and Voyager. Each essay lists the pertinent data of the mission, launch vehicle, and spacecraft. There is a brief summary of the program, the knowledge gained by the probes, and the historical significance of each mission. Each essay contains an annotated bibliography and cross-references to other essays in the set.

Mason, Robert Grant, ed. "Exploring Deep Space." In *Life in Space*. Alexandria, Va.: Time-Life Books, 1983.
The editors of *Life* magazine have sifted through hundreds of NASA's and their own photographs taken during the first twenty-five years of the space age. What has resulted is a superb collection of photographs of each U.S. manned spaceflight, from Alan Shepard's suborbital hop in *Freedom 7* through the STS-

52 *America in Space*

6 Space Shuttle mission. Throughout the work are breathtaking color and startling black-and-white photographs. These cover a range of topics, including the spacecraft and launch vehicles. The focus of this segment is on flights to neighboring planets in the solar system, with spectacular views of Mercury, Venus, Mars, Jupiter, and Saturn.

Melton, Robert G. "The Interplanetary Monitoring Platform Satellites." In *Magill's Survey of Science: Space Exploration Series*, vol. 2, edited by Frank N. Magill. Pasadena, Calif.: Salem Press, 1989.
One of the essays on the history of space exploration in this five-volume set, which covers every aspect of the U.S. and Soviet manned and unmanned space programs, as well as those of nations newer to the space race. The ten Interplanetary Monitoring Platform (IMP) satellites were deployed during the ten-year period beginning November, 1963. They measured cosmic radiation levels, magnetic field intensities, and solar wind properties in the near-Earth and interplanetary environments. This work chronicles the IMP program. Provides an annotated bibliography and cross-references.

Murray, Bruce. *Journey into Space: The First Three Decades of Space Exploration*. New York: W. W. Norton, 1989.
A comprehensive look at the U.S. and Soviet unmanned probes to Venus, Mercury, Mars, Jupiter, Saturn, and Uranus. Murray, director of the Jet Propulsion Laboratory from 1976 to 1982, shares the triumphs and mishaps of the quest to explore the solar system. The details of planning and executing these missions are discussed, providing an insider's look at what it takes to get a probe off the ground. The problems of working through NASA and the politics of space exploration are scrutinized with the scientist's eye. There is an extensive, annotated bibliography, although some of the entries are mentioned only in passing. Dozens of black-and-white photographs and drawings add to the text.

Powers, Robert M. *Planetary Encounters*. Harrisburg, Pa.: Stackpole Books, 1978.
Written at the time of the launch of the two Voyager spacecraft, this work discusses the unmanned exploration of the solar system. The Pioneer, Mariner, Viking, and Voyager spacecraft are detailed, along with many of the color and black-and-white photographs they snapped at Mercury, Venus, and Mars. Each of these planets is described and predictions are made as to what the probes will find at Jupiter, Saturn, Uranus, and Neptune. Appendices list information about the planets and their moons, planetary encounters, space and astronomy magazines, sources for obtaining space photographs, and a glossary of terms. Also provides a bibliography and an index.

Sagan, Carl. *Cosmos.* New York: Random House, 1980.
In 1980, the Public Broadcasting Service aired the series *Cosmos*, which tells the story of man's discovery of the universe. This book is based upon that series. It presents, in a very interesting way, how man is exploring, with modern ground- and space-based instruments, the solar system and beyond. The history of the universe, as understood in 1980, is chronicled. The book is filled with color and black-and-white photographs, paintings, and etchings of the universe and its examiners—both human and mechanical. The author describes the probabilities of galactic civilizations and our search for them, as well as plans to go calling on them. There is an extensive bibliography and an index.

Taylor, John W. R., ed. *Jane's All the World's Aircraft.* 17 vols. London: Jane's, 1957- .
Considered by some to be the most complete reference on aircraft, the biennial publication began to include rockets, missiles, and spacecraft after the first Sputnik was orbited. The most reliable sources of information are used to provide as much technical data about the vehicle, engine, or program as possible. Each issue highlights those systems or components that were introduced or made a significant contribution during the previous two-year period. The major manned and unmanned spaceflights are also detailed. There are black-and-white photographs and drawings of each vehicle or component.

Thompson, Tina D., ed. *Space Log: 1957-1987.* Redondo Beach, Calif.: TRW Space & Technology Group, 1988.
Each year, TRW publishes a log of worldwide space activities. Any new spacecraft, launch vehicle, engine, or program, or one which made a significant contribution to the exploration of space during the year, is detailed. Tables include a "box score" of U.S. launches, worldwide successful space launches, Space Transportation System payload deployment records, payloads in orbit, and manned spaceflight records. The highlight of each volume is the summary of space launches, which details (in a table) the name, international designation, program direction, launch data, weight, orbital data, and status. This particular volume was published in conjunction with the thirtieth anniversary of the space age and contains data for the entire era. Most major libraries have or can obtain copies of these logs directly from the publisher.

U.S. General Accounting Office. *Space Exploration: NASA's Deep Space Missions Are Experiencing Long Delays.* Washington, D.C.: Government Printing Office, 1988.
This work is the report of the GAO's findings on four of NASA's proposed deep space missions. The report covers the Galileo mission to Jupiter, the Ulysses mission to the Sun, the Magellan mission to Venus, and the Mars Observer mission. The report provides a general overview of the program,

including its objectives, scope, and methodology. There are spacecraft configuration drawings and information relating to cost, schedule, and performance. A chronology of the project, to the date of the report, is presented. There is a glossary of terms used.

U.S. House of Representatives. *United States Civilian Space Programs 1958-1978.* Vol. 1. Washington, D.C.: Government Printing Office, 1981.
In a very concise report, the Committee on Space Science and Applications has compiled data on all U.S. space activity during its first two decades. After a brief introduction and summary chapter, the volume is divided into fourteen additional sections. The second chapter deals with the space-related issues under consideration by Congress. The remaining sections cover the history of NASA and its relationship to U.S. space policy, NASA facilities and tracking systems, launch vehicles and propulsion, manned spaceflight through 1975, the Space Transportation System, space life sciences, space science programs, materials processing in space, international cooperation in space, interagency and non-NASA governmental space activities, industrial and university support for NASA, space program benefits, and selected future space programs. Appendices contain Department of Defense manned spaceflight plans, NASA funding history, international space agreements, texts of President Jimmy Carter's space directives, documents relating to the legal aspects of the Space Shuttle, major U.S. space organizations, a master log of U.S. spaceflights, and a table of U.S. space orbital payloads by mission from 1957 through 1979.

U.S. National Aeronautics and Space Administration and U.S. Air Force. *STS Inertial Upper Stage (IUS) Systems Handbook, Basic,* Rev., G. Washington, D.C.: Government Printing Office, 1988.
The Inertial Upper Stage (IUS) is a high-altitude booster that is used in conjunction with either the Space Shuttle or the Titan launch vehicle. It was originally designed as a temporary stand-in for a reusable space tug and was called the "Interim" Upper Stage. When it became apparent that the space tug would not be developed in the foreseeable future, the Interim Upper Stage began its gradual evolution into the Inertial Upper Stage ("inertial" refers to its guidance technique). This volume is the official handbook on the IUS used by everyone associated with its development, construction, deployment, and use. It contains hundreds of detailed drawings and schematics. Although much of it is highly technical, the illustrations make it easy to understand.

Von Braun, Wernher, and Frederick I. Ordway III. *History of Rocketry and Space Travel.* 3d rev. ed. New York: Thomas Y. Crowell, 1975.
This is the story of the exploration of space from the earliest experiments with rocketry to the final flight of the Skylab program. Hundreds of experts on every aspect of this broad field contributed to the work. Most of the programs

of the United States, the Soviet Union, and the rest of the nations engaged in space exploration at that time are detailed, both descriptively and with black-and-white and color photographs. It is one of the best references on the subject. The book also contains a large, chapter-by-chapter bibliography. The authors finish their discussion of the space programs with a look at the future, including the Space Transportation System.

Wilson, Andrew. *Solar System Log*. London: Jane's, 1987.
A comprehensive look at the unmanned spacecraft which explored the Moon and our neighboring planets. Each year of the first thirty years of the space age is explored. Each spacecraft is detailed, as is each mission flown. There are dozens of photographs of the extraterrestrial landscapes, the spacecraft, and their launches, as well as drawings diagraming the inner workings of each craft and its trajectory through the heavens. It is truly a comprehensive work and a reliable source for the researcher.

Woods, David. "Probes to the Planets." In *The Illustrated Encyclopedia of Space Technology: A Comprehensive History of Space Exploration*, by Kenneth Gatland et al. New York: Harmony Books, 1981.
This section in the book discusses the interplanetary probes of the United States and the Soviet Union. American spacecraft detailed include Mariner, Viking, Pioneer, and Voyager. There are color drawings of Voyager and the Viking lander and orbiter. A two-page chart lists each of the probes, their mission, weight, booster, and date of launch. There are color and black-and-white photographs of the planets visited by the spacecraft. The major features of the programs, including the spacecraft and launch vehicle, are discussed. In the appendices of the book there is a chronology of the major space events since Sputnik 1, a glossary of terms, and an index.

Pioneer

Bova, Ben, with Trudy E. Bell, eds. *Closeup: New Worlds*. New York: St. Martin's Press, 1977.
A collection of essays written by some of the best-known science and science-fiction writers in the world. This fact-filled book details our solar system, its planets, moons, and other phenomena. There are plenty of color and black-and-white photographs of these extraterrestrial entities and a description of the efforts to obtain these pictures with space probes. Photographs taken from ground-based observatories are compared with those taken from the visiting spacecraft, such as Mariner, Viking, and Pioneer, as well as those originating in the Soviet Union. Descriptions of each spacecraft and the story of their travels are included.

Corliss, William R. *Interplanetary Pioneers.* 3 vols. Washington, D.C.: Government Printing Office, 1972.
This work, part of the NASA Special Publication series (SP-278 through SP-280), discusses the Pioneer 6 through 9 spacecraft, which explored the interplanetary space around the Sun. They measured and transmitted back to Earth data on solar plasma, solar and galactic cosmic radiation, magnetic and electric fields, and the specks of cosmic dust that pervade interplanetary space. These three volumes summarize the missions, detail the system design and development, and discuss the operations surrounding the launches and return of data. There are numerous black-and-white photographs and line drawings. Each volume has its own index and bibliography.

Fimmel, Richard O., James A. Van Allen, and Eric Burgess. *Pioneer: First to Jupiter, Saturn, and Beyond.* Washington, D.C.: National Technical Information Service, 1980.
This work takes a look at the scientific and photographic data returned by Pioneer 10 and 11. The Pioneer 10 spacecraft was launched on March 3, 1972, followed a year later by Pioneer 11. Each was sent on its interplanetary journey by an Atlas-Centaur launch vehicle. Pioneer 10 went to Jupiter, arriving in December, 1973. After photographing and collecting other data about the giant planet, Pioneer 10 began its journey out of the solar system. Although it passed the orbits of Saturn, Uranus, and Neptune, it was not close enough to photograph any of them. In 1987, it became the first man-made object to leave the solar system. Pioneer 11 began its study of Jupiter on December 3, 1974, and encountered Saturn five years later. In addition to providing data on Jupiter, and some of its moons, this work details the Pioneer spacecraft. Color and black-and-white images fill the book. There are appendices covering Pioneer's imaging photopolarimeter, technical details of Jupiter images, the Pioneer Jupiter team, and the 1974 Pioneer 10 award recipients. There is an index and a brief bibliography.

Magill, Frank N., ed. *Magill's Survey of Science: Space Exploration Series.* Vol. 3. Pasadena, Calif.: Salem Press, 1989, pp. 1116-1158.
Six essays from this five-volume set on the history of space exploration, which covers every aspect of the U.S. and Soviet manned and unmanned space programs, as well as those of nations newer to the space race. The Pioneer spacecraft explored the Moon, the Sun, Venus, Jupiter, and Saturn. The essays discuss the development of the spacecraft and details each of the missions. Contains an annotated bibliography and cross-references.

Powers, Robert M. *Planetary Encounters.* Harrisburg, Pa.: Stackpole Books, 1978.

Written at the time of the launch of the two Voyager spacecraft, this work discusses the unmanned exploration of the solar system. The Pioneer, Mariner, Viking, and Voyager spacecraft are detailed, along with many of the color and black-and-white photographs they snapped at Mercury, Venus, and Mars. Each of these planets is described and predictions are made as to what the probes will find at Jupiter, Saturn, Uranus, and Neptune. Appendices list information about the planets and their moons, planetary encounters, space and astronomy magazines, sources for obtaining space photographs, and a glossary of terms. There are a bibliography and an index.

Mariner

Bova, Ben, with Trudy E. Bell, eds. *Closeup: New Worlds.* New York: St. Martin's Press, 1977.
A collection of essays written by some of the best-known science and science-fiction writers in the world. This fact-filled book details our solar system, its planets, moons, and other phenomena. There are plenty of color and black-and-white photographs of these extraterrestrial entities and a description of the efforts to obtain these pictures with space probes. Photographs taken from ground-based observatories are compared with those taken by visiting spacecraft, such as Mariner, Viking, and Pioneer, as well as those originating in the Soviet Union. Descriptions of each spacecraft and the story of their travels are included.

Davies, M. E., S. E. Dornik, D. E. Gault, and R. G. Strom. *Atlas of Mercury.* Washington, D.C.: National Technical Information Service, 1978.
This work presents a photomosaic study of the planet closest to the Sun. Mariner 10 was launched atop an Atlas-Centaur launch vehicle on November 3, 1973. It visited Venus the following February before swinging on to Mercury, where it arrived on March 29. It swept past Mercury and returned for another look on September 21. During the two flybys, Mariner 10 returned eight thousand photographs of the cratered planet. There are numerous black-and-white photographs, photomosaics, and maps of Mercury, as well as some of the scientific data returned by Mariner.

Dunne, J. A., and E. Burgess. *The Voyage of Mariner 10: Mission to Venus and Mercury.* Washington, D.C.: National Technical Information Service, 1978.
Mariner 10 was launched to make photographic surveys of Mercury using a gravity assist from Venus. After studying the planned trajectory, it was noted that Mariner would swing past Mercury a second time. This would permit additional photography of the Sun's closest offspring. Mariner 10 was fitted with seven experiments: television imaging camera, infrared radiometer,

extreme ultraviolet spectroscope, magnetometer, plasma science package, charged particles collector, and radio wave propagation experiment package. This book details the Mariner 10 spacecraft and its experiments. It also presents mosaics and maps of Mercury. There are dozens of color and black-and-white photographs in addition to the black-and-white photomaps. Provides a bibliography and an index.

Magill, Frank N., ed. *Magill's Survey of Science: Space Exploration Series.* Vol. 2. Pasadena, Calif.: Salem Press, 1989, pp. 835-877.
Six essays from this five-volume set on the history of space exploration, which covers every aspect of the U.S. and Soviet manned and unmanned space programs, as well as those of nations newer to the space race. The Mariner spacecraft explored Mercury, Venus, and Mars between 1962 and 1975. The essays discuss the development of the spacecraft and details each of the ten missions. Contains an annotated bibliography and cross-references.

Mitchum, Ellen F. "Atlas Launch Vehicles." In *Magill's Survey of Science: Space Exploration Series*, vol. 1, edited by Frank N. Magill. Pasadena, Calif.: Salem Press, 1989.
One of the essays on the history of space exploration in this five-volume set, which covers every aspect of the U.S. and Soviet manned and unmanned space programs, as well as those of nations newer to the space race. The Atlas vehicle was first built as an intercontinental ballistic missile (ICBM) for the Air Force. It was later modified to launch a variety of manned and unmanned spacecraft. Some of these include the Mercury spacecraft, the Gemini Agena Target Vehicle, Mariner, Ranger, Lunar Orbiter, Surveyor, and many other military and civilian spacecraft. This essay discusses the development of the vehicle and its contributions to space exploration. Contains an annotated bibliography and cross-references.

Murray, Bruce. *Journey into Space: The First Three Decades of Space Exploration.* New York: W. W. Norton, 1989.
Extensive coverage of the Mariner programs to explore Mars, Venus, and Mercury is included in Murray's inside look at the efforts to send unmanned probes through the solar system. Details of the planning and execution of these journeys show the delicate maneuvering it takes, not only through outer space but also through bureaucratic space. There is an extensive, annotated bibliography, although some of the entries are mentioned only in passing. Dozens of black-and-white photographs and drawings add to the text.

Powers, Robert M. *Planetary Encounters.* Harrisburg, Pa.: Stackpole Books, 1978.

Written at the time of the launch of the two Voyager spacecraft, this work discusses the unmanned exploration of the solar system. The Pioneer, Mariner, Viking, and Voyager spacecraft are detailed, along with many of the color and black-and-white photographs they snapped at Mercury, Venus, and Mars. Each of these planets is described, and predictions are made as to what the probes will find at Jupiter, Saturn, Uranus, and Neptune. Appendices list information about the planets and their moons, planetary encounters, space and astronomy magazines, sources for obtaining space photographs, and a glossary of terms. There is a bibliography and an index.

Rovin, Jeff. *Mars!* Los Angeles: Corwin Books, 1978.
A look at Mars in fact and fiction, this work combines man's images of the Martian landscape before and after spacecraft "invaded" the red planet. About half of the book studies the popular ideas about Mars which grew from the imagination of science-fiction writers, including photographs from such cinematic classics as *War of the Worlds* and *Invasion of the Saucer Men*. The American missions to Mars, Mariner and Viking, are discussed in detail. Black-and-white photographs taken by the spacecraft fill the later part of the work. There is a very good bibliography, listing a number of fictional and nonfictional works; unfortunately, it is not annotated.

Viking

Bova, Ben, with Trudy E. Bell, eds. *Closeup: New Worlds*. New York: St. Martin's Press, 1977.
A collection of essays written by some of the best-known science and science-fiction writers in the world. This fact-filled book details the solar system, including its planets, moons, and other phenomena. There are plenty of color and black-and-white photographs of these extraterrestrial entities and a description of the efforts to obtain these pictures with space probes. Photographs taken from ground-based observatories are compared with those taken from the visiting spacecraft, such as Mariner, Viking, and Pioneer, as well as those originating in the Soviet Union. Descriptions of each spacecraft and the story of their travels are included.

Burgess, Eric. *To the Red Planet*. New York: Columbia University Press, 1978.
Mars has always intrigued man, perhaps for its red color or for the dark lines which were thought to be vegetation or Martian-made canals. Burgess writes about the Viking missions to Mars. He details the spacecraft (each flight consisted of an orbiter and a lander) and describes the scientific results they obtained. He also speculates about future expeditions, including manned flights.

This is a well-written book with dozens of color and black-and-white photographs taken both from Martian orbit and on the surface.

Carr, Michael, and Nancy Evans, comps. *Images of Mars: The Viking Extended Mission.* Washington, D.C.: National Technical Information Service, 1980.
When the Viking project was conceived in 1968, scientists and engineers designed the landers to operate for about three months but believed that they probably would not last three weeks. As this and subsequent publications have shown, the spacecraft exceeded the expectations by a great deal. The first Viking landed on Mars on July 20, 1976, and continued to send back pictures of the surface for more than six years. This short work is full of color and black-and-white photographs taken of Mars from above by the orbiters. There is a brief chronology of the two orbiters. The foreword was written by Thomas A. Mutch, Associate Administrator for NASA's Office of Space Science, for whom the Viking 1 landing site was later renamed after his untimely death.

Corliss, William R. *The Viking Mission to Mars.* Rev. ed. Washington, D.C.: National Technical Information Service, 1975.
This preview of the Viking missions to Mars presents one of the most comprehensive looks at the machines sent to study the red planet up close. The author discusses Mars, based upon information obtained by ground-based observatories and Mariner missions. The plan of the Viking missions is detailed, along with the launch vehicle designated to send the craft on their way. The most detailed sections are devoted to the Viking orbiter and lander. Each of the scientific experiments is discussed at length and accompanied by black-and-white photographs and line drawings. Some forecasts of what results are expected from the missions are also given. There is a list of references and suggested reading.

Ezell, Edward C., and Linda N. Ezell. *On Mars: Exploration of the Red Planet, 1958-1978.* Washington, D.C.: Government Printing Office, 1984.
One title in the NASA History Series, this book chronicles the Viking program and its search for answers at Mars. The two Viking spacecraft, each consisting of an orbiter and a lander, were launched to Mars in 1975. The orbiters surveyed the planet from orbit and served as a communications relay between the landers and Earth. The landers made soft landings on the surface of Mars and studied the chemical and physical properties of its surface and atmosphere. There are dozens of black-and-white photographs of Mars, as well as line drawings of the spacecraft and experimental equipment. There is an extensive appendix listing source notes and bibliographic references.

French, Bevan M. *Mars: The Viking Discoveries.* Washington, D.C.: Government Printing Office, 1977.

This work is part of the NASA educational publications series and briefly describes some of the early results of the Viking missions to Mars. It was prepared in a format useful to the teacher of basic courses in Earth science, Earth-space science, astronomy, physics, and geology. The author is a geologist, so the emphasis is on this particular discipline. There are numerous color and black-and-white photographs of Mars. There is an appendix of suggested experiments and activities for the classroom, as well as a brief annotated bibliography.

Newman, John. "Titan Launch Vehicles." In *Magill's Survey of Science: Space Exploration Series*, vol. 5, edited by Frank N. Magill. Pasadena, Calif.: Salem Press, 1989.
The first intercontinental ballistic missile (ICBM) designed to be used as such, rather than one modified from an existing research vehicle, was the mighty Titan. Titan was designed to fit into an underground silo and it used fuels which could be stored inside the vehicle's propellant tanks for long periods of time. In addition, the fuel and oxidizer were chosen because they ignited on contact and did not need a bulky, sometimes unreliable, ignition system. This chapter discusses the many faces of Titan and the spacecraft it launched, including the Gemini two-man spacecraft, Viking, Voyager, and many military satellites. Contains an annotated bibliography and cross-references.

Powers, Robert M. *Planetary Encounters*. Harrisburg, Pa.: Stackpole Books, 1978.
Written at the time of the launch of the two Voyager spacecraft, this work discusses the unmanned exploration of the solar system. The Pioneer, Mariner, Viking, and Voyager spacecraft are detailed, along with many of the color and black-and-white photographs they snapped at Mercury, Venus, and Mars. Each of these planets is described, and predictions are made as to what the probes will find at Jupiter, Saturn, Uranus, and Neptune. Appendices list information about the planets and their moons, planetary encounters, space and astronomy magazines, sources for obtaining space photographs, and a glossary of terms. Contains a bibliography and an index.

Rovin, Jeff. *Mars!* Los Angeles: Corwin Books, 1978.
A look at Mars in fact and fiction, this work combines our images of the Martian landscape before and after spacecraft "invaded" the red planet. About half of the book studies popular ideas about Mars which grew from the imagination of science-fiction writers, including still photographs from such cinematic classics as *War of the Worlds* and *Invasion of the Saucer Men*. The U.S. missions to Mars, Mariner and Viking, are discussed in detail. Black-and-white photographs taken by the spacecraft fill the later part of the work. There

is a very good bibliography, listing a number of fictional and nonfictional works. Unfortunately, it is not annotated.

Sakimoto, Phillip J. "Viking 1 and 2." In *Magill's Survey of Science: Space Exploration Series*, vol. 5, edited by Frank N. Magill. Pasadena, Calif.: Salem Press, 1989.
Since 1877, when Italian astronomer Giovanni Schiaparelli detected a number of straight lines on Mars and called them *canali*, meaning channels, man has envisioned the red planet to be inhabited by strange creatures. Famed American astronomer Percival Lowell was firmly convinced that the *canali* were artificial waterways constructed by Martians. Orson Welles, with the aid of author H. G. Wells, convinced the American public that Martians were landing in New Jersey one October evening. We have always wanted to know if there were indeed Martians. Although the Viking orbiters and landers were not designed to prove it one way or the other, they were sent to examine Mars up close. So far, neither of the two landers has found traces of life (as we know it). This chapter looks at the Viking missions to Mars and the results of their exploratory missions. Contains an annotated bibliography and cross-references.

Spitzer, C. R., ed. *Viking Orbiter Views of Mars*. Washington, D.C.: National Technical Information Service, 1980.
Some breathtaking photographs of Mars are presented in this outstanding work. The pictures returned by the two Viking orbiters help scientists study the planet in detail and make comparisons of it with Earth. Some of the features studied include the equatorial canyons, channels, volcanic features, deformational features, craters, surface processes, the polar regions, and the atmosphere. They also studied the two Martian moons, Phobos and Deimos. There are hundreds of color and black-and-white photographs, including several stereographic shots. A stereographic viewer is included with the book. A glossary of terms and details of the Viking orbiter imaging system are provided.

U.S. National Aeronautics and Space Administration. *The Martian Landscape*. Washington, D.C.: National Technical Information Service, 1978.
Snapshots from the surface of Mars fill this volume on the results of the two Viking missions to the red planet. The story of the program from its concept to the historic landings is told, mostly in pictures. There are hundreds of color and black-and-white photographs, some in stereo. Each photograph is accompanied by a detailed caption describing the view. The spacecraft are described, as is the scientific equipment sent to study the conditions at the surface and to search for traces of life.

Voyager

Magill, Frank N., ed. *Magill's Survey of Science: Space Exploration Series*. Vol. 5. Pasadena, Calif.: Salem Press, 1989, pp. 2219-2261.
Six essays from the five-volume set on the history of space exploration which covers every aspect of the U.S. and Soviet manned and unmanned space programs, as well as those of nations newer to the space race. The Voyager spacecraft explored the larger, outer planets of the solar system between 1979 and 1989. During the decade, the two wanderers sent back photographs from Jupiter, Saturn, Uranus, and Neptune; discovered many new moons; and unlocked many of the secrets these worlds held for billions of years. The essays discuss the development of the spacecraft and details of each of the missions. Each contains an annotated bibliography and cross-references.

Morrison, David, and Jane Samz. *Voyage to Jupiter*. Washington, D.C.: National Technical Information Service, 1980.
The two Voyager spacecraft encountered Jupiter in July, 1979, sending back thousands of images of the giant planet. The scientific experiments packages investigated infrared radiation, ultraviolet spectroscopy, photopolarimetry, planetary radio astronomy, magnetic fields, plasma particles, plasma waves, low-energy charged particles, cosmic ray particles, and radio science. This report documents the early results of the encounters with Jupiter and its moons. There are hundreds of color and black-and-white photographs of Jupiter and pictorial maps of the Galilean satellites. A brief bibliography is included.

Newman, John. "Titan Launch Vehicles." In *Magill's Survey of Science: Space Exploration Series*, vol. 5, edited by Frank N. Magill. Pasadena, Calif.: Salem Press, 1989.
The first intercontinental ballistic missile (ICBM) designed to be used as such, rather than one modified from an existing research vehicle, was the mighty Titan. Titan was designed to fit into an underground silo and used fuels that could be stored inside the vehicle's propellant tanks for long periods of time. In addition, the fuel and oxidizer were chosen because they ignited on contact and did not need a bulky, sometimes unreliable, ignition system. This chapter discusses the many faces of Titan and the spacecraft it launched, including the Gemini two-man spacecraft, Viking, Voyager, and many military satellites. Provides an annotated bibliography and cross-references.

Powers, Robert M. *Planetary Encounters*. Harrisburg, Pa.: Stackpole Books, 1978.
Written at the time of the launch of the two Voyager spacecraft, this work discusses the unmanned exploration of the solar system. The Pioneer, Mariner, Viking, and Voyager spacecraft are detailed, along with many of the color and

black-and-white photographs they snapped at Mercury, Venus, and Mars. Each of these planets is described and predictions are made as to what the probes will find at Jupiter, Saturn, Uranus, and Neptune. Appendices list information about the planets and their moons, planetary encounters, space and astronomy magazines, sources for obtaining space photographs, and a glossary of terms. There are a bibliography and an index.

Sagan, Carl, et al. *Murmurs of Earth.* New York: Random House, 1978.
When the two Voyager spacecraft were launched, they carried with them a record of human existence in the hope that one day another civilization would find it, unravel its mysteries, and discover it is not alone. These records are just that, gold-coated copper phonograph record. There are even instructions on how to construct a machine to play the record. The contents of the Voyager record includes 118 pictures, the first bars of the Beethoven Cavatina, greetings from the president of the United States and from the secretary general of the United Nations, a congressional list, U.N. greetings, whale greetings, the sounds of Earth, and music. Sagan details every entry on the record and the logic of its being placed there. This work is filled with black-and-white photographs and diagrams. There is also an index.

U.S. National Aeronautics and Space Administration. *To Uranus and Beyond.* Washington, D.C.: Government Printing Office, 1987.
This is a brief look at the Voyager 2 encounter with Uranus in January, 1986. Much of the glory of the encounter was lost, since it occurred so close to the *Challenger* accident. There are a few dozen photographs of Uranus, several of its moons, and its ring system. The fact that Voyager was able to transmit these photographs over such a long distance, after such a long journey, is worth the effort to find this book.

——————————. *Voyager Encounters Jupiter.* Washington, D.C.: Government Printing Office, 1979.
This is one of the first reports on the photographic images of Jupiter and some of its satellites taken by the two Voyager spacecraft. Most of this work consists of these photographs. In themselves, they are worth the effort to read the book. There are dozens of color photographs. Each image was obtained by photographing the scene through a series of colored filters. The images were computer-combined back on Earth to produce the final images. There is a brief description of the spacecraft and their journey to the Jovian system.

——————————. *Voyager 1 Encounters Saturn.* Washington, D.C.: Government Printing Office, 1980.
Voyager 1 came within seventy-seven thousand miles of Saturn on November 12, 1980. It was programmed to travel up through the Saturnian ring system

for close-up examination of this phenomenon. In doing so, its trajectory was altered so that Voyager 1 crossed the plane of the ecliptic (the imaginary plane formed by the orbital paths of the planets around the Sun). This meant that it would have no further planetary encounters and would miss the celebrity of its sister ship, Voyager 2, which traveled on to Uranus and Neptune. This work presents a brief photographic essay on Saturn, its rings and several of its moons. There is a description of the spacecraft and its scientific equipment.

Magellan

U.S. General Accounting Office. *Space Exploration: Cost, Schedule, and Performance of NASA's Magellan Mission to Venus.* Washington, D.C.: Government Printing Office, 1988.
This work is the report of the GAO's findings on the Magellan mission to Venus, which was launched from the Space Shuttle *Atlantis* in May, 1989. The report provides a general overview of the program, including its objectives, scope, and methodology. There are spacecraft configuration drawings and information relating to cost, schedule, and performance. A chronology of the project, through the date of the report, is presented. There is a glossary of terms used.

_____. *Space Exploration: NASA's Deep Space Missions Are Experiencing Long Delays.* Washington, D.C.: Government Printing Office, 1988.
This work is the report of the GAO's findings on four of NASA's proposed deep space missions. The report covers the Galileo mission to Jupiter, the Ulysses mission to the Sun, the Magellan mission to Venus, and the Mars Observer mission. The report provides a general overview of the program, including its objectives, scope, and methodology. There are spacecraft configuration drawings and information relating to cost, schedule, and performance. A chronology of the project, through the date of the report, is presented. There is a glossary of terms used.

U.S. National Aeronautics and Space Administration. *Magellan: The Unveiling of Venus.* Pasadena, Calif.: Jet Propulsion Laboratory, 1989.
This is a preflight guide to the Magellan spacecraft deployed from the Space Shuttle *Atlantis* on May 4, 1989, as part of the STS-30 mission. Magellan's primary goal is to make radar studies of the surface of Venus while in orbit around the cloud-covered planet. The spacecraft was built mostly of spare parts from other planetary projects, most notably Voyager and Galileo. The booklet is filled with color and black-and-white photographs, line drawings, and artists' renditions. The project is detailed, as is the spacecraft and its one main scientific instrument, the synthetic aperture radar (SAR). SAR uses the phenom-

enon known as the Doppler shift to create a three-dimensional image of the surface. It will greatly enhance our knowledge of Venus.

Galileo

U.S. General Accounting Office. *Space Exploration: Cost, Schedule, and Performance of NASA's Galileo Mission to Jupiter.* Washington, D.C.: Government Printing Office, 1988.
The chairman of the Senate Committee on Commerce, Science, and Transportation asked the GAO to assess the cost, schedule, and performance of several NASA projects. This work is the report of their findings. The report provides a general overview of the program, including its objectives, scope, and methodology. There are spacecraft configuration drawings and information relating to cost, schedule, and performance. A chronology of the project, through the date of the report, is presented. There is a glossary of terms used.

_____. *Space Exploration: NASA's Deep Space Missions Are Experiencing Long Delays.* Washington, D.C.: Government Printing Office, 1988.
This work is the report of the GAO's findings on four of NASA's proposed deep space missions. The report covers the Galileo mission to Jupiter, the Ulysses mission to the Sun, the Magellan mission to Venus, and the Mars Observer mission. The report provides a general overview of the program, including its objectives, scope, and methodology. There are spacecraft configuration drawings and information relating to cost, schedule, and performance. A chronology of the project, through the date of the report, is presented. There is a glossary of terms used.

U.S. National Aeronautics and Space Administration. *Galileo to Jupiter.* Washington, D.C.: Government Printing Office, 1979.
A brief preflight guide to the Galileo spacecraft, which will orbit Jupiter and send a probe to explore its atmosphere. Although the mission described in this booklet is not the one which was flown, it does give the researcher an insight into the spacecraft. The mission depicted would have been launched from the Space Shuttle in 1982 and used an Inertial Upper Stage (IUS) to boost it to Jupiter. Unlike the two-stage IUS used in 1989 during its actual deployment, the IUS for this mission was to have three stages. It would propel Galileo toward Mars, where the spacecraft would get a gravity assist from the red planet. Development problems with the three-stage IUS forced NASA to switch to the more powerful, liquid-propellant Centaur upper stage. The *Challenger* accident forced NASA to drop plans for Centaur and switch to the already proven two-stage IUS. There are a number of color drawings of the spacecraft

and its mission, as well as color photographs taken by the Voyager 1 spacecraft.

U.S. Senate. *Space Shuttle and Galileo Mission.* Washington, D.C.: Government Printing Office, 1980.
The main reason for including this document in this bibliography is to permit a review of the early days of the Galileo mission to Jupiter. However, it serves a dual purpose by providing Senator William Proxmire's own words on the subject of the project, the Space Transportation System, and the U.S. space program. In his opening statement he says, "[The Galileo] program is a program that has great merit and very, very substantial support in the country and the Congress, but it is also a program, as you know, that is very expensive and involves a great deal of money." The report also presents a discussion of the safety and reliability of the Space Shuttle. It is not a very large work, but it does present some insight into the behind-the-scenes struggles to get the Shuttle and some of its most important payloads off the ground.

Ulysses

European Space Agency. *The International Solar Polar Mission: Its Scientific Investigations.* Washington, D.C.: Government Printing Office, 1983.
A series of essays written by some of the scientific investigators who have developed the Ulysses program. Ulysses, originally known as the International Solar Polar Mission, is designed to orbit the Sun from a unique vantage point. Its orbit will carry it over the Sun's polar regions. It will be launched from the payload bay of the Space Shuttle toward Jupiter. There it will use the giant planet's gravitational field to alter its trajectory in order for it to move out of the plane of the ecliptic. The essays discuss the mission of Ulysses and the equipment it will use in its study of the Sun.

U.S. General Accounting Office. *Space Exploration: Cost, Schedule, and Performance of NASA's Ulysses Mission to the Sun.* Washington, D.C.: Government Printing Office, 1988.
The chairman of the Senate Committee on Commerce, Science, and Transportation asked the GAO to assess the cost, schedule, and performance of several NASA projects. This work is the report of their findings. The report provides a general overview of the program, including its objectives, scope, and methodology. There are spacecraft configuration drawings and information relating to cost, schedule, and performance. A chronology of the project, through the date of the report, is presented. There is a glossary of terms used.

_____. *Space Exploration: NASA's Deep Space Missions Are Experiencing Long Delays.* Washington, D.C.: Government Printing Office, 1988.
This work is the report of the GAO's findings on four of NASA's proposed deep space missions. The report covers the Galileo mission to Jupiter, the Ulysses mission to the Sun, the Magellan mission to Venus, and the Mars Observer mission. The report provides a general overview of the program, including its objectives, scope, and methodology. There are spacecraft configuration drawings and information relating to cost, schedule, and performance. A chronology of the project, through the date of the report, is presented. There is a glossary of terms used.

Applications Satellites

General Studies

Ameigh, Michael S. "Applications Technology Satellites." In *Magill's Survey of Science: Space Exploration Series*, vol. 1, edited by Frank N. Magill. Pasadena, Calif.: Salem Press, 1989.
One of the essays on the history of space exploration in this five-volume set, which covers every aspect of the U.S. and Soviet manned and unmanned space programs, as well as those of nations newer to the space race. The Applications Technology Satellites, designed to demonstrate direct broadcast communications and meteorological monitoring, were placed into orbit from 1966 through 1979. This essay discusses in some detail the design of these satellites and their contributions to our knowledge about the world. Includes an annotated bibliography and cross-references.

Caidin, Martin. *Vanguard! The Story of the First Man-Made Satellite.* New York: E. P. Dutton, 1957.
This is one of the earlier works of this fine science writer. He has taken what was still very much under wraps and presented a look at the forthcoming space age. Vanguard was indeed to have been the first man-made satellite, but no one told that to the Soviet Union, which launched Sputnik shortly after this book was published. While many books on the exploration of space skim over the period of development before October 4, 1957, this work details every aspect. The author writes about Project Bumper, the Aerobee, the Viking rocket from which Vanguard evolved, the X-405 which would propel the vehicle through the atmosphere, and the satellite it would orbit. There are dozens of

black-and-white photographs and line drawings. It may be difficult to track down a copy of this work, but it is well worth the effort.

Gatland, Kenneth, et al. *The Illustrated Encyclopedia of Space Technology: A Comprehensive History of Space Exploration.* New York: Harmony Books, 1981.
"Illustrated" should be underscored in the title of this work, because it is the color and black-and-white photographs, drawings, paintings, and charts that are the highlight of this work. Every spacecraft, launch vehicle, space center, and major component of each U.S. space endeavor is included, as are those from the other countries which have entered the space race. There is a chronology of the major space events since Sputnik 1, a glossary of terms, and an index. There is a great deal of text, which does not bog down the work but merely enhances the illustrations. Each chapter has its own list of references.

Green, Constance McLaughlin, and Milton Lomask. *Vanguard: A History.* Washington, D.C.: Smithsonian Institution Press, 1970.
The Vanguard program was designed to place the world's first artificial satellite into orbit in 1957. What it is most remembered for is the disastrous attempt to launch the first Vanguard satellite. The flight lasted an instant, as the vehicle lifted from its launchpad and slowly settled back down in a ball of flames. The tiny satellite tucked inside its nose cone rolled along the ground, beeping laconically. Vanguard would have its successes—after the Soviet Union launched Sputnik and after the United States orbited Explorer 1. This work chronicles the Navy's satellite program and details its spacecraft and launch vehicles. It also discusses the Cold War political climate which pressured the scientists, engineers, and technicians to get a satellite up before the Soviets. There are numerous black-and-white photographs, line drawings, and an index.

Ley, Willy. *Satellites, Rockets, and Outer Space.* New York: New American Library of World Literature, 1956, rev. ed. 1962.
This pocketbook is a fascinating look at the U.S. space programs to put satellites into orbit. The author discusses these early satellites and some of the feuding that went on between the Army and the Navy over who would be the first to launch a satellite. Some of the earliest space launch vehicles are described. Nontechnical physics lessons are presented in a discussion of propulsion and orbital mechanics. There is a section devoted to the solar system, with emphasis on the third planet. In the final chapter there is a discussion of some future plans, including Moon cars and men on Mars. This last chapter is perhaps the most interesting, especially in the light of events that occurred during the subsequent quarter century. There are several line drawings and a few color photographs.

Magill, Frank N., ed. *Magill's Survey of Science: Space Exploration Series.* 5 vols. Pasadena, Calif.: Salem Press, 1989.
This five-volume set covers every aspect of the U.S. and Soviet manned and unmanned space programs, as well as those of nations newer to the space race. The United States has launched a variety of satellites to study Earth and the rest of the solar system from Earth orbit, to map our planet and look at its weather, and to improve communications with our neighbors. Spacecraft and programs covered in this work are divided into six groups: Earth resources, meteorological, military, scientific, telecommunications, and miscellaneous. The essays discuss examples of spacecraft in each category, its contributions to our knowledge, and the historical significance of each mission. Each article includes an annotated bibliography and cross-references to other articles in the set.

Newell, Homer. *Beyond the Atmosphere: Early Years of Space Science.* Washington, D.C.: Government Printing Office, 1980.
This is one of the volumes in the NASA History Series, the official history of the U.S. space programs. This book covers the scientific investigations made possible by sounding rockets, satellites, and space probes. The author begins with a look at the early pioneers of rocketry and some of the first space scientists. The National Aeronautics and Space Administration was created in response to the launch of Sputnik 1 and the desire to release the military from its role in space exploration. NASA's design and organization are discussed, along with its interaction with other agencies, the military, and universities. Particular attention is paid to the California Institute of Technology's Jet Propulsion Laboratory. There are dozens of black-and-white photographs, line drawings, tables, and charts, as well as an impressive appendix listing source notes and bibliographic references and an index.

Taylor, John W. R., ed. *Jane's All the World's Aircraft.* 17 vols. London: Jane's, 1957-   .
Considered by some to be the most complete reference on aircraft, the biennial publication began to include rockets, missiles, and spacecraft after the first Sputnik was orbited. The most reliable sources of information are used to provide as much technical data about the vehicle, engine, or program as possible. Each issue highlights those systems or components which were introduced or made a significant contribution during the previous two-year period. The major manned and unmanned spaceflights are also detailed. There are black-and-white photographs and drawings of each vehicle or component.

Thompson, Tina D., ed. *Space Log: 1957-1987.* Redondo Beach, Calif.: TRW Space & Technology Group, 1988.
Each year, TRW publishes a log of worldwide space activities. Any new spacecraft, launch vehicle, engine, or program, or one that made a significant

contribution to the exploration of space during the year, is detailed. Tables include a "box score" of U.S. launches, worldwide successful space launches, Space Transportation System payload deployment records, payloads in orbit, and manned spaceflight records. The highlight of each volume is the summary of space launches which details (in a table) the name, international designation, program direction, launch data, weight, orbital data, and status. This particular volume was published in conjunction with the thirtieth anniversary of the space age and contains data for the entire era. Most major libraries have or can obtain copies of these logs directly from the publisher.

U.S. House of Representatives. *United States Civilian Space Programs 1958-1978.* Vol. 1. Washington, D.C.: Government Printing Office, 1981.
In a very concise report, the Committee on Space Science and Applications has compiled data on all U.S. space activity during its first two decades. After a brief introduction and summary chapter, the volume is divided into fourteen additional sections. The second chapter deals with the space-related issues under consideration by Congress. The remaining sections cover the history of NASA and its relationship to U.S. space policy, NASA facilities and tracking systems, launch vehicles and propulsion, manned spaceflight through 1975, the Space Transportation System, space life sciences, space science programs, materials processing in space, international cooperation in space, interagency and non-NASA governmental space activities, industrial and university support for NASA, space program benefits, and selected future space programs. Appendices contain Department of Defense manned spaceflight plans, NASA funding history, international space agreements, texts of President Jimmy Carter's space directives, documents relating to the legal aspects of the Space Shuttle, major U.S. space organizations, a master log of U.S. spaceflights, and a table of U.S. space orbital payloads by mission from 1957 through 1979.

U.S. National Aeronautics and Space Administration. *Scientific Results of Project Pegasus: Interim Report.* Washington, D.C.: National Technical Information Service, 1967.
The designers of the Saturn I were looking for "ballast" for the boilerplate Apollo spacecraft they would be launching atop the booster. What resulted was a large, winged structure called *Pegasus*. *Pegasus*, named for the flying horse of Greek mythology, was designed to collect data on micrometeoroid impacts during low-Earth-orbit flights. Three spacecraft were flown, one on each of the final Saturn I missions. This paper discusses the history of the project and the scientific results obtained. There are several charts and drawings and a list of references.

_____. *Spartan: Science with Efficiency and Simplicity.* Washington, D.C.: Government Printing Office, 1984.

This is a preflight look at the Shuttle Pointed Autonomous Research Tool for Astronomy (Spartan), a retrievable free- flying platform for high-energy astrophysics, solar physics, and ultraviolet astronomy studies. Spartan is carried to orbit inside the payload bay of the Space Shuttle, where it is deployed by the orbiter's remote manipulator system arm. It can then operate independent of the Shuttle for periods up to forty hours. After completing its mission, it is recaptured by the manipulator arm and placed back in the stowed position for return to Earth. This brief work has several color photographs and color renditions of Spartan in flight. Despite its simplicity, the work gives a lot of information about this unique satellite.

Von Braun, Wernher, and Frederick I. Ordway III. *History of Rocketry and Space Travel*. 3d rev. ed. New York: Thomas Y. Crowell, 1975.
This is the story of the exploration of space from the earliest experiments with rocketry to the final flight of the Skylab program. Hundreds of experts on every aspect of this broad field contributed to the work. Most of the programs of the United States, the Soviet Union, and the rest of the nations engaged in space exploration at that time are detailed, both descriptively and with black-and-white and color photographs. It is one of the best references on the subject. The book also contains a large, chapter-by-chapter bibliography. The authors finish their discussion of the space programs with a look at the future, including the Space Transportation System.

Astronomical Observatories

Bentley, Alan F. "The Infrared Astronomical Satellite." In *Magill's Survey of Science: Space Exploration Series*, vol. 2, edited by Frank N. Magill. Pasadena, Calif.: Salem Press, 1989.
One of the essays on the history of space exploration in this five-volume set, which covers every aspect of the U.S. and Soviet manned and unmanned space programs, as well as those of nations newer to the space race. For nearly a year, the Infrared Astronomical Satellite (IRAS) studied the heat emitted by astronomical sources. This work surveys the program and details the satellite and its findings. Provides an annotated bibliography and cross-references.

Dooling, Dave. "The High-Energy Astronomical Observatories." In *Magill's Survey of Science: Space Exploration Series*, vol. 2, edited by Frank N. Magill. Pasadena, Calif.: Salem Press, 1989.
One of the essays on the history of space exploration in this five-volume set, which covers every aspect of the U.S. and Soviet manned and unmanned space programs, as well as those of nations newer to the space race. This essay is about the satellites launched to provide a detailed survey of the celestial sphere

and the sources of X rays, gamma rays, and cosmic radiation. The High-Energy Astronomical Observatory (HEAO) program is explained, and the results of the studies are presented. Includes an annotated bibliography and cross-references.

Ghitelman, David. *The Space Telescope.* New York: Gallery Books, 1987.
This work is a preview of the Hubble Space Telescope. It discusses Earth-based telescopes and their advantages and disadvantages, as well as their limitations. The author traces the development of the Hubble Space Telescope and the problems of polishing the world's smoothest mirror, the 94-inch-diameter primary reflecting mirror. The design and construction of the Hubble Space Telescope are detailed, as are the plans for its deployment by the Space Shuttle. During its life, the telescope will be periodically serviced by the Shuttle and, if necessary, can be returned to Earth for refurbishment. A look at the expected increase in knowledge of the universe is included. There is a chapter about the life of the telescope's namesake, Dr. Edward Powell Hubble, the American astronomer who, among other things, discovered that all galaxies are red-shifted (their motion away from us causes their light to shift toward the red end of the visible spectrum due to the Doppler effect). There are dozens of color and black-and-white photographs and paintings, an index, and a brief bibliography.

Hall, Donald N. B., ed. *The Space Telescope Observatory.* Washington, D.C.: Government Printing Office, 1982.
This is a compendium of information about the Hubble Space Telescope, written by individuals or groups that have played a major role in the development of the first large-aperture, long-term optical and ultraviolet observatory to be launched into space. Most of the papers are highly technical and deal with the projected performance of the telescope. The dissertations represent an overview of the Hubble Space Telescope's scientific potential as perceived by the scientists involved in its development. Detailed line drawings and black-and-white photographs of the telescope's equipment are included. Each of the observatory's individual telescopes and cameras is detailed.

McRoberts, Joseph J. *Space Telescope.* Washington, D.C.: Government Printing Office, 1982.
The Hubble Space Telescope will allow scientists to view the universe from a vantage point three hundred miles above Earth. There, unobstructed by the atmosphere, it will peer back into time, seven times farther than previously seen. It will be able to image the planets of our solar system at a resolution greater than before possible. Even a planet as far away as Saturn will be viewed with the clarity available from the Voyager spacecraft. This is a preview guide to the deployment mission. It uses a great number of color and

black-and-white photographs, as well as drawings to illustrate the telescope and its mission. Despite the age of the book, the information presented has changed relatively little since it was published. This is an excellent source of information about this project.

Magill, Frank N., ed. *Magill's Survey of Science: Space Exploration Series*. Vol. 3. Pasadena, Calif.: Salem Press, 1989, pp. 1092-1110.
Three essays in this five-volume set on the history of space exploration, which covers every aspect of the U.S. and Soviet manned and unmanned space programs, as well as those of nations newer to the space race. These articles discuss the Orbiting Astronomical Observatories, the Orbiting Geophysical Observatories, and the Orbiting Solar Observatories. These satellites provide astronomers with an opportunity to conduct observations at specific wavelengths, which could not be conducted through Earth's atmosphere. Each essay includes a brief summary of the satellite and its development, the knowledge gained from the observations, an annotated bibliography, and cross-references.

Merguerian, Charles. "The Vanguard Program." In *Magill's Survey of Science: Space Exploration Series*, vol. 5, edited by Frank N. Magill. Pasadena, Calif.: Salem Press, 1989.
By its very name, Vanguard was meant to lead the United States into space. Instead, it became our first "goat." Vanguard was the name of the pencil-thin launch vehicle (as well as the satellite it would carry). The Navy vehicle was given the task to place the first U.S. satellite into orbit soon after Sputnik 1 beeped its taunting message from above. Instead, it crumpled into a ball of fire moments after liftoff. It was not until the fourth Vanguard launch that a success was realized—two months after an Army Juno 1 launched Explorer 1. This essay discusses the origins of Vanguard, which developed from the Viking rocket, and its contributions to the space program. Includes an annotated bibliography and cross-references.

Ogier, Divonna. "The Solar Maximum Mission." In *Magill's Survey of Science: Space Exploration Series*, vol. 3, edited by Frank N. Magill. Pasadena, Calif.: Salem Press, 1989.
Every eleven years, or so, the Sun begins a period of dynamic activity. Scientists have attempted to study this liveliness from the vantage point of orbit. The Solar Maximum satellite (commonly known as "Solar Max") was launched in 1980 to study the Sun during that cycle's peak year. For ten months, Max gathered valuable data, then suddenly suffered a major malfunction. Scientists determined that it would be possible to repair the satellite on orbit. This was accomplished on the eleventh Space Shuttle mission (STS 41-C). This article discusses the Solar Max satellite and its mission, as well as the successful rescue. Contains an annotated bibliography and cross-references.

Smith, Robert W. *The Space Telescope: A Study of NASA, Science, Technology, and Politics.* Cambridge, Mass.: Cambridge University Press, 1989.
A behind-the-scenes look at the Hubble Space Telescope program. The author looks at the economic and political influences that shaped the telescope's design. According to Smith, NASA's main reason for the orbiting telescope was to help sell the idea that the Space Shuttle was necessary. By its very size, the telescope could be launched by the Shuttle. NASA even deliberately underestimated its cost because Congress would not have approved of the program. Smith lets his facts speak for themselves and does not attempt to prove any of his speculation. Black-and-white photographs are included.

U.S. General Accounting Office. *Space Science: Status of the Hubble Space Telescope Program.* Washington, D.C.: Government Printing Office, 1988.
This work is the report of the GAO's findings on the Hubble Space Telescope, which was launched from the Space Shuttle *Discovery* in 1990. The report provides a general overview of the program, including its objectives, scope, and methodology. There are spacecraft configuration drawings and information relating to cost, schedule, and performance. A chronology of the project, through the date of the report, is presented. There is a glossary of terms used.

U.S. National Aeronautics and Space Administration. *Spartan: Science with Efficiency and Simplicity.* Washington, D.C.: Government Printing Office, 1984.
This is a preflight look at the Shuttle Pointed Autonomous Research Tool for Astronomy (Spartan), a retrievable free- flying platform for high-energy astrophysics, solar physics, and ultraviolet astronomy studies. Spartan is carried to orbit inside the payload bay of the Space Shuttle where it is deployed by the orbiter's remote manipulator system arm. It can then operate independent of the Shuttle for periods up to forty hours. After completing its mission, it is recaptured by the manipulator arm and placed back in the stowed position for return to Earth. This brief work has several color photographs and color renditions of Spartan in flight. Despite its simplicity, the work gives a lot of information about this unique satellite.

Biosatellites

Kennedy, George P. "U.S. Biosatellites." In *Magill's Survey of Science: Space Exploration Series*, vol. 1, edited by Frank N. Magill. Pasadena, Calif.: Salem Press, 1989.
One of the essays on the history of space exploration in the five-volume set which covers every aspect of the U.S. and Soviet manned and unmanned space programs, as well as those of nations newer to the space race. The author

summarizes the satellites and gives a brief history of the biosatellite program. Contains an annotated bibliography and cross-references.

Communications

Bishop, T. Parker. "Amateur Radio Satellites." In *Magill's Survey of Science: Space Exploration Series*, vol. 1, edited by Frank N. Magill. Pasadena, Calif.: Salem Press, 1989.
The essay summarizes the OSCAR (Orbiting Satellite Carrying Amateur Radio) Association, formed in 1959, and the satellites its members designed and built to be flown either as ballast for other missions or "piggyback" with another satellite. A brief description of each satellite launched is given, as well as the historical context of the program. Provides an annotated bibliography and cross-references.

Dooling, Dave. "Voices from the Sky." In *The Illustrated Encyclopedia of Space Technology: A Comprehensive History of Space Exploration*, by Kenneth Gatland et al. New York: Harmony Books, 1981.
This section of the book discusses the communications satellites, including the passive ones as well as the active. Passive communications satellites, such as Echo, serve only as reflectors for radio signals transmitted from one ground station and then bounced back down to another. There is a full-color cutaway view of Comstar 1, an active satellite. There are many color and black-and-white photographs, drawings, and charts. Includes a chronology of the major space events since Sputnik 1, a glossary of terms, and an index.

Froehlich, Walter. *The New Space Network: The Tracking and Data Relay Satellite System*. Washington, D.C.: Government Printing Office, 1986.
This work looks at NASA's Tracking and Data Relay Satellite System (TDRSS), which permits continuous radio contact between Earth-orbiting spacecraft and ground stations. This system helps to eliminate costly ground-based tracking stations. It also permits radio communications with the Space Shuttle during reentry. Prior to TDRSS (pronounced "tea dress"), this was not possible, because of the communications blackout that occurred during the period when a returning spacecraft began to ionize the air around it. The booklet is filled with color photographs and artists' renditions of the TDRSS, as well as a description of the system's operations.

Magill, Frank N., ed. *Magill's Survey of Science: Space Exploration Series*. 5 vols. Pasadena, Calif.: Salem Press, 1989.
This five-volume set covers every aspect of the U.S. and Soviet manned and unmanned space programs, as well as those of nations newer to the space race.

From the beginning of time, man has tried to communicate with his neighbors. Since that first "hello" was transmitted over the airwaves, he has worked to improve it to a point where one can actually hear (and later, see) the person with whom one is speaking. The problems associated with communicating around a sphere such as the Earth using equipment that transmits only in a straight line have been solved to some extent with the advent of communications satellites. Several articles in this set are devoted to these spacecraft and the technology that has come with satellite communications. Each article includes an annotated bibliography and cross-references.

Rayman, Marc D. "Space Shuttle Mission 14." In *Magill's Survey of Science: Space Exploration Series*, vol. 4, edited by Frank N. Magill. Pasadena, Calif.: Salem Press, 1989.
One of the goals set for the Space Shuttle program at its inception was the capability to service and retrieve disabled satellites. The first demonstration of this capability came during the STS 51-A mission. In February, 1984, the Space Shuttle *Challenger* successfully deployed two communications satellites. Unfortunately, their solid rocket motors failed to perform properly, leaving the satellites in useless elliptical orbits rather than in their desired geosynchronous orbit. NASA and the contractors (and their insurance companies) decided it would be cheaper to retrieve the satellites, refit them with new motors, and relaunch them either aboard another Shuttle mission or atop a Delta launch vehicle. This article details the event-filled mission which, in addition to the rescue of the two satellites, deployed two satellites and conducted numerous experiments. The particulars of the mission are presented in a concise format with important data given and technical jargon eliminated. There is a brief annotated bibliography. As a footnote to the story, the two satellites were successfully relaunched in April, 1990.

Taylor, L. B., Jr. *For All Mankind: America's Space Programs of the 1970s and Beyond*. New York: E. P. Dutton, 1974.
The author discusses the benefits of the United States' space programs of the early 1970's, especially the multiple benefits derived from communications satellites and Earth resources satellites. He describes these programs as well as the Space Transportation System, which was in the latter stages of planning and development. The book discusses the full range of possibilities for the Space Shuttle and some of its payloads. Much is to be gained by comparing the goals of the system in 1974 and its accomplishments through the next decade and a half. There are black-and-white photographs and an index.

U.S. National Aeronautics and Space Administration. *Relay Program Final Report*. Washington, D.C.: National Technical Information Service, 1968.

Two Relay communications satellites were launched on separate Thor Delta boosters. Relay 1 went into orbit on December 13, 1962, followed thirteen months later by Relay 2. The spacecraft were built by the Radio Corporation of America and were designed to test intercontinental microwave communications with a low-altitude repeater satellite and to measure radiation levels. The spacecraft were capable of television and voice communications. This is the official report of the Relay program. There are numerous black-and-white photographs and line drawings.

_____. *Tracking and Data Relay Satellite System (TDRSS) Users' Guide.* Washington, D.C.: Government Printing Office, 1984.
Although most people will not have a direct need to use NASA's Tracking and Data Relay Satellite System, many will find this book to be quite informative. The TDRSS (pronounced "tea dress") is a network of three geosynchronous satellites used to communicate with and track other spacecraft. One of the two operational TDRS's is located over the equator at 41 degrees west longitude, while the second is at 171 degrees west. The third, an on-orbit spare, is at 62 degrees west longitude. The operational satellites are spaced 130 degrees apart to permit the use of only one ground tracking station, which is located at White Sands, New Mexico. Each satellite is carried into low Earth orbit by the Space Shuttle and propelled to its operational position by the Inertial Upper Stage. This document was written to assist in user planning activities, but it provides the researcher with a great deal of technical information available nowhere else. There are numerous line drawings, schematic diagrams, and charts to augment the text.

Explorer Series

Christensen, Eric. "Active Magnetospheric Particle Tracer Explorers." In *Magill's Survey of Science: Space Exploration Series*, vol. 1, edited by Frank N. Magill. Pasadena, Calif.: Salem Press, 1989.
One of the essays on the history of space exploration in this five-volume set, which covers every aspect of the U.S. and Soviet manned and unmanned space programs, as well as those of nations newer to the space race. This essay looks at the spacecraft designed to perform active experiments on the Sun's effects on Earth's magnetosphere (the region of the upper atmosphere which extends out for thousands of miles and is dominated by Earth's magnetic field) and radiation belts. Includes an annotated bibliography and cross-references.

Heelis, Rod. "Dynamics Explorers." In *Magill's Survey of Science: Space Exploration Series*, vol. 1, edited by Frank N. Magill. Pasadena, Calif.: Salem Press, 1989.

One of the essays on the history of space exploration in this five-volume set, which covers every aspect of the U.S. and Soviet manned and unmanned space programs, as well as those of nations newer to the space race. These satellites were designed to investigate the interactions of the region of charged particles surrounding Earth, called the magnetosphere. This essay describes these satellites and their missions. Includes an annotated bibliography and cross-references.

Magill, Frank N., ed. *Magill's Survey of Science: Space Exploration Series.* Vol. 1. Pasadena, Calif.: Salem Press, 1989, pp. 394-446.
One of the finest collections of essays on the history of space exploration, this five-volume set covers every aspect of the U.S. and Soviet manned and unmanned space programs, as well as those of nations newer to the space race. Each of the essays on the Explorer satellites lists the pertinent data of the mission, launch vehicle, or spacecraft. Includes a brief summary of the subject, the knowledge gained, its historical context, an annotated bibliography, and cross-references.

Melton, Robert G. "The Interplanetary Monitoring Platform Satellites." In *Magill's Survey of Science: Space Exploration Series*, vol. 2, edited by Frank N. Magill. Pasadena, Calif.: Salem Press, 1989.
One of the essays on the history of space exploration in this five-volume set, which covers every aspect of the U.S. and Soviet manned and unmanned space programs, as well as those of nations newer to the space race. The ten Interplanetary Monitoring Platform (IMP) satellites were deployed during the ten-year period beginning November, 1963. They measured cosmic radiation levels, magnetic field intensities, and solar wind properties in the near-Earth and interplanetary environments. This work chronicles the IMP program. Includes an annotated bibliography and cross-references.

Military

Gomery, Douglas. "Military Meteorological Satellites." In *Magill's Survey of Science: Space Exploration Series*, vol. 3, edited by Frank N. Magill. Pasadena, Calif.: Salem Press, 1989.
One of the essays on the history of space exploration in this five-volume set, which covers every aspect of the U.S. and Soviet manned and unmanned space programs, as well as those of nations newer to the space race. These satellites provide weather data which are used for a variety of military uses, including the scheduling of reconnaissance satellite launchings and the planning of military operations. Although very little unclassified information is available,

this work does discuss some of the better-known satellites. Includes an annotated bibliography and cross-references.

Hussain, Farooq, and Curtis Peebles. "Military Space Systems." In *The Illustrated Encyclopedia of Space Technology: A Comprehensive History of Space Exploration*, by Kenneth Gatland et al. New York: Harmony Books, 1981.
This section in the book discusses many of the so-called "spy" satellites of the United States and the Soviet Union, including some of the earlier U.S. projects, such as the Discovery series of satellites and the proposed Manned Orbiting Laboratory. There are color and black-and-white photographs, drawings, charts, a brief bibliography, a chronology of the major space events since Sputnik 1, a glossary of terms, and an index.

Peebles, Curtis. "Electronic Intelligence Satellites." In *Magill's Survey of Science: Space Exploration Series*, vol. 1, edited by Frank N. Magill. Pasadena, Calif.: Salem Press, 1989.
One of the essays on the history of space exploration in this five-volume set, which covers every aspect of the U.S. and Soviet manned and unmanned space programs, as well as those of nations newer to the space race. The electronic "eavesdropper" satellites of the United States, Soviet Union, and Great Britain are discussed in this essay. Although little information is provided because of the classified nature of the subject, the basics of electronic surveillance are sketched in broad strokes. Includes an annotated bibliography and cross-references.

Remote Sensing

Bodechtel, Johann, and Hans-Günter Gieroff-Emden. *The Earth from Space*. New York: Arco, 1974.
This is a fine collection of color photographs of Earth taken by manned and unmanned spacecraft. It discusses the history of space photography from the first crude black-and-white image, transmitted from the orbiting Explorer 6 satellite in 1959, through the long-distance portraits taken by the crew of Apollo 17 as they journeyed from the Moon. The technical aspects of space photography are presented, including how many of the photographs were taken and what they reveal.

Gatland, Kenneth. "Observing Planet Earth." In *The Illustrated Encyclopedia of Space Technology: A Comprehensive History of Space Exploration*, by Kenneth Gatland et al. New York: Harmony Books, 1981.
This section in the book discusses Earth resources satellites, which study the planet in the areas of cartography, agriculture, rangelands, forestry, oceanogra-

phy, ice reconnaissance, pollution, and geology. There are color and black-and-white photographs, drawings, and charts. The major features of the programs, including some of the satellites, are discussed. Includes a chronology of the major space events since Sputnik 1, a glossary of terms, and an index.

Gomery, Douglas. "Environmental Science Services Administration Satellites." In *Magill's Survey of Science: Space Exploration Series*, vol. 1, edited by Frank N. Magill. Pasadena, Calif.: Salem Press, 1989.
One of the essays on the history of space exploration in this five-volume set, which covers every aspect of the U.S. and Soviet manned and unmanned space programs, as well as those of nations newer to the space race. The meteorological satellites of NASA's Environmental Science Service Administration are summarized in this essay, including TIROS, ESSA-1 through ESSA-9, and the NOAA (National Oceanic and Atmospheric Administration) satellites. Provides an annotated bibliography and cross-references.

_____. "U.S. Meteorological Satellites." In *Magill's Survey of Science: Space Exploration Series*, vol. 3, edited by Frank N. Magill. Pasadena, Calif.: Salem Press, 1989.
One of the essays on the history of space exploration in this five-volume set, which covers every aspect of the U.S. and Soviet manned and unmanned space programs, as well as those of nations newer to the space race. This article looks at the variety of weather satellites launched since the first successful meteorological experiment flown on Explorer 7 in 1959. The major programs, such as TIROS (Television Infrared Observations Satellite) and GOES (Geostationary Operational Environmental Satellite), are discussed. There are an annotated bibliography and cross-references.

Hartmann, William K., Ron Miller, and Pamela Lee. *Out of the Cradle: Exploring the Frontiers Beyond Earth*. New York: Workman, 1984.
This is an interesting portrait of the solar system as seen by the remote explorers of the United States at some future date. Although much of the work is based upon speculation, there is a very good chance that our children and their children will see the scenes portrayed in the book. The book is filled with colorful paintings of exotic landscapes and yet-to-be-built spacecraft. There are also some photographs taken by Viking, Voyager, Mariner, and several other unmanned spacecraft.

McMahan, Tracy, and Valerie Neal. *Repairing Solar Max: The Solar Maximum Repair Mission*. Washington, D.C.: Government Printing Office, 1984.
The Solar Maximum Satellite was launched on Valentine's Day, 1980, to study the Sun during one of its peak periods of activity. The satellite functioned for nearly a year before suffering what normally would be a fatal failure. NASA,

however, would not let the patient die so easily. Once the Space Shuttle had become more or less operational, the engineers who had built it hit upon a plan whereby astronauts from the Shuttle would zip over to Solar Max, grab it, lock it into their garage in the back of the orbiter's payload bay, fix the ailing satellite, and send it on its way. There are many reasons for fixing the satellite, the most obvious being that repairs would cost about one-quarter of the price of a replacement satellite. This colorful booklet previews the rescue mission, the equipment needed to fix Max, and the astronauts who would attempt it.

Magill, Frank N., ed. *Magill's Survey of Science: Space Exploration Series*. Vol. 2. Pasadena, Calif.: Salem Press, 1989, pp. 710-721.
Two of the essays on the history of space exploration in this five-volume set, which covers every aspect of the U.S. and Soviet manned and unmanned space programs, as well as those of nations newer to the space race. The articles on these pages take a look at the Landsat programs, which studied Earth resources, including agriculture, forests, flatlands, minerals, waters, and environment. The five satellites were launched between 1972 and 1982. These essays detail each satellite and its scientific applications. Each article contains an annotated bibliography and cross-references.

Mika, Aram M. "Earth Resources Mapped from Satellites." In *Magill's Survey of Science: Space Exploration Series*, vol. 1, edited by Frank N. Magill. Pasadena, Calif.: Salem Press, 1989.
One of the essays on the history of space exploration in this five-volume set, which covers every aspect of the U.S. and Soviet manned and unmanned space programs, as well as those of nations newer to the space race. This work takes a look at the U.S. satellite programs which studied Earth resources, including TIROS, Nimbus, and Landsat, as well as the programs of other countries. Contains an annotated bibliography and cross-references.

Neal, Valerie. *Renewing Solar Science: The Solar Maximum Mission*. Washington, D.C.: Government Printing Office, 1984.
This is a preview of the attempted Space Shuttle rescue of the Solar Maximum Satellite. It differs from the account by McMahan and Neal (cited above) because its emphasis is on the satellite rather than on the rescue. There are numerous color photographs, including some that were transmitted from Solar Max before it developed problems. The scientific results returned by Max are highlighted and guide the reader to an understanding of the importance of repairing the satellite. There is a short preview of the repair mission and a fine drawing of the satellite, detailing its major components.

Schnapf, Abraham. "Weather Patrol in Space." In *The Illustrated Encyclopedia of Space Technology: A Comprehensive History of Space Exploration*, by Kenneth Gatland et al. New York: Harmony Books, 1981.
This section in the book discusses the satellites that study Earth's weather patterns and provides an indication of how these patterns will affect us. A color chart chronicles the advancements in weather satellites. There are color and black-and-white photographs and drawings. The major features of the various programs, including the particular satellites, are discussed. Includes a chronology of the major space events since Sputnik 1, a glossary of terms, and an index.

Short, Nicholas M., et al. *Mission to Earth: Landsat Views the World*. Washington, D.C.: National Technical Information Service, 1976.
The Landsat satellites are part of the Earth Resources Technology Satellite (ERTS) program, designed to utilize unmanned spacecraft to survey Earth's surface. Photographs taken by these satellites are in the visible and infrared portions of the spectrum and are taken on a repetitive basis. Landsat spacecraft are also used to investigate the practical commercial and scientific application of the results. This book, filled with images transmitted by the Landsat spacecraft, was designed to be used in a classroom and is provided with an accompanying teacher's reference. There are dozens of color and false-color images of Earth, a brief bibliography, and an index.

Taylor, F. W. "Nimbus Meteorological Satellites." In *Magill's Survey of Science: Space Exploration Series*, vol. 3, edited by Frank N. Magill. Pasadena, Calif.: Salem Press, 1989.
One of the essays on the history of space exploration in this five-volume set, which covers every aspect of the U.S. and Soviet manned and unmanned space programs, as well as those of nations newer to the space race. The Nimbus satellites (*nimbus* is Latin for raincloud), launched since 1964, are used to develop new techniques for observing Earth, particularly its oceans and atmosphere. This essay chronicles the development of the spacecraft and discusses some of the technology generated by them. Includes an annotated bibliography and cross-references.

Taylor, L. B., Jr. *For All Mankind: America's Space Programs of the 1970s and Beyond*. New York: E. P. Dutton, 1974.
The author discusses the benefits of the United States' space programs of the early 1970's, especially the multiple benefits derived from communications satellites and Earth resources satellites. He describes these programs as well as the Space Transportation System, which was in the latter stages of planning and development. The book discusses the full range of possibilities for the Space Shuttle and some of its payloads. Much is to be gained by comparing

the goals of the system in 1974 and its accomplishments through the next decade and a half. There are black-and-white photographs and an index.

U.S. National Aeronautics and Space Administration. *Orbiting Solar Observatory Satellite OSO-1: The Project Summary.* Washington, D.C.: National Technical Information Service, 1965.

The Orbiting Solar Observatory spacecraft were developed to conduct observations of the Sun and solar physics experiments investigating a broad spectral range of solar radiation. Most of the OSO spacecraft were launched during the peak of the Sun's eleven-year sunspot activity cycle. This report details the first spacecraft mission. OSO-1 was launched aboard a Delta booster on March 7, 1962, and continued to transmit data for seventeen months. The report discusses each phase of the mission and some of the results of its observations. There are numerous black-and-white photographs and line drawings, tables, and charts. Includes an index and a bibliography.

Yearley, Clifton K., and Kerrie L. MacPherson. "U.S. Geodetic Satellites." In *Magill's Survey of Science: Space Exploration Series*, vol. 2, edited by Frank N. Magill. Pasadena, Calif.: Salem Press, 1989.

One of the essays on the history of space exploration in this five-volume set, which covers every aspect of the U.S. and Soviet manned and unmanned space programs, as well as those of nations newer to the space race. This article discusses the measurement and mapping of Earth (geodesy). The history of the satellite programs, as well as their contribution to the study of Earth, is detailed. Satellites such as GEOS (Geodetic Earth-Orbiting Satellite), PAGEOS (Passive Geodetic Earth-Orbiting Satellite), LAGEOS (Laser Geodynamics Satellite), and Landsat (Land Satellite) are discussed in detail. Provides an annotated bibliography and cross-references.

85

MANNED SPACECRAFT

General Studies

Baker, David. *The Rocket: The History and Development of Rocket and Missile Technology.* New York: Crown, 1978.
This large, "coffee-table" book covers the technological and political development of manned and unmanned missiles and rockets. It provides a complete history of solid and liquid propulsion systems from fire-sticks to moon rockets. Propulsion systems are examined for their advantages and faults and how they influence the design of the overall vehicle. The ancestry of U.S. and Soviet launch vehicles is traced to the war machines from which they were derived, all the way back to their common grandparent, the German *Vergeltungswaffe Zwei*, or V-2. The author concludes the work with a forecast about future vehicles, including reusable, atomic-powered, and interplanetary launch vehicles. A compendium of launch vehicles and ballistic missiles and of rocket-powered aircraft is provided. Each vehicle is detailed with information about its origin, configuration, development and flight history, and its descendants. There is a silhouette of the vehicle, scaled for comparison with the others in the compendium. Hundreds of color and black-and-white photographs and illustrations enhance the comprehensive text. There are tables of data on space launch vehicles; research rockets; strategic and tactical ballistic missiles; and antiballistic, air-to-ground, surface-to-air, air-to-air, antiship, antisubmarine, and anti-armor missiles. Contains an index and a bibliography.

Gatland, Kenneth. *Manned Spacecraft.* New York: Macmillan, 1967.
This is a brief "pocketbook" covering the manned spacecraft of the United States and the Soviet Union. Most of these spacecraft are detailed with color photographs and cutaway drawings. There are lists of specifications, as well as the history of these spacecraft. The author also discusses the launch vehicles used to place these craft in space. Includes a glossary of terms and an index.

_____. *Missiles and Rockets: A Pocket Encyclopedia of Spaceflight in Color.* New York: Macmillan, 1975.
A compact history of the missiles and rockets of the world, more specifically, the United States and the Soviet Union. Each vehicle is described, including its configuration and use. There are color and black-and-white photographs of each vehicle, as well as cutaway drawings of the most familiar ones. The history of the missiles and rockets, from Pennemünde to the Space Shuttle, is traced in a concise discussion. The politics and technology which influenced the design of each vehicle are also presented. The work is indexed.

Gatland, Kenneth, et al. *The Illustrated Encyclopedia of Space Technology: A Comprehensive History of Space Exploration.* New York: Harmony Books, 1981.

"Illustrated" should be underscored in the title of this work, because it is the color and black-and-white photographs, drawings, paintings, and charts that are the highlight of this work. Every launch vehicle of the major space powers is discussed in an appropriate chapter. There are two four-page, full-color drawings of the major launch vehicles. Each is drawn to scale for comparison. Contains a chronology of the major space events since Sputnik 1, a glossary of terms, and an index. There is a great amount of text, which does not bog down the work but merely enhances the illustrations. Each chapter has its own list of references.

Hall, Al, ed. *Petersen's Book of Man in Space.* 5 vols. Los Angeles: Petersen, 1974.

This is a colorful presentation of the history of spaceflight, from the early pioneers through the last Apollo flight. There are hundreds of color and black-and-white photographs and drawings. The focus of this work is the U.S. manned programs, perhaps because of the abundance of available photographs. The text is concise and enhances the pictures, although they really do not need enhancement. All of the spacecraft and launch vehicles of the American programs are covered, as are the contributions of the pioneers of spaceflight and the astronauts.

Harrison, Harry, and Malcolm Edwards. *Spacecraft in Fact and Fantasy.* New York: Exeter Books, 1979.

This is an interesting work which compares some of our modern launch vehicles and spacecraft with those created in the minds of science-fiction writers. The work covers the history of spacecraft, primarily American, from the early pioneers through the pre-Shuttle era. There are numerous color and black-and-white photographs, as well as artwork from some of the science-fiction publications. The authors show how some of the predictions of early writers have paralleled fact, and take a look at the future with an eye on the science fiction of today. Includes a brief bibliography and an index.

Magill, Frank N., ed. *Magill's Survey of Science: Space Exploration Series.* 5 vols. Pasadena, Calif.: Salem Press, 1989.

This five-volume set covers every aspect of the U.S. and Soviet manned and unmanned space programs, as well as those of nations newer to the space race. The United States has launched six different types of manned spacecraft into orbit and to the Moon. Essays in this work cover each of the manned programs: Mercury, Gemini, Apollo, Skylab, Apollo Soyuz, and the Space Shuttle. Each essay lists the pertinent data of the mission, launch vehicle, and spacecraft in a brief summary of the program; the knowledge gained by each flight; and the historical significance of the mission. Each also includes an annotated bibliography and cross-references.

Ordway, Frederick I., III, and Mitchell R. Sharpe. *The Rocket Team.* Foreword by Wernher von Braun. New York: Thomas Y. Crowell, 1979.
The men responsible for the launch vehicles that put humans on the Moon also were responsible for the missiles of World War II that brought destruction from the sky. This is the story of the group of German scientists and engineers, headed by von Braun, who developed the science of rocketry from the early 1930's through the Saturn family of launch vehicles. Much of the information about their days at Pennemünde was classified until this book was written. This is fascinating reading about scientists, dedicated to the betterment of human-kind, being forced to develop war machines. There are black-and-white photographs, a bibliography, and an index.

Shortal, Joseph A. *A New Dimension—Wallops Island Flight Test Range: The First Fifteen Years.* Washington, D.C.: National Technical Information Service, 1978.
The Wallops Station, located on Wallops Island, Virginia, was established by the National Advisory Committee for Aeronautics in 1945 to gather information about Earth's atmosphere and its near-space environment. During its first fifteen years, the facility launched more than six thousand research vehicles. Consisting of from one to seven stages, these vehicles were used to gather scientific information on the flight characteristics of airplanes, launch vehicles, and spacecraft, and to increase our understanding of the upper atmosphere and space environment. This large volume details the history of the facility, includ-ing its role in the development of wartime aircraft and missiles, ramjets, supersonic bodies, hypersonic vehicles, high-temperature research, ballistic missile nose cones, guided missiles, sounding rockets, and Project Mercury. There are numerous black-and-white photographs and drawings, and an index. Appendices detail rocket motors used at Wallops, program identification, flight operations, preflight jet operations, and rocket propulsion systems developed at Wallops.

Taylor, John W. R., ed. *Jane's All the World's Aircraft.* 17 vols. London: Jane's, 1957- .
Considered by some to be the most complete reference on aircraft, the biennial publication began to include rockets, missiles, and spacecraft after the first Sputnik was orbited. The most reliable sources of information are used to provide as much technical data about the vehicle, engine, or program as possible. Each issue highlights those systems or components that were intro-duced or made a significant contribution during the previous two-year period.

The major manned and unmanned spaceflights are also detailed. There are black-and-white photographs and drawings of each vehicle or component.

Thompson, Tina D., ed. *Space Log: 1957-1987.* Redondo Beach, Calif.: TRW Space & Technology Group, 1988.
Each year, TRW publishes a log of worldwide space activities. Any new spacecraft, launch vehicle, engine, or program, or one which made a significant contribution to the exploration of space during the year, is detailed. Tables include a "box score" of U.S. launches, worldwide successful space launches, Space Transportation System payload deployment records, payloads in orbit, and manned spaceflight records. The highlight of each volume is the summary of space launches, which details (in a table) the name, international designation, program direction, launch data, weight, orbital data, and status. This particular volume was published in conjunction with the thirtieth anniversary of the space age and contains data for the entire era. Most major libraries have or can obtain copies of these logs directly from the publisher.

Turnill, Reginald, ed. *Jane's Spaceflight Directory.* London: Jane's, 1985-1989.
After publishing spacecraft, missile, and rocket engine data in *Jane's All the World's Aircraft* for a number of years, the publisher found the information too great not to be included in its own book. The biennial publication, like its parent, uses only the most reliable sources of information to provide as much technical data about the vehicle, engine, or program as possible. Each issue highlights those systems or components that were introduced or made a significant contribution during the previous two-year period. The major manned and unmanned spaceflights are also detailed. There are black-and-white photographs and drawings of each vehicle or component.

U.S. House of Representatives. *United States Civilian Space Programs 1958-1978.* Vol. 1. Washington, D.C.: Government Printing Office, 1981.
In a very concise report, the Committee on Space Science and Applications has compiled data on all U.S. space activity during its first two decades. After a brief introduction and summary chapter, the volume is divided into fourteen additional sections. The second chapter deals with the space-related issues under consideration by Congress. The remaining sections cover the history of NASA and its relationship to U.S. space policy, NASA facilities and tracking systems, launch vehicles and propulsion, manned spaceflight through 1975, the Space Transportation System, space life sciences, space science programs, materials processing in space, international cooperation in space, interagency and non-NASA governmental space activities, industrial and university support for NASA, space program benefits, and selected future space programs. Appendices contain Department of Defense manned spaceflight plans, NASA funding history, international space agreements, texts of President Jimmy Carter's space

directives, documents relating to the legal aspects of the Space Shuttle, major U.S. space organizations, a master log of U.S. spaceflights, and a table of U.S. space orbital payloads by mission from 1957 through 1979.

Van Nimmen, Jane, and Leonard C. Bruno, with Robert L. Rosholt. *NASA Historical Data Book 1958-1968*. Vol. 1, *NASA Resources*. Washington, D.C.: National Technical Information Service, 1976.
This is the first in what was intended to be a series of volumes providing a comprehensive statistical summary of the first decade of the National Aeronautics and Space Administration, from its post-Sputnik creation until the Apollo 8 astronauts became the first men to circle the Moon. This volume measures dollars, people, and things and is designed to provide a reference source for a variety of purposes. The summary documents the immense growth and eventual leveling off of the agency's programs. It covers NASA's budget and financial history, its scattered installations, its manpower resources, and a statistical summary of its contractual history. This work is ideal for the "number cruncher," but it is difficult for the common researcher to wade through its 547 pages. There is no table of contents or index, and one is forced to find things by the "hunt and peck" method. However, it does provide a great deal of information about how the mighty dollar influences the decisions of the NASA. There are scores of tables and charts.

Von Braun, Wernher, and Frederick I. Ordway III. *History of Rocketry and Space Travel*. 3d rev. ed. New York: Thomas Y. Crowell, 1975.
This is the story of the exploration of space from the earliest experiments with rocketry to the final flight of the Skylab program. Hundreds of experts on every aspect of this broad field contributed to the work. Most of the programs of the United States, the Soviet Union, and the rest of the nations engaged in space exploration at that time are detailed, both descriptively and with black-and-white and color photographs. It is one of the best references on the subject. The book also contains a large, chapter-by-chapter bibliography. The authors finish their discussion of the space programs with a look at the future, including the Space Transportation System.

Wells, Helen T., Susan Whiteley, and Carrie E. Karegeannes. "Manned Space Flight." In *Origins of NASA Names*. Washington, D.C.: National Technical Information Service, 1976.
Ever wonder how a particular spacecraft, launch vehicle, or program derived its name? Although this work is dated, it provides a great number of answers regarding these names. This is one of the volumes in the NASA History Series, and it is a wonderful book for trivia buffs. It discusses the major NASA projects, launch vehicles, satellites, space probes, sounding rockets, manned spacecraft, and NASA installations. This chapter deals with the manned space

programs and spacecraft, including Mercury, Gemini, Apollo, Skylab, and the Space Shuttle. Appendices list abbreviations, acronyms, and terms; international designation of spacecraft; NASA major launch records, 1958-1974; and NASA naming committees. There are dozens of black-and-white photographs, an index, and an in-depth bibliography.

Yenne, Bill. *The Encyclopedia of U.S. Spacecraft*. New York: Exeter Books, 1985.
A complete encyclopedia of U.S. spacecraft is presented in a book filled with color and black-and-white photographs. General information on the programs is provided in alphabetical order, with individual spacecraft, probes, or launch vehicles listed chronologically. Data on all of the manned spacecraft, including Apollo, Gemini, Mercury, Skylab, and the Space Shuttle, are furnished. Includes lists of acronyms and abbreviations, and an index.

_____. *The Pictorial History of World Spacecraft*. New York: Exeter Books, 1988.
The history of the world's spacecraft and probes is told in chronological order from Sputnik 1 through Cosmos 1870, and spans the first thirty years of the space age. Included are all of the manned spacecraft and launch vehicles. Each is detailed with charts, diagrams, illustrations, and color and black-and-white photographs. Data on all of the manned spacecraft, including the Mercury, Gemini, Apollo, Skylab, and Space Shuttle, are provided. An appendix lists all of the spacecraft in service as of July, 1987, grouped according to the countries or organizations responsible for them.

Astronauts

Aldrin, Buzz, and Malcolm McConnell. *Men from Earth*. New York: Bantam Books, 1989.
Aldrin, the second man to walk on the Moon, writes a brief history of the U.S. manned space program, with emphasis on his own Gemini XII and Apollo 11 flights. He discusses the manned programs leading to Apollo with an insider's knowledge. The book is well written and provides the reader with some information obtainable nowhere else. His description of his Gemini spacewalks and the lunar landing and subsequent moonwalk is quite vivid. The reader can almost picture the events as if he were there when they happened. There are black-and-white photographs and an extensive bibliography.

Aldrin, Edwin E. "Buzz," Jr., with Wayne Warga. *Return to Earth*. New York: Random House, 1973.

For years Buzz Aldrin, Mike Collins, and Neil Armstrong trained to become the crew to make the first landing on the Moon. They were taught the intricacies of the spacecraft, launch vehicle, and equipment they would use. They rehearsed the details of every aspect of their mission from launch to splashdown in the Pacific. Armstrong and Aldrin practiced the lunar landing and liftoff in simulators. One-sixth-G trainers were used to simulate the conditions expected during their sojourn on the Moon. The one thing NASA forgot to teach them was how to be ordinary human beings after they returned to Earth. Aldrin chronicles his career from his glory days as an astronaut to his post-Apollo battle with alcohol and depression.

Allen, Joseph P., with Russell Martin. *Entering Space.* New York: Stewart, Tabori & Chang, 1984.
The story of an astronaut's journey in space, told in conjunction with a study of the U.S. exploration of space. This work is filled with colorful words and spectacular photographs of space travel from the ground up, and back again. There are hundreds of color photographs taken during the manned Gemini, Apollo, Skylab, Apollo Soyuz, and Space Shuttle programs, as well as those shots of our neighbors in the solar system taken from unmanned probes. The spacecraft, launch vehicles, spacefarers, and their equipment are discussed in some detail, although this is primarily done from the perspective of a single trip into orbit and back again. There is a very real sense of "being there" as Astronaut Allen describes his feelings during the various phases of flight. Contains a brief bibliography and an index.

Barbour, John. *Footprints on the Moon.* New York: Associated Press, 1969.
A documentary look at the United States' efforts to place a man on the Moon. Barbour chronicles the U.S. space program from the early days of Project Mercury through the successful completion of the Apollo 11 mission. Written right after *Columbia* splashed down in the Pacific Ocean, the book tells of both the glory and the misfortune of Apollo. Barbour's reporter-like presentation could well be used as a history book. Most of the information is presented in an unbiased style, neither giving NASA a pat on the back nor kicking it when it is down.

Bergwin, Clyde R., and William T. Coleman. *Animal Astronauts: They Opened the Way to the Stars.* Englewood Cliffs, N.J.: Prentice-Hall, 1963.
Man was not the first of God's creatures to venture into space. In fact, he was one of the last. Dogs, monkeys, mice, rats, chimpanzees, insects, and even pigs were lofted into the heavens atop the future man-carriers. The first individual reported to have been placed into Earth orbit was a dog named Laika. This book looks at the suborbital and orbital flights of the United States' animal pioneers. The two most famous were chimpanzees. Ham (named for

the Holloman Aerospace Medical Center, New Mexico) made a successful suborbital flight in a Mercury spacecraft on January 31, 1961. Enos, a forty-two-pound chimpanzee, completed the first orbital flight of a Mercury spacecraft on November 29, 1961, after two orbits. This is an interesting book about some very important but often overlooked characters in the history of space exploration.

Bodechtel, Johann, and Hans-Günter Gieroff-Emden. *The Earth from Space*. New York: Arco, 1974.
This is a fine collection of color photographs of Earth taken by manned and unmanned spacecraft. It discusses the history of space photography from the first crude black-and-white image transmitted from the orbiting Explorer 6 satellite in 1959 through the long-distance portraits taken by the crew of Apollo 17 as they journeyed from the Moon. The technical aspects of space photography are presented, including how many of the photographs were taken and what they reveal.

Bond, Peter. *Heroes in Space: From Gagarin to Challenger*. Oxford, England: Basil Blackwell, 1987.
This is one of the first books to cover the astronauts and cosmonauts of the first quarter century of the space age. It is also the story of the two countries' manned space programs. Each mission is discussed, with the more notable ones getting the most coverage. The author, on occasion, gets carried away with his story. For the most part, however, the book holds the reader's interest. There are several black-and-white photographs, an index, and a brief bibliography.

Booker, Peter, Gerald Frewer, and Geoffrey Pardoe. *Project Apollo: The Way to the Moon*. New York: American Elsevier, 1970.
The authors write about the efforts to place men on the Moon, as well as the Mercury and Gemini programs, which paved the way for Apollo. They look at the spacecraft, launch vehicles, flights, and astronauts involved. They also discuss the problems and accomplishments of each. Since the book is broad in coverage, there is very little detail on individual flights. The text is illustrated with black-and-white photographs and line drawings.

Borman, Frank, with Robert J. Sterling. *Countdown: An Autobiography*. New York: Silver Arrow Books, 1988.
What does it take to be an astronaut? A little skill and a lot of luck. That is the impression Frank Borman gives in his look at the life of an astronaut. He also shows that it is not all guts and glory. Sacrifices have to be made and, most often, it is the astronaut's family that is pushed down the list of priorities. The book also looks at life after being a space traveler. Although he was at times treated like a conquering hero, Borman often found it difficult to be the

person he was made out to be. After succeeding in space, the failure to "complete his mission" with Eastern Airlines could have crushed his spirit, but Frank Borman was able to pick up the pieces and move on to the next assignment.

Boynton, John H., ed. *First United States Manned Three-Pass Orbital Mission (Mercury-Atlas 6, Spacecraft 13): Part 1—Description and Performance Analysis.* Washington, D.C.: National Technical Information Service, 1964.
This is part 1 of the two-volume official NASA report on the flight of Mercury-Atlas 6 with astronaut John Glenn. The contents were prepared by a flight evaluation team. A description of the space vehicle and launch vehicle is presented, detailing each of the major systems as configured for the mission. The performance of these systems is given in the form of charts and tables. Each phase of the mission operation is described: prelaunch, including astronaut training and spacecraft and launch vehicle preparation; launch operations; flight-control operations; and recovery operations. There is an aeromedical analysis of the astronaut and a description of pilot flight activities. The sequence of events is enumerated along with trajectory data. Black-and-white photographs, line drawings, and a brief reference list are included.

_____, ed. *Second United States Manned Three-Pass Orbital Mission (Mercury-Atlas 7, Spacecraft 18).* Washington, D.C.: Government Printing Office, 1967.
This is the first of two official NASA reports on the flight of Mercury-Atlas 7 with astronaut Scott Carpenter. The contents were prepared by a flight evaluation team and are more detailed than the other report. A description of the space vehicle and launch vehicle is presented, detailing each of the major systems as configured for the mission. The performance of these systems is given in the form of charts and tables. Each phase of the mission operation is described: prelaunch, including astronaut training and spacecraft and launch vehicle preparation; launch operations; flight-control operations; and recovery operations. There is an aeromedical analysis of the astronaut and a description of pilot flight activities. The sequence of events is enumerated along with trajectory data. There is a complete transcript of the air-to-ground communications between the astronaut and tracking stations. Black-and-white photographs, line drawings, and a brief reference list are included in each section of the work.

_____, ed. *First U.S. Manned Six-Pass Orbital Mission (Mercury- Atlas 8, Spacecraft 16).* Washington, D.C.: National Technical Information Service, 1968.
This is the first of two official NASA reports on the flight of Mercury-Atlas 8 with astronaut Wally Schirra. The contents were prepared by a flight evalua-

tion team and are more detailed than the other report. A description of the space vehicle and launch vehicle is presented, detailing each of the major systems as configured for the mission. The performance of these systems is given in the form of charts and tables. Each phase of the mission operation is described: prelaunch, including astronaut training and spacecraft and launch vehicle preparation; launch operations; flight-control operations; and recovery operations. There is an aeromedical analysis of the astronaut and a description of pilot flight activities. The sequence of events is enumerated along with trajectory data. There is a complete transcript of the air-to-ground communications between the astronaut and tracking stations. Black-and-white photographs, line drawings, and a brief reference list are included in each section of the work.

Carpenter, M. Scott, et al. *We Seven, by the Astronauts Themselves.* New York: Simon & Schuster, 1962.
The seven Mercury astronauts write about the man-in-space program with a little help from the editors of *Life* magazine. The main focus is on John Glenn's flight in Mercury-Atlas 6. He discusses the mission in some detail, while the others talk about their roles in the flight. Some of the chapters are written by one, while many are a team effort, much like Project Mercury itself. The stories are personal narratives of many aspects of the project, including the spacecraft and the flights that preceded Glenn's. Scott Carpenter writes the closing chapter, about his Mercury-Atlas 7 flight, which confirmed the feasibility of placing a man into orbit. There are many black-and-white photographs and an index. It would be safe to presume that the astronauts did not sit down at the typewriter to compose this work, but rather told their stories to other writers. The book does, however, give an introspective look at the pioneers of manned spaceflight.

Cassutt, Michael. *Who's Who in Space (The First Twenty-five Years).* Boston: G. K. Hall, 1987.
While a lot has been written about the U.S. astronauts and Soviet cosmonauts, there are few books which include the lesser known ones. This work not only covers them, it does so in great detail. There is an individual biography for each of the astronauts of the Mercury, Gemini, Apollo, Skylab, Apollo Soyuz, and Space Shuttle programs. In addition, the author details the lives of the X-15, X-20, and Manned Orbiting Laboratory projects, as well as the civilian and military Shuttle payload specialists. A black-and-white photograph accompanies each biography. There is a chronological log of the astronauts and cosmonauts, in the order in which they made their first spaceflights, and a log of the manned spaceflights and X-15 spaceflights. There is an index.

Christensen, Eric. "Astronauts and the U.S. Astronaut Program." In *Magill's Survey of Science: Space Exploration Series*, vol. 1, edited by Frank N. Magill. Pasadena, Calif.: Salem Press, 1989.
One of the essays on the history of space exploration in this five-volume set, which covers every aspect of the U.S. and Soviet manned and unmanned space programs, as well as those of nations newer to the space race. The author briefly discusses the astronaut program and the contributions the astronauts have made to the design of spacecraft and equipment, in addition to their scientific contributions during their flights. Mission assignments are also discussed, as are the roles of backup and mission support crews. Provides an annotated bibliography and cross-references.

Collins, Michael. *Carrying the Fire: An Astronaut's Journeys*. New York: Farrar, Straus & Giroux, 1983.
Collins, pilot on Gemini X and command module pilot on Apollo 11, offers an intriguing look at life as a test pilot. He takes the reader into the mysterious world of space travel and behind the scenes at the Manned Spacecraft Center in Houston. Always the test pilot, he does not consider spaceflight any more dangerous than air flight, as long as the pilot trains well and has a "good machine." In a very personal way, Collins captures the spirit of adventure that so intrigues nonastronauts and gives a down-to-earth feeling to the extraterrestrial experience.

_____. *Liftoff: The Story of America's Adventure in Space*. New York: Grove Press, 1988.
Who better to write a historical look at the U.S. manned space programs than someone who lived it? Collins did so at the request of NASA, but with the provision that he could write without anyone looking over his shoulder. His book is dedicated to the five deceased members of his fourteen-person astronaut class. As a friend, he tells their stories as well as those of others who achieved the glory of spaceflight. It is an evenly written tale of accomplishments and failures. It is also a personal look at space travel from a perspective inaccessible to the majority of us. The book is illustrated with eighty-eight line drawings by James Dean, former NASA art director.

Columbia Broadcasting System. *10:56:20 P.M., EDT, 7/20/69: The Historic Conquest of the Moon as Reported to the American People by CBS News Over the CBS Television Network*. New York: Author, 1970.
This interesting look at the televising of the most significant event in the history of exploration is filled with glimpses into the personal lives of the participants. One not only learns of the Apollo 11 crew's experiences which brought them to the mission but also meets some of the crew members' relatives. How would you feel if your son just landed on the moon? Mrs.

Armstrong said, "Praise the Lord." This moment-by-moment chronicle gives a true feeling of what the world thought about man's greatest adventure.

Compton, William David. *Where No Man Has Gone Before: A History of Apollo Lunar Exploration Missions.* Washington, D.C.: Government Printing Office, 1989.
This is one title in the NASA History Series, and it tells of the courage of the astronauts chosen to participate in man's greatest adventure. It also introduces the people behind the scenes who made it all possible. The author, having interviewed most of those associated with the program, allows the reader to share their experiences as part of the team. Illustrated with many black-and-white photographs and drawings, the work takes the reader inside NASA and the lunar landing program. A completely annotated source listing is almost as valuable as the manuscript.

Compton, William David, and Charles D. Benson. *Living and Working in Space: A History of Skylab.* Washington, D.C.: Government Printing Office, 1983.
One title in the NASA History Series, this book chronicles the Skylab program, from its conception during the early days of the Apollo program to the orbiting workshop's fiery plunge in 1979. There are dozens of black-and-white photographs of the three manned missions, as well as the launch of the unmanned workshop. Color photographs, taken from orbit, are in the back of the book. Line drawings show the inner workings of much of the equipment related to the missions. There is an index and an impressive hundred-page appendix listing source notes and bibliographic references. Other appendices include a summary of the missions, astronaut biographies, in-flight experiments, Comet Kohoutek, and the International Aeronautical Federation world records set by Skylab.

Cooper, Henry S. F., Jr. *Before Liftoff: The Making of a Space Shuttle Crew.* Baltimore: The Johns Hopkins University Press, 1987.
Space Shuttle Mission 41-G, with seven astronauts aboard *Challenger*, spent eight days in space. The crew included veteran Commander Robert Crippen and Mission Specialist Sally Ride, along with rookie Pilot Jon McBride, Mission Specialists Kathy Sullivan and David Leetsma, and Payload Specialists Paul Scully-Power and Canadian Marc Garneau. During the mission, the crew deployed the Earth Radiation Budget Satellite and conducted experiments. Two of the astronauts performed a spacewalk to demonstrate an on-orbit refueling system. Author Cooper made special arrangements with NASA to follow the crew from its formation through the completion of the mission. This is an engrossing look at the everyday life of an astronaut crew. The reader gets to sit in on briefings, join the crew for simulations, and even swim underwater

for spacewalk practice. There are a few black-and-white photographs and an index.

_____. *A House in Space.* New York: Holt, Rinehart and Winston, 1976. This work is about the nine-month period from May 14, 1973, through February 8, 1974—the active life of the Skylab orbiting workshop. During this time it was inhabited by three crews of astronauts for periods of twenty-eight, fifty-nine, and eighty-four days. The book was derived from articles written by Cooper, which appeared in *The New Yorker* magazine during this period. It looks more at the human aspect of the program than at its technical side, but still contains information useful to the researcher. There are many black-and-white photographs and color diagrams.

_____. *Thirteen: The Flight That Failed.* New York: Dial Press, 1973. An interesting look at the astronauts involved in the dramatic rescue of the Apollo 13 crew. Cooper gives an account of the flight and how it affected the people on the ground as well as in space. Based upon interviews with NASA astronauts and other personnel, the book explores the drama of the accident without jumping to conclusions about its cause. It is as engrossing as any novel, mostly because the story is true.

Cortright, Edgar M., ed. *Apollo Expeditions to the Moon.* Washington, D.C.: National Technical Information Service, 1976. A compilation of articles about the Apollo lunar landing program from the people who made it happen. Each of the later Apollo flights (Apollo 11 through 17) is discussed by the astronauts who flew the mission. Jim Lovell tells the tale of Apollo 13 from inside the crippled spacecraft. The crew, unaware of the media coverage their flight was getting, was surprised by the greeting they received upon their return to Earth. Harrison Schmitt, Apollo 17 lunar module pilot, discusses the wealth of information returned during the expeditions, and Wernher von Braun himself discusses the mighty launch vehicles of Apollo. Filled with color photographs and lengthy captions, the book truly captures the spirit of adventure that was Apollo.

Cunningham, Walter. *The All-American Boys.* New York: Macmillan, 1977. A personal look inside the halls of NASA by an astronaut determined "to share the enthusiasm and skill we brought to our work as well as to tell about the warts and moles which sometimes compromised it." Cunningham takes an uncompromising look at his days as a test pilot and as an astronaut. He reveals the strain that the life he chose had on relations with his family, friends, and coworkers. While most autobiographies are a personal view of history, Cunningham tries to remove himself from the story and put his experiences in perspective.

DeWaard, E. John, and Nancy DeWaard. *History of NASA: America's Voyage to the Stars.* New York: Exeter Books, 1984.
This is a brief, photo-filled look at NASA's programs more than it is a look at NASA itself. Each of the manned and unmanned programs, including Mercury, Gemini, Apollo, Skylab, the Space Shuttle, Voyager, and Viking, is discussed in general. There is very little "new" information provided, but there are dozens of color and black-and-white photographs which, in themselves, make the book worthwhile. An index is included.

Dryden, Hugh L. *Proceedings of a Conference on Results of the First U.S. Manned Suborbital Space Flight.* Washington, D.C.: National Technical Information Service, 1961.
This is the official NASA report on the flight of Mercury-Redstone 3 with astronaut Alan Shepard. The contents were prepared by a flight evaluation team, in cooperation with the National Institutes of Health and the National Academy of Sciences. A description of the space vehicle and launch vehicle is presented, detailing each of the major systems as configured for the mission. The performance of these systems is given in the form of charts and tables. Each phase of the mission is described: prelaunch, including astronaut training and spacecraft and launch vehicle preparation; launch operations; flight-control operations; and recovery operations. There is an aeromedical analysis of the astronaut and a description of pilot flight activities. The sequence of events is enumerated along with trajectory data. Black-and-white photographs, line drawings, and a brief reference list are included.

Elliot, James C. "Food and Diet for Space Travel." In *Magill's Survey of Science: Space Exploration Series*, vol. 1, edited by Frank N. Magill. Pasadena, Calif.: Salem Press, 1989.
One of the essays on the history of space exploration in this five-volume set, which covers every aspect of the U.S. and Soviet manned and unmanned space programs, as well as those of nations newer to the space race. This essay discusses the attempts to develop palatable food for spaceflight, which could be stored for long periods of time and retain all of its nutritional qualities. Although some of the early programs are mentioned, the main focus of the essay is on the Space Shuttle program. Includes an annotated bibliography and cross-references.

Ezell, Edward C., and Linda N. Ezell. *The Partnership: A History of the Apollo-Soyuz Test Project.* Washington, D.C.: Government Printing Office, 1978.
One title in the NASA History Series, this book chronicles the Apollo Soyuz Test Project, to date the only joint American-Soviet manned spaceflight. The origins of the project, immediately following the successful completion of the Apollo 11 Moon landing mission, are traced. Also discussed are the political

aspects of the venture. There are dozens of black-and-white photographs of the flight. Color photographs, taken from orbit, are in the back of the book. Line drawings show the inner workings of much of the equipment related to the mission. There is an impressive seventy-page appendix listing source notes and bibliographic references, and an index. Other appendices include NASA organization charts, development of U.S. and Soviet manned spaceflight, a summary of the U.S./U.S.S.R. meetings, and descriptions of the ASTP launch vehicles.

Farmer, Gene, and Dora Jane Hamblin. *First on the Moon.* Boston: Little, Brown, 1970.
The journey of Neil Armstrong, Buzz Aldrin, and Michael Collins to the Moon and back. An account of the historic trip as told by the astronauts who made the trek. The book adds very little in the way of historical data about the flight, but it does make interesting reading. This is one of the first published accounts of the mission by the Apollo 11 crew and conveys their thoughts while relatively fresh in their minds. A speculative epilogue by Arthur Clarke on the future of spaceflight concludes the book.

Fisher, David G. "Mercury-Redstone 3." In *Magill's Survey of Science: Space Exploration Series,* vol. 3, edited by Frank N. Magill. Pasadena, Calif.: Salem Press, 1989.
For some reason when the subject of "firsts" in manned space exploration comes up in a discussion, the United States' first astronaut gets ignored. Everyone knows which American was the first in orbit, the first spacewalker, the first on the Moon, and the first to fly the Shuttle. However, most people (those who are not avid followers of the space program) will identify John Glenn as the first American in space. Actually, it was Alan Shepard. Shepard's historic fifteen-minute venture into space is detailed in this concise, information-filled article. The author discusses the mission and gives a brief biography of the pilot. He also points out the importance of this first flight, including the fact that it was all President John F. Kennedy needed to challenge the United States to be first on the Moon.

Froehlich, Walter. *Apollo Soyuz.* Washington, D.C.: Government Printing Office, 1976.
This is an entertaining look at the Apollo Soyuz Test Project, the United States' last manned mission using expendable spacecraft and launch vehicles. It was designed to test a rescue method for astronauts or cosmonauts stranded in orbit and unable to be saved by their own country. The U.S. spacecraft, an Apollo command and service module and a docking module (stored in the adapter used to house the Apollo lunar module during launch), were boosted into orbit by a Saturn IB. The Soviets used their standard Soyuz spacecraft and A-2 booster.

The book briefly looks at the mission's origin, the spacecraft, the astronauts and cosmonauts, the experiments, and the results of the joint endeavor. There are numerous color photographs and appendices listing the times of major events, "firsts" achieved by Apollo Soyuz, major officials involved, scientific experiments, and principal Apollo contractors.

Furniss, Tim. *Manned Spaceflight Log.* London: Jane's, 1983.
This work covers the manned spaceflights of the Soviet Union and the United States from 1961 through 1986. A synopsis of each mission is given, along with pertinent data (date, crew, site, recovery, duration, spacecraft weight, and so forth) and several black-and-white photographs. The Mercury, Gemini, Apollo, Skylab, Apollo Soyuz, and Space Shuttle flights are listed chronologically. Included are the thirteen flights of the X-15 research aircraft, which exceeded the fifty-mile altitude necessary to qualify its pilot as an astronaut under Air Force rules. There are astronaut photographs and, in the appendices, listings of space seniority and the current status of the astronaut and cosmonaut classes.

_____. *One Small Step.* Newbury Park, Calif.: Haynes, 1989.
Written to coincide with the twentieth anniversary of the first manned lunar landing, this book takes a look back at the origins of Apollo and updates the reader on the twelve men who walked on the Moon. In fact, one of the most interesting features of this work is the section (or rather, chapters) on each of them. Using titles which the author feels best describes the astronauts (for example, Buzz Aldrin is "The Second," Alan Bean, "The Painter"), he talks about their backgrounds, contributions to Apollo, and current status. A large portion of the book details the ancestors of Apollo: Project Mercury and the Gemini program. It is well written and contains a listing of references.

_____. *Space Flight: The Records.* London: Guiness Books, 1985.
Do you know the first manned spaceflight to be curtailed? It was Gemini V, which landed one orbit early to miss hurricane Betsy. Were you aware that the first spaceflight with more than one fifty-year-old person on board was that of STS 51-B/Spacelab 3, in April, 1985? These and dozens of other interesting and significant—or not so significant—facts are covered in this work. The first part of the book is a "diary" of manned spaceflight, listing each of the missions of the United States and Soviet Union. There is a chapter on manned spaceflight "firsts" and one on the manned space machines. Basic biographical information on each of the space travelers is given, accompanied by the person's photograph. The major information section is last and includes tables on manned spaceflight duration, space seniority, space experience, lunar spacemen, space walks, astroflights of the X-15, all known cosmonauts, NASA astronauts, Space Shuttle passengers, NASA flight crew selections, and the

Space Shuttle schedule. There are hundreds of black-and-white photographs, a glossary of terms, and an index.

_____. *Space Shuttle Log.* London: Jane's, 1986.
The first twenty-two flights of the Space Shuttle are chronicled in this concise work about the Space Transportation System. The first chapter traces the development and testing of the system, detailing the earlier designs of the vehicle and some of the research aircraft which paved the way for the orbiter. There is a section on the astronauts who fly the Shuttle, which includes their photographs and brief biographical listings. Perhaps the most ironic segment is the listing of future flights, including the ill-fated STS 51-L mission. There are hundreds of black-and-white photographs and replicas of each of the individual crew emblems.

Gagarin, Yuri, and V. Lebedev. *Survival in Space.* New York: Frederick A. Praeger, 1969.
The first man in space and a noted Soviet psychologist write about the psychological changes and strenuous demands of spaceflight. Their essay discusses both the U.S. and Soviet missions to date. They compare the ideal temperament required for space travel with the actual responses of Soviet cosmonauts. They also speak of the requirements of future lunar and planetary flights. An interesting look at the Soviet philosophy of manned space missions and hope to cope with the possible problems of long-term cohabitation.

Gatland, Kenneth, et al. *The Illustrated Encyclopedia of Space Technology: A Comprehensive History of Space Exploration.* New York: Harmony Books, 1981.
"Illustrated" should be underscored in the title of this work, because it is the color and black-and-white photographs, drawings, paintings, and charts that are the highlight of this work. Every spacecraft, launch vehicle, space center, and major component of each U.S. space endeavor is included, as are those from the other countries which have entered the space race. Contains a chronology of the major space events since Sputnik 1, a glossary of terms, and an index. There is a great deal of text, which does not bog down the work but merely enhances the illustrations. Each chapter has its own list of references.

Goldstein, Norm, ed. *Moments in Space.* New York: Gallery Books, 1986.
Newspaper photographs from the Associated Press are the highlight of this book, which offers little text to accompany them. Much of the discussion is not to be relied on for accuracy, especially because the information included with the photographs has not been updated from what was known at the time of the event. Many of the photographs are grainy, but it is for their historical context that they should be viewed, not for their clarity.

Grimwood, James M. *Project Mercury: A Chronology.* Washington, D.C.: National Technical Information Service, 1963.
This is NASA's official record of Project Mercury, covering events on a day-to-day basis. Mercury was the United States' first attempt to place a man into low Earth orbit. Embarking on a trip into the unknown environment of space, while developing the technology "on the fly," the scientists, engineers, technicians, and astronauts created spacecraft systems to accomplish the deed, and they did it in less than four years. Included in the coverage are the development of the spacecraft and launch vehicles, astronaut training, and mission results. There are dozens of black-and-white photographs and line drawings of components. Appendices provide a summary of the Mercury flights: mission objectives, orbital activities, and experiments. There are tables of vehicle manufacturing and test histories; program costs; contractors, subcontractors, and vendors; and the flight record of Project Mercury.

Grimwood, James M., and Barton C. Hacker, with Peter J. Vorzimmer. *Project Gemini Technology and Operations: A Chronology.* Washington, D.C.: National Technical Information Service, 1969.
This is NASA's official record of the Gemini program, covering events on a day-to-day basis. Gemini was developed as an "in-between" program. What evolved was a test program that proved that the theoretical concepts of rendezvous and docking with another orbiting spacecraft could be accomplished. Included in the coverage are the development of the spacecraft and launch vehicles, astronaut training, and mission results. There are dozens of black-and-white photographs and line drawings of components. Appendices provide a summary of the Gemini flights: mission objectives, orbital activities, experiments, and extravehicular activity. There are tables of vehicle manufacturing and test histories; program costs; contractors, subcontractors, and vendors; and the flight records of Project Mercury and the Gemini program.

Grissom, Betty, and Henry S. Still. *Starfall.* New York: Thomas Y. Crowell, 1974.
A gutsy, sometimes bitter look at the Apollo program from a point of view not offered to many. Betty Grissom, widow of Gus Grissom, who was killed in the Apollo 204 pad fire, talks about how her husband and she got caught up in the drive to conquer the Moon. The woman who wrote this book is nothing like the character portrayal of her in the film *The Right Stuff.* Her characterization of her husband seems more like the test pilot he was and less like the bumbling fool in *The Right Stuff.*

Gurney, Gene. *Americans on the Moon: The Story of Project Apollo.* New York: Random House, 1970.

A review of the Apollo program from the first circumlunar flight through the first lunar landing. Although only four manned missions are discussed (Apollo 8 through 11), the goals of Apollo are explained, as well as the means used to accomplish them. Nontechnical in content, it brings the technology of manned spaceflight down to earth. The are a number of photographs, many of which are not presented in other works. A short preview of upcoming lunar exploration flights is included.

Hallion, Richard. *Supersonic Flight: Breaking the Sound Barrier and Beyond.* New York: Macmillan, 1972.
This is the history of the two research aircraft families—the Bell X-1 and the Douglas D-558. It chronicles the two craft from the first attempts at breaking the sound barrier to the end of their respective programs. Much has been written about the X-1, but this is perhaps the best source of information about the D-558-I *Skystreak* and the D-558-II *Skyrocket*. Technical specifications are given for all members of both families, as well as their flight test records. The test pilots who flew these supersonic aircraft are also profiled. There are numerous black-and-white photographs and drawings, and an index.

Hallion, Richard, and Tom O. Crouch, eds. *Ten Years Since Tranquility: Reflections upon Apollo 11.* Washington, D.C.: Smithsonian Institution Press, 1979.
The editors, now former curators at the National Air and Space Museum, have collected essays reviewing the social and political factors that led to the first lunar landing. Those who were involved wrote the essay about a particular aspect of the Apollo program. The technological developments, spin-offs, accomplishments in rocket science, and scientific results of the lunar surface and orbital experiments are discussed. Illustrated with black-and-white photographs, the work is a concise view of America's journey to the Moon. A bibliography is included.

Henry, James P., and John D. Mosely, eds. *Results of the Project Mercury Ballistic and Orbital Chimpanzee Flights.* Washington, D.C.: National Technical Information Service, 1963.
Prepared by the personnel of NASA's Manned Spacecraft Center in Houston, Texas, this publication presents a full account of the flights of the Project Mercury chimpanzees. Before committing man to the unknowns of space travel, these pioneers rode atop the fiery missiles. The suborbital flight of Ham preceded Alan Shepard's by a little more than three months. Enos went into orbit three months before John Glenn. This compilation of essays elaborates on the contributions these two primates made to Mercury. Black-and-white photographs, line drawings, charts, and tables are used to illustrate the volume. Each section has its own reference list.

Irwin, James B., with William A. Emerson, Jr. *To Rule the Night: The Discovery Voyage of Astronaut Jim Irwin.* Nashville: A. J. Holman, 1973.
Astronaut Irwin provides a different view of the nature of an astronaut and how a trip to the Moon can change one's perspective on life. Although Irwin could not be considered the typical hard-driving test pilot, his spiritual well-being took a turn for the better after his God's-eye view of Earth. After retiring from NASA and the Air Force in 1972, Irwin founded the High Flight Foundation, a nonprofit organization he uses to share his faith in God and to serve humanity, through speaking engagements, publications, retreats, and training activities. Illustrated with black-and-white photographs.

Irwin, Mary, with Madalene Harris. *The Moon Is Not Enough: An Astronaut's Wife Finds Peace with God and Herself.* Grand Rapids, Mich.: Sondervan, 1978.
An astronaut's wife is not the model of perfection, waiting patiently while her husband soars through the cosmos. This book, by the wife of astronaut James Irwin, shows us just how human the spouse of an astronaut really is. She chronicles the career of her husband while telling her own story. The reader gets to share the anxious moments as well as the happy ones. It takes as much intestinal fortitude to stay at home and smile for the television cameras as it does to climb atop a Saturn V. Black-and-white photographs help to share some of the private memories with the reader.

Johnston, Richard S., and Lawrence F. Dietlein, eds. *Biomedical Results from Skylab.* Washington, D.C.: National Technical Information Service, 1977.
Biomedical testing under the conditions of orbital flight was studied for relatively brief periods during the Mercury, Gemini, and Apollo programs. With Skylab, scientists would be able to conduct experiments on astronauts spending a month or more in space. The editors of this work have compiled a concise review of each experiment, including the theory behind the test, the means by which is was completed, and the results. The experiments were divided into four disciplines: neurophysiology; musculoskeletal function; biochemistry, hematology, and cytology; and cardiovascular and metabolic function. The text is supplemented with photographs and drawings, as well as charts of the conclusions reached by each examiner. Every section of the book has its own reference listing, which will guide the researcher to more detailed works. Appendices detail the experimental support hardware and the operational life sciences support hardware.

Kaplan, Judith, and Robert Muniz. *Space Patches from Mercury to the Space Shuttle.* New York: Sterling, 1986.
This work, written and published by one of the manufacturers and distributors of cloth patches and vinyl decals, discusses the emblems' design by the astro-

naut crews and other participants in space programs. Overall, the work has been well researched and contains many interesting facts about the origins of these patches. Few people realize how the practice of designing crew patches began. The authors discuss Gemini V's "covered wagon" patch, the first ever flown, and the story behind the hidden "8 Days or Bust." The only major error concerns the Apollo 1 patch. It is an error that did not originate with this book, but is perpetuated by reference to the story of the patch's design. The crew of Apollo 1, officially known as Apollo 204, were killed in a fire that swept through their command module during a ground test. According to the authors, the crew patch has a black overlock border "as a sign of mourning for the lost crew." The patch does have this black border, but if one looks carefully at color photographs or films of the crew, the black border can be seen on the patch. Unless someone went back and airbrushed black borders on these prints, the crew must have been wearing the black-bordered patches before the accident. The book is filled with color photographs of the patches from various manned and unmanned missions, as well as space centers and miscellaneous events. There is an appendix listing the U.S. manned flights and an index.

Kelley, Kevin W., ed. *The Home Planet.* Reading, Mass.: Addison-Wesley, 1988. This is a large-format, "coffee-table" book of the finest photographs ever taken of Earth from space. These images are combined with the thoughts of the astronauts who snapped the pictures as they whirled around Earth or traveled to the Moon. The author looked at every medium- and large-format handheld image in the NASA archives, as well as every available image in the Soviet archives. There are images taken from as many parts of the globe as possible. Each was selected for its beauty first. There are also images of the spacecraft and some of the spacewalking astronauts and cosmonauts. The comments made by the spacefarers are in their native language and translated into English. They combine with the photographs to create a remarkable work of art. An appendix details each of the scenes captured by the cameras. Includes a list of source notes.

Kerrod, Robin. *The Illustrated History of NASA.* New York: Gallery Books, 1986. One of the better books about the manned and unmanned space programs undertaken by NASA, this work was written shortly after the *Challenger* accident. Although the book mainly discusses the programs of NASA, there is one chapter devoted to NASA and its facilities throughout the United States. There are hundreds of color and black-and-white photographs. An appendix lists some of the highlights of NASA's first quarter century in chronological order. Contains an epilogue devoted to the STS 51-L mission, and an index.

Lattimer, Richard L. *All We Did Was Fly to the Moon.* History-Alive Series, vol.
1. Alachula, Fla.: Whispering Eagle Press, 1983.
An interesting collection of photographs and anecdotes by the astronauts, this
work is filled with space trivia. The Apollo 15 crew emblem, for example, was
designed by a dress designer. Front pages from newspapers and color replicas
of the crew emblem from each manned mission are included. Every flight is
detailed, although briefly. The most fascinating part of each segment is the
explanation, by the astronaut crew members, of how each crew emblem came
to be. They also tell about the selection of the call signs for their spacecraft.
Many color and black-and-white photographs highlight the text. Unfortunately,
no bibliography is included.

Lee, Chester M., ed. *Apollo Soyuz Mission Report.* AAS Advances in the Astronautical Sciences, vol. 34. San Diego, Calif.: American Astronomical Society,
1975.
The official report on the Apollo Soyuz Test Project, prepared by the Mission
Evaluation Team, contains a wealth of data on the flight of Apollo 18. Included
are a mission summary and sections which detail the flight, spacecraft, crew
activities, orbital experiments, in-flight demonstrations, biomedical evaluations,
and mission ground support. An assessment of the mission objectives, as well
as anomalies, is included. Tables summarize the flight trajectory and activity
time lines. Appendices include descriptions and drawings of the spacecraft and
launch vehicles, the as-flown ASTP flight plan, spacecraft history and mass
properties, postflight testing, and a glossary of terms. There is also a summary
of lightning activities by NASA for the mission.

Lewis, Richard S. *Appointment on the Moon.* New York: Ballantine Books, 1969.
This is one of the most complete accounts of the U.S. space program through
the Apollo 11 lunar landing mission. The author takes the reader through the
manned phase of Apollo, beginning with the Apollo 204 pad fire, which killed
three astronauts. Unfortunately, he almost completely ignores the unmanned
flights of the Saturn I and Saturn IB. He makes up for it, somewhat, by
discussing the unmanned lunar probes which helped to make the Apollo 11
mission possible. There are several pages of black-and-white photographs and
an excellent listing of reference material.

_____. *The Voyages of Apollo: The Exploration of the Moon.* New York:
Quadrangle/New York Times, 1974.
This is the sequel to *Appointment on the Moon* and covers in depth the seven
manned Apollo flights to the Moon, beginning with Apollo 11. For some
reason, the author chose to ignore Apollo 10, perhaps because it was not
intended to land on the Moon. Of the seven missions, though, six did land and
the other turned into the most dramatic rescue of the space age. Lewis views

these journeys as "personal adventures, mass communication events and evolutionary episodes in our movement out of our earthly cradle."

Link, Mae Mills. *Space Medicine in Project Mercury.* Washington, D.C.: National Technical Information Service, 1965.
Since it provided the United States' first orbiting laboratory for the study of the physiological effects of space travel, Project Mercury marked the transition from what was known as aviation medicine to what would become space medicine. In addition to studying the effects of space travel on an astronaut, NASA was concerned with the entire spectrum of the life sciences, including ecology and exobiology. In cooperation with those associated with Project Mercury, the author prepared a comprehensive look at the experiments and tests performed during the program, in the unmanned as well as manned flights. One chapter discusses the medical aspects of astronaut selection. Black-and-white photographs and an index enhance the well-written text.

Lord, Douglas R. *Spacelab: An International Success Story.* Washington, D.C.: Government Printing Office, 1987.
One of the main purposes for building the Space Transportation System was to provide the capability of taking scientific work stations into orbit. What started as a plan for a space station developed into the Spacelab, an interchangeable set of modules and pallets that can be adapted for an unlimited number of experiment packages. This book, although not listed as part of the official NASA History Series, was written for NASA and is a thorough look at the development and construction of Spacelab. There are discussions of the countries that helped build and pay for Spacelab and a look at its first three missions. There are hundreds of color and black-and-white photographs and a summary of the program to date. Appendices present the Memorandum of Understanding, which provided for the implementation of the cooperative program to build Spacelab; the Joint Programme Plan; Programme Requirements; and a list of key program participants. Like other NASA historical references, this one contains an extensive bibliography.

McConnell, Malcolm. *Challenger: A Major Malfunction.* New York: Doubleday, 1987.
One of several "witch-hunt" books written in the wake of the *Challenger* accident of January, 1986. The resident space "expert" at *Reader's Digest*, McConnell levels his biased attacks at anyone and everyone within a hundred miles of the accident. He accuses then-NASA Administrator James Fletcher of having rigged the awarding of the solid rocket booster contract to Morton Thiokol; the joint between two of the lower segments of the right-hand booster is believed to be the culprit in the accident. McConnell attacks President Ronald Reagan for pressuring NASA to launch the first teacher in space in

time for his State of the Union Address. The author claims to have sources no one else could find, yet he is unable to reveal one fact not found in the President's Commission report. For facts about the accident, the reader should consult *Report of the Presidential Commission on the Space Shuttle Challenger Accident* by former Secretary of State William P. Rogers et al. (detailed below).

McKann, Robert E., ed. *First United States Manned Three-Pass Orbital Mission (Mercury-Atlas 6, Spacecraft 13): Part II—Flight Data.* Washington, D.C.: National Technical Information Service, 1964.
This is part 2 of the two-volume official NASA report on the flight of Mercury-Atlas 6 with astronaut John Glenn. The contents were prepared by a flight evaluation team. In this volume, actual flight data are presented, from which the analyses in part 1 are derived. Voice, radar, and telemetry contacts were maintained with ground stations at intervals throughout the flight to permit in-flight ground monitoring of the astronaut's physiological condition, the spacecraft trajectory, and the operations of onboard systems. Continuous recording of spacecraft measurements was achieved by means of an onboard tape recorder. This work contains a complete presentation of the data record. It is filled with charts, tables, and line drawings. A reference list is included.

MacKinnon, Douglas, and Joseph Baldanza. *Footprints: The Twelve Men Who Walked on the Moon Reflect on Their Flights, Their Lives, and the Future.* Washington, D.C.: Acropolis Books, 1989.
As the twentieth anniversary of the first lunar landing approached, there was a rush to publish books on the Apollo 11 mission. Many good books were written, as well as a number of poor ones. This is one of the best. The authors sat down with twelve men who probably understand the most about moonwalks. They were the twelve who had actually done the walking. The questions ranged from the technical to the sublime, but each interview revealed more about the inner feelings of the astronauts than any prior essay. The book is illustrated with color paintings by astronaut-artist Alan Bean. He has annotated each painting with the ideas he had when he created them.

Mason, Robert Grant, ed. *Life in Space.* Alexandria, Va.: Time-Life Books, 1983.
The editors of *Life* magazine have sifted through hundreds of NASA's and their own photographs taken during the first twenty-five years of the space age. What has resulted is a superb collection of photographs of each U.S. manned spaceflight, from Alan Shepard's suborbital hop in *Freedom 7* through the STS-6 Space Shuttle mission. Throughout the work are breathtaking color and startling black-and-white photographs. The major characters in the book are, of course, the astronauts who flew the missions. Interestingly enough, the book ends with the flight of the last all-male crew. The astronauts' families are

included in this historical portrait. The unmanned probes to the planets are highlighted in the final section of the book.

Masursky, Harold, G. W. Colton, and Farouk El-Baz, eds. *Apollo Over the Moon: A View from Orbit.* Washington, D.C.: National Technical Information Service, 1978.
Everyone who takes a trip to faraway places tries to capture some of the magic of the moment through photographs. The Apollo astronauts were no exception. Of course, a great deal of their photography was done in the name of science, but that does not take away any of their beauty. There are dozens of black-and-white photographs, each one documented as to when and where it was taken. The stark beauty of the lunar landscape is enhanced by the black-and-white images. The most spectacular photographs are the stereographic pairs. Unfortunately, a stereographic viewer is not provided, but with a little work one can obtain fairly good stereo.

Murray, Charles, and Catherine Bly Cox. *Apollo: The Race to the Moon.* New York: Simon & Schuster, 1989.
An intriguing look at the people behind the accomplishment, this book details those whose unenviable task it was to translate a president's dream into reality. Much research has gone into this work. The reader gets an insight into the background of the Apollo program team members, as well as a look at their extracurricular activities. They were, after all, only human—they simply had an inhuman goal to complete. The book is well written and contains an excellent appendix of reference notes. Several black-and-white photographs give faces to the characters discussed in the book.

Nelson, Bill, with Jamie Buckingham. *Mission.* New York: Harcourt Brace Jovanovich, 1988.
The last successful flight of the Space Shuttle program, prior to the STS 51-L *Challenger* accident, included the second journey of a U.S. congressman. STS 61-C was launched on January 12, 1986, after numerous delays caused by bad weather and technical problems. This is the tale of this mission, as told by Congressman Bill Nelson, who acted as a payload specialist. There is not much technical information contained in this work, but there is a great deal about the inner workings of the Shuttle program. Nelson discusses his role on the flight, as well as those of his six crewmates.

Newkirk, Roland W., and Ivan D. Ertel, with Courtney G. Brooks. *Skylab: A Chronology.* Washington, D.C.: National Technical Information Service, 1977.
This is NASA's official record of the Skylab program, covering events on a day-to-day basis. At its inception, the project was known as the Apollo Applications Program, since it was to use modified equipment from the lunar landing

endeavor. Included in the coverage are the early space station designs, the development of the spacecraft and launch vehicles, astronaut training, and mission results. There are dozens of black-and-white photographs and line drawings of components. Appendices provide a summary of the Skylab flights: mission objectives, orbital activities, experiments, and extravehicular activity. Contains a glossary of abbreviations and acronyms, and an index.

Nicogossian, Arnauld E. *The Apollo Soyuz Test Project Medical Report.* Washington, D.C.: National Technical Information Service, 1977.
This is a summary of the life science experiments performed during the nine-day Apollo 18 flight, the American half of the joint U.S.-Soviet space mission called the Apollo Soyuz Test Project. The researchers involved with each experiment write about their tests and the results. The experiments are divided into two groups: crew health and flight monitoring; and preflight, in-flight, and postflight medical testing. There are dozens of black-and-white photographs, charts, diagrams, and tables to enhance this technical work. The only disappointment is the lack of information about the life science experiments conducted during the Soviet Soyuz 19 flight.

Obregón, Mauricio. "Gagarin to NASA." In *Argonauts to Astronauts.* New York: Harper & Row, 1980.
In this book, Obregón does a study of explorers from the early Greek seafarers through the modern spacefarers. It is a brief but well-written work. This particular chapter compares the early space programs of the United States and Soviet Union and puts them in perspective with respect to the explorers of the past. The researcher should not expect to find any new information; rather, the book should read for its overall assessment of the history of man's ventures into the unknown. There are many black-and-white photographs and line drawings to accentuate the text, and a brief bibliography.

Otto, Dixon P. *On Orbit: Bringing on the Space Shuttle.* Athens, Ohio: Main Stage, 1986.
This book, by the publisher of *Countdown* magazine, is a concise look at what the author calls "The First Space Shuttle Era." It chronicles the Space Transportation System from its inception through the *Challenger* accident. The first part of the work discusses the early design concepts for the Shuttle and some of the factors that influenced its evolution. There is also a brief description of a typical Shuttle mission. The highlight of the book is the coverage of the first twenty-five missions. Each is presented with the particulars of the flight, including crew, launch and landing times, duration, orbits, and payload. There are several black-and-white photographs from each flight and a portfolio of color pictures in the center section.

Otto, Dixon P., and Donald Andrew Gardner. *Moonrise: Apollo Plus Twenty.*
Athens, Ohio: Main Stage, 1989.
A retrospective of the Apollo era through the completion of the Apollo 11 lunar
landing mission. The first half of this work presents a chronology of the major
events leading to Apollo 11. Although the entries are brief, they contain all
the pertinent data. The latter half provides a transcript (with commentary) of
the flight of Apollo 11 as it was broadcast on television. The transcript covers
every phase of the flight from liftoff to splashdown. There are many color and
black-and-white photographs of the Apollo missions, as well as a few of the
other, related flights.

Pitts, John A. *The Human Factor: Biomedicine in the Manned Space Program to
1980.* Washington, D.C.: Government Printing Office, 1985.
One title in the NASA History Series, this book chronicles the life science
programs of the U.S. manned spaceflights of the Mercury, Gemini, Apollo,
and Skylab programs, and of the Apollo Soyuz Test Project. There are dozens
of black-and-white photographs, line drawings, tables, and charts about the
experiments used to test man's ability to live and work in the microgravity
environment of orbital flight. Provides an impressive appendix listing source
notes and bibliographic references, and an index.

Pogue, William R. *How Do You Go to the Bathroom in Space?* New York: Tom
Doherty Associates, 1985.
This and many other interesting questions about living in space are answered
by former astronaut Pogue. He was one of three crew members who spent
eighty-four days in orbit aboard Skylab. Actually, there are 156 questions
which the author has gleaned from thousands that he and his fellow astronauts
have received during a quarter century of manned spaceflight. Many of the
questions lead to humorous answers, but most provide a great amount of
firsthand information about matters of general interest. The questions touch on
each of the U.S. manned space programs. Several appendices provide additional
information, including a summary of the physiological effects of spaceflight,
a list of Earth features recognizable from space, a guide to information and
resources, and a bibliography.

Ride, Sally K. *Leadership and America's Future in Space.* Washington, D.C.:
Government Printing Office, 1987.
In response to a growing concern in both Congress and the Administration over
the long-term direction of the U.S. civilian space program, NASA Administrator Dr. James Fletcher formed a task group to define potential U.S. space
initiatives. This is the report of the group, which identified four candidate
initiatives for study and evaluation: Mission to Planet Earth, Exploration of the
Solar System, Outpost on the Moon, and Humans to Mars. Each of the four

112   *America in Space*

fields is discussed in terms of background; strategy and scenario; technology, transportation, and orbital facilities; and summary of the project. The "leadership in space" status of the United States has dropped considerably since the Apollo program, and Dr. Ride addresses the reasons for this. There a drawings, tables, charts, color photographs, a reference list, and a list of the additional studies that went into the creation of the report.

Ride, Sally K., with Susan Okie. *To Space and Back*. New York: Lothrop, Lee & Shepard Books, 1986.
Former astronaut Ride tells about her two trips into space (aboard *Challenger* on STS-7 and STS 41-G). This work was written mainly for children, but it provides the first look at space travel from a woman's perspective. There are dozens of color photographs from her flights and from the other Space Shuttle missions. Ride talks about each phase of a typical mission and her reactions to the events that occurred during her flights. Includes a glossary of terms and an index.

Rogers, William, et al. *Report of the Presidential Commission on the Space Shuttle Challenger Accident*. 5 vols. Washington, D.C.: Government Printing Office, 1986.
On January 28, 1986, seven astronauts flew the Space Shuttle *Challenger* on its last mission. Seventy-three seconds after lifting off from the Kennedy Space Center, the giant external tank attached to the orbiter disintegrated. This is the official report of the commission appointed by President Ronald Reagan to investigate the accident. The fourteen-person commission included such notable persons as former Secretary of State William P. Rogers (chairman), former astronauts Neil Armstrong (vice chairman) and Sally K. Ride, and former test pilot Charles (Chuck) Yeager. The report, and its four-volume set of appendices and hearings transcripts, indicates that the most probable cause of the accident was a failure in the joint between the lower two segments of the right solid rocket motor. The work details the flight and the subsequent investigation. There are dozens of color and black-and-white photographs and line drawings for emphasis. Many of the photographs have not been made available in any other document. For the truth about the accident (as best it can be known), this work is far superior to the tabloid-style books that have tried to cash in on the disaster.

Schirra, Walter M., Jr., with Richard N. Billings. *Schirra's Space*. Boston: Quinlan Press, 1988.
Astronaut Schirra's account of his aviation career and personal life, with particular emphasis on his astronaut experience. This autobiography gives a private look at the early days of the U.S. space program. Schirra, who flew in the Mercury, Gemini, and Apollo spacecraft (the only person to fly in all

three of them), compares them to the other vessels he has flown. The controversial events of the "Wally, Walt, and Donn Show" (also known as Apollo 7) are retold from inside the command module. Although not filled with any technical details, the book provides the historical perspective only an insider can give.

Smith, Mervyn. *An Illustrated History of Space Shuttle: U.S. Winged Spacecraft, X-15 to Orbiter*. Newbury Park, Calif.: Haynes, 1985.
This work traces the history of the Space Shuttle orbiter and the research aircraft from which it was derived. Each of these ancestors contributed in some way or another to the final design of the orbiter. Included in the discussions are the X-1 series, X-2, X-3, X-20, X-24A, X-24B, HL-10, D-558-I, D-558-II, M2F2, M2F3, and the X-15. There are hundreds of color and black-and-white photographs of these pioneers, as well as the pioneers who flew them. Seven appendices chronicle the flight programs of the X-15, M2F2, HL-10, X-24A, M2F3, X-24B, and the Space Shuttle (through STS 51-C). This is one of the best collections of information on the early research aircraft and lifting bodies.

Steinberg, Florence S. *Aboard the Space Shuttle*. Washington, D.C.: Government Printing Office, 1980.
A preview of the Space Transportation System is presented for the general audience. The major features of the Space Shuttle orbiter are described, accompanied by line drawings and color photographs of its crew compartment. All of the conveniences of home are provided to the astronaut crew. There is a sleeping area, an eating area, and, of course, a space "potty." The extravehicular mobility unit (spacesuit) for taking expeditions outside the orbiter is also discussed, as is the remote manipulator system arm for payload deployment and retrieval. There is not much technical information, but there are plenty of pictures.

Summerlin, Lee B., ed. *Skylab, Classroom in Space*. Washington, D.C.: Government Printing Office, 1977.
The Skylab Student Project was originated by NASA and the National Science Teachers Association as a means of involving schoolchildren, the next generation of scientists, in the study of space sciences. In 1972, twenty-five high school students from across the United States were selected to participate in the program. They were from among the more than four thousand students who had made proposals. This volume, filled with color and black-and-white photographs, details how and why the project was developed, describes the experiments flown aboard Skylab, and relates them to other scientific investigations carried out during the flights.

Swenson, Loyd S., Jr., James M. Grimwood, and Charles C. Alexander. *This New Ocean: A History of Project Mercury.* Washington, D.C.: National Technical Information Service, 1966.

One title in the NASA History Series, this book chronicles Project Mercury, from its conception during the early days of NASA to its completion following the flight of Gordon Cooper in Mercury-Atlas 9. There are dozens of black-and-white photographs of the manned, as well as unmanned, flights. Line drawings show the inner workings of much of the equipment related to the missions. There is an impressive hundred-page appendix listing source notes and bibliographic references. Other appendices include a summary of flight data, functional and workflow organization of Project Mercury, personnel growth, the ground station tracking network, and the cost of the project.

Taylor, L. B., Jr. *Space Shuttle.* New York: Thomas Y. Crowell, 1979.

This is a preview of the Space Transportation System and the plans for making it the main means of taking U.S. (and some foreign) payloads into space. It also discusses the Space Shuttle's potential for the industrialization and colonization of space. The author details the development and testing of the system, how other nations are involved in the program, and the criticism and benefits of a reusable spacecraft. There are black-and-white photographs and line drawings, and a bibliography.

Trento, Joseph J. *Prescription for Disaster.* New York: Crown, 1987.

One of several "witch-hunt" books written in the wake of the *Challenger* accident of January, 1986. According to the publishers, Trento was an "investigative reporter" for Cable News Network. However, very little investigation of the book reveals its obvious bias and attempt to exploit the "newsworthiness" of the subject. For facts about the accident, the reader should turn to the *Report of the Presidential Commission on the Space Shuttle Challenger Accident*, by former Secretary of State William P. Rogers et al. (detailed above).

U.S. General Accounting Office. *Space Station: NASA Efforts to Establish a Design-to-Life-Cycle Cost Process.* Washington, D.C.: Government Printing Office, 1988.

In 1985, the Senate Committee on Commerce, Science, and Transportation directed NASA to outline its plans for the Space Station *Freedom* to ensure that it did not overlook future operations costs during the station's definition, design, and development phases. NASA responded that it would control operations costs by using a design-to-life-cycle cost approach, which establishes the projected total life-cycle cost of a system as a design requirement equal in importance to performance and schedule concerns, and which establishes cost elements as management goals. This is the GAO's report on this approach.

Appendices include a system design tradeoff model and comments from NASA on the report.

U.S. House of Representatives. *The Apollo 13 Accident: Hearings Before the Committee on Science and Astronautics.* Washington, D.C.: Government Printing Office, 1970.
This is the official report of the congressional committee that investigated the Apollo 13 accident. An oxygen tank in the service module ruptured, crippling the spacecraft and nearly costing the lives of its astronaut crew as they traveled to the Moon. The report supports NASA's own investigative conclusions as to the cause and remedy of the problem. There is a wealth of information about the mission and the inner workings of the Apollo command and service modules. Several line drawings complement the text. Although not an extremely large document, it contains a considerable amount of political mumbo jumbo, which the reader must mentally filter out. An appendix contains the entire report of the NASA Review Board.

_____. *Astronauts and Cosmonauts Biographical and Statistical Data.* Washington, D.C.: Government Printing Office, 1978.
This report, prepared for the Committee on Science and Technology, contains updated biographical data on all U.S. astronauts and their known Soviet counterparts. It includes present and former astronauts, astronaut candidates, and the astro-pilots of the X-15, X-20 Dyna-Soar, and Manned Orbiting Laboratory programs. Because of the difficulty in obtaining information from the Soviets during this period, there may be a few inaccuracies in their data. A status report on each of the astronauts by group is presented, accompanied by tables of their flight records. Selection criteria for each group are also included. Tables compare U.S. and Soviet spaceflights. Where available, there is a black-and-white photograph of the astronaut or cosmonaut.

_____. *Investigation into Apollo 204 Accident: Hearings Before the Subcommittee on NASA Oversight of the Committee on Science and Astronautics.* Washington, D.C.: Government Printing Office, 1967.
This is the comprehensive, multivolume report of the congressional committee that investigated the Apollo 1 accident. This work contains all of the testimony by witnesses, test results, and conclusions of the inquiry board established by NASA. Unlike the witch-hunts of the *Challenger* accident investigation, this report supports NASA's results. There are many photographic exhibits in the book, but because of the poor quality of their reproduction they provide very little additional information. It takes quite a while to wade through the mass of data, but a great deal of technical information is provided about the Block I Apollo spacecraft. The entire report of the NASA Review Board is included.

_____. *Investigation of the Challenger Accident: Report of Committee on Science and Technology*. Washington, D.C.: Government Printing Office, 1986. Not content to let the Presidential Commission get all of the "press" for the investigation of the *Challenger* accident, this committee of the House of Representatives conducted its own hearings. The committee held ten formal hearings involving sixty witnesses, made an extensive review of the report of the Rogers Commission, and held numerous briefings and interviews with NASA officials, contractor personnel, outside experts, and other interested parties. According to the report, the committee came to the same conclusions as the Rogers Commission. It concluded, too, that NASA's drive to achieve its launch schedule created pressure throughout the agency that directly contributed to unsafe launch conditions. The committee failed to point out the lack of congressional support for the original Space Transportation System concept, which did not need to rely on "unsafe" solid rocket motors. They also overlooked the fact that, prior to STS 51-L, they considered the Shuttle safe enough to carry a senator and a congressman into space. Contains many (poorly reproduced) black-and-white photographs and line drawings.

_____. *United States Civilian Space Programs 1958-1978*. Vol. 1. Washington, D.C.: Government Printing Office, 1981.
In a very concise report, the Committee on Space Science and Applications has compiled data on all U.S. space activity during its first two decades. After a brief introduction and summary chapter, the volume is divided into fourteen additional sections. The second chapter deals with the space-related issues under consideration by Congress. The remaining sections cover the history of NASA and its relationship to U.S. space policy, NASA facilities and tracking systems, launch vehicles and propulsion, manned spaceflight through 1975, the Space Transportation System, space life sciences, space science programs, materials processing in space, international cooperation in space, interagency and non-NASA governmental space activities, industrial and university support for NASA, space program benefits, and selected future space programs. Appendices contain Department of Defense manned spaceflight plans, NASA funding history, international space agreements, texts of President Jimmy Carter's space directives, documents relating to the legal aspects of the Space Shuttle, major U.S. space organizations, a master log of U.S. spaceflights, and a table of U.S. space orbital payloads by mission from 1957 through 1979.

U.S. National Aeronautics and Space Administration. *Apollo Mission Report: Apollo 7 Through 17*. 10 vols. Washington, D.C.: National Technical Information Service, 1968-1973.
The official report on each of the manned flights in the Apollo program. Each volume was prepared by the Mission Evaluation Team and contains a wealth of data on each particular flight. There is a mission summary and sections

which detail the flight, spacecraft, crew activities, orbital and surface experiments, in-flight demonstrations, biomedical evaluations, and mission ground support. An assessment of the mission objectives, as well as anomalies, is included. Tables summarize the flight trajectory and activity time lines. Descriptions and drawings of the spacecraft, launch vehicles, and experiment packages are included. This publication provides the definitive study of each flight. Some volumes might have to be obtained directly from NASA.

_____. *Apollo Program Summary Report*. Washington, D.C.: National Technical Information Service, 1975.
Several chapters provide an in-depth look at the training and mission experience of the astronauts who participated in the Apollo program. The work examines the development of flight plans and how effective their implementation was. Also discussed are the biomedical experiments conducted during the flights and the Apollo Lunar Quarantine Program. Several medical studies were completed during the program to determine the effect of prolonged spaceflight on humans. There are many photographs and line drawings to highlight the extensive text, as well as references for further research.

_____. *EASE/ACCESS: Framework for the Future*. Washington, D.C.: Government Printing Office, 1985.
In preparation for permanent space construction, NASA's Marshall Space Flight Center in Huntsville, Alabama, developed two experiments to demonstrate the ability of astronauts to build large structures in space. The experiments were flown aboard the Space Shuttle *Atlantis* on mission STS 61-B in November, 1985. The first of the experiments is the Experimental Assembly of Structures in Extravehicular Activity (EASE). EASE consists of six aluminum beams, each 12 feet long, which form a tetrahedral cell when pieced together. The Assembly Concept for Construction of Erectable Space Structures (ACCESS) consists of mastlike, 4.5-foot assembly fixtures. These are raised to a vertical position and the fixture's three guide rails unfold like an umbrella. When fully erected, the structure is 45 feet tall. This booklet is filled with color photographs and it discusses the experiments in detail.

_____. *Gemini Program Mission Report: Gemini 3 Through XII*. 10 vols. Washington, D.C.: Government Printing Office, 1964-1966.
These are the official records of the Gemini program missions. Each volume was prepared by the Mission Evaluation Team and contains a wealth of data on each particular flight. There is a mission summary and sections which detail the flight, spacecraft and launch vehicle performance, crew activities, orbital experiments, in-flight demonstrations, biomedical evaluations, and mission ground support. An assessment of the mission objectives, as well as anomalies, is included. Tables summarize the vehicle histories, weather conditions, flight

safety reviews, and postflight inspection of the spacecraft. Descriptions and drawings of the spacecraft, launch vehicles, and experiment packages are included. This publication presents the definitive study of each flight. Some volumes might have to be obtained directly from NASA.

_____. *Mercury Project Summary Including Results of the Fourth Manned Orbital Flight.* Washington, D.C.: National Technical Information Service, 1963.
This document presents a summary of the planning, preparation, experiences, and results of Project Mercury and includes the results of the Mercury-Atlas 9 flight with Gordon Cooper. The essays were written by Mercury scientists, engineers, and technicians and are grouped into four main technical areas: space-vehicle development, mission support development, flight operations, and mission results. Line drawings, black-and-white photographs, tables, and charts add to the text. Appendices list typical documents prepared for Mercury, NASA centers and other government agencies, prime contractors, subcontractors, NASA personnel, and Mercury-Atlas 9 air-to-ground voice communications. There is an aeromedical analysis of Aatronaut Cooper and a description of his flight activities. The sequence of events is enumerated along with trajectory data.

_____. *National Space Transportation System Reference.* 2 vols. Washington, D.C.: Government Printing Office, 1988.
This is the most complete technical reference about the Space Transportation System written in nontechnical terminology. It is an enlarged and updated version of the *Press Information* books published by Rockwell International, maker of the Space Shuttle Orbiter. The last Rockwell version was printed in 1984, but because of budget reductions instituted at Rockwell in 1985, their Media Relations Office could not update and reprint it. NASA, however, wanted a new edition when the Shuttle resumed operations after the *Challenger* accident. They contracted with Rockwell to provide the text and artwork. Volume 1 details the systems and facilities, while the second volume covers NASA centers and management. There are hundreds of line drawings and black-and-white photographs. Each system and subsystem is presented in great detail. Emphasis, of course, has been placed on the orbiter systems, but there is still a great deal of data about the solid rocket boosters and external tank. Also detailed are the crew equipment and escape systems, NASA centers and responsibilities, and payloads. Provides a summary of mission events, a chronology of the Space Shuttle program, a list of contractors, and a glossary of acronyms and abbreviations.

_____. *Portable Life Support Systems.* Washington, D.C.: National Technical Information Service, 1970.

This is a collection of dissertations by noted specialists in the field of portable life support systems. The systems discussed include those used by astronauts outside the spacecraft and ground support personnel working in toxic atmospheres. The technology has been translated into many uses outside the space program, in such fields as aircraft crew flight suits and breathing apparatus for firefighters and mine workers. Each report discusses the particular problem being studied, the researcher's approach to the problem, experiments performed, results of the tests, conclusions drawn from the findings, and recommendations for the application of the knowledge gained. A detailed bibliography accompanies each article, as do black-and-white photographs and line drawings.

_____. *Report to the President: Actions to Implement the Recommendations of the Presidential Commission on the Space Shuttle Challenger Accident.* Washington, D.C.: Government Printing Office, 1986.

On June 6, 1986, the Rogers Commission presented the report of its findings and recommendations to President Ronald Reagan. After reviewing the Report, the president instructed NASA Administrator James C. Fletcher to undertake a program to implement these recommendations. On July 14, 1986, Fletcher delivered NASA's plans to comply with the order. This report addresses the nine recommendations of the commission and presents a detailed plan for the implementation status for each.

_____. *Results of the First United States Manned Orbital Space Flight, February 20, 1962.* Washington, D.C.: National Technical Information Service, 1962.

This is the second of two official NASA reports on the flight of Mercury-Atlas 6 with astronaut John Glenn. The contents were prepared by a flight evaluation team. A description of the space vehicle and launch vehicle is presented, detailing each of the major systems as configured for the mission. The performance of these systems is given in the form of charts and tables. Each phase of the mission operation is described: prelaunch, including astronaut training and spacecraft and launch vehicle preparation; launch operations; flight-control operations; and recovery operations. There is an aeromedical analysis of the astronaut and a description of pilot flight activities. The sequence of events is enumerated along with trajectory data. There is a complete transcript of the air-to-ground communications between the astronaut and tracking stations. Black-and-white photographs, line drawings, and a brief reference list are included in each section of the work.

_____. *Results of the Second U.S. Manned Suborbital Space Flight, July 21, 1961.* Washington, D.C.: National Technical Information Service, 1961.

This is the official NASA report on the flight of Mercury-Redstone 4 with astronaut Virgil Grissom. The contents were prepared by a flight evaluation team. A description of the space vehicle and launch vehicle is presented, detailing each of the major systems as configured for the mission. The performance of these systems is given in the form of charts and tables. Each phase of the mission operation is described: prelaunch, including astronaut training and spacecraft and launch vehicle preparation; launch operations; flight-control operations; and recovery operations. There is an aeromedical analysis of the astronaut and a description of pilot flight activities. The sequence of events is enumerated along with trajectory data. Black-and-white photographs, line drawings, and a brief reference list are included.

_____. *Results of the Second United States Manned Orbital Space Flight, May 24, 1962.* Washington, D.C.: National Technical Information Service, 1962.

This is the second of two official NASA reports on the flight of Mercury-Atlas 7 with astronaut M. Scott Carpenter. The contents were prepared by a flight evaluation team. A description of the space vehicle and launch vehicle is presented, detailing each of the major systems as configured for the mission. The performance of these systems is given in the form of charts and tables. Each phase of the mission operation is described: prelaunch, including astronaut training and spacecraft and launch vehicle preparation; launch operations; flight-control operations; and recovery operations. There is an aeromedical analysis of the astronaut and a description of pilot flight activities. The sequence of events is enumerated along with trajectory data. There is a complete transcript of the air-to-ground communications between the astronaut and tracking stations. Black-and-white photographs, line drawings, and a brief reference list are included in each section of the work.

_____. *Results of the Third United States Manned Orbital Space Flight, October 3, 1962.* Washington, D.C.: National Technical Information Service, 1962.

This is the second of two official NASA reports on the flight of Mercury-Atlas 8 with astronaut Wally Schirra. The contents were prepared by a flight evaluation team. A description of the space vehicle and launch vehicle is presented, detailing each of the major systems as configured for the mission. The performance of these systems is given in the form of charts and tables. Each phase of the mission operation is described: prelaunch, including astronaut training and spacecraft and launch vehicle preparation; launch operations; flight-control operations; and recovery operations. There is an aeromedical analysis of the astronaut and a description of pilot flight activities. The sequence of events is enumerated along with trajectory data. There is a complete transcript of the air-to-ground communications between the astronaut and tracking stations. Black-and-white photographs, line drawings, and a brief reference list are included in each section of the work.

_____. *Skylab Experiments.* 7 vols. Washington, D.C.: Government Printing Office, 1973.
Prior to the beginning of the Skylab flights, NASA's Education Office, the Skylab Program Office, and the University of Colorado published a series of teaching guides to the experiments that were to be conducted in flight. These experiments were divided into four categories: physical sciences, biomedical sciences, Earth applications, and space applications. Each volume looks at the experiments' background, scientific objectives, description, data, crew activities, related curriculum studies, and suggested classroom demonstrations. Volume 1 covers physical science and solar astronomy; volume 2, remote sensing of Earth resources; volume 3, materials science; volume 4, life sciences; volume 5, astronomy and space physics; volume 6, mechanics; and volume 7, living and working in space. Each volume includes numerous line drawings and a glossary of terms.

_____. *Skylab Explores the Earth.* Washington, D.C.: National Technical Information Service, 1977.
Since the first flight of Project Mercury, one of NASA's primary goals of orbital space missions was the observation of Earth. There is no better vantage point than from above. Observation time for manned spacecraft is limited by life support supplies and, prior to Skylab, the longest mission was the fourteen-day Gemini VII flight in 1965. This book studies the Earth observation experiments of Skylab during the 171 days it was occupied. It is filled with exciting color photographs of Earth, each of which is accompanied by a detailed caption. Several of the photographs are analyzed with the aid of a map of the region shown. Comparisons are made with color and black-and-white photographs taken of geologic sites and meteorologic phenomena during previous manned flights. Contains a glossary of terms and an index of the photographs used, alphabetized by geographic location.

_____. *Skylab Mission Report: Skylab 2 Through Skylab 4.* 3 vols. Washington, D.C.: National Technical Information Service, 1973-1974.
The official report on each of the manned flights in the Skylab program. Each volume was prepared by the Mission Evaluation Team and contains a wealth of data on the particular flight. There is a mission summary and sections which detail the flight, spacecraft, crew activities, orbital experiments, in-flight demonstrations, biomedical evaluations, and mission ground support. An assessment of the mission objectives, as well as anomalies, is included. Tables summarize the flight trajectory and activity time lines. Descriptions and drawings of the spacecraft, launch vehicles, and experiment packages are included. Includes a glossary of terms and a list of references.

_____. *STS-1 Orbiter Final Mission Report.* Washington, D.C.: Government Printing Office, 1981.
This is the official record of the first Space Shuttle mission on April 12, 1981. Since this was a test flight, a great deal of data was collected on all of the Shuttle's systems. This report details each of the tests and measurements made during and after the flight. Nearly every minute of the two-day mission is chronicled. There is a report by the crew as to the effectiveness of preflight training and the handling of *Columbia*. There is a complete biomedical, trajectory, and flight control evaluation. A summary of anomalies and the corrective action taken is included. There are a number of black-and-white photographs, line drawings, charts, and tables.

_____. *STS Orbiter Mission Report: STS-2 Through STS-4.* 3 vols. Washington, D.C.: Government Printing Office, 1981-1982.
These are the official reports for the final three missions of *Columbia* during the Orbiter Flight Test (OFT) program. As with the report on the first flight (see *STS-1 Orbiter Final Mission Report,* cited above), the performance of each of the vehicle's main systems—orbiter, solid rocket motors, and external tank—is detailed. In addition, the orbiter's major subsystems are discussed. There is a report by the individual crews as to the effectiveness of preflight training and the handling of the vehicle. There is a complete biomedical, trajectory, and flight control evaluation. A summary of anomalies and the corrective action taken is included. There are a number of black-and-white photographs, line drawings, charts, and tables.

_____. *STS Space Shuttle Program Mission Report: STS-5 Through STS-7.* 3 vols. Washington, D.C.: Government Printing Office, 1982-1983.
Beginning with *Columbia*'s first operational flight (STS-5) and continuing through *Challenger*'s first two missions (STS-6 and STS-7), mission reports contained much less information. Fewer tests on orbiter subsystems were being conducted and, since commercial and scientific payloads were now being carried, much of the emphasis switched to the cargo and its support equipment. A list of mission objectives and a summary of the flight are given. There is an evaluation of the major Shuttle components, as well as crew equipment assessment. There are very few black-and-white photographs, line drawings, tables, and charts.

_____. *STS National Space Transportation Systems Program Mission Report: STS-8 Through STS-35.* 31 vols. Washington, D.C.: Government Printing Office, 1983-1991.
As Space Shuttle flights became more and more routine, fewer mission objectives relating to the measurement of subsystem performance were necessary. Eventually, these mission reports were reduced to a summary of the flight,

sequence of events, vehicle assessment, remote manipulator system operations, payloads and experiments, detailed test objectives, detailed secondary objectives, and anomalies. Line drawings and black-and-white photographs became scarcer, and there were only a few necessary tables and charts. These reports do detail the mission and provide valuable information about each flight.

_____. *STS 51-L Data and Design Analysis Task Force Historical Summary.* Washington, D.C.: Government Printing Office, 1986.
Immediately following the STS 51-L *Challenger* accident, NASA formed an Interim Mishap Investigation Board, which was replaced by the 51-L Data and Design Analysis Task Force. This replacement (in name only) was necessary to coincide with the official investigation of the Rogers Commission. The task force was to determine, review, and analyze the facts surrounding the launch of *Challenger*; review all factors relating to the accident determined to be relevant; examine all other factors which could relate to the accident; utilize the technical and scientific expertise and resources available within the NASA; document task force findings and determinations and conclusions; and provide this information to the Presidential Commission. This report is the historical summary of the official NASA investigation into the accident. It includes a chronology of the flight and subsequent events through the presentation of the commission's report to the president.

U.S. Senate. *Apollo 13 Mission: Hearing Before the Committee on Aeronautical and Space Sciences.* Washington, D.C.: Government Printing Office, 1970.
This is the official report of the Senate committee hearings to determine the cause of the Apollo 13 accident. An oxygen tank in the service module ruptured, crippling the spacecraft and nearly costing the lives of its astronaut crew as they traveled to the Moon. The report supports NASA's own investigative conclusions as to the cause and remedy of the problem. This work is not as detailed as the House of Representatives' investigation report and provides little additional information.

Ward, Robinson J., Jr., comp. *A Funny Thing Happened on the Way to the Moon.* Greenwich, Conn.: Fawcett, 1969.
Although the exploration of space is a serious, often challenging business, there is still time for humor. Some of the humor presented in this book was unintentional, evolving from the frustrations and failures of the U.S. space program. The author has collected humorous events, jokes, and other tension-relieving anecdotes from the scientists, technicians, engineers, and astronauts involved in man's conquest of space. While this volume does not contain any pertinent data on the history of the space program, it does make these people seem a little more human.

_____. *The Light Stuff: Space Humor—From Sputnik to Shuttle*. Huntsville, Ala.: Jester Books, 1982.
Some of the lighter moments in an otherwise harrowing business are presented in this compendium of anecdotes from the space age. This is not a book for the "serious" researcher, but an amusing compendium of what Walter Cronkite in his introduction calls "the era's choicest anecdotes, its bons mots, putdowns, puns, and pranks." It also contains some cartoons and a reproduction of the front page from the November 4, 1981, edition of *The Detroit News*. The headline reads, "*Columbia* Does Encore." The Shuttle, however, had not been launched.

Wilford, John Noble. *We Reach the Moon*. New York: W. W. Norton, 1971.
The author presents an account of the Apollo 11 lunar landing mission and a brief history of Apollo's predecessors. Most of the work concentrates on Apollo. Written in a journalistic style, the book details each flight in story. It is a well-written work, published within seventy-two hours of the completion of the Apollo 11 flight. The author admits his lack of scientific or engineering expertise, but the two years of research that went into the preparation of this volume is evident. Also evident is the amount of work that occurred during and immediately after the flight. There is a section of color photographs in the center of the book and a few line drawings throughout. A transcript of the major lunar surface activities is included in the back of the book. There is also a brief bibliography.

Wilson, Andrew. *Space Shuttle Story*. New York: Hamlyn, 1986.
Written for a general audience, this book is filled with color photographs. It traces the history of the Space Transportation System from the early design concepts through the twenty-fifth launch. Information is provided on each of the flights, although there is very little detail. There are a few technical errors, so do not rely on its information as the sole source. Many facts about the astronauts who flew the Shuttle during the period are presented.

Wolfe, Tom. *The Right Stuff*. New York: Farrar, Straus & Giroux, 1979.
A very interesting book about the team of men who flew in Project Mercury and about Chuck Yeager, the "loner" of X-1 fame. Wolfe has taken the stories of these men and intertwined them for an exciting and romantic tale of high flight. There are a great number of stories told by the astronauts and related in this book, which the reader will find too fantastic to believe. They really did happen—or, at least, the characters portrayed in this work say they did. It also tells of the women who loved the men and who supported them, who waited for them, and who in some cases mourned their demise. For those who want to know more about the Mercury Seven and Chuck Yeager, this book

is superior to its film adaptation, which did not accurately portray the incidents from the book.

Yeager, General Chuck, and Leo Janos. *Yeager: An Autobiography.* New York: Bantam Books, 1985.
Chuck Yeager was a World War II ace who loved to do nothing more than fly. His incredible record during the war was surpassed only by his records as a test pilot. He was the first person to fly faster than the speed of sound, and he did his best to break his own records when he could. However, he was first a professional; he did not take chances for the sake of glory. This is his story, and if he embellishes a little, that's all right; he has earned it. It is also the story of his two loves—his wife, Glennis, and the aircraft he flew. There are several black-and-white photographs and an index.

Yenne, Bill. *The Astronauts: The First Twenty-five Years of Manned Space Flight.* New York: Exeter Books, 1986.
This book discusses the astronauts and cosmonauts who flew into space during the first quarter century of manned spaceflight—or, more correctly, it discusses the manned flights of the United States and Soviet Union and lists the crew members. There is very little biographical information about the astronauts, except for mentioning where a crew member was born, or when. There are scores of color and black-and-white photographs of the astronauts, most of them taken during flight. There is also an index.

Spacesuits

Collins, Michael. *Liftoff: The Story of America's Adventure in Space.* New York: Grove Press, 1988.
Collins discusses the various types of suits designed to keep an astronaut alive in case something happened to the air inside the spacecraft. As a former astronaut, he presents an inside view of these man-sized "balloons." Prior to the Space Shuttle, each suit was tailored to the measurements of its wearer, but it still proved to be difficult to bend in the right places. The suits provided little comfort both physically and mentally, since there were no backup systems built into the suit. If it ripped, if the helmet's visor opened, if a glove flew off, there would be no hope for the wearer.

Hays, Edward L. "Space Suits." In *Manned Spacecraft: Engineering Design and Operation*, edited by Paul E. Purser, Maxime A. Faget, and Norman F. Smith. New York: Fairchild, 1964.
A compilation of essays based upon a series of lectures delivered at NASA's Manned Spacecraft Center, Louisiana State University, University of Houston,

and William Marsh Rice University in 1963 and 1964. This paper discusses in some detail the technical side of spacesuits, with particular emphasis on the ones used in the Mercury and Gemini programs. The history of the pressurized flying suit is traced from its beginnings with such great aviation pioneers as Wiley Post. The essay is highlighted with black-and-white photographs and line drawings of the components, as well as a list of references.

Kosmo, Joseph J. "The Development of Spacesuits." In *Magill's Survey of Science: Space Exploration Series*, vol. 5, edited by Frank N. Magill. Pasadena, Calif.: Salem Press, 1989.
One of the essays on the history of space exploration in this five-volume set, which covers every aspect of the U.S. and Soviet manned and unmanned space programs, as well as those of nations newer to the space race. If machines were perfect and sealed cabins did not spring leaks, there would be no need for spacesuits. Since man first rode an aircraft up to where the air is too thin to support life, he has found a need to take his atmosphere with him. Initially, spacesuits were used for emergency situations inside the spacecraft and were known as intravehicular mobility units. Later, they became known as extravehicular mobility units, when men started taking walks in space. This article takes a look at the development of these mobility units and how the technology has been adapted for earthbound use. Contains an annotated bibliography and cross-references.

Machell, Reginald M., ed. *Summary of Gemini Extravehicular Activity.* Washington, D.C.: National Technical Information Service, 1967.
This is a collection of reports from NASA summarizing the Gemini program's extravehicular activity (EVA) operations. EVAs, or "spacewalks," were initiated during Gemini and were featured on six of the ten manned flights, from Ed White's thirty-six-minute stroll during Gemini IV to Buzz Aldrin's five-and-one-half-hour marathon during Gemini XII. The book evaluates the techniques developed during the program and the problems associated with the EVAs. There are dozens of black-and-white photographs and line drawings to supplement the text. Topics covered include life support systems, body positioning and restraint systems, maneuvering equipment, training and simulation, operational and medical aspects of extravehicular activity, results, and conclusions. There is a short list of references at the end of the book.

Pogue, William R. *How Do You Go to the Bathroom in Space?* New York: Tom Doherty Associates, 1985.
This and many other interesting questions about living in space are answered by former astronaut Pogue. He was one of three crew members who spent eighty-four days in orbit aboard Skylab. Actually, there are 156 questions which the author has gleaned from thousands that he and his fellow astronauts

have received in a quarter century of manned spaceflight. Many of the questions lead to humorous answers, but most provide a great deal of firsthand information about matters of general interest. The questions touch on each of the U.S. manned space programs. Several appendices provide additional information, including a summary of the physiological effects of spaceflight, a list of Earth features recognizable from space, a guide to information and resources, and a bibliography.

U.S. House of Representatives. *United States Civilian Space Programs 1958-1978.* Vol. 1. Washington, D.C.: Government Printing Office, 1981.
In a very concise report, the Committee on Space Science and Applications has compiled data on all U.S. space activity during its first two decades. After a brief introduction and summary chapter, the volume is divided into fourteen additional sections. The second chapter deals with the space-related issues under consideration by Congress. The remaining sections cover the history of NASA and its relationship to U.S. space policy, NASA facilities and tracking systems, launch vehicles and propulsion, manned spaceflight through 1975, the Space Transportation System, space life sciences, space science programs, materials processing in space, international cooperation in space, interagency and non-NASA governmental space activities, industrial and university support for NASA, space program benefits, and selected future space programs. Appendices contain Department of Defense manned spaceflight plans, NASA funding history, international space agreements, texts of President Jimmy Carter's space directives, documents relating to the legal aspects of the Space Shuttle, major U.S. space organizations, a master log of U.S. spaceflights, and a table of U.S. space orbital payloads by mission from 1957 through 1979.

U.S. National Aeronautics and Space Administration. *EASE/ACCESS: Framework for the Future.* Washington, D.C.: Government Printing Office, 1985.
In preparation for permanent space construction, NASA's Marshall Space Flight Center in Huntsville, Alabama, developed two experiments to demonstrate the ability of astronauts to build large structures in space. The experiments were flown aboard the Space Shuttle *Atlantis* on mission STS 61-B in November, 1985. The first of the experiments is the Experimental Assembly of Structures in Extravehicular Activity (EASE). EASE consists of six aluminum beams, each 12 feet long, which form a tetrahedral cell when pieced together. The Assembly Concept for Construction of Erectable Space Structures (ACCESS) consists of mastlike, 4.5-foot assembly fixtures. These are raised to a vertical position, and the fixture's three guide rails unfold like an umbrella. When fully erected the structure is 45 feet tall. This booklet is filled with color photographs, and it discusses the experiments in detail.

_____. *National Space Transportation System Reference.* 2 vols. Washington, D.C.: Government Printing Office, 1988.
This is the most complete technical reference about the Space Transportation System written in nontechnical terminology. It is an enlarged and updated version of the *Press Information* books published by Rockwell International, maker of the Space Shuttle Orbiter. The last Rockwell version was printed in 1984, but because of budget reductions instituted at Rockwell in 1985, their Media Relations Office could not update and reprint it. NASA, however, wanted a new edition when the Shuttle resumed operations after the *Challenger* accident. They contracted with Rockwell to provide the text and artwork. Volume 1 details the systems and facilities, while the second volume covers NASA centers and management. There are hundreds of line drawings and black-and-white photographs. Each system and subsystem is presented in great detail. Emphasis, of course, has been placed on the orbiter systems, but there is still a great deal of information about the solid rocket boosters and external tank. Also detailed are the crew equipment and escape systems, NASA centers and responsibilities, and payloads. Provides a summary of mission events, a chronology of the Space Shuttle program, a list of contractors, and a glossary of acronyms and abbreviations.

_____. *Portable Life Support Systems.* Washington, D.C.: National Technical Information Service, 1969.
This is a collection of dissertations by noted specialists in the field of portable life support systems. The systems discussed include those used by astronauts outside the spacecraft and ground support personnel working in toxic atmospheres. The technology has been translated into many uses outside the space program, such as aircraft crew flight suits and breathing apparatus for firefighters and mine workers. Each report discusses the particular problem being studied, the researcher's approach to the problem, experiments performed, results of the tests, conclusions drawn from the findings, and recommendations for the application of the knowledge gained. A detailed bibliography accompanies each article, as do black-and-white photographs and line drawings.

Space Medicine

Bergwin, Clyde R., and William T. Coleman. *Animal Astronauts: They Opened the Way to the Stars.* Englewood Cliffs, N.J.: Prentice-Hall, 1963.
Man was not the first of God's creatures to venture into space. In fact, he was one of the last. Dogs, monkeys, mice, rats, chimpanzees, insects, and even pigs were lofted into the heavens atop the future man-carriers. The first individual reported to have been placed into Earth orbit was a dog named Laika. This book looks at the suborbital and orbital flights of the United States'

animal pioneers. The two most famous were chimpanzees. Ham (named for the Holloman Aerospace Medical Center, New Mexico) made a successful suborbital flight in a Mercury spacecraft on January 31, 1961. Enos, a forty-two-pound chimpanzee, completed the first orbital flight of a Mercury spacecraft on November 29, 1961, after two orbits. This is an interesting book about some very important but often overlooked characters in the history of space exploration.

Ezell, Edward C., and Linda N. Ezell. *The Partnership: A History of the Apollo-Soyuz Test Project.* Washington, D.C.: Government Printing Office, 1978.
One title in the NASA History Series, this book chronicles the Apollo Soyuz Test Project, to date the only joint U.S.-Soviet manned spaceflight. The origins of the project, immediately following the successful completion of the Apollo 11 Moon landing mission, are traced. Also discussed are the political aspects of the venture. There are dozens of black-and-white photographs of the flight. Color photographs, taken from orbit, are in the back of the book. Line drawings show the inner workings of much of the equipment related to the mission. Contains an impressive seventy-page appendix listing source notes and bibliographic references, and an index. Other appendices include NASA organization charts, development of U.S. and Soviet manned spaceflight, a summary of the U.S./U.S.S.R. meetings, and descriptions of the ASTP launch vehicles.

Johnston, Richard S., Lawrence F. Dietlein, and Charles A. Berry. *Biomedical Results of Apollo.* Washington, D.C.: National Technical Information Service, 1975.
Biomedical testing, under ideal conditions, is by its very nature an iffy proposition. Take your subjects 250,000 miles away from the laboratory and the chances of getting accurate data are next to none. These were the conditions under which scientists had to work during the Apollo program. The editors of this work have compiled a concise review of each experiment, including the theory behind the test, the means by which is was completed, and the results. The text is supplemented with photographs and drawings, as well as charts of the conclusions reached by each examiner. Every section of the book has its own reference listing, which will guide the researcher to more detailed works.

Johnston, Richard S., and Lawrence F. Dietlein, eds. *Biomedical Results from Skylab.* Washington, D.C.: National Technical Information Service, 1977.
Biomedical testing under the conditions of orbital flight was done for relatively brief periods during the Mercury, Gemini, and Apollo programs. With Skylab, scientists would be able to conduct experiments on astronauts spending a month or more in space. The editors of this work have compiled a concise review of each experiment, including the theory behind the test, the means by which it was completed, and the results. The experiments were divided into four

disciplines: neurophysiology; musculoskeletal function; biochemistry, hematology, and cytology; and cardiovascular and metabolic function. The text is supplemented with photographs and drawings, as well as charts of the conclusions reached by each examiner. Every section of the book has its own reference listing, which will guide the researcher to more detailed works. Appendices detail the experimental support hardware and the operational life sciences support hardware.

Lee, Chester M., ed. *Apollo Soyuz Mission Report*. AAS Advances in the Astronautical Sciences, vol. 34. San Diego, Calif.: American Astronomical Society, 1975.
The official report on the Apollo Soyuz Test Project, prepared by the Mission Evaluation Team, contains a wealth of data on the flight of Apollo 18. Included are a mission summary and sections which detail the flight, spacecraft, crew activities, orbital experiments, in-flight demonstrations, biomedical evaluations, and mission ground support. An assessment of the mission objectives, as well as anomalies, is included. Tables summarize the flight trajectory and activity time lines. Appendices include descriptions and drawings of the spacecraft and launch vehicles, the as-flown ASTP flight plan, spacecraft history and mass properties, postflight testing, and a glossary of terms. There is also a summary of lightning activities by NASA for the mission.

Link, Mae Mills. *Space Medicine in Project Mercury.* Washington, D.C.: National Technical Information Service, 1965.
Since it provided the United States' first orbiting laboratory for the study of the physiological effects of space travel, Project Mercury marked the transition from what was known as aviation medicine to what would become space medicine. In addition to studying the effects on an astronaut, NASA was concerned with the entire spectrum of the life sciences. This included ecology and exobiology. In cooperation with those associated with Project Mercury, the author has prepared a comprehensive look at the experiments and tests performed during the program, in the unmanned as well as manned flights. One chapter discusses the medical aspects of astronaut selection. Black-and-white photographs and an index enhance the well-written text.

Lord, Douglas R. *Spacelab: An International Success Story.* Washington, D.C.: Government Printing Office, 1987.
One of the main purposes for building the Space Transportation System was to provide the capability of taking scientific work stations into orbit. What started as a plan for a space station developed into the Spacelab, an interchangeable set of modules and pallets which can be adapted for an unlimited number of experiment packages. This book, although not listed as part of the official NASA History Series, was written for NASA and is a thorough look

at the development and construction of Spacelab. There are discussions on the countries that helped build and pay for Spacelab, and a look at its first three missions. There are hundreds of color and black-and-white photographs and a summary of the program to date. Appendices present the Memorandum of Understanding, which provided for the implementation of the cooperative program to build Spacelab; the Joint Programme Plan; Programme Requirements; and a list of key program participants. Like other NASA historical references, this one contains an extensive bibliography.

Magill, Frank N., ed. *Magill's Survey of Science: Space Exploration Series*. Vol. 4. Pasadena, Calif.: Salem Press, 1989, pp. 1884-1911.
This five-volume set covers every aspect of the U.S. and Soviet manned and unmanned space programs, as well as those of nations newer to the space race. As part of the "advertising" program for the development of the Space Shuttle, NASA began a program to provide scientists with facilities to study the microgravity environment while approximating the conditions of an earthbound laboratory. The result, a joint effort with the European Space Agency, is Spacelab. Using a combination of interchangeable modules and pallets, researchers could perform an unlimited variety of experiments and studies. The first three Spacelab missions flown aboard the Space Shuttle are discussed in separate articles, as well as the overall program. Each essay lists the pertinent data of the mission and the results of its investigations, as well as an annotated bibliography and cross-references.

Messerschmitt-Bölkow-Blohm. *First German SPACELAB: Mission D1*. Bremen, West Germany: MBB/ERNO, 1985.
The "Deutschland Spacelab Mission D1" was the first of a series of dedicated West German missions on the Space Shuttle. It flew aboard *Challenger* in October, 1985, the last successful mission of the orbiter. The modules contained equipment for seventy-six experiments in five disciplines: fluid physics, solidification, biology, medicine, and space-time interaction. This work details each of the experiments and the facilities used to run them. There are dozens of color photographs and drawings of the experiment packages. This publication, although published in West Germany, has been made available through NASA.

Nicogossian, Arnauld E. *The Apollo Soyuz Test Project Medical Report*. Washington, D.C.: National Technical Information Service, 1977.
This is a summary of the life sciences experiments performed during the nine-day Apollo 18 flight, the American half of the joint U.S.-Soviet space mission called the Apollo Soyuz Test Project. The researchers involved with each experiment write about their tests and the results. The experiments are divided into two groups: crew health and flight monitoring; and preflight, in-flight, and

postflight medical testing. There are dozens of black-and-white photographs, charts, diagrams, and tables to enhance this technical work. The only disappointment is the lack of information about life science experiments conducted during the Soviet Soyuz 19 flight.

Pitts, John A. *The Human Factor: Biomedicine in the Manned Space Program to 1980.* Washington, D.C.: Government Printing Office, 1985.
One title in the NASA History Series, this book chronicles the life science programs of the U.S. manned spaceflights of the Mercury, Gemini, Apollo, and Skylab programs, and the Apollo Soyuz Test Project. There are dozens of black-and-white photographs, line drawings, tables, and charts about the experiments used to test man's ability to live and work in the microgravity environment of orbital flight. Includes an impressive appendix listing source notes and bibliographic references, and an index.

Pogue, William R. *How Do You Go to the Bathroom in Space?* New York: Tom Doherty Associates, 1985.
This and many other interesting questions about living in space are answered by former astronaut Pogue. He was one of three crew members who spent eighty-four days in orbit aboard Skylab. Actually, there are 156 questions which the author has gleaned from thousands that he and his fellow astronauts have received in a quarter century of manned spaceflight. Many of the questions lead to humorous answers, but most provide a great deal of firsthand information about matters of general interest. The questions touch on each of the U.S. manned space programs. Several appendices provide additional information, including a summary of the physiological effects of spaceflight, a list of Earth features recognizable from space, a guide to information and resources, and a bibliography.

U.S. National Aeronautics and Space Administration. *Science in Orbit: The Shuttle and Spacelab Experience, 1981-1986.* Washington, D.C.: Government Printing Office, 1988.
The opportunity to conduct large-scale experiments in Earth orbit escaped the U.S. space program for nearly a decade, from the end of the last Skylab mission in February, 1974, to the first Spacelab mission aboard *Columbia* in November, 1983. Now the United States has the capability to obtain the necessary data to launch a permanently manned space station. This book studies the Space Transportation System and the Spacelab research laboratory. It chronicles the two programs and looks at the science gained from the first twenty-four Shuttle flights. Disciplines detailed include life sciences, materials science, solar physics, space plasma physics, atmospheric science, Earth observation, astronomy, and astrophysics. In addition, experiments conducted

to test the technology needed to build the space station *Freedom* are presented. There are dozens of color and black-and-white photographs.

_____. *Spacelab 1.* Washington, D.C.: Government Printing Office, 1983.
This is a preview to the first Spacelab mission flown aboard the Space Shuttle. The work discusses the need for a reusable orbital research facility and the history of Spacelab's development. The experiments to be conducted during the mission are detailed and brief biographies of the two payload specialists, their backups, and the two mission specialists for the flight are provided. Color and black-and-white photographs and drawings accentuate the text. This book is for general audiences, although the researcher will find a great deal of detail about Spacelab's experiments.

_____. *Spacelab 1 Experiments.* Washington, D.C.: Government Printing Office, 1983.
Spacelab 1 was launched aboard the Space Shuttle *Columbia* in November, 1983. It was the inaugural mission of the versatile, reusable research facility funded, developed, and built by the European Space Agency. This work, using black-and-white photographs and drawings, details each of the seventy different experiments in five research disciplines: astronomy and solar physics, space plasma physics, atmospheric physics and Earth observations, life sciences, and materials sciences. The summaries include the purpose, importance, and method of each experiment. The identification number, sponsor, and principal investigator's name and affiliation are provided for each experiment.

_____. *Spacelab 2.* Washington, D.C.: Government Printing Office, 1985.
Spacelab 2 was actually the third mission flown by this scientific research facility. Delays in the development of some of its equipment caused its flight to be switched with the Spacelab 3 mission. Spacelab 2, the first pallet-only mission, was carried into orbit aboard *Challenger* in July, 1985. It consisted of thirteen experiments in six scientific disciplines: solar physics, atmospheric physics, plasma physics, high-energy astrophysics, technology research, and life sciences. This work previews the flight, with emphasis on the experiments. Each is detailed, including the identification number, sponsor, and principal investigator's name and affiliation, and is accompanied by color photographs and drawings.

_____. *Spacelab Mission 2 Experiment Descriptions.* 2d ed. Washington, D.C.: Government Printing Office, 1982.
NASA's official guide to the experiments carried aboard Spacelab 2 contains very detailed information about each experiment. In addition to the discussion of the test, the experimental apparatus is detailed, including a diagram of the equipment and its physical dimensions and characteristics. There is a line

drawing of the Spacelab as it is seen in the Space Shuttle's payload bay. The location of each of the experiments is included.

_____. *Spacelab 3*. Washington, D.C.: Government Printing Office, 1984.
Spacelab 3 was carried into orbit aboard the Space Shuttle *Challenger* in April, 1985. It consisted of a long module and Mission Peculiar Equipment Support Structure (MPESS), which carried the fifteen investigations in five scientific disciplines: materials sciences, life sciences, fluid mechanics, atmospheric science, and astronomy. This booklet discusses the mission and its flight crew, including the two payload specialists and their backups. Each of the experiments is detailed, including the identification number, sponsor, and principal investigator's name and affiliation, and is accompanied by color photographs and drawings.

_____. *Spacelab Mission 3 Experiment Descriptions*. Washington, D.C.: Government Printing Office, 1982.
NASA's official guide to the experiments carried aboard Spacelab 3 contains very detailed information about each experiment. In addition to the discussion of the test, the experimental apparatus is detailed, including a diagram of the equipment and its physical dimensions and characteristics. There is a line drawing of the Spacelab as it is seen in the Space Shuttle's payload bay. The location of each of the experiments is included.

Earth Observation

Anderton, David A. *Space Station*. Washington, D.C.: Government Printing Office, 1985.
This NASA Educational Publication (EP-211) looks at the plans to build the United States' first permanently manned space station, *Freedom*. This work provides an overview of the program and the various design concepts developed by various NASA facilities and major aerospace contractors. At the time of the writing, the exact plans for constructing the space station were not finalized. Although this work does not provide any details, it does give some insight into the evolution of *Freedom*. There are many color photographs of the different design concepts.

Belew, Leland F., ed. *Skylab, Our First Space Station*. Washington, D.C.: National Technical Information Service, 1977.
A colorful retrospective of the Skylab program and its four flights is presented in this work. Technically speaking, the title is a misnomer, since Skylab was not a "space station." By definition, a space station is a permanently manned platform which can be completely resupplied. Astronauts replenished the food,

water, film, and a few other expendables, but Skylab's attitude control and electrical and life support systems were not replenishable. The book is a good reference, chronicling the program from its design and planning phases through the completion of the third manned period. There are dozens of color photographs and drawings, including several spectacular pictures taken on orbit. A mission summary table and an index are included. Belew was the manager of the Skylab program office at the Marshall Space Flight Center, where Skylab was built.

Belew, Leland F., and Ernst Stuhlinger. *Skylab: A Guidebook.* Washington, D.C.: Government Printing Office, 1973.
This is a preflight guide to the Skylab program and provides in-depth, nontechnical information about the orbiting workshop and its components. Skylab, the spacecraft, was built around the S-IVB third stage of the Saturn V launch vehicle. The major components included the Orbital Workshop (OWS), the Instrument Unit (IU), the Airlock Module (AM), the Multiple Docking Adapter (MDA), and the Apollo Telescope Mount (ATM). As much of the spacecraft as possible was made from existing hardware or with hardware requiring little modification. This guide describes the work of several thousand engineers and scientists who conceived, designed, and built Skylab. Each of the experiments to be performed during Skylab's stay in orbit is described, as well as the apparatus to conduct it. Line drawings, black-and-white photographs, a glossary of terms and acronyms, an index, and a brief bibliography are included.

Bodechtel, Johann, and Hans-Günter Gieroff-Emden. *The Earth from Space.* New York: Arco, 1974.
This is a fine collection of color photographs of Earth taken by manned and unmanned spacecraft. It discusses the history of space photography from the first crude black-and-white image transmitted from the orbiting Explorer 6 satellite in 1959 through the long-distance portraits taken by the crew of Apollo 17 as they journeyed from the Moon. The technical aspects of space photography are presented, including how many of the photographs were taken and what they reveal.

Compton, W. David, and Charles D. Benson. *Living and Working in Space: A History of Skylab.* Washington, D.C.: Government Printing Office, 1983.
One title in the NASA History Series, this book chronicles the Skylab program, from its conception during the early days of the Apollo program to the orbiting workshop's fiery plunge in 1979. There are dozens of black-and-white photographs of the three manned missions, as well as the launch of the unmanned workshop. Color photographs, taken from orbit, are in the back of the book. Line drawings show the inner workings of much of the equipment related to the missions. There is an impressive hundred-page appendix listing source notes

and bibliographic references, as well as an index. Other appendices include a summary of the missions, astronaut biographies, in-flight experiments, Comet Kohoutek, and the International Aeronautical Federation world records set by Skylab.

Cooper, Henry S. F., Jr. *Before Liftoff: The Making of a Space Shuttle Crew.* Baltimore: The Johns Hopkins University Press, 1987.
Space Shuttle Mission 41-G, with seven astronauts aboard *Challenger,* spent eight days in space. The crew included veteran Commander Robert Crippen and Mission Specialist Sally Ride, along with rookie Pilot Jon McBride, Mission Specialists Kathy Sullivan and David Leetsma, and Payload Specialists Paul Scully-Power and Canadian Marc Garneau. During the mission, the crew deployed the Earth Radiation Budget Satellite and conducted experiments. Two of the astronauts performed a spacewalk to demonstrate an on-orbit refueling system. Author Cooper made special arrangements with NASA to follow the crew from its formation through the completion of the mission. This is an engrossing look at the everyday life of an astronaut crew. The reader gets to sit in on briefings, join the crew for simulations, and even swim underwater for spacewalk practice. There are a few black-and-white photographs and an index.

_____. *A House in Space.* New York: Holt, Rinehart and Winston, 1976.
This work is about the nine-month period from May 14, 1973, through February 8, 1974—the active life of the Skylab orbiting workshop. During this time, it was inhabited by three crews of astronauts for periods of twenty-eight, fifty-nine, and eighty-four days. The book was derived from articles written by Cooper, which appeared in *The New Yorker* magazine during this period. It looks more at the human aspect of the program than at its technical side, but still contains information useful to the researcher. There are many black-and-white photographs and color diagrams.

Ezell, Edward C., and Linda N. Ezell. *The Partnership: A History of the Apollo-Soyuz Test Project.* Washington, D.C.: Government Printing Office, 1978.
One title in the NASA History Series, this book chronicles the Apollo Soyuz Test Project, to date the only joint American-Soviet manned spaceflight. The origins of the project, immediately following the successful completion of the Apollo 11 Moon landing mission, are traced. Also discussed are the political aspects of the venture. There are dozens of black-and-white photographs of the flight. Color photographs, taken from orbit, are in the back of the book. Line drawings show the inner workings of much of the equipment related to the mission. There is an impressive seventy-page appendix listing source notes and bibliographic references, as well as an index. Other appendices include NASA organization charts, development of U.S. and Soviet manned spaceflight, a

summary of the U.S./U.S.S.R. meetings, and descriptions of the ASTP launch vehicles.

Froehlich, Walter. *Apollo Soyuz*. Washington, D.C.: Government Printing Office, 1976.
This is an entertaining look at the Apollo Soyuz Test Project, the United States' last manned mission using expendable spacecraft and launch vehicles. It was designed to test a rescue method for astronauts or cosmonauts stranded in orbit and unable to be saved by their own country. The U.S. spacecraft, an Apollo command and service module and a docking module (stored in the adapter used to house the Apollo lunar module during launch), were boosted into orbit by a Saturn IB. The Soviets used their standard Soyuz spacecraft and A-2 booster. The book briefly looks at the mission's origin, spacecraft, astronauts and cosmonauts, experiments, and results of the joint endeavor. There are numerous color photographs and appendices listing the times of major events, "firsts" achieved by Apollo Soyuz, major officials involved, scientific experiments, and principal Apollo contractors.

_____. *Spacelab: An International Short-Stay Orbiting Laboratory*. Washington, D.C.: Government Printing Office, 1983.
International cooperation is the status quo for the Spacelab program. Ten nations of the European Space Agency (ESA)—Austria, Belgium, Denmark, France, West Germany, Italy, The Netherlands, Spain, Switzerland, and the United Kingdom—have designed, built, and financed Spacelab. This Space Shuttle payload consists of interchangeable modules and pallets, which can be combined into a nearly unlimited mixture for a variety of scientific experimentation. This work looks at the Spacelab: what it does, how it came to be, and what its users expect from it. It is for the general audience and contains dozens of color photographs and artist's renditions. There is a very detailed cutaway drawing of the Spacelab 1 module and pallet.

Furniss, Tim. *Manned Spaceflight Log*. London: Jane's, 1983, rev. ed. 1987.
This work covers the manned spaceflights of the Soviet Union and the United States from 1961 through 1986. A synopsis of each mission is given, along with pertinent data (date, crew, site, recovery, duration, spacecraft weight, and so forth) and several black-and-white photographs. The Mercury, Gemini, Apollo, Skylab, Apollo Soyuz, and Space Shuttle flights are listed chronologically. Included are the thirteen flights of the X-15 research aircraft which exceeded the fifty-mile altitude necessary to qualify its pilot as an astronaut under Air Force rules. There are astronaut photographs and, in the appendices, listings of space seniority and the current status of the astronaut and cosmonaut classes.

_____. *Space Flight: The Records*. London: Guiness Books, 1985.
Do you know the first manned spaceflight to be curtailed? It was Gemini V, which landed one orbit early to miss hurricane Betsy. Were you aware that the first spaceflight with more than one fifty-year-old person on board was that of STS 51-B/Spacelab 3, in April, 1985? These and dozens of other interesting and significant—or not so significant—facts are covered in this work. The first part of the book is a "diary" of manned spaceflight, listing each of the missions of the United States and Soviet Union. There is a chapter on manned spaceflight "firsts" and one on the manned space machines. Basic biographical information on each of the space travelers is given, accompanied by the person's photograph. The major information section is last and includes tables on manned spaceflight duration, space seniority, space experience, lunar spacemen, spacewalks, astroflights of the X-15, all known cosmonauts, NASA astronauts, Space Shuttle passengers, NASA flight crew selections, and the Space Shuttle schedule. There are hundreds of black-and-white photographs, a glossary of terms, and an index.

_____. *Space Shuttle Log*. London: Jane's, 1986.
The first twenty-two flights of the Space Shuttle are chronicled in this concise work about the Space Transportation System. The first chapter traces the development and testing of the system, detailing the earlier designs of the vehicle and some of the research aircraft that paved the way for the orbiter. There is a section on the astronauts who fly the Shuttle, which includes photographs and brief biographical listings. Perhaps the most ironic segment is the listing of future flights, including the ill-fated STS 51-L mission. There are hundreds of black-and-white photographs and replicas of each of the individual crew emblems.

Gatland, Kenneth. "The First Space Stations." In *The Illustrated Encyclopedia of Space Technology: A Comprehensive History of Space Exploration*, by Kenneth Gatland et al. New York: Harmony Books, 1981.
This section in the book discusses the early space stations of the United States and the Soviet Union. There is a fine four-page, full-color cutaway drawing of the Skylab workshop and the Soviets' Salyut space station. There are color and black-and-white photographs, drawings, and charts. The major features of the program, including the spacecraft and launch vehicle, are discussed. Includes a chronology of the major space events since Sputnik 1, a glossary of terms, and an index.

Kelley, Kevin W., ed. *The Home Planet*. Reading, Mass.: Addison-Wesley, 1988.
This is a large-format, "coffee-table" book of the finest photographs ever taken of Earth from space. These images are combined with the thoughts of the astronauts who snapped the pictures as they whirled around Earth or traveled

to the Moon. The author looked at every medium- and large-format handheld image in the NASA archives, as well as every available image in the Soviet archives. There are images taken from as many parts of the globe as possible. Each was selected for its beauty first. There are also images of the spacecraft and some of the spacewalking astronauts and cosmonauts. The comments made by the spacefarers are in their native language and are translated into English. They combine with the photographs to create a remarkable work of art. Provides an appendix detailing each of the scenes captured by the cameras and a listing of source notes.

Lee, Chester M., ed. *Apollo Soyuz Mission Report.* AAS Advances in the Astronautical Sciences, vol. 34. San Diego, Calif.: American Astronomical Society, 1975.
The official report on the Apollo Soyuz Test Project, prepared by the Mission Evaluation Team, contains a wealth of data on the flight of Apollo 18. Included are a mission summary and sections which detail the flight, spacecraft, crew activities, orbital experiments, in-flight demonstrations, biomedical evaluations, and mission ground support. An assessment of the mission objectives, as well as anomalies, is included. Tables summarize the flight trajectory and activity time lines. Appendices include descriptions and drawings of the spacecraft and launch vehicles, the as-flown ASTP flight plan, spacecraft history and mass properties, postflight testing, and a glossary of terms. There is also a summary of lightning activities by NASA for the mission.

Lord, Douglas R. *Spacelab: An International Success Story.* Washington, D.C.: Government Printing Office, 1987.
One of the main purposes for building the Space Transportation System was to provide the capability of taking scientific work stations into orbit. What started as a plan for a space station developed into the Spacelab, an interchangeable set of modules and pallets that can be adapted for an unlimited number of experiment packages. This book, although not listed as part of the official NASA History Series, was written for NASA and provides a thorough look at the development and construction of Spacelab. There are discussions of the countries that helped build and pay for Spacelab and a look at its first three missions. There are hundreds of color and black-and-white photographs and a summary of the program to date. Appendices present the Memorandum of Understanding, which provided for the implementation of the cooperative program to build Spacelab; the Joint Programme Plan; Programme Requirements; and a list of key program participants. Like other NASA historical references, this one has an extensive bibliography.

Messerschmitt-Bölkow-Blohm. *First German SPACELAB: Mission D1.* Bremen, West Germany: MBB/ERNO, 1985.

The "Deutschland Spacelab Mission D1" was the first of a series of dedicated West German missions on the Space Shuttle. It flew aboard *Challenger* in October, 1985, the last successful mission of the orbiter. The modules contained equipment for seventy-six experiments in five disciplines: fluid physics, solidification, biology, medicine, and space-time interaction. This work details each of the experiments and the facilities used to run them. There are dozens of color photographs and drawings of the experiment packages. This publication, although published in West Germany, has been made available through NASA.

Newkirk, Roland W., and Ivan D. Ertel, with Courtney G. Brooks. *Skylab: A Chronology*. Washington, D.C.: National Technical Information Service, 1977.
This is NASA's official record of the Skylab program, covering events on a day-to-day basis. At its inception, the project was known as the Apollo Applications Program, since it was to use modified equipment from the lunar landing endeavor. Included in the coverage are the early space station designs, the development of the spacecraft and launch vehicles, astronaut training, and mission results. There are dozens of black-and-white photographs and line drawings of components. Appendices provide a summary of the Skylab flights: mission objectives, orbital activities, experiments, and extravehicular activity. Contains a glossary of abbreviations and acronyms, and an index.

O'Leary, Brian. *Project Space Station*. Harrisburg, Pa.: Government Printing Office, 1983.
The author takes a look at the space station programs of the United States and the Soviet Union and discusses their practical applications and benefits. He traces the history of manned space platforms and, in the process, touches upon Skylab, Spacelab, and the Space Transportation System. The major systems of an orbiting space station, similar to the United States' *Freedom*, are described. Much of the emphasis is on the political aspects of the program. Includes black-and-white photographs, a brief bibliography, and an index.

Pogue, William R. *How Do You Go to the Bathroom in Space?* New York: Tom Doherty Associates, 1985.
This and many other interesting questions about living in space are answered by former astronaut Pogue. He was one of three crew members who spent eighty-four days in orbit aboard Skylab. Actually, there are 156 questions which the author has gleaned from thousands that he and his fellow astronauts have received in a quarter century of manned spaceflight. Many of the questions lead to humorous answers, but most provide a great deal of firsthand information about matters of general interest. The questions touch on each of the U.S. manned space programs. Several appendices provide additional information, including a summary of the physiological effects of spaceflight,

a list of Earth features recognizable from space, a guide to information and resources, and a bibliography.

Summerlin, Lee B., ed. *Skylab, Classroom in Space.* Washington, D.C.: Government Printing Office, 1977.

The Skylab Student Project was originated by NASA and the National Science Teachers Association as a means of involving schoolchildren, the next generation of scientists, in the study of space sciences. In 1972, twenty-five high school students from across the United States were selected to participate in the program. They were from among the more than four thousand students who had made proposals. This volume, filled with color and black-and-white photographs, details how and why the project was developed, describes the experiments flown aboard Skylab, and relates them to other scientific investigations carried out during the flights.

U.S. House of Representatives. *United States Civilian Space Programs 1958-1978.* Vol. 1. Washington, D.C.: Government Printing Office, 1981.

In a very concise report, the Committee on Space Science and Applications has compiled data on all U.S. space activity during its first two decades. After a brief introduction and summary chapter, the volume is divided into fourteen additional sections. The second chapter deals with the space-related issues under consideration by Congress. The remaining sections cover the history of NASA and its relationship to U.S. space policy, NASA facilities and tracking systems, launch vehicles and propulsion, manned spaceflight through 1975, the Space Transportation System, space life sciences, space science programs, materials processing in space, international cooperation in space, interagency and non-NASA governmental space activities, industrial and university support for NASA, space program benefits, and selected future space programs. Appendices contain Department of Defense manned spaceflight plans, NASA funding history, international space agreements, texts of President Jimmy Carter's space directives, documents relating to the legal aspects of the Space Shuttle, major U.S. space organizations, a master log of U.S. spaceflights, and a table of U.S. space orbital payloads by mission from 1957 through 1979.

U.S. National Aeronautics and Space Administration. *Earth Photographs from Gemini III, IV, and V.* Washington, D.C.: National Technical Information Service, 1967.

NASA's own scrapbook, this work presents color photographs taken by the astronauts while in Earth orbit. They resulted from two of twenty-two scientific experiments that were part of the Gemini program: synoptic terrain photography (S-005) and synoptic weather photography (S-006). Each of the spectacular photographs is captioned with information about the locations shown. Appendices list the mission, revolution, date, time, location, and area description for each photograph taken during the flights. World maps on the inside covers show the location of each photograph presented in the book. There is also a glossary.

_____. *Earth Photographs from Gemini VI Through XII*. Washington, D.C.: National Technical Information Service, 1968.
This book is the sequel to the first (listed above), covering the last seven missions of the program. The same format is used and the pictures are just as spectacular.

_____. *Office of Space Sciences-1 Experiment Investigation Descriptions*. Washington, D.C.: Government Printing Office, 1982.
The OSS-1 experiments package was flown onboard the Space Shuttle *Columbia* in March, 1982, during the third flight of the Space Transportation System program. The investigations studied space plasma physics, the orbiter environment, solar physics, life sciences, space technology, and astronomy. This booklet discusses each of the experiments in detail and provides a technical description of the equipment. Line drawings and a detailed bibliography are included.

_____. *OSTA-1 Experiments*. Washington, D.C.: Government Printing Office, 1981.
On its second flight, the Space Shuttle *Columbia* carried the first science and applications payload scheduled by the Space Transportation System. This payload, called OSTA-1, was developed by NASA's Office of Space and Terrestrial Applications (OSTA) to provide an early demonstration of the Shuttle's research capabilities. The payload consisted of the Shuttle Imaging Radar-A, Shuttle Multispectral Infrared Radiometer, Feature Identification and Location Experiment, Measurement of Air Pollution from Satellites, Ocean Color Experiment, Night/Day Optical Survey of Lightning, and Heflex Bioengineering Test. The booklet previews the flight of STS-2 and discusses the OSTA-1 experiments in great detail. There are black-and-white photographs and line drawings and a bibliography.

_____. *OSTA-2 Payload*. Washington, D.C.: Government Printing Office, 1982.
The OSTA-2 payload was carried into orbit during the second flight of *Challenger*, STS-7, in June, 1983. The experiments package consisted of two facilities that operated automatically. These were the Materials Experiment Assembly, sponsored by NASA, and the Materialwissenschaftliche Autonome Experimente unter Schwerelosigkeit, sponsored by the German Ministry for Research and Technology. The booklet discusses the two experiment packages

and their Mission Peculiar Support Structure in great detail. There are several line drawings to show the inner workings of the equipment.

_____. *OSTA-3 Experiments.* Washington, D.C.: Government Printing Office, 1984.

The OSTA-3 experiments were carried aboard *Challenger* during the STS 41-G mission, which was flown in October, 1984. It was the second generation of the first science and applications payload carried by the Space Shuttle. Three of the OSTA-1 experiments were reflown in modified form: the Shuttle Imaging Radar, Feature Identification and Location Experiment, and the Measurement of Air Pollution from Satellites. In addition, there was the Large Format Camera, designed to take stereoscopic, wide-angle, high-resolution metric photographs of Earth. The booklet describes the experiments and uses black-and-white photographs and line drawings to detail the experiment equipment.

_____. *Science in Orbit: The Shuttle and Spacelab Experience, 1981-1986.* Washington, D.C.: Government Printing Office, 1988.

The opportunity to conduct large-scale experiments in Earth orbit escaped the U.S. space program for nearly a decade, from the end of the last Skylab mission in February, 1974, to the first Spacelab mission aboard *Columbia* in November, 1983. Now the United States has the capability to obtain the necessary data to launch a permanently manned space station. This book studies the Space Transportation System and the Spacelab research laboratory. It chronicles the two programs and looks at the science gained from the first twenty-four Shuttle flights. Disciplines detailed include life sciences, materials science, solar physics, space plasma physics, atmospheric science, Earth observation, astronomy, and astrophysics. In addition, experiments conducted to test the technology needed to build the space station *Freedom* are presented. There are dozens of color and black-and-white photographs.

_____. *Skylab Experiments.* 7 vols. Washington, D.C.: Government Printing Office, 1973.

Prior to the beginning of the Skylab flights, NASA's Education Office, the Skylab Program Office, and the University of Colorado published a series of teaching guides to the experiments that were to be conducted in flight. These experiments were divided into four categories: physical sciences, biomedical sciences, Earth applications, and space applications. Each volume looks at the experiments' background, scientific objectives, description, data, crew activities, related curriculum studies, and suggested classroom demonstrations. Volume 1 covers physical science and solar astronomy; volume 2, remote sensing of Earth resources; volume 3, materials science; volume 4, life sciences; volume 5, astronomy and space physics; volume 6, mechanics; and volume 7, living and working in space. Each volume includes numerous line drawings and a glossary of terms.

_____. *Skylab Explores the Earth*. Washington, D.C.: National Technical Information Service, 1977.
Since the first flight of Project Mercury, one of the primary goals of NASA's orbital space missions was the observation of Earth. There is no better vantage point than from above. Observation time for manned spacecraft is limited by life support supplies, and, prior to Skylab, the longest mission was the fourteen-day Gemini VII flight, in 1965. This book studies the Earth observation experiments of Skylab during the 171 days it was occupied. It is filled with exciting color photographs of Earth, each of which is accompanied by a detailed caption. Several of the photographs are analyzed with the aid of a map of the region shown. Comparisons are made with color and black-and-white photographs taken of geologic sites and meteorologic phenomena during previous manned flights. Contains a glossary of terms and an index of the photographs used, alphabetized by geographic location.

_____. *Skylab Mission Report: Skylab 2 Through Skylab 4*.
3 vols. Washington, D.C.: National Technical Information Service, 1973-1974.
The official report on each of the manned flights in the Skylab program. Each volume was prepared by the Mission Evaluation Team and contains a wealth of data on the particular flight. There is a mission summary and sections which detail the flight, spacecraft, crew activities, orbital experiments, in-flight demonstrations, biomedical evaluations, and mission ground support. An assessment of the mission objectives, as well as anomalies, is included. Tables summarize the flight trajectory and activity time lines. Descriptions and drawings of the spacecraft, launch vehicles, and experiment packages are included. Provides a glossary of terms and a list of references.

_____. *The Space Station: A Description of the Configuration Established at the Systems Requirements Review (SRR)*. Washington, D.C.: Government Printing Office, 1986.
This work takes a brief yet in-depth look at the planned Space Station *Freedom*. In response to President Ronald Reagan's 1984 commitment to develop a permanently manned space station within a decade, NASA undertook an examination of the many missions that a space station might carry out, and of the many ways in which the station might be configured. This effort reached a major milestone in 1986, called the Systems Requirements Review (SRR). SRR decisions established the "baseline" configuration for *Freedom*. The report details this configuration, as well as the process from which it was derived. There are many pages of black-and-white photographs and line drawings, as

well as a chart depicting the assembly sequence for *Freedom*. There is also a brief history of the space station concept.

_____. *Space Station Development Plan Submitted to the Committee on Science, Space, and Technology, U.S. House of Representatives*. Washington, D.C.: Government Printing Office, 1987.
This plan for the development of a permanently manned space station was submitted by NASA in response to a request by the committee. The plan submitted was based on internal planning and budgetary considerations. Included in the plan are program objectives and requirements, development strategy, management approach, and program schedule. The work reads like most government documents, but the reader can get an idea of the work involved in planning and implementing a program of this magnitude. There are numerous line drawings and charts, a list of reference documents, and a glossary of acronyms and abbreviations. One large appendix details the space station's components and the auxiliary equipment necessary to run it.

_____. *Space Station Reference Configuration Description*. Washington, D.C.: Government Printing Office, 1984.
In order for potential contractors to bid on a particular project, they must have some information about the item on which they will be bidding. This document presents such a guideline for the Space Station *Freedom*. The information was generated to provide a focal point for the definition and assessment of program requirements, establish a basis for estimating program cost, and define a reference configuration in sufficient detail to allow its inclusion in the definition phase of the program. This is the first official look at how the station will appear in orbit during each phase of its construction. It details the manned core, unmanned platforms, payload accommodations, crew accommodations, and related subsystems. There are dozens of line drawings, a bibliography, and an evaluation of the assembly operations crew time lines.

_____. *Spacelab 1*. Washington, D.C.: Government Printing Office, 1983.
This is a preview of the first Spacelab mission flown aboard the Space Shuttle. The work discusses the need for a reusable orbital research facility and the history of Spacelab's development. The experiments to be conducted during the mission are detailed, and brief biographies of the two payload specialists, their backups, and the two mission specialists are provided. Color and black-and-white photographs and drawings accentuate the text. This is for general audiences, although the researcher will find a great deal of detail about Spacelab's experiments.

_____. *Spacelab 1 Experiments*. Washington, D.C.: Government Printing Office, 1983.

Spacelab 1 was launched aboard the Space Shuttle *Columbia* in November, 1983. It was the inaugural mission of the versatile, reusable research facility funded, developed, and built by the European Space Agency. This work, using black-and-white photographs and drawings, details each of the seventy different experiments in five research disciplines: astronomy and solar physics, space plasma physics, atmospheric physics and Earth observations, life sciences, and materials sciences. The summaries include the purpose, importance, and method of each experiment. The identification number, sponsor, and principal investigator's name and affiliation are provided for each experiment.

_____. *Spacelab 2*. Washington, D.C.: Government Printing Office, 1985.
Spacelab 2 was actually the third mission flown by this scientific research facility. Delays in the development of some of its equipment caused its flight to be switched with the Spacelab 3 mission. Spacelab 2, the first pallet-only mission, was carried into orbit aboard *Challenger* in July, 1985. It consisted of thirteen experiments in six scientific disciplines: solar physics, atmospheric physics, plasma physics, high-energy astrophysics, technology research, and life sciences. This work previews the flight, with emphasis on the experiments. Each is detailed, including the identification number, sponsor, and principal investigator's name and affiliation, and is accompanied by color photographs and drawings.

_____. *Spacelab Mission 2 Experiment Descriptions*. 2d ed. Washington, D.C.: Government Printing Office, 1982.
NASA's official guide to the experiments carried aboard Spacelab 2 contains very detailed information about each experiment. In addition to the discussion of the test, the experimental apparatus is detailed, including a diagram of the equipment and its physical dimensions and characteristics. There is a line drawing of the Spacelab as it is seen in the Space Shuttle's payload bay. The location of each of the experiments is included.

_____. *Spacelab 3*. Washington, D.C.: Government Printing Office, 1984.
Spacelab 3 was carried into orbit aboard the Space Shuttle *Challenger* in April, 1985. It consisted of a long module and Mission Peculiar Equipment Support Structure (MPESS), which carried the fifteen investigations in five scientific disciplines: materials sciences, life sciences, fluid mechanics, atmospheric science, and astronomy. This booklet discusses the mission and its flight crew, including the two payload specialists and their backups. Each of the experiments is detailed, including the identification number, sponsor, and principal investigator's name and affiliation, and is accompanied by color photographs and drawings.

_____. *Spacelab Mission 3 Experiment Descriptions.* Washington, D.C.: Government Printing Office, 1982.
NASA's official guide to the experiments carried aboard Spacelab 3 contains very detailed information about each experiment. In addition to the discussion of the test, the experimental apparatus is detailed, including a diagram of the equipment and its physical dimensions and characteristics. There is a line drawing of the Spacelab as it is seen in the Space Shuttle's payload bay. The location of each of the experiments is included.

_____. *STS-1 Orbiter Final Mission Report.* Washington, D.C.: Government Printing Office, 1981.
This is the official record of the first Space Shuttle mission on April 12, 1981. Since this was a test flight, a great deal of information was collected on all of the Shuttle's systems. This report details each of the tests and measurements made during and after the flight. Nearly every minute of the two-day mission is chronicled. There is a report by the crew as to the effectiveness of preflight training and the handling of *Columbia*. There is a complete biomedical, trajectory, and flight control evaluation. A complete anomaly summary, with the corrective action taken, is included. Black-and-white photographs, line drawings, charts, and tables are also included.

_____. *STS Orbiter Mission Report: STS-2 Through STS-4.* 3 vols. Washington, D.C.: Government Printing Office, 1981-1982.
These are the official reports for the final three missions of *Columbia* during the Orbiter Flight Test (OFT) program. As with the report on the first flight (see *STS-1 Orbiter Final Mission Report,* listed above) the performance of each of the vehicle's main systems—orbiter, solid rocket motors, and external tank— is detailed. In addition, the orbiter's major subsystems are discussed. There is a report by the individual crews as to the effectiveness of preflight training and the handling of the vehicle. There is a complete biomedical, trajectory, and flight control evaluation. A complete anomaly summary, with the corrective action taken, is included. There are a number of black-and-white photographs, line drawings, charts, and tables.

_____. *STS Space Shuttle Program Mission Report: STS-5 Through STS-7.* 3 vols. Washington, D.C.: Government Printing Office, 1982-1983.
Beginning with *Columbia*'s first operational flight (STS-5) and continuing through *Challenger*'s first two missions (STS-6 and STS-7), mission reports contained much less information. Fewer tests on orbiter subsystems were being conducted and, since commercial and scientific payloads were now being carried, much of the emphasis switched to the cargo and its support equipment. A list of mission objectives and a summary of the flight are given. There is

an evaluation of the major Shuttle components, as well as crew equipment assessment. There are very few black-and-white photographs, line drawings, tables, and charts.

_____. *STS National Space Transportation Systems Program Mission Report: STS-8 Through STS-35.* 31 vols. Washington, D.C.: Government Printing Office, 1983-1991.
As Space Shuttle flights became more and more routine, fewer mission objectives relating to the measurement of subsystem performance were necessary. Eventually, these mission reports were reduced to a summary of the flight, sequence of events, vehicle assessment, remote manipulator system operations, payloads and experiments, detailed test objectives, detailed secondary objectives, and anomalies. Line drawings and black-and-white photographs became scarcer, and there were only a few necessary tables and charts. These reports do detail the mission and provide valuable information about each flight.

Astronomy from Space

Anderton, David A. *Space Station.* Washington, D.C.: Government Printing Office, 1985.
This NASA Educational Publication (EP-211) looks at the plans to build the United States' first permanently manned space station, *Freedom.* This work provides an overview of the program and the various design concepts developed by various NASA facilities and major aerospace contractors. At the time of the writing, the exact plans for constructing the space station were not finalized. Although this work does not provide any details, it does give some insight into the evolution of *Freedom.* There are many color photographs of the different design concept.

Froehlich, Walter. *Spacelab: An International Short-Stay Orbiting Laboratory.* Washington, D.C.: Government Printing Office, 1983.
International cooperation is the status quo for the Spacelab program. Ten nations of the European Space Agency (ESA)—Austria, Belgium, Denmark, France, West Germany, Italy, The Netherlands, Spain, Switzerland, and the United Kingdom—have designed, built, and financed Spacelab. This Space Shuttle payload consists of interchangeable modules and pallets, which can be combined into a nearly unlimited mixture for a variety of scientific experimentation. This work looks at the Spacelab, what it does, how it came to be, and what its users expect from it. It is for the general audience and contains dozens of color photographs and artist's renditions. There is a very detailed cutaway drawing of the Spacelab 1 module and pallet.

Furniss, Tim. *Manned Spaceflight Log*. London: Jane's, 1983, rev. ed. 1987. This work covers the manned spaceflights of the Soviet Union and the United States from 1961 through 1986. A synopsis of each mission is given, along with pertinent data (date, crew, site, recovery, duration, spacecraft weight, and so forth) and several black-and-white photographs. The Mercury, Gemini, Apollo, Skylab, Apollo Soyuz, and Space Shuttle flights are listed chronologically. Included are the thirteen flights of the X-15 research aircraft which exceeded the fifty-mile altitude necessary to qualify its pilot as an astronaut under Air Force rules. There are astronaut photographs and, in the appendices, listings of space seniority and the current status of the astronaut and cosmonaut classes.

_____. *Space Flight: The Records*. London: Guiness Books, 1985. Do you know the first manned spaceflight to be curtailed? It was Gemini V, which landed one orbit early to miss hurricane Betsy. Were you aware that the first spaceflight with more than one fifty-year-old person on board was that of STS 51-B/Spacelab 3, in April, 1985? These and dozens of other interesting and significant—or not so significant—facts are covered in this work. The first part of the book is a "diary" of manned spaceflight, listing each of the missions of the United States and Soviet Union. There is a chapter on manned spaceflight "firsts," and one on the manned space machines. Basic biographical information on each of the space travelers is given, accompanied by the person's photograph. The major information section is last and includes tables on manned spaceflight duration, space seniority, space experience, lunar spacemen, spacewalks, astroflights of the X-15, all known cosmonauts, NASA astronauts, Space Shuttle passengers, NASA flight crew selections, and the Space Shuttle schedule. There are hundreds of black-and-white photographs, a glossary of terms, and an index.

_____. *Space Shuttle Log*. London: Jane's, 1986. The first twenty-two flights of the Space Shuttle are chronicled in this concise work about the Space Transportation System. The first chapter traces the development and testing of the system, detailing the earlier designs of the vehicle and some of the research aircraft which paved the way for the orbiter. There is a section on the astronauts who fly the Shuttle, which includes photographs and brief biographical listings. Perhaps the most ironic segment is the listing of future flights, including the ill-fated STS 51-L mission. There are hundreds of black-and-white photographs and replicas of each of the individual crew emblems.

Ghitelman, David. *The Space Telescope*. New York: Gallery Books, 1987. This work is a preview of the Hubble Space Telescope. It discusses Earth-based telescopes and their advantages and disadvantages. The author traces the development of the Hubble Space Telescope and the problems of polishing the world's smoothest mirror—the 94-inch-diameter primary reflecting mirror. The design and construction of the Hubble Space Telescope are detailed, as are the plans for its deployment by the Space Shuttle. During its life the Hubble Space Telescope will be periodically serviced by the Shuttle and, if necessary, can be returned to Earth for refurbishment. A look at the expected increase in knowledge of the universe is included. There is a chapter about the life of the telescope's namesake, Dr. Edward Powell Hubble, the American astronomer who, among other things, discovered that all galaxies are red-shifted (their motion away from us causes their light to shift toward the red end of the visible spectrum as a result of the phenomenon known as the Doppler effect). There are dozens of color and black-and-white photographs and paintings, an index, and a brief bibliography.

Hall, Donald N. B., ed. *The Space Telescope Observatory.* Washington, D.C.: Government Printing Office, 1982.
This is a compendium of information about the Hubble Space Telescope, written by individuals or groups who have played a major role in the development of the first large-aperture, long-term optical and ultraviolet observatory to be launched into space. Most of the papers are highly technical and deal with the projected performance of the telescope. The dissertations represent an overview of the Hubble Space Telescope's scientific potential as perceived by the scientists involved in its development. Detailed line drawings and black-and-white photographs of the telescope's equipment are included. Each of the observatory's individual telescopes and cameras is detailed.

Lord, Douglas R. *Spacelab: An International Success Story.* Washington, D.C.: Government Printing Office, 1987.
One of the main purposes for building the Space Transportation System was to provide the capability of taking scientific work stations into orbit. What started as a plan for a space station developed into the Spacelab, an interchangeable set of modules and pallets which can be adapted for an unlimited number of experiment packages. This book, although not listed as part of the official NASA History Series, was written for NASA and is a thorough look at the development and construction of Spacelab. There are discussions of the countries that helped build and pay for Spacelab, and a look at its first three missions. There are hundreds of color and black-and-white photographs and a summary of the program to date. Appendices present the Memorandum of Understanding, which provided for the implementation of the cooperative program to build Spacelab; the Joint Programme Plan; Programme Requirements; and a list of key program participants. Like other NASA historical references, this one has an extensive bibliography.

Lundquist, Charles A., ed. *Skylab's Astronomy and Space Sciences.* Washington, D.C.: Government Printing Office, 1979.
One of Skylab's main objectives was to perform experiments in the microgravity conditions of orbital flight over extended periods of time. Another was to look at the rest of the universe, especially the Sun, with the unblinking eye of the telescope. This study details these two aspects of the Skylab missions. Subjects covered in this work include stellar and galactic astronomy, interplanetary dust, Comet Kohoutek, energetic particles, Earth's atmosphere, and the orbital environment. Color photographs and art highlight this informative book.

McRoberts, Joseph J. *Space Telescope.* Washington, D.C.: Government Printing Office, 1982.
The Hubble Space Telescope will allow scientists to view the universe from a vantage point three hundred miles above Earth. There, unobstructed by our atmosphere, it will peer back into time, seven times farther than previously seen. It will be able to image the planets of the solar system at a resolution greater than before possible. Even a planet as far away as Saturn will be viewed with the clarity available from the Voyager spacecraft. This is a preview guide to the deployment mission. It uses a great number of color and black-and-white photographs, as well as drawings, to illustrate the telescope and its mission. An excellent source of information about this project.

Page, Lou Williams, and Thorton Page. *Apollo Soyuz Experiments in Space.* 9 vols. Washington, D.C.: Government Printing Office, 1977.
This nine-part series of curriculum-related pamphlets for teachers and students of space science discusses the Apollo Soyuz mission. After the authors collected the data and assembled draft versions of the pamphlets, selected teachers from high schools and universities throughout the United States reviewed them and made suggestions. The result is a well-written, illustrated set. Each volume contains an introduction, discussion of the topic, questions and answers, a table of conversion units, a glossary of terms, and a briefly annotated bibliography. Topics covered are the flight, X rays and gamma rays, the Sun, stars and in between, the gravitational field, the Earth from orbit, cosmic ray dosage, biology in zero-gravity conditions, zero-gravity technology, and general science.

Pogue, William R. *How Do You Go to the Bathroom in Space?* New York: Tom Doherty Associates, 1985.
This and many other interesting questions about living in space are answered by former astronaut Pogue. He was one of three crew members who spent eighty-four days in orbit aboard Skylab. Actually, there are 156 questions which the author has gleaned from thousands that he and his fellow astronauts have received in a quarter century of manned spaceflight. Many of the questions lead to humorous answers, but most provide a great deal of firsthand

information about matters of general interest. The questions touch on each of the U.S. manned space programs. Several appendices provide additional information, including a summary of the physiological effects of spaceflight, a list of Earth features recognizable from space, a guide to information and resources, and a bibliography.

U.S. General Accounting Office. *Space Science: Status of the Hubble Space Telescope Program.* Washington, D.C.: Government Printing Office, 1988.
This work is the report of the GAO's findings on the Hubble Space Telescope, which was launched from the Space Shuttle *Discovery* in April, 1990. The report provides a general overview of the program, including its objectives, scope, and methodology. There are spacecraft configuration drawings and information relating to cost, schedule, and performance. A chronology of the project, through the date of the report, is presented. There is a glossary of terms used.

U.S. House of Representatives. *United States Civilian Space Programs 1958-1978.* Vol. 1. Washington, D.C.: Government Printing Office, 1981.
In a very concise report, the Committee on Space Science and Applications has compiled data on all U.S. space activity during its first two decades. After a brief introduction and summary chapter, the volume is divided into fourteen additional sections. The second chapter deals with the space-related issues under consideration by Congress. The remaining sections cover the history of NASA and its relationship to U.S. space policy, NASA facilities and tracking systems, launch vehicles and propulsion, manned spaceflight through 1975, the Space Transportation System, space life sciences, space science programs, materials processing in space, international cooperation in space, interagency and non-NASA governmental space activities, industrial and university support for NASA, space program benefits, and selected future space programs. Appendices contain Department of Defense manned spaceflight plans, NASA funding history, international space agreements, texts of President Jimmy Carter's space directives, documents relating to the legal aspects of the Space Shuttle, major U.S. space organizations, a master log of U.S. spaceflights, and a table of U.S. space orbital payloads by mission from 1957 through 1979.

U.S. National Aeronautics and Space Administration. *Apollo Soyuz Test Project: Summary Science Report.* 2 vols. Washington, D.C.: Government Printing Office, 1977.
Upon completion of the Apollo Soyuz flight, engineers, scientists from the various disciplines, and the astronauts who flew the mission wrote summaries of the venture. Topics covered in these two volumes include astronomy, Earth's atmosphere and gravity field, life sciences, materials processing, earth observations, and photography. There are dozens of color and black-and-white photo-

graphs, line drawings, and data tables. Each section has its own comprehensive reference list. Appendices contain glossaries, acronyms, and unit conversion tables. These books provide the researcher with a bounty of facts and figures about the flight. Much of it has to be filtered, however, because it is filled with scientific terminology beyond the range of the general reader.

_____. *Science in Orbit: The Shuttle and Spacelab Experience, 1981-1986.* Washington, D.C.: Government Printing Office, 1988.
The opportunity to conduct large-scale experiments in Earth orbit escaped the U.S. space program for nearly a decade, from the end of the last Skylab mission in February, 1974, to the first Spacelab mission aboard *Columbia* in November, 1983. Now the United States has the capability to obtain the necessary data to launch a permanently manned space station. This book studies the Space Transportation System and the Spacelab research laboratory. It chronicles the two programs and looks at the knowledge gained from the first twenty-four Shuttle flights. Disciplines detailed include life sciences, materials science, solar physics, space plasma physics, atmospheric science, Earth observation, astronomy, and astrophysics. In addition, experiments conducted to test the technology needed to build the space station *Freedom* are presented. There are dozens of color and black-and-white photographs.

_____. *Skylab and the Sun.* Washington, D.C.: Government Printing Office, 1973.
The Apollo Telescope Mount (ATM) on the Skylab orbiting workshop was used to study the Sun in depth. This work was written to familiarize the reader with the Sun and what the Skylab program expected to gain by observing it. Scientists, astronauts, engineers, and other individuals closely associated with the ATM program wrote the articles. There is a brief overview of the program and the facts known about the Sun prior to Skylab. The studies proposed for the ATM, as well as the equipment designed to carry out the observations, are detailed. Appendices tell the reader where to obtain additional information about the program and the data to be received.

_____. *Spacelab 1.* Washington, D.C.: Government Printing Office, 1983.
This is a preview of the first Spacelab mission flown aboard the Space Shuttle. The work discusses the need for a reusable orbital research facility and the history of Spacelab's development. The experiments to be conducted during the mission are detailed and brief biographies of the two payload specialists, their backups, and the two mission specialists for the flight are provided. Color and black-and-white photographs and drawings accentuate the text. This is for general audiences, although the researcher will find a great deal of detail about Spacelab's experiments.

_____. *Spacelab 1 Experiments*. Washington, D.C.: Government Printing Office, 1983.
Spacelab 1 was launched aboard the Space Shuttle *Columbia* in November, 1983. It was the inaugural mission of the versatile, reusable research facility funded, developed, and built by the European Space Agency. This work, using black-and-white photographs and drawings, details each of the seventy different experiments in five research disciplines: astronomy and solar physics, space plasma physics, atmospheric physics and Earth observations, life sciences, and materials sciences. The summaries include the purpose, importance, and method of each experiment. The identification number, sponsor, and principal investigator's name and affiliation are provided for each experiment.

_____. *Spacelab 2*. Washington, D.C.: Government Printing Office, 1985.
Spacelab 2 was actually the third mission flown by this scientific research facility. Delays in the development of some of its equipment caused its flight to be switched with the Spacelab 3 mission. Spacelab 2, the first pallet-only mission, was carried into orbit aboard *Challenger* in July, 1985. It consisted of thirteen experiments in six scientific disciplines: solar physics, atmospheric physics, plasma physics, high-energy astrophysics, technology research, and life sciences. This work previews the flight, with emphasis on the experiments. Each is detailed, including the identification number, sponsor, and principal investigator's name and affiliation, and is accompanied by color photographs and drawings.

_____. *Spacelab Mission 2 Experiment Descriptions*. 2d ed. Washington, D.C.: Government Printing Office, 1982.
NASA's official guide to the experiments carried aboard Spacelab 2 contains very detailed information about each experiment. In addition to the discussion of the test, the experimental apparatus is detailed, including a diagram of the equipment and its physical dimensions and characteristics. There is a line drawing of the Spacelab as it is seen in the Space Shuttle's payload bay. The location of each of the experiments is included.

_____. *Spacelab 3*. Washington, D.C.: Government Printing Office, 1984.
Spacelab 3 was carried into orbit aboard the Space Shuttle *Challenger* in April, 1985. It consisted of a long module and Mission Peculiar Equipment Support Structure (MPESS), which carried the fifteen investigations in five scientific disciplines: materials sciences, life sciences, fluid mechanics, atmospheric science, and astronomy. This booklet discusses the mission and its flight crew, including the two payload specialists and their backups. Each of the experiments is detailed, including the identification number, sponsor, and principal investigator's name and affiliation and is accompanied by color photographs and drawings.

_____. *Spacelab Mission 3 Experiment Descriptions.* Washington, D.C.: Government Printing Office, 1982.

NASA's official guide to the experiments carried aboard Spacelab 3 contains very detailed information about each experiment. In addition to the discussion of the test, the experimental apparatus is detailed, including a diagram of the equipment and its physical dimensions and characteristics. There is a line drawing of the Spacelab as it is seen in the Space Shuttle's payload bay. The location of each of the experiments is included.

_____. *Spartan: Science with Efficiency and Simplicity.* Washington, D.C.: Government Printing Office, 1984.

This is a preflight look at the Shuttle Pointed Autonomous Research Tool for Astronomy (Spartan), a retrievable free- flying platform for high-energy astrophysics, solar physics, and ultraviolet astronomy studies. Spartan is carried to orbit inside the payload bay of the Space Shuttle, where it is deployed by the orbiter's remote manipulator system arm. It can then operate independent of the Shuttle for periods up to forty hours. After completing its mission, it is recaptured by the manipulator arm and placed back in the stowed position for return to Earth. This brief work has several color photographs and color renditions of Spartan in flight. Despite its simplicity, the work gives a lot of information about this unique satellite.

Science in Orbit

Anderton, David A. *Space Station.* Washington, D.C.: Government Printing Office, 1985.

This NASA Educational Publication (EP-211) looks at the plans to build the United States' first permanently manned space station, *Freedom.* This work provides an overview of the program and the various design concepts developed by various NASA facilities and major aerospace contractors. At the time of the writing, the exact plans for constructing the space station were not finalized. Although this work does not provide any details, it does give some insight into the evolution of *Freedom.* There are many color photographs of the different design concepts.

Belew, Leland F., ed. *Skylab, Our First Space Station.* Washington, D.C.: National Technical Information Service, 1977.

A colorful retrospective of the Skylab program and its four flights is presented in this work. Technically speaking, the title is a misnomer, since Skylab was not a "space station." By definition, a space station is a permanently manned platform which can be completely resupplied. Astronauts replenished the food, water, film, and a few other expendables, but Skylab's attitude control and electrical and life support systems were not replenishable. The book is a good reference, chronicling the program from its design and planning phases through the completion of the third manned period. There are dozens of color photographs and drawings, including several spectacular pictures taken on orbit. A mission summary table and an index are included. Belew was the manager of the Skylab Program Office at the Marshall Space Flight Center, where Skylab was built.

Belew, Leland F., and Ernst Stuhlinger. *Skylab: A Guidebook.* Washington, D.C.: Government Printing Office, 1973.
This is a preflight guide to the Skylab program and provides in-depth, nontechnical information about the orbiting workshop and its components. Skylab, the spacecraft, was built around the S-IVB third stage of the Saturn V launch vehicle. The major components included the Orbital Workshop (OWS), Instrument Unit (IU), Airlock Module (AM), Multiple Docking Adapter (MDA), and the Apollo Telescope Mount (ATM). As much of the spacecraft as possible was made from existing hardware or with hardware requiring little modification. This guide describes the work of several thousand engineers and scientists who conceived, designed, and built Skylab. Each of the experiments to be performed during Skylab's stay in orbit is described, as well as the apparatus to conduct it. Line drawings, black-and-white photographs, a glossary of terms and acronyms, an index, and a brief bibliography are included.

Clark, Lenwood G., et al., eds. *Long Duration Exposure Facility (LDEF): Mission 1 Experiments.* Washington, D.C.: Government Printing Office, 1984.
The LDEF is a twelve-sided, open-grid reusable space platform which can be deployed from the Shuttle's cargo bay and later retrieved for return to Earth. It has been designed to provide a large number of economical opportunities for science and technology experiments that require modest electrical power and data processing while in space and that benefit from postflight laboratory investigations with the retrieved equipment hardware. The first LDEF was deployed from the Space Shuttle *Challenger* on April 7, 1984, for a one-year mission in Earth orbit. LDEF-1 carried fifty-seven science and technology experiments, including 12.5 million tomato seeds, packaged in kits, for later distribution to students from the upper elementary through university level. As a result of scheduling difficulties and the STS 51-L accident, the LDEF was not retrieved until January 12, 1990. This book discusses in great detail each of the experiments, using black-and-white photographs and line drawings. The location of each experiment package on the LDEF is shown.

Compton, W. David, and Charles D. Benson. *Living and Working in Space: A History of Skylab.* Washington, D.C.: Government Printing Office, 1983.

One title in the NASA History Series, this book chronicles the Skylab program, from its conception during the early days of the Apollo program to the orbiting workshop's fiery plunge in 1979. There are dozens of black-and-white photographs of the three manned missions, as well as the launch of the unmanned workshop. Color photographs, taken from orbit, are in the back of the book. Line drawings show the inner workings of much of the equipment related to the missions. There is an index and an impressive hundred-page appendix listing source notes and bibliographic references. Other appendices include a summary of the missions, astronaut biographies, in-flight experiments, Comet Kohoutek, and the International Aeronautical Federation world records set by Skylab.

Cooper, Henry S. F., Jr. *Before Liftoff: The Making of a Space Shuttle Crew.* Baltimore: The Johns Hopkins University Press, 1987.
Space Shuttle Mission 41-G, with seven astronauts aboard *Challenger*, spent eight days in space. The crew included veteran Commander Robert Crippen and Mission Specialist Sally Ride, along with rookie Pilot Jon McBride, Mission Specialists Kathy Sullivan and David Leetsma, and Payload Specialists Paul Scully-Power and Canadian Marc Garneau. During the mission, the crew deployed the Earth Radiation Budget Satellite and conducted experiments. Two of the astronauts performed a spacewalk to demonstrate an on-orbit refueling system. Author Cooper made special arrangements with NASA to follow the crew from its formation through the completion of the mission. This is an engrossing look at the everyday life of an astronaut crew. The reader gets to sit in on briefings, join the crew for simulations, and even swim underwater for spacewalk practice. There are a few black-and-white photographs and an index.

_____. *A House in Space.* New York: Holt, Rinehart and Winston, 1976.
This work is about the nine-month period from May 14, 1973, through February 8, 1974—the active life of the Skylab orbiting workshop. During this time, it was inhabited by three crews of astronauts for periods of twenty-eight, fifty-nine, and eighty-four days. The book was derived from articles written by Cooper, which appeared in *The New Yorker* magazine during this period. It looks more at the human aspect of the program than at its technical side, but still contains information useful to the researcher. There are many black-and-white photographs and color diagrams.

David, Leonard. *Space Station Freedom: A Foothold on the Future.* Washington, D.C.: Government Printing Office, 1988.
This is a colorful booklet on the proposed Space Station *Freedom* and what it will mean to us in the future. There are dozens of color and black-and-white photographs and artists' conceptions to highlight the text. The history of the

space station is chronicled from the early 1950's through the Skylab program. There are descriptions of the scientific missions and experiments conceived for *Freedom*. The individual components and how they will be assembled in orbit are described. The text is readable at all levels of understanding, and there is a lot of information packed into this work.

Eddy, John A. *A New Sun: The Solar Results from Skylab*. Washington, D.C.: National Technical Information Service, 1979.
    Countless volumes of data about the biological and physiological effects of long-duration spaceflight on humans, plants, and animals were obtained during the Skylab program. In addition, the first space telescopes (combined in a structure called the Apollo Telescope Mount, or ATM) were used to study the Sun. The ATM derived its name from a study that was conducted to determine the feasibility of mounting a stable telescope on the Apollo service module. In actuality, the ATM was built around the lunar module descent stage. There is very little technical information, but the color and black-and-white photographs of the Sun make this book worthwhile.

Ezell, Edward C., and Linda N. Ezell. *The Partnership: A History of the Apollo-Soyuz Test Project*. Washington, D.C.: Government Printing Office, 1978.
    One title in the NASA History Series, this book chronicles the Apollo Soyuz Test Project, to date the only joint U.S.-Soviet manned spaceflight. The origins of the project, immediately following the successful completion of the Apollo 11 Moon landing mission, are traced. Also discussed are the political aspects of the venture. There are dozens of black-and-white photographs of the flight. Color photographs, taken from orbit, are in the back of the book. Line drawings show the inner workings of much of the equipment related to the mission. Includes an impressive seventy-page appendix listing source notes and bibliographic references, and an index. Other appendices include NASA organization charts, development of U.S. and Soviet manned spaceflight, a summary of the U.S./U.S.S.R. meetings, and descriptions of the ASTP launch vehicles.

Froehlich, Walter. *Apollo Soyuz*. Washington, D.C.: Government Printing Office, 1976.
    This is an entertaining look at the Apollo Soyuz Test Project, the United States' last manned mission using expendable spacecraft and launch vehicles. It was designed to test a rescue method for astronauts or cosmonauts stranded in orbit and unable to be saved by their own country. The U.S. spacecraft, an Apollo command and service module and a docking module (stored in the adapter used to house the Apollo lunar module during launch), were boosted into orbit by a Saturn IB. The Soviets used their standard Soyuz spacecraft and A-2 booster. The book briefly looks at the mission's origin, the spacecraft, astronauts and cosmonauts, experiments, and results of the joint endeavor. There are numerous

color photographs and appendices listing the times of major events, "firsts" achieved by Apollo Soyuz, major officials involved, scientific experiments, and principal Apollo contractors.

_____. *Spacelab: An International Short-Stay Orbiting Laboratory.* Washington, D.C.: Government Printing Office, 1983.
International cooperation is the status quo for the Spacelab program. Ten nations of the European Space Agency (ESA)—Austria, Belgium, Denmark, France, West Germany, Italy, The Netherlands, Spain, Switzerland, and the United Kingdom—have designed, built, and financed Spacelab. This Space Shuttle payload consists of interchangeable modules and pallets, which can be combined into a nearly unlimited mixture for a variety of scientific experimentation. This work looks at the Spacelab: what it does, how it came to be, and what its users expect from it. It is for the general audience and contains dozens of color photographs and artist's renditions. There is a very detailed cutaway drawing of the Spacelab 1 module and pallet.

Furniss, Tim. *Manned Spaceflight Log.* London: Jane's, 1983, rev. ed. 1987.
This work covers the manned spaceflights of the Soviet Union and the United States from 1961 through 1986. A synopsis of each mission is given, along with pertinent data (date, crew, site, recovery, duration, spacecraft weight, and so forth) and several black-and-white photographs. The Mercury, Gemini, Apollo, Skylab, Apollo Soyuz, and Space Shuttle flights are listed chronologically. Included are the thirteen flights of the X-15 research aircraft which exceeded the fifty-mile altitude necessary to qualify its pilot as an astronaut under Air Force rules. There are astronaut photographs and, in the appendices, listings of space seniority and the current status of the astronaut and cosmonaut classes.

_____. *Space Flight: The Records.* London: Guiness Books, 1985.
Do you know the first manned spaceflight to be curtailed? It was Gemini V, which landed one orbit early to miss hurricane Betsy. Were you aware that the first spaceflight with more than one fifty-year-old person on board was that of STS 51-B/Spacelab 3, in April, 1985? These and dozens of other interesting and significant—or not so significant—facts are covered in this work. The first part of the book is a "diary" of manned spaceflight, listing each of the missions of the United States and Soviet Union. There is a chapter on manned spaceflight "firsts" and one on the manned space machines. Basic biographical information on each of the space travelers is given, accompanied by the person's photograph. The major information section is last and includes tables on manned spaceflight duration, space seniority, space experience, lunar spacemen, spacewalks, astroflights of the X-15, all known cosmonauts, NASA astronauts, Space Shuttle passengers, NASA flight crew selections, and the

Space Shuttle schedule. There are hundreds of black-and-white photographs, a glossary of terms, and an index.

_____. *Space Shuttle Log*. London: Jane's, 1986.
The first twenty-two flights of the Space Shuttle are chronicled in this concise work about the Space Transportation System. The first chapter traces the development and testing of the system, detailing the earlier designs of the vehicle and some of the research aircraft that paved the way for the orbiter. There is a section on the astronauts who fly the Shuttle, which includes photographs and brief biographical listings. Perhaps the most ironic segment is the listing of future flights, including the ill-fated STS 51-L mission. There are hundreds of black-and-white photographs and replicas of each of the individual crew emblems.

Gatland, Kenneth. "The First Space Stations." In *The Illustrated Encyclopedia of Space Technology: A Comprehensive History of Space Exploration*, by Kenneth Gatland et al. New York: Harmony Books, 1981.
This section in the book discusses the early space stations of the United States and the Soviet Union. There is a fine four-page, full-color cutaway drawing of the Skylab workshop and the Soviets' Salyut space station. There are color and black-and-white photographs, drawings, and charts. The major features of the program, including the spacecraft and launch vehicle, are discussed. Appendices include a chronology of the major space events since Sputnik 1, a glossary of terms, and an index.

Ghitelman, David. *The Space Telescope*. New York: Gallery Books, 1987.
This work is a preview of the Hubble Space Telescope. It discusses Earth-based telescopes and their advantages and disadvantages. The author traces the development of the Hubble Space Telescope and the problems of polishing the world's smoothest mirror—the 94-inch-diameter primary reflecting mirror. The design and construction of the Hubble Space Telescope are detailed, as are the plans for its deployment by the Space Shuttle. During its life the telescope will be periodically serviced by the Shuttle and, if necessary, can be returned to Earth for refurbishment. A look at the expected increase in knowledge of the universe is included. There is a chapter about the life of the telescope's namesake, Dr. Edward Powell Hubble, the American astronomer who, among other things, discovered that all galaxies are red-shifted (their motion away from us causes their light to shift toward the red end of the visible spectrum as a result of the phenomenon known as the Doppler effect). There are dozens of color and black-and-white photographs and paintings, an index, and a brief bibliography.

Johnston, Richard S., and Lawrence F. Dietlein, eds. *Biomedical Results from Skylab*. Washington, D.C.: National Technical Information Service, 1977.
Biomedical testing under the conditions of orbital flight was studied for relatively brief periods during the Mercury, Gemini, and Apollo programs. With Skylab, scientists would be able to conduct experiments on astronauts spending a month or more in space. The editors of this work have compiled a concise review of each experiment, including the theory behind the test, the means by which is was completed, and the results. The experiments were divided into four disciplines: neurophysiology; musculoskeletal function; biochemistry, hematology, and cytology; and cardiovascular and metabolic function. The text is supplemented with photographs and drawings, as well as charts of the conclusions reached by each examiner. Every section of the book has its own reference listing, which will guide the researcher to more detailed works. Appendices detail the experimental support hardware and the operational life sciences support hardware.

Lee, Chester M., ed. *Apollo Soyuz Mission Report*. AAS Advances in the Astronautical Sciences, vol. 34. San Diego, Calif.: American Astronomical Society, 1975.
The official report on the Apollo Soyuz Test Project, prepared by the Mission Evaluation Team, contains a wealth of data on the flight of Apollo 18. Included are a mission summary and sections which detail the flight, spacecraft, crew activities, orbital experiments, in-flight demonstrations, biomedical evaluations, and mission ground support. An assessment of the mission objectives, as well as anomalies, is included. Tables summarize the flight trajectory and activity time lines. Appendices include descriptions and drawings of the spacecraft and launch vehicles, the as-flown ASTP flight plan, spacecraft history and mass properties, postflight testing, and a glossary of terms. There is also a summary of lightning activities by NASA for the mission.

Lord, Douglas R. *Spacelab: An International Success Story*. Washington, D.C.: Government Printing Office, 1987.
One of the main purposes for building the Space Transportation System was to provide the capability of taking scientific work stations into orbit. What started as a plan for a space station developed into the Spacelab, an interchangeable set of modules and pallets that can be adapted for an unlimited number of experiment packages. This book, although not listed as part of the official NASA History Series, is a thorough look at the development and construction of Spacelab. There are discussions of the countries that helped build and pay for Spacelab and a look at its first three missions. There are hundreds of color and black-and-white photographs and a summary of the program to date. Appendices present the Memorandum of Understanding, which provided for the implementation of the cooperative program to build Spacelab;

the Joint Programme Plan; Programme Requirements; and a list of key program participants. Like other NASA historical references, this one has an extensive bibliography.

Lundquist, Charles A., ed. *Skylab's Astronomy and Space Sciences*. Washington, D.C.: Government Printing Office, 1979.

One of Skylab's main objectives was to perform experiments in the microgravity conditions of orbital flight over extended periods of time. Another was to look at the rest of the universe, especially the Sun, with the unblinking eye of the telescope. This study details these two aspects of the Skylab missions. Subjects covered in this work include stellar and galactic astronomy, interplanetary dust, Comet Kohoutek, energetic particles, Earth's atmosphere, and the orbital environment. Color photographs and art highlight this informative book.

Magill, Frank N., ed. *Magill's Survey of Science: Space Exploration Series*. Vol. 5. Pasadena, Calif.: Salem Press, 1989, pp. 1828-1863.

This five-volume set covers every aspect of the U.S. and Soviet manned and unmanned space programs, as well as those of nations newer to the space race. Since 1971, the Soviet Union has had a permanently manned space station in orbit. The United States had Skylab for nine months in 1973-1974, but that was not a "real" space station. By the end of this century, the United States plans to have the *Freedom* space station orbiting. Five articles are devoted to the design and uses of *Freedom*, its development, international contributions to *Freedom*, the modules and nodes from which it will be constructed, and what it will be like working and living aboard it. Included are an annotated bibliography and cross-references for each article.

Messerschmitt-Bölkow-Blohm. *First German SPACELAB: Mission D1*. Bremen, West Germany: MBB/ERNO, 1985.

The "Deutschland Spacelab Mission D1" was the first of a series of dedicated West German missions on the Space Shuttle. It flew aboard *Challenger* in October, 1985, the last successful mission of the orbiter. The modules contained equipment for seventy-six experiments in five disciplines: fluid physics, solidification, biology, medicine, and space-time interaction. This work details each of the experiments and the facilities used to run them. There are dozens of color photographs and drawings of the experiment packages. This publication, although published in West Germany, has been made available through NASA.

Newkirk, Roland W., and Ivan D. Ertel, with Courtney G. Brooks. *Skylab: A Chronology*. Washington, D.C.: National Technical Information Service, 1977.

This is NASA's official record of the Skylab program, covering events on a day-to-day basis. At its inception, the project was known as the Apollo Applications Program since it was to use modified equipment from the lunar landing endeavor. Included in the coverage are the early space station designs, the development of the spacecraft and launch vehicles, astronaut training, and mission results. There are dozens of black-and-white photographs and line drawings of components. Appendices provide a summary of the Skylab flights: mission objectives, orbital activities, experiments, and extravehicular activity. Includes a glossary of abbreviations and acronyms and an index.

O'Leary, Brian. *Project Space Station.* Harrisburg, Pa.: Government Printing Office, 1983.
The author takes a look at the space station programs of the United States and the Soviet Union, and discusses their practical applications and benefits. He traces the history of manned space platforms and, in the process, touches upon Skylab, Spacelab, and the Space Transportation System. The major systems of an orbiting space station, similar to America's *Freedom*, are described. Much of the emphasis of the book is on the political aspects of the program. Contains black-and-white photographs, a brief bibliography, and an index.

Page, Lou Williams, and Thorton Page. *Apollo Soyuz Experiments in Space.* 9 vols. Washington, D.C.: Government Printing Office, 1977.
This nine-part series of curriculum-related pamphlets for teachers and students of space science discusses the Apollo Soyuz mission. After the authors collected the data and assembled draft versions of the pamphlets, selected teachers from high schools and universities throughout the United States reviewed them and made suggestions. The result is a well-written, illustrated set. Each volume contains an introduction, discussion of the topic, questions and answers, a table of conversion units, a glossary of terms, and a briefly annotated bibliography. Topics covered are the flight, X rays and gamma rays, the Sun, stars and in between, the gravitational field, the Earth from orbit, cosmic ray dosage, biology in zero gravity, zero-gravity technology, and general science.

Pogue, William R. *How Do You Go to the Bathroom in Space?* New York: Tom Doherty Associates, 1985.
This and many other interesting questions about living in space are answered by former astronaut Pogue. He was one of three crew members who spent eighty-four days in orbit aboard Skylab. Actually, there are 156 questions which the author has gleaned from thousands that he and his fellow astronauts have received in a quarter century of manned spaceflight. Many of the questions lead to humorous answers, but most provide a great deal of firsthand information about matters of general interest. The questions touch on each of the U.S. manned space programs. Several appendices provide additional information, including a summary of the physiological effects of spaceflight,

a list of Earth features recognizable from space, a guide to information and resources, and a bibliography.

Ride, Sally K. *Leadership and America's Future in Space.* Washington, D.C.: Government Printing Office, 1987.

In response to growing concern in both Congress and the Administration over the long-term direction of the U.S. civilian space program, NASA Administrator Dr. James Fletcher formed a task group to define potential U.S. space initiatives. This is the report of the group which identified four candidate initiatives for study and evaluation: Mission to Planet Earth, Exploration of the Solar System, Outpost on the Moon, and Humans to Mars. Each of the four fields is discussed in terms of background; strategy and scenario; technology, transportation, and orbital facilities; and summary of the project. The "leadership in space" status of the United States has dropped considerably since the Apollo program, and Dr. Ride addresses the reasons for this. There a drawings, tables, charts, color photographs, a reference list, and a list of the additional studies which went into the creation of the report.

Summerlin, Lee B., ed. *Skylab, Classroom in Space.* Washington, D.C.: Government Printing Office, 1977.

The Skylab Student Project was originated by NASA and the National Science Teachers Association as a means of involving schoolchildren, the next generation of scientists, in the study of space sciences. In 1972, twenty-five high school students from across the United States were selected to participate in the program. They were from among the more than four thousand students who had made proposals. This volume, filled with color and black-and-white photographs, details how and why the project was developed, describes the experiments flown aboard Skylab, and relates them to other scientific investigations carried out during the flights.

U.S. House of Representatives. *Skylab 1 Investigation Report: Hearing Before the Subcommittee on Manned Space Flight of the Committee on Science and Astronautics.* Washington, D.C.: National Technical Information Service, 1973.

In August, 1973, the subcommittee opened its investigation into the incident which had occurred during the launch of the Skylab 1 spacecraft. At sixty-three seconds into the flight, there were indications that the workshop's micrometeoroid shield had deployed and that the workshop solar array wing 2 was no longer secured in its launch position. This, coupled with the failure of solar array wing 1 to deploy on orbit, should have terminated the mission. Fortunately, the first manned crew was able to free the stuck wing and install a shield over the sunside of the workshop. The workshop was usable. This report documents the accident, as best it could be reconstructed, and the procedures developed and implemented to recover from the effects of the incident. There are many black-and-white photographs and drawings to give the reader a great deal of technical information. Most of the contents are transcripts of the testimony of witnesses.

_____. *United States Civilian Space Programs 1958-1978*. Vol. 1. Washington, D.C.: Government Printing Office, 1981.
In a very concise report, the Committee on Space Science and Applications has compiled data on all U.S. space activity during its first two decades. After a brief introduction and summary chapter, the volume is divided into fourteen additional sections. The second chapter deals with the space-related issues under consideration by Congress. The remaining sections cover the history of NASA and its relationship to U.S. space policy, NASA facilities and tracking systems, launch vehicles and propulsion, manned spaceflight through 1975, the Space Transportation System, space life sciences, space science programs, materials processing in space, international cooperation in space, interagency and non-NASA governmental space activities, industrial and university support for NASA, space program benefits, and selected future space programs. Appendices contain Department of Defense manned spaceflight plans, NASA funding history, international space agreements, texts of President Jimmy Carter's space directives, documents relating to the legal aspects of the Space Shuttle, major U.S. space organizations, a master log of U.S. spaceflights, and a table of U.S. space orbital payloads by mission from 1957 through 1979.

U.S. National Aeronautics and Space Administration. *Apollo Soyuz Test Project: Summary Science Report*. 2 vols. Washington, D.C.: Government Printing Office, 1977.
Upon completion of the Apollo Soyuz flight, engineers, scientists from the various disciplines, and the astronauts who flew the mission wrote summaries of the venture. Topics covered in these two volumes include astronomy, Earth's atmosphere and gravity field, life sciences, materials processing, Earth observations, and photography. There are dozens of color and black-and-white photographs, line drawings, and data tables. Each section has its own comprehensive reference list. Appendices contain glossaries, acronyms, and unit conversion tables. These books provide the researcher with a bounty of facts and figures about the flight. Much of it has to be filtered, however, because it is filled with scientific terminology beyond the range of the average reader.

_____. *Gemini Midprogram Conference, Including Experiment Results*. Washington, D.C.: National Technical Information Service, 1966.
A four-day conference was held at NASA's Manned Spacecraft Center in Houston, Texas, February 23-25, 1966. The purpose of the meeting was to have key members of Gemini report on the progress of the program at the midway point. This work presents the reports, divided into the following

categories: spacecraft, launch vehicle, flight operations, mission results, physical science experiments, and medical science experiments. Each dissertation is accompanied by black-and-white photographs, line drawings, tables, and charts. There is a two-segment report on the planning and execution of the Gemini VII and VI-A rendezvous mission.

_____. *Gemini Program Mission Report: Gemini 3 Through XII.* 10 vols. Washington, D.C.: Government Printing Office, 1964-1966.
The official record of the Gemini program missions. Each volume was prepared by the Mission Evaluation Team and contains a wealth of data on the particular flight. There is a mission summary and sections that detail the flight, spacecraft and launch vehicle performance, crew activities, orbital experiments, in-flight demonstrations, biomedical evaluations, and mission ground support. An assessment of the mission objectives, as well as anomalies, is included. Tables summarize the vehicle histories, weather conditions, flight safety reviews, and postflight inspection of the spacecraft. Descriptions and drawings of the spacecraft, launch vehicles, and experiment packages are included. These volumes present the definitive study of each flight. Some volumes might have to be obtained directly from NASA.

_____. *Gemini Summary Conference.* Washington, D.C.: National Technical Information Service, 1967.
A two-day conference was held at NASA's Manned Spacecraft Center in Houston, Texas, on February 1-2, 1967. The purpose of the symposium was to report on the results of the last five missions of the Gemini program. The technical papers presented were divided into five sections: The first describes the rendezvous, docking, and tethered-vehicle operations involving the spacecraft and a target vehicle; the second presents various aspects of extravehicular activity; the third concerns the operational support of the missions; the fourth covers the experiments conducted during the missions; and the fifth compares the astronaut flight and simulation experiences and relates the Gemini results to the Apollo program. Each dissertation is accompanied by black-and-white photographs, line drawings, tables, and charts.

_____. *Get Away Special (GAS) Small Self-Contained Payloads: Experimenter Handbook.* Washington, D.C.: Government Printing Office, 1984.
The purpose of NASA's Get Away Special (GAS) program is to encourage the use of space by all researchers, foster enthusiasm in the younger generation, increase knowledge of space, be alert to possible growth of GAS investigation into a prime experiment, and generate new activities unique to space. The GAS payloads are self-contained and are not permitted to draw upon any Shuttle services beyond three on-off controls that are operated by an astronaut. The experimenter is required to provide any electrical power, heating, data handling

facilities, and other necessities within the GAS container. This document provides the experimenter with all the information necessary to develop a payload for one or more of these containers. Specifications for each of the available containers, as well as safety requirements, are included. There are tips for the experimenter and a brief, annotated bibliography to guide the investigator to books that might be useful in the design of the experiment.

_____. *MSFC Skylab Orbital Workshop Final Technical Report.* 5 vols. Washington, D.C.: National Technical Information Service, 1974.
The definitive technical reference on the Skylab orbiting workshop, this work covers all aspects of the program, including concepts, goals, design philosophy, hardware, and testing. The evolution of the workshop from a "wet" configuration (one flown as the fuel tank of the second stage of the Saturn IB into orbit, drained, purged, and then converted to a habitation area by the crew) to a "dry" structure (one launched completely outfitted in orbital configuration) is chronicled. The final configuration is discussed in detail, including structures, systems, and components. The testing program is reviewed, as well as the mission results and performance during launch and flight. Detailed line drawings, tables, and charts add to the text, as does a complete reference listing.

_____. *National Space Transportation System Reference.* 2 vols. Washington, D.C.: Government Printing Office, 1988.
This is the most complete technical reference about the Space Transportation System written in nontechnical terminology. It is an enlarged and updated version of the *Press Information* books published by Rockwell International, maker of the Space Shuttle Orbiter. The last Rockwell version was printed in 1984, but because of budget reductions instituted at Rockwell in 1985, their Media Relations office could not update and reprint it. NASA, however, wanted a new edition when the Shuttle resumed operations after the *Challenger* accident. They contracted with Rockwell to provide the text and artwork. Volume 1 details the systems and facilities, while the second volume covers NASA centers and management. There are hundreds of line drawings and black-and-white photographs. Each system and subsystem is presented in great detail. Emphasis, of course, has been placed on the orbiter systems, but there is still a great deal of information about the solid rocket boosters and external tank. Also detailed are the crew equipment and escape systems, NASA centers and responsibilities, and payloads. Contains a summary of mission events, a chronology of the Space Shuttle program, a list of contractors, and a glossary of acronyms and abbreviations.

_____. *Office of Space Sciences-1 Experiment Investigation Descriptions.* Washington, D.C.: Government Printing Office, 1982.

168 America in Space

The OSS-1 experiments package was flown onboard the Space Shuttle *Columbia* in March, 1982, during the third flight of the Space Transportation System program. The investigations studied space plasma physics, the orbiter environment, solar physics, life sciences, space technology, and astronomy. This booklet discusses each of the experiments in detail and provides a technical description of the equipment. Line drawings and a detailed bibliography are included.

_____. *OSTA-1 Experiments.* Washington, D.C.: Government Printing Office, 1981.
On its second flight, the Space Shuttle *Columbia* carried the first science and applications payload scheduled by the Space Transportation System. This payload, called OSTA-1, was developed by NASA's Office of Space and Terrestrial Applications (OSTA) to provide an early demonstration of the Shuttle's research capabilities. The payload consisted of the Shuttle Imaging Radar-A, Shuttle Multispectral Infrared Radiometer, Feature Identification and Location Experiment, Measurement of Air Pollution from Satellites, Ocean Color Experiment, Night/Day Optical Survey of Lightning, and Heflex Bioengineering Test. The booklet previews the flight of STS-2 and discusses the OSTA-1 experiments in great detail. There are black-and-white photographs and line drawings and a bibliography.

_____. *OSTA-2 Payload.* Washington, D.C.: Government Printing Office, 1982.
The OSTA-2 payload was carried into orbit during the second flight of *Challenger*, STS-7, in June, 1983. The experiments package consisted of two facilities that operated automatically. These were the Materials Experiment Assembly, sponsored by NASA, and the Materialwissenschaftliche Autonome Experimente unter Schwerelosigkeit, sponsored by the German Ministry for Research and Technology. The booklet discusses the two experiment packages and their Mission Peculiar Support Structure in great detail. There are several line drawings to show the inner workings of the equipment.

_____. *OSTA-3 Experiments.* Washington, D.C.: Government Printing Office, 1984.
The OSTA-3 experiments were carried aboard *Challenger* during the STS 41-G mission, which was flown in October, 1984. It was the second generation of the first science and applications payload carried by the Space Shuttle. Three of the OSTA-1 experiments were reflown in modified form: the Shuttle Imaging Radar, Feature Identification and Location Experiment, and the Measurement of Air Pollution from Satellites. In addition, there was the Large Format Camera, designed to take stereoscopic, wide-angle, high-resolution metric

photographs of Earth. The booklet describes the experiments and uses black-and-white photographs and line drawings to detail the experiment equipment.

_____. *Science in Orbit: The Shuttle and Spacelab Experience, 1981-1986.* Washington, D.C.: Government Printing Office, 1988.
The opportunity to conduct large-scale experiments in Earth orbit escaped the U.S. space program for nearly a decade, from the end of the last Skylab mission in February, 1974, to the first Spacelab mission aboard *Columbia* in November, 1983. Now the United States has the capability to obtain the necessary data to launch a permanently manned space station. This book studies the Space Transportation System and the Spacelab research laboratory. It chronicles the two programs and looks at the knowledge gained from the first twenty-four Shuttle flights. Disciplines detailed include life sciences, materials science, solar physics, space plasma physics, atmospheric science, Earth observation, astronomy, and astrophysics. In addition, experiments conducted to test the technology needed to build the space station *Freedom* are presented. There are dozens of color and black-and-white photographs.

_____. *Skylab and the Sun.* Washington, D.C.: Government Printing Office, 1973.
The Apollo Telescope Mount (ATM) on the Skylab orbiting workshop was used to study the Sun in depth. This work was written to familiarize the reader with the Sun and what the Skylab program expected to gain by observing it. Scientists, astronauts, engineers, and other individuals closely associated with the ATM program wrote the articles. There is a brief overview of the program and the facts known about the Sun prior to Skylab. The studies proposed for the ATM, as well as the equipment designed to carry out the observations, are detailed. Appendices tell the reader where to obtain additional information about the program and the data to be received.

_____. *Skylab Experiments.* 7 vols. Washington, D.C.: Government Printing Office, 1973.
Prior to the beginning of the Skylab flights, NASA's Education Office, the Skylab Program Office, and the University of Colorado published a series of teaching guides to the experiments which were to be conducted in flight. These experiments were divided into four categories: physical sciences, biomedical sciences, Earth applications, and space applications. Each volume looks at the experiments' background, scientific objectives, description, data, crew activities, related curriculum studies, and suggested classroom demonstrations. Volume 1 covers physical science and solar astronomy; volume 2, remote sensing of Earth resources; volume 3, materials science; volume 4, life sciences; volume 5, astronomy and space physics; volume 6, mechanics; and volume 7, living

and working in space. Each volume includes numerous line drawings and a glossary of terms.

_____. *Skylab Explores the Earth*. Washington, D.C.: National Technical Information Service, 1977.
Since the first flight of Project Mercury, one of NASA's primary goals of orbital space missions was the observation of Earth. There is no better vantage point than from above. Observation time for manned spacecraft is limited by life support supplies and, prior to Skylab, the longest mission was the fourteen-day Gemini VII flight in 1965. This book studies the Earth observation experiments of Skylab during the 171 days it was occupied. It is filled with exciting color photographs of Earth, each of which is accompanied by a detailed caption. Several of the photographs are analyzed with the aid of a map of the region shown. Comparisons are made with color and black-and-white photographs taken of geologic sites and meteorologic phenomena during previous manned flights. Provides a glossary of terms and an index of the photographs used, alphabetized by geographic location.

_____. *Skylab Mission Report: Skylab 2 Through Skylab 4*. 3 vols. Washington, D.C.: National Technical Information Service, 1973-1974.
The official report on each of the manned flights in the Skylab program. Each volume was prepared by the Mission Evaluation Team and contains a wealth of data on the particular flight. Included are a mission summary and sections which detail the flight, spacecraft, crew activities, orbital experiments, in-flight demonstrations, biomedical evaluations, and mission ground support. An assessment of the mission objectives, as well as anomalies, is included. Tables summarize the flight trajectory and activity time lines. Descriptions and drawings of the spacecraft, launch vehicles, and experiment packages are included. Contains a glossary of terms and a list of references.

_____. *Skylab Mission Report, Saturn Workshop*. Washington, D.C.: National Technical Information Service, 1974.
The official NASA report on the performance of the Skylab orbiting workshop from launch until the end of the last manned period. Included are summaries of the three manned periods and the intervals when it was unmanned. Descriptions of the structural components and mechanisms are given, as well as their anomalies. A report is provided on each of the major systems and subsystems. Each of the experiments, involving solar physics, astrophysics, materials science and manufacturing, engineering and technology, student investigations, and science demonstrations, is detailed. Line drawings, black-and-white photographs, tables, charts, and an extensive reference listing add to the text.

_____. *Spacelab 1*. Washington, D.C.: Government Printing Office, 1983. This is a preview to the first Spacelab mission flown aboard the Space Shuttle. The work discusses the need for a reusable orbital research facility and the history of Spacelab's development. The experiments to be conducted during the mission are detailed, and brief biographies of the two payload specialists, their backups, and the two mission specialists for the flight are provided. Color and black-and-white photographs and drawings accentuate the text. This is for general audiences, although the researcher will find a great deal of detail about Spacelab's experiments.

_____. *Spacelab 1 Experiments*. Washington, D.C.: Government Printing Office, 1983.
Spacelab 1 was launched aboard the Space Shuttle *Columbia* in November, 1983. It was the inaugural mission of the versatile, reusable research facility funded, developed, and built by the European Space Agency. This work, using black-and-white photographs and drawings, details each of the seventy different experiments in five research disciplines: astronomy and solar physics, space plasma physics, atmospheric physics and Earth observations, life sciences, and materials sciences. The summaries include the purpose, importance, and method of each experiment. The identification number, sponsor, and principal investigator's name and affiliation are provided for each experiment.

_____. *Spacelab 2*. Washington, D.C.: Government Printing Office, 1985.
Spacelab 2 was actually the third mission flown by this scientific research facility. Delays in the development of some of its equipment caused its flight to be switched with the Spacelab 3 mission. Spacelab 2, the first pallet-only mission, was carried into orbit aboard *Challenger* in July, 1985. It consisted of thirteen experiments in six scientific disciplines: solar physics, atmospheric physics, plasma physics, high-energy astrophysics, technology research, and life sciences. This work previews the flight, with emphasis on the experiments. Each is detailed, including the identification number, sponsor, and principal investigator's name and affiliation, and is accompanied by color photographs and drawings.

_____. *Spacelab Mission 2 Experiment Descriptions*. 2d ed. Washington, D.C.: Government Printing Office, 1982.
NASA's official guide to the experiments carried aboard Spacelab 2 contains very detailed information about each experiment. In addition to the discussion of the test, the experimental apparatus is detailed, including a diagram of the equipment and its physical dimensions and characteristics. There is a line drawing of the Spacelab as it is seen in the Space Shuttle's payload bay. The location of each of the experiments is included.

_____. *Spacelab 3*. Washington, D.C.: Government Printing Office, 1984.
Spacelab 3 was carried into orbit aboard the Space Shuttle *Challenger* in April,
1985. It consisted of a long module and Mission Peculiar Equipment Support
Structure (MPESS), which carried the fifteen investigations in five scientific
disciplines: materials sciences, life sciences, fluid mechanics, atmospheric
science, and astronomy. This booklet discusses the mission and its flight crew,
including the two payload specialists and their backups. Each of the experiments is detailed, including the identification number, sponsor, and principal
investigator's name and affiliation, and is accompanied by color photographs
and drawings.

_____. *Spacelab Mission 3 Experiment Descriptions*. Washington, D.C.:
Government Printing Office, 1982.
NASA's official guide to the experiments carried aboard Spacelab 3 contains
very detailed information about each experiment. In addition to the discussion
of the test, the experimental apparatus is detailed, including a diagram of the
equipment and its physical dimensions and characteristics. There is a line
drawing of the Spacelab as it is seen in the Space Shuttle's payload bay. The
location of each of the experiments is included.

_____. *The Space Station: A Description of the Configuration Established
at the Systems Requirements Review (SRR)*. Washington, D.C.: Government
Printing Office, 1986.
This work takes a brief yet in-depth look at the planned space station *Freedom*.
In response to President Ronald Reagan's 1984 commitment to develop a
permanently manned space station within a decade, NASA undertook an
examination of the many missions that a space station might carry out, and of
the many ways in which the station might be configured. This effort reached
a major milestone in 1986, called the Systems Requirements Review (SRR).
SRR decisions established the "baseline" configuration for *Freedom*. The report
details this configuration, as well as the process which derived it. There are
many pages of black-and-white photographs and line drawings. There is a chart
depicting the assembly sequence for *Freedom*. There is also a brief history of
the space station concept.

_____. *Space Station Development Plan Submitted to the Committee on
Science, Space, and Technology, U.S. House of Representatives*. Washington,
D.C.: Government Printing Office, 1987.
This plan for the development of a permanently manned space station was
submitted by NASA in response to a request by the committee. The plan
submitted was based on internal planning and on budgetary considerations.
Included in the plan are program objectives and requirements, development
strategy, management approach, and program schedule. The work reads like

most government documents, but the reader can get an idea of the work involved in getting a program of this magnitude off the ground. There are numerous line drawings and charts, a list of reference documents, and a glossary of acronyms and abbreviations. One large appendix details the space station's components and the auxiliary equipment necessary to run it.

_____. *Space Station Reference Configuration Description.* Washington, D.C.: Government Printing Office, 1984.
In order for potential contractors to bid on a particular project, they must have some information about the item on which they will be bidding. This document presents such a guideline for the space station *Freedom.* The information was generated to provide a focal point for the definition and assessment of program requirements, establish a basis for estimating program cost, and define a reference configuration in sufficient detail to allow its inclusion in the definition phase of the program. This is the first official look at how the space station will appear in orbit during each phase of construction. It details the manned core, unmanned platforms, payload accommodations, crew accommodations, and related subsystems. There are dozens of line drawings, a bibliography, and an evaluation of the assembly operations crew time lines.

_____. *Space Transportation System and Associated Payloads: Glossary, Acronyms, and Abbreviations.* Washington, D.C.: National Technical Information Service, 1985.
In the fast-paced world of space travel, it has become necessary to develop a large set of new words and abbreviations. At the moment that the solid rocket boosters (SRBs) expend their fuel and are jettisoned, a lot can happen and it can happen rapidly. Since the Space Shuttle is traveling at about five times the speed of sound when this occurs, it is important to say things in a swift, compact, and clearly understood manner. Instead of the flight controllers reporting, "Everything looks fine right now and your solid rocket boosters are being separated at this point in the flight," they say, "Go at SRB sep." This book, which NASA tries to update regularly (although these updates are not published very often), contains an alphabetical listing of these special words. The glossary contains definitions of some of the terms commonly used in conjunction with the Shuttle and its payloads. It is a very good reference, especially when used in conjunction with some of the more technical documents.

_____. *STS-1 Orbiter Final Mission Report.* Washington, D.C.: Government Printing Office, 1981.
This is the official record of the first Space Shuttle mission, on April 12, 1981. Since this was a test flight, a great deal of information was collected on all of the Shuttle's systems. This report details each of the tests and measurements

made during and after the flight. Nearly every minute of the two-day mission is chronicled. There is a report by the crew as to the effectiveness of preflight training and the handling of *Columbia*. There is a complete biomedical, trajectory, and flight control evaluation. A summary of anomalies and the corrective action taken is included. There are a number of black-and-white photographs, line drawings, charts, and tables.

_____. *STS Orbiter Mission Report: STS-2 Through STS-4*. 3 vols. Washington, D.C.: Government Printing Office, 1981-1982.
These are the official reports for the final three missions of *Columbia* during the Orbiter Flight Test (OFT) program. As with the report on the first flight (see *STS-1 Orbiter Final Mission Report*, cited above) the performance of each of the vehicle's main systems—orbiter, solid rocket motors, and external tank—is detailed. In addition, the orbiter's major subsystems are discussed. There is a report by the individual crews as to the effectiveness of preflight training and the handling of the vehicle. There is a complete biomedical, trajectory, and flight control evaluation. A complete anomaly summary, with the corrective action taken, is included. Finally, there are a number of black-and-white photographs, line drawings, charts, and tables.

_____. *STS Space Shuttle Program Mission Report: STS-5 Through STS-7*. 3 vols. Washington, D.C.: Government Printing Office, 1982-1983.
Beginning with *Columbia*'s first operational flight (STS-5) and continuing through *Challenger*'s first two missions (STS-6 and STS-7), mission reports contained much less information. Fewer tests on orbiter subsystems were being conducted and, since commercial and scientific payloads were now being carried, much of the emphasis switched to the cargo and its support equipment. A list of mission objectives and a summary of the flight are given. There is an evaluation of the major Shuttle components, as well as crew equipment assessment. There are very few black-and-white photographs, line drawings, tables, and charts.

_____. *STS National Space Transportation Systems Program Mission Report: STS-8 Through STS-35*. 31 vols. Washington, D.C.: Government Printing Office, 1983-1991.
As Space Shuttle flights became more and more routine, fewer mission objectives relating to the measurement of subsystem performance were necessary. Eventually, these mission reports were reduced to a summary of the flight, sequence of events, vehicle assessment, remote manipulator system operations, payloads and experiments, detailed test objectives, detailed secondary objectives, and anomalies. Line drawings and black-and-white photographs became scarcer, and there were only a few necessary tables and charts. These reports do detail the mission and provide valuable information about each flight.

Manned Programs

General Studies

Allen, Joseph P., with Russell Martin. *Entering Space.* New York: Stewart, Tabori & Chang, 1984.
The story of an astronaut's journey in space, told in conjunction with a study of the U.S. exploration of space. This work is filled with colorful words and spectacular photographs of space travel from the ground up, and back again. There are hundreds of color photographs taken during the manned Gemini, Apollo, Skylab, Apollo Soyuz, and Space Shuttle programs, as well as those shots of our neighbors in the solar system taken from unmanned probes. The spacecraft, launch vehicles, spacefarers, and their equipment are discussed in some detail, although primarily from the perspective of a single trip into orbit and back again. There is a very real sense of "being there" as Astronaut Allen describes his feelings during the various phases of flight. Contains a brief bibliography and an index.

Baker, David. *The Rocket: The History and Development of Rocket and Missile Technology.* New York: Crown, 1978.
This large, "coffee-table" book covers the technological and political development of manned and unmanned missiles and rockets. It provides a complete history of solid and liquid propulsion systems from fire-sticks to moon rockets. Propulsion systems are examined for their advantages and faults, and how they influence the design of the overall vehicle. The ancestry of U.S. and Soviet launch vehicles is traced to the war machines from which they were derived, all the way back to their common grandparent, the German *Vergeltungswaffe Zwei*, or V-2. The author concludes the work with a forecast about future vehicles, including reusable, atomic-powered, and interplanetary launch vehicles. A compendium of launch vehicles and ballistic missiles, as well as rocket-powered aircraft, is provided. Each vehicle is detailed with information about its origin, configuration, development and flight history, and descendants. There is a silhouette of the vehicle, scaled for comparison with the others in the compendium. Rocket-powered aircraft, from the Messerschmitt Me-163 of World War II Germany to the Space Shuttle, are discussed. Hundreds of color and black-and-white photographs and illustrations enhance the comprehensive text. There are tables of data on space launch vehicles; research rockets; strategic and tactical ballistic missiles; and antiballistic, air-to-ground, surface-to-air, air-to-air, antiship, antisubmarine, and anti-armor missiles. Includes an index and a bibliography.

Bilstein, Roger E. *Orders of Magnitude: A History of the NACA and NASA, 1915-1990*. Washington, D.C.: Government Printing Office, 1989.
This is the third edition of the concise history of the National Advisory Committee for Aeronautics (NACA) and its successor agency, the National Aeronautics and Space Administration (NASA). This edition was published to coincide with the twentieth-anniversary celebration of the flight of Apollo 11. The author traces the history of the NACA and NASA in concise chapters divided into chronological eras. This is an interesting look at these aerospace pioneers and some of the programs they developed to study air and space phenomena. There are dozens of black-and-white photographs and an index.

Bodechtel, Johann, and Hans-Günter Gieroff-Emden. *The Earth from Space*. New York: Arco, 1974.
This is a fine collection of color photographs of Earth taken by manned and unmanned spacecraft. It discusses the history of space photography from the first crude black-and-white image transmitted from the orbiting Explorer 6 satellite in 1959 through the long-distance portraits taken by the crew of Apollo 17 as they journeyed from the Moon. The technical aspects of space photography are presented, including how many of the photographs were taken and what they reveal.

Bond, Peter. *Heroes in Space: From Gagarin to Challenger*. Oxford, England: Basil Blackwell, 1987.
This is one of the first books to cover the astronauts and cosmonauts of the first quarter century of the space age. It is also the story of the two countries' manned space programs. Each mission is discussed, with the more notable ones getting the most coverage. The author, on occasion, gets carried away with his story, but, for the most part, it is an interesting book. There are several black-and-white photographs, an index, and a brief bibliography.

Cassutt, Michael. *Who's Who in Space (The First Twenty-five Years)*. Boston: G. K. Hall, 1987.
While a lot has been written about the U.S. astronauts and Soviet cosmonauts, there are few books that include the lesser known ones. This work not only covers them, it does so in great detail. There is an individual biography for each of the astronauts of the Mercury, Gemini, Apollo, Skylab, Apollo Soyuz, and Space Shuttle programs. In addition, the author details the lives of the X-15, X-20, and Manned Orbiting Laboratory projects, as well as the civilian and military Shuttle payload specialists. A black-and-white photograph accompanies each biography. There is a chronological log of the astronauts and cosmonauts, in the order in which they made their first spaceflight, and a log of the manned spaceflights and X-15 spaceflights. There is an index for cross-referencing.

DeWaard, E. John, and Nancy DeWaard. *History of NASA: America's Voyage to the Stars.* New York: Exeter Books, 1984.
This is a brief, photo-filled look at NASA's programs more than it is a look at NASA itself. Each of the manned and unmanned programs, including Mercury, Gemini, Apollo, Skylab, the Space Shuttle, Voyager, and Viking, is discussed in general. There is very little "new" information provided. There are dozens of color and black-and-white photographs which, in themselves, make the book worthwhile. An index is included.

Furniss, Tim. *Manned Spaceflight Log.* London: Jane's, 1983.
This work covers the manned spaceflights of the Soviet Union and the United States from 1961 through 1986. A synopsis of each mission is given, along with pertinent data (date, crew, site, recovery, duration, spacecraft weight, and so forth) and several black-and-white photographs. The Mercury, Gemini, Apollo, Skylab, Apollo Soyuz, and Space Shuttle flights are listed chronologically. Included are the thirteen flights of the X-15 research aircraft which exceeded the fifty-mile altitude necessary to qualify its pilot as an astronaut under Air Force rules. There are astronaut photographs and, in the appendices, listings of space seniority and the current status of the astronaut and cosmonaut classes.

_____. *Space Flight: The Records.* London: Guiness Books, 1985.
Do you know the first manned spaceflight to be curtailed? It was Gemini V, which landed one orbit early to miss hurricane Betsy. Were you aware that the first spaceflight with more than one fifty-year-old person on board was that of STS 51-B/Spacelab 3, in April, 1985? These and dozens of other interesting and significant—or not so significant—facts are covered in this work. The first part of the book is a "diary" of manned spaceflight, listing each of the missions of the United States and Soviet Union. There is a chapter on manned spaceflight "firsts," and one on the manned space machines. Basic biographical information on each of the space travelers is given, accompanied by the person's photograph. The major information section is last and includes tables on manned spaceflight duration, space seniority, space experience, lunar spacemen, spacewalks, astroflights of the X-15, all known cosmonauts, NASA astronauts, Space Shuttle passengers, NASA flight crew selections, and the Space Shuttle schedule. There are hundreds of black-and-white photographs, a glossary of terms, and an index.

Hall, Al, ed. *Petersen's Book of Man in Space.* 5 vols. Los Angeles: Petersen, 1974.
This is a very colorful presentation of the history of spaceflight from the early pioneers through the last Apollo flight. There are hundreds of color and black-and-white photographs and drawings. The focus of this work is on the U.S.

manned programs, perhaps because of the abundance of available photographs. The text is concise and enhances the pictures, although they really do not need enhancement. All of the spacecraft and launch vehicles of the U.S. programs are covered, as are the contributions of the pioneers of spaceflight and the astronauts.

Kaplan, Judith, and Robert Muniz. *Space Patches from Mercury to the Space Shuttle*. New York: Sterling, 1986, rev. ed. 1988.
This work, written and published by one of the manufacturers and distributors of cloth patches and vinyl decals, discusses the emblems' design by the astronaut crews and other participants in space programs. Overall, the work has been well researched and contains many interesting facts about the origins of these patches. Few people realize how the practice of designing crew patches began. The authors discuss Gemini V's "covered wagon" patch, the first ever flown, and the story behind the hidden "8 Days or Bust." The only major error concerns the Apollo 1 patch. It is an error that did not originate with this book but is perpetuated by reference to the story of the patch's design. The crew of Apollo 1, officially known as Apollo 204, were killed in a fire that swept through their command module during a ground test. According to the authors, the crew patch has a black overlock border "as a sign of mourning for the lost crew." The patch does have this black border, but if one looks carefully at color photographs or films of the crew, the black border can be seen on the patch they wear. Unless someone went back and airbrushed black borders on these prints, the crew must have been wearing the black-bordered patches before the accident. The book is filled with color photographs of the patches from various manned and unmanned missions, as well as space centers and other miscellaneous events. There is an appendix listing the U.S. manned flights and an index.

Kelley, Kevin W., ed. *The Home Planet*. Reading, Mass.: Addison-Wesley, 1988.
This is a large-format, "coffee-table" book of the finest photographs ever taken of Earth from space. These images are combined with the thoughts of the astronauts who snapped the pictures as they whirled around Earth or traveled to the Moon. The author looked at every medium- and large-format handheld image in the NASA archives, as well as every available image in the Soviet archives. There are images taken from as many parts of the globe as possible. Each was selected for its beauty first. There are also images of the spacecraft and some of the spacewalking astronauts and cosmonauts. The comments made by the spacefarers are in their native language and translated into English. They combine with the photographs to create a remarkable work of art. There is an appendix detailing each of the scenes captured by the cameras, as well as a bibliography of source notes.

Kerrod, Robin. *The Illustrated History of NASA*. New York: Gallery Books, 1986. One of the better books about the manned and unmanned space programs undertaken by NASA, this work was written shortly after the *Challenger* accident. Although the book mainly discusses the programs of NASA, there is one chapter devoted to NASA and its facilities throughout the United States. There are hundreds of color and black-and-white photographs. An appendix lists some of the highlights of NASA's first quarter century in chronological order. An epilogue is devoted to the STS 51-L mission, and there is an index.

Mason, Robert Grant, ed. *Life in Space*. Alexandria, Va.: Time-Life Books, 1983. The editors of *Life* magazine have sifted through hundreds of NASA's and their own photographs taken during the first twenty-five years of the space age. What has resulted is a superb collection of photographs of each U.S. manned spaceflight, from Alan Shepard's suborbital hop in *Freedom 7* through the STS-6 Space Shuttle mission. Throughout the work are breathtaking color and startling black-and-white photographs. The major characters in the book are, of course, the astronauts who flew the missions. Interestingly enough, the book ends with the flight of the last all-male crew. The astronauts' families are included in this historical portrait. The unmanned probes to the planets are highlighted in the final section of the book.

U.S. House of Representatives. *United States Civilian Space Programs 1958-1978*. Vol. 1. Washington, D.C.: Government Printing Office, 1981. In a very concise report, the Committee on Space Science and Applications has compiled data on all U.S. space activity during its first two decades. After a brief introduction and summary chapter, the volume is divided into fourteen additional sections. The second chapter deals with the space-related issues under consideration by Congress. The remaining sections cover the history of NASA and its relationship to U.S. space policy, NASA facilities and tracking systems, launch vehicles and propulsion, manned spaceflight through 1975, the Space Transportation System, space life sciences, space science programs, materials processing in space, international cooperation in space, interagency and non-NASA governmental space activities, industrial and university support for NASA, space program benefits, and selected future space programs. Appendices contain Department of Defense manned spaceflight plans, NASA funding history, international space agreements, texts of President Jimmy Carter's space directives, documents relating to the legal aspects of the Space Shuttle, major U.S. space organizations, a master log of U.S. spaceflights, and a table of U.S. space orbital payloads by mission from 1957 through 1979.

Von Braun, Wernher, and Frederick I. Ordway III. *History of Rocketry and Space Travel*. 3d rev. ed. New York: Thomas Y. Crowell, 1975.

This is the story of the exploration of space from the earliest experiments with rocketry to the final flight of the Skylab program. Hundreds of experts on every aspect of this broad field contributed to the work. Most of the programs of the United States, the Soviet Union, and the rest of the nations engaged in space exploration at that time are detailed, both descriptively and with black-and-white and color photographs. It is one of the best references on the subject. The book contains a large, chapter-by-chapter bibliography. The authors finish their discussion of the space programs with a look at the future, including the Space Transportation System.

Ward, Robinson J., Jr. *The Light Stuff: Space Humor—From Sputnik to Shuttle.* Huntsville, Ala.: Jester Books, 1982.
Some of the lighter moments in an otherwise harrowing business are presented in this compendium of anecdotes from the space age. This is not a book for the "serious" researcher, but the humorous side of space exploration is revealed by what Walter Cronkite in his introduction calls "the era's choicest anecdotes, its bons mots, putdowns, puns, and pranks." The book also contains some cartoons and a reproduction of the front page from the November 4, 1981, edition of *The Detroit News.* The headline reads, "*Columbia* Does Encore." The Shuttle, however, had not been launched.

Yenne, Bill. *The Astronauts: The First Twenty-five Years of Manned Space Flight.* New York: Exeter Books, 1986.
This book discusses the astronauts and cosmonauts who flew into space during the first quarter century of manned spaceflight. Or, more correctly, it discusses the manned flights of the United States and Soviet Union and lists the crew members. There is very little biographical information about the astronauts, except for where a crew member was born or when. There are scores of color and black-and-white photographs of the astronauts, most of them taken during flight. There is also an index.

Research Aircraft

Anderson, Fred. *Northrop: An Aeronautical History.* Los Angeles: Northrop Corp., 1976.
This book relates the story of Northrop Corporation from 1939 through 1976. This giant of aircraft design and construction was created in a leased Hawthorne, California, hotel in August, 1939, by engineer John K. Northrop. The author leads the reader through Northrop's illustrative history from pre-World War II N-3PB Patrol Bombers to the F-18 Navy Air Combat Fighter of today. Each craft is detailed in configuration and contribution to aviation history. There are numerous black-and-white photographs. Research aircraft, the

forerunners of the Space Shuttle, are discussed. These include the X-4, and the M2F2, M2F3, and HL-10 lifting bodies. Northrop also makes the F-5 fighter and its derivative, the T-38 Talon, used as a training aircraft by astronauts.

Guenther, Ben, and Jay Miller. *Bell X-1 Variants.* Arlington, Tex.: Aerofax, 1989.
The Bell X-1, with pilot Chuck Yeager on board, became the first aircraft to break the sound barrier, doing so on October 14, 1947. This "Datagraph" contains hundreds of color and black-and-white photographs and drawings of the original X-1 (there were three of them), as well as its descendants. The X-1 flew a total of 157 flights. Three second-generation aircraft were built, the X-1A, X-1B, and X-1D. The X-1C was ordered but later was canceled prior to construction. The X-1D made only one flight, while the other two completed a total of fifty-two flights. The third generation, the X-1E, was created by modification to the number two X-1. It made twenty-six test flights and now resides on a pedestal in front of NASA's Ames Dryden Flight Research Center, where all of the X-1 flights were conducted. There are a number of rare shots of the X-1's, many close-ups, and several in-flight pictures. In addition to the description of the aircraft, the authors present a history of these aviation pioneers.

Guenther, Ben, Jay Miller, and Terry Panopalis. *North American X-15/X-15A-2.* Arlington, Tex.: Aerofax, 1985.
The first true "spaceplane" was the X-15. It was carried to its test altitude under the right-hand wing of a Boeing B-52. Once released, its large XLR99 powerplant (the first twenty-five flights used two XLR11 engines, similar to the one used in the X-1, in tandem), propelled the craft. During the 199 flights, the three X-15's set many speed and altitude records. The fastest speed attained by an X-15 was 4,534 miles per hour, and the highest altitude was 354,200 feet (about 67 miles). The X-15 flew above the 50-mile mark on thirteen occasions, qualifying eight of its pilots for astronaut wings, including future Space Shuttle commander Joe Engle. One pilot would have to wait until he joined NASA to qualify. He was Neil Armstrong. The book chronicles the X-15 from its initial design to its last flight. Of the three X-15's, number three was destroyed in a fatal crash; number two was damaged on landing, converted into the X-15A-2, and now is on permanent display at Wright-Patterson Air Force Base, Ohio. The first X-15 is permanently displayed in the main hall of the National Air and Space Museum. Like the other "Datagraphs," this work is filled with color and black-and-white photographs and illustrations.

Hallion, Richard. *On the Frontier: Flight Research at Dryden, 1946-1981.* Washington, D.C.: Government Printing Office, 1984.

This is one of the titles in the NASA History Series, which provide an official look at the space agency, its programs and facilities. Just a bit northeast of Los Angeles lies a desert region just perfect for testing aircraft. In the southwest corner of the Mojave Desert is the Antelope Valley, a mecca for the aerospace industry. That is where the United States placed its Edwards Air Force Base, and that is where, in 1946, the National Advisory Committee for Aeronautics (NACA) sent a group of engineers and technicians to assist in a supersonic test program. The NACA High-Speed Flight Research Station became the NACA High-Speed Flight Station in 1954. With the coming of NASA, the station was redesignated the NASA Flight Research Center in 1959. In 1976, NASA renamed it the Hugh L. Dryden Flight Research Center. This is the story of the center and the flight testing which occurred there during its first thirty-five years. The information is presented in chronological order and covers such noted aerospace craft as the X-1, X-15, HL-10, X-24A, X-24B, and the Space Shuttle. Also detailed is the research which assisted the development of the Gemini and Apollo spacecraft. There are many black-and-white photographs and line drawings, an index, and an impressive bibliography. Appendices include program flight chronologies on the X-1, D-558, X-2, X-3, X-4, X-5, XF-92A, X-15, lifting bodies, XB-70A, and Space Shuttle approach and landing test program.

_____. *Supersonic Flight: Breaking the Sound Barrier and Beyond*. New York: Macmillan, 1972.
This is the history of the two research aircraft families—the Bell X-1 and the Douglas D-558. It chronicles the two craft from the first attempts at breaking the sound barrier to the end of their respective programs. Much has been written about the X-1, but this is perhaps the best source of information about the D-558-I *Skystreak* and the D-558-II *Skyrocket*. Technical specifications are given for all members of both families, as well as their flight test records. There are numerous black-and-white photographs and drawings, and an index.

Hartman, Edwin P. *Adventures in Research: A History of Ames Research Center, 1940-1965*. Washington, D.C.: National Technical Information Service, 1970.
This is one of the titles in the NASA History Series. It discusses the Ames Research Center, located near San Francisco, California. Ames was established at its present location in 1940, because of ready electric power availability, a climate ideal for flight research (when the fog lifts), a nearby university community, and an urgent need for increasing the United States' aeronautical research capability. It is named for the late Dr. Joseph S. Ames, Chairman of NASA's predecessor organization, the National Advisory Committee for Aeronautics. The facility is best known for its many wind tunnels, but it also houses laboratory facilities for research and technology development in aeronautics, space science, life science, spacecraft missions, and applications of new

science and technology from the space program to contemporary national needs. There are numerous black-and-white photographs, an index, and an impressive bibliography of resources.

Lewis, Richard. "The Space Shuttle." In *The Illustrated Encyclopedia of Space Technology: A Comprehensive History of Space Exploration*, by Kenneth Gatland et al. New York: Harmony Books, 1981.
This section in the book takes a brief historical look at the Space Transportation System and the research aircraft which helped to develop the technology to make the Shuttle possible. Some of these early winged spacecraft and lifting bodies—the X-15, X-24A, X-24B, HL-10, M2F2, and M2F3—are pictured. There are color cutaway diagrams of the Space Shuttle's major systems: the orbiter, solid rocket boosters, and external tank. Some early designs of the Shuttle are included. There are color and black-and-white photographs and drawings. Also included are a chronology of the major space events since Sputnik 1, a glossary of terms, and an index.

Miller, Jay. *The X-Planes: X-1 to X-31*. Arlington, Tex.: Aerofax, 1988.
Each of the experimental aircraft, and its derivatives, is chronicled in this pictorial history. The aircraft, including the X-1 family, X-2, X-3, X-4, X-11, X-12, X-15, X-20 Dyna-Soar, X-23A PRIME, X-24A, and X-24B, are detailed. Specifications relating to airframe and powerplant, as well as a complete flight record, are provided. There are dozens of black-and-white photographs and drawings. Appendices detail the launch aircraft and chase planes, and discuss two "famous" problems: the Ulmer leather gasket problem of the X-1A, and the inertial coupling phenomenon of the X-2. There is an index, a list of abbreviations, a bibliography of books and manuscripts, and a bibliography of magazines and miscellany. This is one of the finest collections of data on these important research vehicles.

Smith, Mervyn. *An Illustrated History of Space Shuttle: U.S. Winged Spacecraft, X-15 to Orbiter*. Newbury Park, Calif.: Haynes, 1985.
This work traces the history of the Space Shuttle orbiter and the research aircraft from which it was derived. Each of these ancestors contributed in some way or another to the final design of the orbiter. Included in the discussions are the X-1 series, X-2, X-3, X-20, X-24A, X-24B, HL-10, D-558-I, D-558-II, M2F2, M2F3, and the X-15. There are hundreds of color and black-and-white photographs of these pioneers, as well as the pioneers who flew them. Seven appendices chronicle the flight programs of the X-15, M2F2, HL-10, X-24A, M2F3, X-24B, and the Space Shuttle (through STS 51-C). This is one of the best collections of information on the early research aircraft and lifting bodies.

Taylor, L. B., Jr. *Space Shuttle*. New York: Thomas Y. Crowell, 1979.
This is a preview of the Space Transportation System and the plans for making it the main means of taking U.S. (and some foreign) payloads into space. It also discusses the Space Shuttle's potential for the industrialization and colonization of space. The author details the development and testing of the system, how other nations are involved in the program, and the criticism and benefits of a reusable spacecraft. There are black-and-white photographs and line drawings, and a bibliography.

U.S. General Accounting Office. *A Technology Development and Demonstration Program to Build the X-30*. Washington, D.C.: Stackpole Books, 1988.
The chairman of the Senate Committee on Commerce, Science, and Transportation asked the GAO to assess the cost, schedule, and performance of several NASA projects. This work is the report of their findings on the National Aero Space Plane program, a technology development and demonstration program to build and test the X-30 experimental flight vehicle. The X-30 is designed to take off horizontally from a conventional runway, reach hypersonic speeds up to twenty-five times the speed of sound, attain low Earth orbit, and return to land on a conventional runway. The report provides a general overview of the program, including its objectives, scope, and methodology. There are spacecraft configuration drawings and information relating to cost, schedule, and performance. A chronology of the project, through the date of the report, is presented. There is a glossary of terms used. This is a look at the program from a purely financial point of view.

U.S. House of Representatives. *United States Civilian Space Programs 1958-1978*. Vol. 1. Washington, D.C.: Government Printing Office, 1981.
In a very concise report, the Committee on Space Science and Applications has compiled data on all U.S. space activity during its first two decades. After a brief introduction and summary chapter, the volume is divided into fourteen additional sections. The second chapter deals with the space-related issues under consideration by Congress. The remaining sections cover the history of NASA and its relationship to U.S. space policy, NASA facilities and tracking systems, launch vehicles and propulsion, manned spaceflight through 1975, the Space Transportation System, space life sciences, space science programs, materials processing in space, international cooperation in space, interagency and non-NASA governmental space activities, industrial and university support for NASA, space program benefits, and selected future space programs. Appendices contain Department of Defense manned spaceflight plans, NASA funding history, international space agreements, texts of President Jimmy Carter's space directives, documents relating to the legal aspects of the Space Shuttle, major U.S. space organizations, a master log of U.S. spaceflights, and a table of U.S. space orbital payloads by mission from 1957 through 1979.

Wolfe, Tom. *The Right Stuff.* New York: Farrar, Straus & Giroux, 1979.
A very interesting book about the team of men who flew in Project Mercury and about Chuck Yeager, the "loner" of X-1 fame. Wolfe has taken the stories of these men and intertwined them for an exciting and romantic tale of high flight. There are a great number of stories told by the astronauts and related in this book, which the reader will find too fantastic to believe. They really did happen—or, at least, the characters portrayed in this work say they did. It also tells of the women who loved the men, and who supported them, waited for them, and in some cases mourned their demise. For those who want to know more about the Mercury Seven and Chuck Yeager, this book is highly recommended. The film adaptation does not accurately portray the incidents from the book.

Yeager, General Chuck, and Leo Janos. *Yeager: An Autobiography.* New York: Bantam Books, 1985.
Chuck Yeager was a World War II ace who loved to do nothing more than fly. His incredible record during the war was surpassed only by his records as a test pilot. He was the first person to fly faster than the speed of sound, and he did his best to break his own records when he could. He was first a professional, however; he did not take chances for the sake of glory. This is his story, and if he embellishes a little, that's all right; he has earned it. It is also the story of his two loves: his wife, Glennis, and the aircraft he flew. There are several black-and-white photographs and an index.

Mercury

Aldrin, Buzz, and Malcolm McConnell. "Lead-Footed Mercury." In *Men from Earth*. New York: Bantam Books, 1989.
Aldrin, the second man to walk on the Moon, writes a brief history of the U.S. manned space program with coverage of Project Mercury, but with emphasis on his own Gemini XII and Apollo 11 flights. He discusses the manned programs leading to Apollo with an insider's knowledge. The book is well written and provides the reader with some information obtainable nowhere else. His description of his Gemini spacewalks and the lunar landing and subsequent moonwalk is quite vivid. The reader can almost picture the events as if he were there when they happened. There are black-and-white photographs and an extensive bibliography.

Allen, Joseph P., with Russell Martin. *Entering Space*. New York: Stewart, Tabori & Chang, 1984.
The story of an astronaut's journey in space, told in conjunction with a study of the U.S. exploration of space. This work is filled with colorful words and

spectacular photographs of space travel from the ground up, and back again. There are hundreds of color photographs taken during the manned Gemini, Apollo, Skylab, Apollo Soyuz, and Space Shuttle programs, as well as those shots of our neighbors in the solar system taken from unmanned probes. The spacecraft, launch vehicles, spacefarers, and their equipment are discussed in some detail, although primarily from the perspective of a single trip into orbit and back again. The is a very real sense of "being there" as Astronaut Allen describes his feelings during the various phases of flight. Contains a brief bibliography and an index.

Anderson, Sally. *Final Report: Mercury/Atlas Launch Vehicle Program.* El Segundo, Calif.: Aerospace Corp., 1963.
A comprehensive report summarizing the management techniques employed in the development, systems test, and launching of the Mercury-Atlas launch vehicle in support of Project Mercury. The vehicle is discussed in great detail, including sections on the airframe/structures, engines, vehicle propulsion systems, flight control systems, instrumentation, abort sensing and implementation system, and propellant delivery systems. Each section contains line drawings, tables, and charts, as well as references and a glossary of definitions. Very little is presented in overly technical language. This is the most informative book available on this vehicle. The researcher will find it an invaluable reference, although it will probably have to be obtained directly from NASA.

Bergwin, Clyde R., and William T. Coleman. *Animal Astronauts: They Opened the Way to the Stars.* Englewood Cliffs, N.J.: Prentice-Hall, 1963.
Man was not the first of God's creatures to venture into space. In fact, he was one of the last. Dogs, monkeys, mice, rats, chimpanzees, insects, and even pigs were lofted into the heavens atop the future man-carriers. The first individual reported to have been placed into Earth orbit was a dog named Laika. This book looks at the suborbital and orbital flights of the United States' animal pioneers. The two most famous were chimpanzees. Ham (named for the Holloman Aerospace Medical Center, New Mexico) made a successful suborbital flight in a Mercury spacecraft on January 31, 1961. Enos, a forty-two-pound chimpanzee, completed the first orbital flight of a Mercury spacecraft on November 29, 1961, after two orbits. This is an interesting book about some very important but often overlooked characters in the history of space exploration.

Booker, Peter, Gerald Frewer, and Geoffrey Pardoe. *Project Apollo: The Way to the Moon.* New York: American Elsevier, 1970.
The authors write about the efforts to place men on the moon, as well as the Mercury and Gemini programs, which paved the way for Apollo. They look at the spacecraft, launch vehicles, flights, and astronauts involved. They also

discuss the problems and accomplishments of each. Since the book is broad in coverage, there is very little detail on individual flights. The book is illustrated with black-and-white photographs and line drawings.

Boynton, John H., ed. *First United States Manned Three-Pass Orbital Mission (Mercury-Atlas 6, Spacecraft 13): Part I— Description and Performance Analysis.* Washington, D.C.: National Technical Information Service, 1964.
This is part 1 of the two-volume official NASA report on the flight of Mercury-Atlas 6 with astronaut John Glenn. The contents were prepared by a flight evaluation team. A description of the space vehicle and launch vehicle is presented, detailing each of the major systems as configured for the mission. The performance of these systems is given in the form of charts and tables. Each phase of the mission operation is described: prelaunch, including astronaut training and spacecraft and launch vehicle preparation; launch operations; flight-control operations; and recovery operations. There is an aeromedical analysis of the astronaut and a description of pilot flight activities. The sequence of events is enumerated along with trajectory data. Black-and-white photographs, line drawings, and a brief reference list are included.

_____, ed. *Second United States Manned Three-Pass Orbital Mission (Mercury-Atlas 7, Spacecraft 18).* Washington, D.C.: Government Printing Office, 1967.
This is the first of two official NASA reports on the flight of Mercury-Atlas 7 with astronaut Scott Carpenter. The contents were prepared by a flight evaluation team and are more detailed than those of the other report. A description of the space vehicle and launch vehicle is presented, detailing each of the major systems as configured for the mission. The performance of these systems is given in the form of charts and tables. Each phase of the mission operation is described: prelaunch, including astronaut training and spacecraft and launch vehicle preparation; launch operations; flight-control operations; and recovery operations. There is an aeromedical analysis of the astronaut and a description of pilot flight activities. The sequence of events is enumerated along with trajectory data. There is a complete transcript of the air-to-ground communications between the astronaut and tracking stations. Black-and-white photographs, line drawings, and a brief reference list are included in each section of the work.

_____, ed. *First U.S. Manned Six-Pass Orbital Mission (Mercury-Atlas 8, Spacecraft 16).* Washington, D.C.: National Technical Information Service, 1968.
This is the first of two official NASA reports on the flight of Mercury-Atlas 8 with astronaut Wally Schirra. The contents were prepared by a flight evaluation team and are more detailed than those of the other report. A description

of the space vehicle and launch vehicle is presented, detailing each of the major systems as configured for the mission. The performance of these systems is given in the form of charts and tables. Each phase of the mission operation is described: prelaunch, including astronaut training and spacecraft and launch vehicle preparation; launch operations; flight-control operations; and recovery operations. There is an aeromedical analysis of the astronaut and a description of pilot flight activities. The sequence of events is enumerated, along with trajectory data. There is a complete transcript of the air-to-ground communications between the astronaut and tracking stations. Black-and-white photographs, line drawings, and a brief reference list are included in each section of the work.

Carpenter, M. Scott, et al. *We Seven, by the Astronauts Themselves.* New York: Simon & Schuster, 1962.
The seven Mercury astronauts write about the man-in-space program with a little help from the editors of *Life* magazine. The main focus is on John Glenn's flight in Mercury-Atlas 6. He discusses the mission in some detail, while the others talk about their roles in the flight. Some of the chapters are written by one, while many are a team effort, much like Project Mercury itself. The stories are personal narratives of many aspects of the project, including the spacecraft and the flights that preceded Glenn's. Scott Carpenter writes the closing chapter about his Mercury-Atlas 7 flight, which confirmed the feasibility of placing a man in orbit. There are many black-and-white photographs and an index. It would be safe to presume that the astronauts did not sit down at the typewriter to compose this work, but rather told their stories to writers. The end product does, however, give an introspective look at the pioneers of manned spaceflight.

Chapman, John L. *Atlas: The Story of a Missile.* New York: Harper & Brothers, 1960.
This is the "biography" of the United States' premier intercontinental ballistic missile, which would soon be used to put a man into orbit. Although the information in this work is very dated and limited to what the Air Force would reveal, it does give an insight into the creation of a missile. The text is well written and not at all technical. If one compares the data about the Atlas in this book with later works on the missile, it is surprising how much was available to the writer. The major attraction of this publication is that it is contemporaneous with the Atlas program.

Collins, Michael. *Liftoff: The Story of America's Adventure in Space.* New York: Grove Press, 1988.
Collins takes a look at Project Mercury in this personal view of the U.S. manned space program. He talks about the seven original astronauts and some

of the difficulties they encountered. According to Collins, federal prison specifications require a minimum cell space of 475 cubic feet per inmate. The Mercury spacecraft had a habitable volume of 40 cubic feet. Illustrated with eighty-eight line drawings that give the reader a view of space unavailable to the camera's eye.

Dooling, Dave. "Cape Canaveral and the Kennedy Space Center." In *Magill's Survey of Science: Space Exploration Series*, vol. 1, edited by Frank N. Magill. Pasadena, Calif.: Salem Press, 1989.
One of the essays on the history of space exploration in this five-volume set, which covers every aspect of the U.S. and Soviet manned and unmanned space programs, as well as those of nations newer to the space race. The essay looks at the two separate launch facilities: Cape Canaveral Air Force Station, located on Cape Canaveral, Florida, and the Kennedy Space Center, located on Merritt Island to the northwest. It traces the history of the sites and discusses their historical contributions to the United States' space programs. Includes an annotated bibliography and cross-references.

Dryden, Hugh L. *Proceedings of a Conference on Results of the First U.S. Manned Suborbital Space Flight*. Washington, D.C.: National Technical Information Service, 1961.
This is the official NASA report on the flight of Mercury-Redstone 3 with astronaut Alan Shepard. The contents were prepared by a flight evaluation team, in cooperation with the National Institutes of Health and the National Academy of Sciences. A description of the space vehicle and launch vehicle is presented, detailing each of the major systems as configured for the mission. The performance of these systems is given in the form of charts and tables. Each phase of the mission operation is described: prelaunch, including astronaut training and spacecraft and launch vehicle preparation; launch operations; flight-control operations; and recovery operations. There is an aeromedical analysis of the astronaut, as well as a description of pilot flight activities. The sequence of events is enumerated along with trajectory data. Black-and-white photographs, line drawings, and a brief reference list are included.

Fisher, David G. "Mercury-Redstone 3." In *Magill's Survey of Science: Space Exploration Series*, vol. 3, edited by Frank N. Magill. Pasadena, Calif.: Salem Press, 1989.
For some reason when the subject of "firsts" in manned space exploration pops up in a discussion, the United States' first astronaut gets ignored. Everyone knows which American was the first in orbit, the first spacewalker, the first on the moon, or the first to fly the Shuttle, but when asked who was the first American in space, most people (those who are not avid followers of the space program) will say, "John Glenn." Well, actually it was Alan Shepard. Shep-

ard's historic fifteen-minute venture into space is detailed in a concise, information-filled article. The author discusses the mission and gives a brief biography
of the pilot. He also points out the importance of this first flight, including the
fact that it was all President John F. Kennedy needed to challenge America
to be first on the Moon.

Furniss, Tim. *Manned Spaceflight Log.* London: Jane's, 1983, rev. ed. 1987.
This work covers the manned spaceflights of the Soviet Union and the United
States from 1961 through 1986. A synopsis of each mission is given, along
with pertinent data (date, crew, site, recovery, duration, spacecraft weight, and
so forth) and several black-and-white photographs. The Mercury, Gemini,
Apollo, Skylab, Apollo Soyuz, and Space Shuttle flights are listed chronologically. Included are the thirteen flights of the X-15 research aircraft which
exceeded the fifty-mile altitude necessary to qualify its pilot as an astronaut
under Air Force rules. There are astronaut photographs and, in the appendices,
listings of space seniority and the current status of the astronaut and cosmonaut
classes.

_____. *One Small Step.* Newbury Park, Calif.: Haynes, 1989.
Written to coincide with the twentieth anniversary of the first manned lunar
landing, this book takes a look back at the origins of Apollo and updates the
reader on the twelve men who walked on the Moon. In fact, one of the most
interesting features of this work is the section (or rather, chapters) on each of
them. Using titles which the author feels best describes each astronaut (for
example, Buzz Aldrin is "The Second," Alan Bean, "The Painter"), he talks
about their backgrounds, contributions to Apollo, and current status. A large
portion of the manuscript details the ancestors of Apollo: Project Mercury and
the Gemini program. The book is well written and contains a listing of references.

_____. *Space Flight: The Records.* London: Guiness Books, 1985.
Do you know the first manned spaceflight to be curtailed? It was Gemini V,
which landed one orbit early to miss hurricane Betsy. Were you aware that the
first spaceflight with more than one fifty-year-old person on board was that of
STS 51-B/Spacelab 3, in April, 1985? These and dozens of other interesting
and significant—or not so significant— facts are covered in this work. The first
part of the book is a "diary" of manned spaceflight, listing each of the missions of the United States and Soviet Union. There is a chapter on manned
spaceflight "firsts" and one on the manned space machines. Basic biographical
information on each of the space travelers is given, accompanied by the
person's photograph. The major information section is last and includes tables
on manned spaceflight duration, space seniority, space experience, lunar
spacemen, spacewalks, astroflights of the X-15, all known cosmonauts, NASA

astronauts, Space Shuttle passengers, NASA flight crew selections, and the Space Shuttle schedule. There are hundreds of black-and-white photographs, a glossary of terms, and an index.

Goldstein, Norm, ed. *Moments in Space.* New York: Gallery Books, 1986, pp. 36-61.
Black-and-white photographs from the files of the Associated Press tell the story of Project Mercury. Very little text is included and most of the pictures are familiar, since they are official NASA photographs. However, one does get a good look at the public's view of the project, spacecraft, launch vehicles, and astronauts. Each of the manned flights is chronicled, as well as the two chimp missions. The book should not be considered a reliable historical source, as it contains several errors, but rather a glimpse of life in the 1960's.

Grimwood, James M. *Project Mercury: A Chronology.* Washington, D.C.: National Technical Information Service, 1963.
This is NASA's official record of Project Mercury, covering events on a day-to-day basis. Mercury was the United States' first attempt to place a man into low Earth orbit. Embarking on a trip into the unknown environment of space, while developing the technology "on the fly," the scientists, engineers, technicians, and astronauts created spacecraft systems to accomplish the deed, and they did it in less than four years. Included in the coverage are the development of the spacecraft and launch vehicles, astronaut training, and mission results. There are dozens of black-and-white photographs and line drawings of components. Appendices provide a summary of the Mercury flights: mission objectives, orbital activities, and experiments. There are tables of vehicle manufacturing and test histories; program costs; contractors, subcontractors, and vendors; and the flight record of Project Mercury.

Hall, Al, ed. *Petersen's Book of Man in Space.* Vol. 1, *The First Small Step.* Los Angeles: Petersen, 1974.
This first volume in a five-volume set of photographic essays covers the beginnings of the space age. In addition to chronicling the manned Mercury flights, the work looks at the contribution of animals to the race for space. There is an in-depth introduction to the Mercury astronauts and their families. The editor relies on the photographs to tell the story, utilizing very little text.

Hays, Edward L. "Space Suits." In *Manned Spacecraft: Engineering Design and Operation*, edited by Paul E. Purser, Maxime A. Faget, and Norman F. Smith. New York: Fairchild, 1964.
A compilation of essays based upon a series of lectures delivered at NASA's Manned Spacecraft Center, Louisiana State University, University of Houston, and William Marsh Rice University in 1963 and 1964. This paper discusses

in some detail the technical side of spacesuits, with particular emphasis on the ones used in the Mercury and Gemini programs. The history of the pressurized flying suit is traced from its beginnings with such great aviation pioneers as Wiley Post. The essay is highlighted with black-and-white photographs and line drawings of the components, as well as a list of references.

Henry, James P., and John D. Mosely, eds. *Results of the Project Mercury Ballistic and Orbital Chimpanzee Flights.* Washington, D.C.: National Technical Information Service, 1963.
Prepared by the personnel of NASA's Manned Spacecraft Center in Houston, Texas, this publication presents a full account of the flights of the Project Mercury chimpanzees. Before committing man to the unknowns of space travel, these pioneers rode atop the fiery missiles. The suborbital flight of Ham preceded Alan Shepard's by a little more than three months. Enos went into orbit three months before John Glenn. This compilation of essays elaborates on the contributions these two primates made to Mercury. Black-and-white photographs, line drawings, charts, and tables are used to illustrate the volume. Each section has its own reference list.

Kerrod, Robin. *Apollo.* London: Multimedia Books, 1989.
The story of the Apollo program is told in this concise, well-written work. The work begins with the early achievements of Project Mercury and the Gemini program. Mercury was man's first tentative step into the unknown region of the universe only a hundred miles above. Gemini developed and perfected the rendezvous techniques so vital the success of the Moon missions. The story would not be complete without mention of the "children" of Apollo: Skylab and the Apollo Soyuz Test Project. The work goes into detail about the development of the hardware for Apollo. In addition to the discussion of flight hardware, the author looks at the massive Launch Umbilical Towers that were used to service the vehicle on the ground and that served as the launching pad. The spacecraft are detailed. Photographs, drawings, and a log of the Apollo missions add to the text.

Lattimer, Richard L. *All We Did Was Fly to the Moon.* History-Alive Series, vol. 1. Alachula, Fla.: Whispering Eagle Press, 1983, pp. 2-17.
The book is an appealing study of Project Mercury and the United States' other pre-Shuttle manned space programs. Using photographs and reproductions of the spacecraft names as they appeared on the side of each capsule, the author briefly details each flight. Each of the six astronauts who flew in Mercury tells about how his spacecraft was named. Quoting from the book *We Seven,* Lattimer tells how the "crack" was painted on the side of *Liberty Bell 7* before the Mercury-Redstone flight of Gus Grissom. According to Grissom, they copied it from the "tails" side of a fifty-cent piece. Since *Liberty Bell 7*

subsequently sank in the Atlantic Ocean, the practice of painting cracks on the sides of spacecraft quickly ended.

Lee, John B. "Earth-Landing Systems: Systems Applications." In *Manned Spacecraft: Engineering Design and Operation*, edited by Paul E. Purser, Maxime A. Faget, and Norman F. Smith. New York: Fairchild, 1964.
A compilation of essays based upon a series of lectures delivered at NASA's Manned Spacecraft Center, Louisiana State University, University of Houston, and William Marsh Rice University in 1963 and 1964. This paper discusses in some detail the systems designed to slow a spacecraft sufficiently to permit a safe landing. The parachute recovery systems used in the Mercury and Apollo spacecraft are compared. Also discussed is the paraglider designed for the Gemini program. The paraglider was to be used to allow the spacecraft to glide to a landing by means of a deployable, inflatable wing. The concept was eventually dropped because of development problems. The essay is highlighted with black-and-white photographs and line drawings of the components, as well as a list of references.

Lewis, Richard S. *Appointment on the Moon*. New York: Ballantine Books, 1969, pp. 100-229.
This is a thorough chronicle of the U.S. effort to put man in space, from its roots in Germany's V-2 of World War II to the first lunar landing of Apollo 11. Project Mercury, being the United States' earliest attempt at manned spaceflight, is discussed in some detail. However, most of the discussion centers on the flight of John Glenn. This is not to say that the author does not provide adequate details on the other six manned flights. The unmanned launches and the Mercury-Redstone flights are barely mentioned. Given the scope of the work, some missions had to be shorted, but it does not detract from the overall appeal of the work. There are several pages of black-and-white photographs and an excellent listing of reference material.

Link, Mae Mills. *Space Medicine in Project Mercury*. Washington, D.C.: National Technical Information Service, 1965.
Since it provided the United States' first orbiting laboratory for the study of the physiological effects of space travel, Project Mercury marked the transition from what was known as aviation medicine to what would become space medicine. In addition to studying the effects of space travel on an astronaut, NASA was concerned with the entire spectrum of the life sciences. This included ecology and exobiology. In cooperation with those associated with Project Mercury, the author has prepared a comprehensive look at the experiments and tests performed during the program, in the unmanned as well as manned flights. One chapter discusses the medical aspects of astronaut selection. Black-and-white photographs and an index enhance the well-written text.

McDonnell Aircraft Corporation. *Project Mercury Familiarization Manual.* St. Louis: Author, 1961.
This manual was used to describe the Mercury spacecraft systems and major components. It was intended as a familiarization and indoctrination aid and as a ready reference for detailed information on a specific system or component. It is the handbook used by engineers, technicians, and astronauts. The text covers major structural assemblies; cabin interior arrangement; electrical, hydraulic, and pneumatic systems; instrumentation; and propulsion, docking, and landing systems. There are hundreds of highly detailed line drawings of each component. The researcher will find it an invaluable reference, although it will probably have to be obtained directly from NASA.

McKann, Robert E., ed. *First United States Manned Three-Pass Orbital Mission (Mercury-Atlas 6, Spacecraft 13): Part II—Flight Data.* Washington, D.C.: National Technical Information Service, 1964.
This is part 2 of the two-volume official NASA report on the flight of Mercury-Atlas 6 with astronaut John Glenn. The contents were prepared by a flight evaluation team. In this volume, actual flight data are presented, from which the analyses in part 1 are derived. During the flight, voice, radar, and telemetry contacts were maintained with ground stations at intervals throughout the flight to permit in-flight ground monitoring of the astronaut's physiological condition, the spacecraft trajectory, and the operations of onboard systems. Continuous recording of spacecraft measurements was achieved by means of an onboard tape recorder. This work contains a complete presentation of the data record. It is filled with charts, tables, and line drawings. A reference list is included.

Magill, Frank N., ed. *Magill's Survey of Science: Space Exploration Series.* Vols. 2 and 3. Pasadena, Calif.: Salem Press, 1989, pp. 940-990.
This five-volume set covers every aspect of the U.S. and Soviet manned and unmanned space programs, as well as those of nations newer to the space race. Project Mercury was the United States' first tentative step into space. By comparison to the Space Shuttle, the Mercury spacecraft was a Tinkertoy. To the men who rode in it, it was a fast little buggy they "put on" instead of getting into it. One article is devoted to an overview of Project Mercury. The others list the pertinent data for each mission, including its launch vehicle and spacecraft. There is a brief summary of the flight, the knowledge gained, and the historical significance of each mission. Each article includes an annotated bibliography and cross-references.

Mason, Robert Grant, ed. "Mercury's Bold Seven." In *Life in Space.* Alexandria, Va.: Time-Life Books, 1983.

The editors of *Life* magazine have sifted through hundreds of NASA's and their own photographs taken during the first twenty-five years of the space age. What has resulted is a superb collection of photographs of each U.S. manned spaceflight from Alan Shepard's suborbital hop in *Freedom 7* through the STS-6 Space Shuttle mission. Throughout the work are breathtaking color and startling black-and-white photographs. The photographs cover a range of topics, including the spacecraft and launch vehicles. The focus of this segment is the flights of Project Mercury, with spectacular views of Earth, the launches, splashdowns, and everything in between. Since *Life* had exclusive rights to the astronauts' stories, there is a great deal of coverage of them in this part.

Miller, F. E., J. L. Cassidy, J. C. Leveye, and R. I. Johnson. *The Mercury-Redstone Project.* Washington, D.C.: National Technical Information Service, 1964.

This is a concise record of the development of the Redstone intermediate-range ballistic missile for use in the Mercury project. The Redstone was first used in space exploration in its Juno 1 configuration to launch Explorer 1. This configuration was modified and fitted with an adapter for the Mercury spacecraft. It flew five missions, including two manned, during the program. The work is divided into nine sections and covers the following topics: Mercury-Redstone mission, vehicle description, man-rating, development test program, checkout and launch operations, flight test program, and contributions to manned launch vehicles. There are numerous black-and-white photographs, line drawings, charts, and tables. A large reference list will lead the researcher to numerous technical publications about the missile and its contribution to manned spaceflight.

Mitchum, Ellen F. "Atlas Launch Vehicles." In *Magill's Survey of Science: Space Exploration Series*, vol. 1, edited by Frank N. Magill. Pasadena, Calif.: Salem Press, 1989.

One of the essays on the history of space exploration in this five-volume set, which covers every aspect of the U.S. and Soviet manned and unmanned space programs, as well as those of nations newer to the space race. The Atlas vehicle was first built as an intercontinental ballistic missile (ICBM) for the Air Force. It was later modified to launch a variety of manned and unmanned spacecraft. Some of these include the Mercury spacecraft, the Gemini Agena Target Vehicle, Mariner, Ranger, Lunar Orbiter, Surveyor, and many other military and civilian spacecraft. This essay discusses the development of the vehicle and its contributions to space exploration. Contains an annotated bibliography and cross-references.

Pitts, John A. *The Human Factor: Biomedicine in the Manned Space Program to 1980.* Washington, D.C.: Government Printing Office, 1985.

One title in the NASA History Series, this book chronicles the life sciences programs of the U.S. manned spaceflights of the Mercury, Gemini, Apollo, and Skylab programs, and the Apollo Soyuz Test Project. There are dozens of black-and-white photographs, line drawings, tables, and charts about the tests and experiments used to test man's ability to live and work in the microgravity environment of orbital flight. Includes an impressive appendix listing source notes and bibliographic references and an index.

Pogue, William R. *How Do You Go to the Bathroom in Space?* New York: Tom Doherty Associates, 1985.
This and many other interesting questions about living in space are answered by former astronaut Pogue. He was one of three crew members who spent eighty-four days in orbit aboard Skylab. Actually, there are 156 questions which the author has gleaned from thousands that he and his fellow astronauts have received in a quarter century of manned spaceflight. Many of the questions lead to humorous answers, but most provide a great deal of firsthand information about matters of general interest. The questions touch on each of the U.S. manned space programs. Several appendices provide additional information, including a summary of the physiological effects of spaceflight, a list of Earth features recognizable from space, a guide to information and resources, and a bibliography.

Purser, Paul E., Maxime A. Faget, and Norman F. Smith, eds. *Manned Spacecraft: Engineering Design and Operation.* New York: Fairchild, 1964.
A compilation of essays based upon a series of lectures delivered at NASA's Manned Spacecraft Center, Louisiana State University, University of Houston, and William Marsh Rice University in 1963 and 1964. The papers discuss in some detail the technical side of the Mercury spacecraft and how its design will affect Gemini and Apollo craft. Each essay is highlighted with black-and-white photographs and line drawings of the systems or components, as well as a list of references. This is a very comprehensive volume and represents technology at its finest. Comparisons should be made between the way problems were resolved in the pre-microchip days and the way they are approached today.

Schirra, Walter M., Jr., with Richard N. Billings. *Schirra's Space.* Boston: Quinlan Press, 1988, pp. 57-96.
As a career Navy test pilot, Schirra was determined to remain a pilot, even in space. He was one of the original seven Mercury astronauts who lobbied to put a window in the Mercury capsule and manual controls so that the pilot could fly the machine. It is an intriguing tale, filled with examples of Schirra's wry humor. However, when he was doing his job, he was all business. He made it clear to NASA that he was a pilot and an engineer, and not a media

spokesman. Black-and-white photographs enhance this story of the only person to fly the Mercury, Gemini, and Apollo spacecraft.

Sharpe, Mitchell. "Man in Space." In *The Illustrated Encyclopedia of Space Technology: A Comprehensive History of Space Exploration,* by Kenneth Gatland et al. New York: Harmony Books, 1981.
This section in the book discusses Project Mercury and the Gemini program, as well as the manned programs of the Soviet Union. Each of the programs is briefly discussed, but a great deal of detail is given to the spacecraft. Each is shown in a full-color cutaway drawing with key components indicated. There are color and black-and-white photographs, drawings, and charts. There is a brief bibliography. Includes a chronology of the major space events since Sputnik 1, a glossary of terms, and an index.

Shortal, Joseph A. *A New Dimension—Wallops Island Flight Test Range: The First Fifteen Years.* Washington, D.C.: National Technical Information Service, 1978.
The Wallops Station, located on Wallops Island, Virginia, was established by the National Advisory Committee for Aeronautics in 1945 to gather information about Earth's atmosphere and its near-space environment. During its first fifteen years, the facility launched more than six thousand research vehicles. Consisting of from one to seven stages, these vehicles were used to gather scientific information on the flight characteristics of airplanes, launch vehicles, and spacecraft and to increase our understanding of the upper atmosphere and space environment. This large volume details the history of the facility, including its role in the development of wartime aircraft and missiles, ramjets, supersonic bodies, hypersonic vehicles, high-temperature research, ballistic missile nose cones, guided missiles, sounding rockets, and Project Mercury. There are numerous black-and-white photographs and drawings, and an index. Appendices detail rocket motors used at Wallops, program identification, flight operations, preflight jet operations, and rocket propulsion systems developed at Wallops.

Swenson, Loyd S., Jr., James M. Grimwood, and Charles C. Alexander. *This New Ocean: A History of Project Mercury.* Washington, D.C.: National Technical Information Service, 1966.
One title in the NASA History Series, this book chronicles Project Mercury, from its conception during the early days of NASA to its completion following the flight of Gordon Cooper in Mercury-Atlas 9. There are dozens of black-and-white photographs of the manned, as well as unmanned, flights. Line drawings show the inner workings of much of the equipment related to the missions. There is an impressive hundred-page appendix listing source notes and bibliographic references. Other appendices include a summary of flight

data, functional and workflow organization of Project Mercury, personnel growth, the ground station tracking network, and the cost of the project.

U.S. House of Representatives. *United States Civilian Space Programs 1958-1978.* Vol. 1. Washington, D.C.: Government Printing Office, 1981.
In a very concise report, the Committee on Space Science and Applications has compiled data on all U.S. space activity during its first two decades. After a brief introduction and summary chapter, the volume is divided into fourteen additional sections. The second chapter deals with the space-related issues under consideration by Congress. The remaining sections cover the history of NASA and its relationship to U.S. space policy, NASA facilities and tracking systems, launch vehicles and propulsion, manned spaceflight through 1975, the Space Transportation System, space life sciences, space science programs, materials processing in space, international cooperation in space, interagency and non-NASA governmental space activities, industrial and university support for NASA, space program benefits, and selected future space programs. Appendices contain Department of Defense manned spaceflight plans, NASA funding history, international space agreements, texts of President Jimmy Carter's space directives, documents relating to the legal aspects of the Space Shuttle, major U.S. space organizations, a master log of U.S. spaceflights, and a table of U.S. space orbital payloads by mission from 1957 through 1979.

U.S. National Aeronautics and Space Administration. *"In This Decade . . .": Mission to the Moon.* Washington, D.C.: Government Printing Office, 1969.
This is a preflight look at the Apollo 11 lunar landing mission and the Mercury, Gemini, and Apollo flights which preceded it. The narration is very simple and adds little to the information available in larger works, but it provides a concise glimpse at these ancestral efforts. In addition, the booklet previews the first manned lunar landing attempt and future programs including Skylab. At the time of the writing, Skylab was still called the Apollo Applications Program. Color and black-and-white photographs highlight the work.

_____. *Mercury Project Summary Including Results of the Fourth Manned Orbital Flight.* Washington, D.C.: National Technical Information Service, 1963.
This document presents a summary of the planning, preparation, experiences, and results of Project Mercury and includes the results of the Mercury-Atlas 9 flight with Gordon Cooper. The essays were written by Mercury scientists, engineers, and technicians and are grouped into four main technical areas: space-vehicle development, mission support development, flight operations, and mission results. Line drawings, black-and-white photographs, tables, and charts add to the text. Appendices list typical documents prepared for Mercury, NASA centers and other government agencies, prime contractors, subcontractors,

NASA personnel, and Mercury-Atlas 9 air-to-ground voice communications. Includes an aeromedical analysis of astronaut Cooper and a description of his flight activities. The sequence of events is enumerated along with trajectory data.

_____. *Results of the First United States Manned Orbital Space Flight, February 20, 1962.* Washington, D.C.: National Technical Information Service, 1962.
This is the second of two official NASA reports on the flight of Mercury-Atlas 6 with astronaut John Glenn. The contents were prepared by a flight evaluation team. A description of the space vehicle and launch vehicle is presented, detailing each of the major systems as configured for the mission. The performance of these systems is given in the form of charts and tables. Each phase of the mission operation is described: prelaunch, including astronaut training and spacecraft and launch vehicle preparation; launch operations; flight-control operations; and recovery operations. Includes an aeromedical analysis of the astronaut and a description of pilot flight activities. The sequence of events is enumerated along with trajectory data. There is a complete transcript of the air-to-ground communications between the astronaut and tracking stations. Black-and-white photographs, line drawings, and a brief reference list are included in each section of the work.

_____. *Results of the Second U.S. Manned Suborbital Space Flight, July 21, 1961.* Washington, D.C.: National Technical Information Service, 1961.
This is the official NASA report on the flight of Mercury-Redstone 4 with astronaut Virgil Grissom. The contents were prepared by a flight evaluation team. A description of the space vehicle and launch vehicle is presented, detailing each of the major systems as configured for the mission. The performance of these systems is given in the form of charts and tables. Each phase of the mission operation is described: prelaunch, including astronaut training and spacecraft and launch vehicle preparation; launch operations; flight-control operations; and recovery operations. Includes an aeromedical analysis of the astronaut and a description of pilot flight activities. The sequence of events is enumerated along with trajectory data. Black-and-white photographs, line drawings, and a brief reference list are included.

_____. *Results of the Second United States Manned Orbital Space Flight, May 24, 1962.* Washington, D.C.: National Technical Information Service, 1962.
This is the second of two official NASA reports on the flight of Mercury-Atlas 7 with astronaut Scott Carpenter. The contents were prepared by a flight evaluation team. A description of the space vehicle and launch vehicle is

presented, detailing each of the major systems as configured for the mission. The performance of these systems is given in the form of charts and tables. Each phase of the mission operation is described: prelaunch, including astronaut training and spacecraft and launch vehicle preparation; launch operations; flight-control operations; and recovery operations. Includes an aeromedical analysis of the astronaut and a description of pilot flight activities. The sequence of events is enumerated along with trajectory data. There is a complete transcript of the air-to-ground communications between the astronaut and tracking stations. Black-and-white photographs, line drawings, and a brief reference list are included in each section of the work.

_____. *Results of the Third United States Manned Orbital Space Flight, October 3, 1962.* Washington, D.C.: National Technical Information Service, 1962.
This is the second of two official NASA reports on the flight of Mercury-Atlas 8 with astronaut Wally Schirra. The contents were prepared by a flight evaluation team. A description of the space vehicle and launch vehicle is presented, detailing each of the major systems as configured for the mission. The performance of these systems is given in the form of charts and tables. Each phase of the mission operation is described: prelaunch, including astronaut training and spacecraft and launch vehicle preparation; launch operations; flight-control operations; and recovery operations. Includes an aeromedical analysis of the astronaut and a description of pilot flight activities. The sequence of events is enumerated along with trajectory data. There is a complete transcript of the air-to-ground communications between the astronaut and tracking stations. Black-and-white photographs, line drawings and a brief reference list are included in each section of the work.

Von Braun, Wernher, and Frederick I. Ordway III. *History of Rocketry and Space Travel.* 3d rev. ed. New York: Thomas Y. Crowell, 1975.
This is the story of the exploration of space from the earliest experiments with rocketry to the final flight of the Skylab program. Hundreds of experts on every aspect of this broad field contributed to the work. Most of the programs of the United States, the Soviet Union, and the rest of the nations engaged in space exploration at that time are detailed, both descriptively and with black-and-white and color photographs. It is one of the best references on the subject. The book also contains a large, chapter-by-chapter bibliography. The authors finish their discussion of the space programs with a look at the future, including the Space Transportation System.

Ward, Robinson J., Jr., comp. *A Funny Thing Happened on the Way to the Moon.* Greenwich, Conn.: Fawcett, 1969.

Although the exploration of space is a serious, often challenging business, there is still time for humor. Some of the humor presented in this book was unintentional, evolving from the frustrations and failures of the U.S. space program. The author has collected amusing events, jokes, and other tension-relieving anecdotes from the scientists, technicians, engineers, and astronauts involved in man's conquest of space. While the book does not contain any pertinent data on the history of the space program, it does make these people seem a little more human.

Wolfe, Tom. *The Right Stuff.* New York: Farrar, Straus & Giroux, 1979.
A very interesting book about the team of men who flew in Project Mercury and about Chuck Yeager, the "loner" of X-1 fame. Wolfe has taken the stories of these men and intertwined them for an exciting and romantic tale of high flight. There are a great number of stories told by the astronauts and related in this book, which the reader will find too fantastic to believe. They really did happen—or, at least, the characters portrayed in this work say they did. It also tells of the women who loved the men, and who supported them, waited for them, and in some cases mourned their demise. For those who want to know more about the Mercury Seven and Chuck Yeager, this book far surpasses the film adaptation, which does not accurately portray the incidents from the book.

Yenne, Bill. *The Encyclopedia of U.S. Spacecraft.* New York: Exeter Books, 1985.
A complete encyclopedia of U.S. spacecraft is presented in a book filled with color and black-and-white photographs. General information on the programs is provided in alphabetical order, with individual spacecraft, probes, or launch vehicles listed chronologically. Data on all of the manned spacecraft, including the Mercury spacecraft, and Atlas, Redstone, and Little Joe boosters, are furnished. An appendix lists acronyms and abbreviations, and there is an index.

_____. *The Pictorial History of World Spacecraft.* New York: Exeter Books, 1988.
The history of the world's spacecraft and probes is told in chronological order from Sputnik 1 through Cosmos 1870, spanning the first thirty years of the space age. Included are all of the manned spacecraft and launch vehicles. Each is detailed with charts, diagrams, illustrations, and color and black-and-white photographs. Data on all of the manned spacecraft, including the Mercury spacecraft, are provided. An appendix lists all of the spacecraft in service as of July, 1987, grouped according to the countries or organizations responsible for them.

Gemini

Aldrin, Buzz, and Malcolm McConnell. *Men from Earth*. New York: Bantam Books, 1989, pp. 113-160.

Aldrin, the second man to walk on the Moon, writes a brief history of the United States' manned space program, with emphasis on his own Gemini XII and Apollo 11 flights. He discusses the manned programs leading to Apollo with an insider's knowledge. The book is well written and provides the reader with some information obtainable nowhere else. His description of his Gemini spacewalks and the lunar landing and subsequent moonwalk is quite vivid. The reader can almost picture the events as if he were there when they happened. There are black-and-white photographs and an extensive bibliography.

Allen, Joseph P., with Russell Martin. *Entering Space*. New York: Stewart, Tabori & Chang, 1984.

The story of an astronaut's journey in space, told in conjunction with a study of the U.S. exploration of space. This work is filled with colorful words and spectacular photographs of space travel from the ground up, and back again. There are hundreds of color photographs taken during the manned Gemini, Apollo, Skylab, Apollo Soyuz, and Space Shuttle programs, as well as those shots of our neighbors in the solar system taken from unmanned probes. The spacecraft, launch vehicles, spacefarers, and their equipment are discussed in some detail, although primarily from the perspective of a single trip into orbit and back again. There is a very real sense of "being there" as Astronaut Allen describes his feelings during the various phases of flight. Includes a brief bibliography and an index.

Booker, Peter, Gerald Frewer, and Geoffrey Pardoe. *Project Apollo: The Way to the Moon*. New York: American Elsevier, 1970.

The authors write about the efforts to place men on the Moon, as well as the Mercury and Gemini programs, which paved the way for Apollo. They look at the spacecraft, launch vehicles, flights, and astronauts involved. They also discuss the problems and accomplishments of each. Since the book is broad in coverage, there is very little detail on individual flights. The book is illustrated with black-and-white photographs and line drawings.

Borman, Frank, with Robert J. Sterling. *Countdown: An Autobiography*. New York: Silver Arrow Books, 1988, pp. 109-167.

Take two men, dress them in deep-sea diver suits, place them in the front seat of a Volkswagen Beetle and then leave them there for two weeks—that is how it was to fly the Gemini VII mission. Borman takes a straightforward look at his Gemini experience with momentary, humorous insights into the workings of an astronaut's mind. Behind-the-scenes tales of his Gemini cohorts add color to this hard look at one man's life. He relates some of the thoughts that went through his mind before and during Gemini VII mission, making the reader feel as if he were crammed inside the spacecraft with Borman and Jim Lovell. Although not a detailed history of the program, the book is a must for those who want to know what it is like to soar with the angels.

Collins, Michael. "The Bridge." In *Liftoff: The Story of America's Adventure in Space*. New York: Grove Press, 1988.
Collins gives a narrative look at the Gemini program, with emphasis on his own Gemini X flight. He takes the reader inside the confines of the small spacecraft as it drifts slowly toward the Agena target vehicle. The monotony of the voyage and the hectic pace of some of the activities provide contrast in this story of the program, which developed the techniques for rendezvous and docking in space. Illustrated with eighty-eight line drawings that give the reader a view of space unavailable to the camera's eye.

_____. *Carrying the Fire: An Astronaut's Journeys*. New York: Farrar, Straus & Giroux, 1983.
Gemini X was, to that point in time, the most daring flight undertaken in the history of spaceflight. Not only would Command Pilot John Young and Pilot Collins rendezvous and dock with a fully loaded Agena vehicle; they would use it to boost them into an orbit high enough to catch a second Agena. Collins describes the sensations associated with the "kick in the pants" he felt when the Agena's engine ignites. He also describes his reaction to floating free of the spacecraft during his spacewalks and what it is like to swing helplessly at the end of a tether, controlled only by Newton's laws of motion.

Dooling, Dave. "Cape Canaveral and the Kennedy Space Center." In *Magill's Survey of Science: Space Exploration Series*, vol. 1, edited by Frank N. Magill. Pasadena, Calif.: Salem Press, 1989.
One of the essays on the history of space exploration in this five-volume set, which covers every aspect of the U.S. and Soviet manned and unmanned space programs, as well as those of nations newer to the space race. The essay looks at the two separate launch facilities: Cape Canaveral Air Force Station, located on Cape Canaveral, Florida, and the Kennedy Space Center, located on Merritt Island to the northwest. It traces the history of the sites and discusses their historical contributions to the United States' space programs. Provides an annotated bibliography and cross-references.

_____. "Johnson Space Center." In *Magill's Survey of Science: Space Exploration Series*, vol. 2, edited by Frank N. Magill. Pasadena, Calif.: Salem Press, 1989.

One of the essays on the history of space exploration in this five-volume set, which covers every aspect of the U.S. and Soviet manned and unmanned space programs, as well as those of nations newer to the space race. The Johnson Space Center, originally called the Manned Spacecraft Center, is located near Houston, Texas. It was first used as the mission control center for manned spaceflights during the Gemini program. This article discusses the center, its origins and its role in the Gemini, Apollo, Skylab, Apollo Soyuz, and Space Shuttle programs. Includes an annotated bibliography and cross-references.

Furniss, Tim. *Manned Spaceflight Log*. London: Jane's, 1983, rev. ed. 1987.
This work covers the manned spaceflights of the Soviet Union and the United States from 1961 through 1986. A synopsis of each mission is given, along with pertinent data (date, crew, site, recovery, duration, spacecraft weight, and so forth) and several black-and-white photographs. The Mercury, Gemini, Apollo, Skylab, Apollo Soyuz, and Space Shuttle flights are listed chronologically. Included are the thirteen flights of the X-15 research aircraft which exceeded the fifty-mile altitude necessary to qualify its pilot as an astronaut under Air Force rules. There are astronaut photographs and, in the appendices, listings of space seniority and the current status of the astronaut and cosmonaut classes.

_____. *One Small Step*. Newbury Park, Calif.: Haynes, 1989.
Written to coincide with the twentieth anniversary of the first manned lunar landing, this book takes a look back at the origins of Apollo and updates the reader on the twelve men who walked on the Moon. In fact, one of the most interesting features of this work is the section (or rather, chapters) on each of them. Using titles that the author feels best describes each astronaut (for example, Buzz Aldrin is "The Second," Alan Bean, "The Painter"), he talks about their backgrounds, contributions to Apollo, and current status. A large portion of the book details the ancestors of Apollo: Project Mercury and the Gemini program. It is well written and contains a listing of references.

_____. *Space Flight: The Records*. London: Guiness Books, 1985.
Do you know the first manned spaceflight to be curtailed? It was Gemini V, which landed one orbit early to miss hurricane Betsy. Were you aware that the first spaceflight with more than one fifty-year-old person on board was that of STS 51-B/Spacelab 3, in April, 1985? These and dozens of other interesting and significant—or not so significant—facts are covered in this work. The first part of the book is a "diary" of manned spaceflight, listing each of the missions of the United States and Soviet Union. There is a chapter on manned spaceflight "firsts" and one on the manned space machines. Basic biographical information on each of the space travelers is given, accompanied by the person's photograph. The major information section is last and includes tables

on manned spaceflight duration, space seniority, space experience, lunar spacemen, spacewalks, astroflights of the X-15, all known cosmonauts, NASA astronauts, Space Shuttle passengers, NASA flight crew selections, and the Space Shuttle schedule. There are hundreds of black-and-white photographs, a glossary of terms, and an index.

Goldstein, Norm, ed. *Moments in Space.* New York: Gallery Books, 1986, pp. 63-72.
Perhaps the weakest section of the book, this photographic look at the Gemini program is exceptionally short. The flight of Gemini IV and Ed White's first extravehicular activity (spacewalk) take up most of the section. Black-and-white photographs and very little text tell the tale of Gemini. It is as if the editor were overlooking the significance of this intermediate program, which played a very important role in the quest for the Moon. In addition, several errors in the book make it little more than a good look at life in the 1960's and how the public saw the space program.

Grimwood, James M., and Barton C. Hacker, with Peter J. Vorzimmer. *Project Gemini Technology and Operations: A Chronology.* Washington, D.C.: National Technical Information Service, 1969.
This is NASA's official record of the Gemini program, covering events on a day-to-day basis. Gemini was developed as an "in-between" program. What evolved was a test program that proved that the theoretical concepts of rendezvous and docking with another orbiting spacecraft could be accomplished. Included in the coverage are the development of the spacecraft and launch vehicles, astronaut training, and mission results. There are dozens of black-and-white photographs and line drawings of components. Appendices provide a summary of the Gemini flights: mission objectives, orbital activities, experiments, and extravehicular activity. There are tables of vehicle manufacturing and test histories; program costs; contractors, subcontractors, and vendors; and the flight record of Project Mercury and the Gemini program.

Grissom, Betty, and Henry S. Still. *Starfall.* New York: Thomas Y. Crowell, 1974.
Although written mostly about Grissom and his life and death during Apollo, this book takes a look at his adventures during the Gemini 3 flight. Grissom, always trying to dispel the rumor that he had panicked and contributed to the loss of his Mercury spacecraft, was extremely cautious about the Gemini flight. He worked harder on this mission than any other and appropriately named his spacecraft *Molly Brown*, after the Broadway character. Perhaps, his spacecraft would be as unsinkable as she was. This is a view of the life of an astronaut from the perspective of a person who was as close to the inner circle as an "outsider" could get.

Hacker, Barton C., and James M. Grimwood. *On the Shoulders of Titans: A History of Project Gemini.* Washington, D.C.: National Technical Information Service, 1977.
One title in the NASA History Series, this book chronicles the Gemini program, from its conception during the early days of Project Mercury to its completion following the Gemini XII flight. There are dozens of black-and-white photographs of the manned, as well as unmanned, flights. Color photographs, taken from orbit, are in the back of the book. Line drawings show the inner workings of much of the equipment related to the missions. There is an impressive hundred-page appendix listing source notes and bibliographic references. Other appendices include a summary of flight data, a glossary of abbreviations and acronyms, astronaut flight assignments, in-flight experiments, and the cost of the program.

Hall, Al, ed. *Petersen's Book of Man in Space.* Vol. 2, *A New Environment.* Los Angeles: Petersen, 1974.
A photographic look at the Gemini program, this volume completely chronicles the flights. Hundreds of black-and-white and color photographs highlight the essay. Very little text is needed, since the pictures tell the story quite well. In addition to covering each flight, the work looks at the Manned Spacecraft Center in Houston and introduces the reader to the latest group of astronauts. Each component of the Gemini spacecraft and launch vehicle is shown, as well as the Gemini Agena Target Vehicle.

Hays, Edward L. "Space Suits." In *Manned Spacecraft: Engineering Design and Operation*, edited by Paul E. Purser, Maxime A. Faget, and Norman F. Smith. New York: Fairchild, 1964.
A compilation of essays based upon a series of lectures delivered at NASA's Manned Spacecraft Center, Louisiana State University, University of Houston, and William Marsh Rice University in 1963 and 1964. This paper discusses in some detail the technical side of spacesuits with particular emphasis on the ones used in the Mercury and Gemini programs. The history of the pressurized flying suit is traced from its beginnings with such great aviation pioneers as Wiley Post. The essay is highlighted with black-and-white photographs and line drawings of the components, as well as a list of references.

Kerrod, Robin. *Apollo.* London: Multimedia Books, 1989.
The story of the Apollo program is told in this concise, well-written work. The work begins with the early achievements of Project Mercury and the Gemini program. Mercury was man's first tentative step into the unknown region of the universe only a hundred miles above. Gemini developed and perfected the rendezvous techniques so vital the success of the Moon missions. The story would not be complete without mention of the "children" of Apollo: Skylab

and the Apollo Soyuz Test Project. The work goes into detail about the development of the hardware for Apollo. In addition to the discussion of flight hardware, the author looks at the massive Launch Umbilical Towers, which were used to service the vehicle on the ground and which served as the launching pad. The spacecraft are detailed. Photographs, drawings, and a log of the Apollo missions add to the text.

Lattimer, Richard L. *All We Did Was Fly to the Moon*. History-Alive Series, vol. 1. Alachula, Fla.: Whispering Eagle Press, 1983, pp. 18-39.
A compilation of brief reports on each of the manned flights of the Gemini program, the work presents a very different look at the project. Color reproductions of the crew emblems from each flight (except for Geminis 3 and IV, which did not have emblems) are the highlight of this book. A summation of the mission is included. The origins of the crew emblems and spacecraft call signs are explained by the astronauts involved. The author has obtained a great deal of information directly from the astronauts. Unfortunately, a bibliography is not included. Black-and-white photographs and reproductions from newspapers from around the nation add to the text.

Lee, John B. "Earth-Landing Systems: Systems Applications." In *Manned Spacecraft: Engineering Design and Operation*, edited by Paul E. Purser, Maxime A. Faget, and Norman F. Smith. New York: Fairchild, 1964.
A compilation of essays based upon a series of lectures delivered at NASA's Manned Spacecraft Center, Louisiana State University, University of Houston, and William Marsh Rice University in 1963 and 1964. This paper discusses in some detail the systems designed to slow a spacecraft sufficiently to permit a safe landing. The parachute recovery systems used in the Mercury and Apollo spacecraft are compared. Also discussed is the paraglider designed for the Gemini program. The paraglider was to be used to allow the spacecraft to glide to a landing by means of a deployable, inflatable wing. The concept was eventually dropped because of development problems. The essay is highlighted with black-and-white photographs and line drawings of the components, as well as a list of references.

Lewis, Richard S. "Gemini." In *Appointment on the Moon*. New York: Ballantine Books, 1969.
This work presents a complete record of the race for space, beginning with the German V-2 missiles of World War II. The author has chronicled each of the manned programs and associated unmanned programs which led to the first manned landing on the Moon. Gemini played a key role in Apollo by proving the theory that two separately launched spacecraft could rendezvous and dock. Lewis limits his discussion of Gemini to the most widely known facts out of necessity, because of the scope of his work. However, the overall volume

contains a wealth of data. There are several pages of black-and-white photographs and an excellent listing of reference material.

Lockheed Missiles and Space Company. *Gemini Agena Target Vehicle Familiarization Handbook.* Sunnyvale, Calif.: Author, 1964.
The Agena Target Vehicle was used in the Gemini program as a orbiting target for the manned spacecraft. It was launched by an Atlas missile and placed into orbit shortly before liftoff of the Gemini spacecraft. The Gemini manned spacecraft would track the Agena by radar, rendezvous with it, dock, and use the Agena's powerful engine to boost the combination to a higher orbit. This manual was used to describe the Agena spacecraft systems and major components. It was intended as a ready reference for detailed information on a specific system or component and is the handbook used by engineers, technicians, and astronauts. The text covers major structural assemblies; electrical, hydraulic, and pneumatic systems; telemetry; and propulsion, docking, and guidance systems. There are hundreds of highly detailed line drawings of each component. The researcher will find it an invaluable reference, although it will probably have to be obtained directly from NASA.

McDonnell Aircraft Corporation. *Project Gemini Familiarization Manual.* 2 vols. St. Louis: Author, 1966.
This manual was used to describe the Gemini spacecraft systems and major components. It was intended as a familiarization-indoctrination aid and as a ready reference for detailed information on a specific system or component. It is the handbook used by engineers, technicians, and astronauts. Volume 1 is applicable to long-range or modified (nonrendezvous) configurations of the spacecraft, while volume 2 is applicable to rendezvous missions. The text covers major structural assemblies; cabin interior arrangement; electrical, hydraulic, and pneumatic systems; instrumentation; and propulsion, docking, and landing systems. There are hundreds of highly detailed line drawings of each component. The researcher will find it an invaluable reference, although it will probably have to be obtained directly from NASA.

Machell, Reginald M., ed. *Summary of Gemini Extravehicular Activity.* Washington, D.C.: National Technical Information Service, 1967.
This is a collection of reports from NASA summarizing the Gemini program extravehicular activity (EVA) operations. EVAs, or "spacewalks," were initiated during Gemini and were featured on six of the ten manned flights, from Ed White's thirty-six-minute stroll during Gemini IV to Buzz Aldrin's five-and-one-half-hour marathon during Gemini XII. The book evaluates the techniques developed during the program and the problems associated with the EVAs. There are dozens of black-and-white photographs and line drawings to supplement the text. Topics covered include life support systems, body position-

ing and restraint systems, maneuvering equipment, training and simulation, operational and medical aspects of extravehicular activity, results, and conclusions. There is a short list of references at the end of the book.

Magill, Frank N., ed. *Magill's Survey of Science: Space Exploration Series*. Vol. 2. Pasadena, Calif.: Salem Press, 1989, pp. 487-539.
This five-volume set covers every aspect of the U.S. and Soviet manned and unmanned space programs, as well as those of nations newer to the space race. As a bridge between the early Project Mercury flights and the Apollo lunar landing missions, NASA developed the Gemini program. Its main purpose was to develop the techniques needed to rendezvous in orbit and to operate outside the spacecraft. One article is devoted to an overview of the program. The others list the pertinent data for each mission, including its launch vehicle and spacecraft. Each article contains a brief summary of the flight, the knowledge gained, the historical significance of each mission, an annotated bibliography, and cross-references.

Malik, P. W., and G. A. Souris. *Project Gemini: A Technical Summary*. Washington, D.C.: National Technical Information Service, 1968.
Prepared by spacecraft prime contractor McDonnell Douglas Corporation, this work provides a brief look at all of the systems of the Gemini manned spacecraft. Included is a description of the reentry module and adapter module. The reentry module contained the crew cabin, rendezvous and recovery section, reentry control system, environmental control system, and heatshield. The adapter module held most of the flight equipment, the Orbit Attitude and Maneuvering System, and the retrorockets. Each system and subsystem is detailed with drawings and text. There is a section on the Target Docking Adapter, which was attached to the Agena Target Vehicle and provided the means for joining the two spacecraft after rendezvous.

Mason, Robert Grant, ed. "Gemini's Record Pace." In *Life in Space*. Alexandria, Va.: Time-Life Books, 1983.
The editors of *Life* magazine have sifted through hundreds of NASA's and their own photographs taken during the first twenty-five years of the space age. What has resulted is a superb collection of photographs of each U.S. manned spaceflight from Alan Shepard's suborbital hop in *Freedom 7* through the STS-6 Space Shuttle mission. Throughout the work are breathtaking color and startling black-and-white photographs. The photographs cover a range of topics, including the spacecraft and launch vehicles. The focus of this segment is the flights of the Gemini program, with spectacular views of Earth, the launches, splashdowns, and everything in between—in particular, Ed White's exciting stroll through the cosmos during Gemini IV.

Mitchum, Ellen F. "Atlas Launch Vehicles." In *Magill's Survey of Science: Space Exploration Series*, vol. 1, edited by Frank N. Magill. Pasadena, Calif.: Salem Press, 1989.
One of the essays on the history of space exploration in this five-volume set, which covers every aspect of the U.S. and Soviet manned and unmanned space programs, as well as those of nations newer to the space race. The Atlas vehicle was first built as an intercontinental ballistic missile (ICBM) for the Air Force. It was later modified to launch a variety of manned and unmanned spacecraft. Some of these include the Mercury spacecraft, the Gemini Agena Target Vehicle, Mariner, Ranger, Lunar Orbiter, Surveyor, and many other military and civilian spacecraft. This essay discusses the development of the vehicle and its contributions to space exploration. Includes an annotated bibliography and cross-references.

Newman, John. "Titan Launch Vehicles." In *Magill's Survey of Science: Space Exploration Series*, vol. 5, edited by Frank N. Magill. Pasadena, Calif.: Salem Press, 1989.
The first intercontinental ballistic missile (ICBM) designed to be used as such, rather than one modified from an existing research vehicle, was the mighty Titan. Titan was designed to fit into an underground silo, and it used fuels that could be stored inside the vehicle's propellant tanks for long periods of time. In addition, the fuel and oxidizer were chosen because they ignited on contact and did not need a bulky, sometimes unreliable, ignition system. This article discusses the many faces of Titan and the spacecraft it launched, including the Gemini two-man spacecraft, Viking, Voyager, and many military satellites. Provides an annotated bibliography and cross-references.

Norman, Leland C., Jerry E. McCullough, and Jerry C. Coffey. *Gemini Land Landing System Development Program*. 2 vols. Washington, D.C.: Government Printing Office, 1967.
While the engineers of Project Mercury were satisfied with their spacecraft landing by parachute into the ocean, when they moved on to Gemini they changed their minds. They theorized that there would be fewer bumps and jolts on the astronaut crew if they were seated upright (in a "heads-up" position) while their spacecraft glided to a landing. What resulted was an inflatable paraglider that would be deployed after the returning craft had been stabilized by parachute. Unfortunately, financial and scheduling constraints spelled the end to the paraglider, but the Gemini spacecraft retained the heads-up landing position by means of a two-point suspension system. This NASA Technical Note contains dozens of line drawings in addition to the text.

Pitts, John A. *The Human Factor: Biomedicine in the Manned Space Program to 1980*. Washington, D.C.: Government Printing Office, 1985.

One title in the NASA History Series, this book chronicles the life sciences programs of the U.S. manned spaceflights of the Mercury, Gemini, Apollo, and Skylab programs, and the Apollo Soyuz Test Project. There are dozens of black-and-white photographs, line drawings, tables, and charts detailing the experiments used to test man's ability to live and work in the microgravity environment of orbital flight. An impressive appendix lists source notes and bibliographic references, and there is an index.

Pogue, William R. *How Do You Go to the Bathroom in Space?* New York: Tom Doherty Associates, 1985.
This and many other interesting questions about living in space are answered by former astronaut Pogue. He was one of three crew members who spent eighty-four days in orbit aboard Skylab. Actually, there are 156 questions which the author has gleaned from thousands that he and his fellow astronauts have received in a quarter century of manned spaceflight. Many of the questions lead to humorous answers, but most provide a great deal of firsthand information about matters of general interest. The questions touch on each of the U.S. manned space programs. Several appendices provide additional information, including a summary of the physiological effects of spaceflight, a list of Earth features recognizable from space, a guide to information and resources, and a bibliography.

Ray, Hilary A., Jr., and Frederick T. Burns. *Development and Qualification of Gemini Escape System.* Washington, D.C.: Government Printing Office, 1967.
Sitting atop a missile loaded with explosive fuel would not be considered by most to be a safe occupation. The engineers of Project Mercury knew this and developed a launch escape system, composed of a tractor rocket system that could rapidly pull the spacecraft away from danger. These systems take a big bite out of the weight available for payloads. Knowing this, the same engineers decided that an ejection seat system could be used for Gemini, since the Titan booster's propellants would not explode as rapidly as those of the Atlas. This essay describes the Gemini escape system, the development program, and the qualification tests for manned use. Line drawings, tables, and charts add detail to this NASA Technical Note.

Schirra, Walter M., Jr., with Richard N. Billings. *Schirra's Space.* Boston: Quinlan Press, 1988, pp. 135-176.
Schirra, the only astronaut to fly in the Mercury, Gemini, and Apollo programs, tells of his Gemini VI-A mission. During the flight he, his crewmate Tom Stafford, and the crew of Gemini VII performed the first rendezvous of two orbiting spacecraft. The book is an interesting study of the life of a test pilot—not the loner, but a member of a team, at work and at home. Schirra

pulls no punches as he conveys his feelings about NASA, spaceflight, and life in general. Many black-and-white photographs add to the text.

Sharpe, Mitchell. "Man in Space." In *The Illustrated Encyclopedia of Space Technology: A Comprehensive History of Space Exploration*, by Kenneth Gatland et al. New York: Harmony Books, 1981.
This section in the book discusses the Mercury project and the Gemini program, as well as the manned programs of the Soviet Union. Each of the programs is briefly discussed, but a great deal of attention is paid to the spacecraft. Each is shown in a full-color cutaway drawing with key components indicated. There are color and black-and-white photographs, drawings, and charts, as well as a brief bibliography. The book includes a chronology of the major space events since Sputnik 1, a glossary of terms, and an index.

U.S. House of Representatives. *United States Civilian Space Programs 1958-1978*. Vol. 1. Washington, D.C.: Government Printing Office, 1981.
In a very concise report, the Committee on Space Science and Applications has compiled data on all U.S. space activity during its first two decades. After a brief introduction and summary chapter, the volume is divided into fourteen additional sections. The second chapter deals with the space-related issues under consideration by Congress. The remaining sections cover the history of NASA and its relationship to U.S. space policy, NASA facilities and tracking systems, launch vehicles and propulsion, manned spaceflight through 1975, the Space Transportation System, space life sciences, space science programs, materials processing in space, international cooperation in space, interagency and non-NASA governmental space activities, industrial and university support for NASA, space program benefits, and selected future space programs. Appendices contain Department of Defense manned spaceflight plans, NASA funding history, international space agreements, texts of President Jimmy Carter's space directives, documents relating to the legal aspects of the Space Shuttle, major U.S. space organizations, a master log of U.S. spaceflights, and a table of U.S. space orbital payloads by mission from 1957 through 1979.

U.S. National Aeronautics and Space Administration. *Earth Photographs from Gemini III, IV, and V.* Washington, D.C.: National Technical Information Service, 1967.
NASA's own scrapbook, this work presents color photographs taken by the astronauts while in Earth orbit. They resulted from two of twenty-two scientific experiments that were part of the Gemini program. The experiments were synoptic terrain photography (S-005) and synoptic weather photography (S-006). Each of the spectacular photographs is captioned with information about the locations shown. Appendices list the mission, revolution, date, time, location, and area description for each photograph taken during the flights. World maps

on the inside covers show the location of each area depicted by the photographs in the book. There is also a glossary of terms used.

_____. *Earth Photographs from Gemini VI Through XII.* Washington, D.C.: National Technical Information Service, 1968.
This book is the sequel to the first (listed above), covering the last seven missions of the program. The same format is used, and the pictures are just as spectacular.

_____. *Gemini Midprogram Conference, Including Experiment Results.* Washington, D.C.: National Technical Information Service, 1966.
A four-day conference was held at NASA's Manned Spacecraft Center in Houston, Texas, February 23-25, 1966. The purpose of the meeting was to have key members of the Gemini program report on the progress of the program at the midway point. This work presents the reports, divided into the following categories: spacecraft, launch vehicle, flight operations, mission results, physical science experiments, and medical science experiments. Each dissertation is accompanied by black-and-white photographs, line drawings, tables, and charts. There is a two-segment report on the planning and execution of the Gemini VII and VI-A rendezvous mission.

_____. *Gemini Program Mission Report: Gemini 1 Through XII.* 12 vols. Washington, D.C.: Government Printing Office, 1964-1966.
These twelve books are the official record of the Gemini program missions. Each volume was prepared by the Mission Evaluation Team and contains a wealth of data on the particular flight. Includes a mission summary and sections which detail the flight, spacecraft and launch vehicle performance, crew activities, orbital experiments, in-flight demonstrations, biomedical evaluations, and mission ground support. An assessment of the mission objectives, as well as anomalies, is included. Tables summarize the vehicle histories, weather conditions, flight safety reviews, and postflight inspection of the spacecraft. Descriptions and drawings of the spacecraft, launch vehicles, and experiments packages are included. Considered to be the definitive study of each flight. Some volumes might have to be obtained directly from NASA.

_____. *Gemini Summary Conference.* Washington, D.C.: National Technical Information Service, 1967.
A two-day conference was held at NASA's Manned Spacecraft Center in Houston, Texas, on February 1-2, 1967. The purpose of the symposium was to report on the results of the last five missions of the Gemini program. The technical papers presented were divided into five sections: The first describes the rendezvous, docking, and tethered-vehicle operations involving the spacecraft and a target vehicle; the second presents various aspects of extravehicular

activity; the third concerns the operational support of the missions; the fourth covers the experiments conducted during the missions; and the fifth compares the astronaut flight and simulation experiences and relates the Gemini results to the Apollo program. Each dissertation is accompanied by black-and-white photographs, line drawings, tables, and charts.

_____. *"In This Decade . . ."*: *Mission to the Moon.* Washington, D.C.: Government Printing Office, 1969.
This is a preflight look at the Apollo 11 lunar landing mission and the Mercury, Gemini, and Apollo flights which preceded it. The narration is very simple and adds little to the information available in larger works, but it provides a concise glimpse at these ancestral efforts. In addition, the booklet previews the first manned lunar landing attempt and future programs, including Skylab. At the time of the writing, Skylab was still called the Apollo Applications Program. Color and black-and-white photographs highlight the work.

Vincze, John. *Gemini Spacecraft Parachute Landing System.* Washington, D.C.: Government Printing Office, 1966.
This work, one of a series of NASA Technical Notes, discusses in great detail the parachute recovery system used on the Gemini spacecraft. While the engineers of Project Mercury were satisfied with their spacecraft's landing by parachute into the ocean, when they moved on to Gemini they changed their minds. They theorized that there would be fewer bumps and jolts on the astronaut crew if they were seated upright (in a "heads-up" position) while their spacecraft glided to a landing. What resulted was an inflatable paraglider that would be deployed after the returning craft had been stabilized by parachute. Unfortunately, financial and scheduling constraints spelled the end to the paraglider, but the Gemini spacecraft retained the heads-up landing position by means of a two-point suspension system. This work discusses the parachute-based system which was used in the program. Line drawings, charts, and tables are used extensively.

Von Braun, Wernher, and Frederick I. Ordway III. *History of Rocketry and Space Travel.* 3d rev. ed. New York: Thomas Y. Crowell, 1975.
This is the story of the exploration of space from the earliest experiments with rocketry to the final flight of the Skylab program. Hundreds of experts on every aspect of this broad field contributed to the work. Most of the programs of the United States, the Soviet Union, and the rest of the nations engaged in space exploration at that time are detailed, both descriptively and with black-and-white and color photographs. It is one of the best references on the subject. The book also contains a large, chapter-by-chapter bibliography. The authors finish their discussion of the space programs with a look at the future, including the Space Transportation System.

Wamboldt, J. F., and S. F. Anderson, eds. *Gemini Program Launch Systems Final Report: Gemini Titan, Agena Target, Atlas SLV-3*. El Segundo, Calif.: Aerospace Corp., 1967.
A comprehensive report summarizing the management techniques employed in the development, systems test, and launching of the Gemini Launch Vehicle, Gemini Agena Target Vehicle, and the Atlas, SLV-3 (Space Launch Vehicle-3) in support of the Gemini program. Each launch vehicle is discussed in great detail, including sections on the airframe/structures, engines, vehicle propulsion systems, flight control systems, instrumentation, and propellant delivery systems. Each section contains line drawings, tables, and charts, as well as references and a glossary of definitions. Very little is presented in overly technical language. This is the most informative book available on these vehicles. The researcher will find it an invaluable reference, although it will probably have to be obtained directly from NASA.

Ward, Robinson J., Jr., comp. *A Funny Thing Happened on the Way to the Moon*. Greenwich, Conn.: Fawcett, 1969.
Although the exploration of space is a serious, often challenging business, there is still time for humor. Some of the humor presented in this book was unintentional, evolving from the frustrations and failures of the U.S. space program. The author has collected humorous events, jokes, and other tension-relieving anecdotes from the scientists, technicians, engineers, and astronauts involved in man's conquest of space. While the book does not contain any pertinent data on the history of the space program, it does make these people seem a little more human.

Yenne, Bill. *The Encyclopedia of U.S. Spacecraft*. New York: Exeter Books, 1985.
A complete encyclopedia of U.S. spacecraft is presented in a book filled with color and black-and-white photographs. General information on the programs is provided in alphabetical order, with individual spacecraft, probes, or launch vehicles listed chronologically. Data on all of the manned spacecraft, including the Gemini spacecraft, the Agena Target Vehicle, and the Titan and Atlas launch vehicles, are furnished. An appendix lists acronyms and abbreviations, and there is an index.

_____. *The Pictorial History of World Spacecraft*. New York: Exeter Books, 1988.
The history of the world's spacecraft and probes is told in chronological order from Sputnik 1 through Cosmos 1870, spanning the first thirty years of the space age. Included are all of the manned spacecraft and launch vehicles. Each is detailed with charts, diagrams, illustrations, and color and black-and-white photographs. Data on all of the manned spacecraft, including the Gemini

spacecraft and the Agena Target Vehicle, are provided. There is an appendix which lists all of the spacecraft in service as of July, 1987, grouped according to the country or organization responsible for it.

Apollo

Akens, David S. *Saturn Illustrated Chronology: Saturn's First Eleven Years, April 1957-April 1968.* Washington, D.C.: National Technical Information Service, 1971.

This is the year-by-year accounting of the activities surrounding the Saturn family of launch vehicles. These boosters include the Saturn I, designed to define the techniques for large, clustered rockets; the Saturn IB, used to test the Apollo spacecraft in low Earth orbit; and the Saturn V, which sent astronauts to the Moon. The first stage of each of the vehicles traces its roots back to two intermediate-range ballistic missiles, the Redstone and the Jupiter. The Saturn boosters, however, were the first launch vehicles designed only for peaceful purposes. Black-and-white photographs and drawings are featured to enhance the text. A reference list and glossary of terms are included.

Aldrin, Buzz, and Malcolm McConnell. *Men from Earth.* New York: Bantam Books, 1989, pp. 161-246.

Everyone knows Neil Armstrong's first words as he stepped onto the Moon, but did you know that during the walk he touched Buzz Aldrin on the shoulder and said, "Isn't it fun?" As one of the first men on the Moon, Aldrin tells the story of the United States' journey to the lunar surface from a perspective unavailable to the vast majority of readers. His description of the Apollo 11 landing reads like a James Michener novel. One of the most difficult questions for an astronaut to answer is, "What is it like?" Aldrin has found a way to answer that question. When he describes the desolation of the lunar surface, the reader can actually see it in his mind's eye. Includes a briefly annotated but extensive bibliography, as well as photographs.

Aldrin, Edwin E. "Buzz," Jr., with Wayne Warga. *Return to Earth.* New York: Random House, 1973.

Buzz Aldrin chronicles his battle with fame and depression, along with the historical events surrounding the Apollo 11 lunar landing mission. To many inside and outside NASA, the flight was more of a political coup than a scientific accomplishment. Through Aldrin's eyes, the reader sees the "party life" an astronaut and his family must endure. Aldrin's purpose in writing this exposé was not to blame NASA for his problems but to "present the reality of [his] life and career not as mere fact but as [he] perceived the truth to be."

Allen, Joseph P., with Russell Martin. *Entering Space.* New York: Stewart, Tabori & Chang, 1984.

The story of an astronaut's journey in space, told in conjunction with a study of the United States' exploration of space. This work is filled with colorful words and spectacular photographs of space travel from the ground up, and back again. There are hundreds of color photographs taken during the manned Gemini, Apollo, Skylab, Apollo Soyuz, and Space Shuttle programs, as well as those shots of our neighbors in the solar system taken from unmanned probes. The spacecraft, launch vehicles, spacefarers, and their equipment are discussed in some detail, although primarily from the perspective of a single trip into orbit and back again. There is a very real sense of "being there" as Astronaut Allen describes his feelings during the various phases of flight. Includes a brief bibliography and an index.

Anderton, David A. *Apollo 17 at Taurus Littrow.* Washington, D.C.: Government Printing Office, 1973.

A short, colorful look at the last in the series of Apollo lunar landing missions, part of NASA's Educational Publications series. The author presents a description of the mission to the Taurus-Littrow region of the Moon and a chronology of the flight. The highlight of the booklet is its detailed drawings and color photographs.

Barbour, John. *Footprints on the Moon.* New York: Associated Press, 1969.

A documentary look at the United States' efforts to place a man on the Moon. Barbour chronicles the U.S. space program from the early days of Project Mercury through the successful completion of the Apollo 11 mission. Written right after *Columbia* splashed down in the Pacific Ocean, the book tells of both the glory and the misfortune of Apollo. Barbour's reportorial presentation could well be used as a history book. Most of the information is presented in an unbiased style, neither giving NASA a pat on the back nor kicking it when it is down.

Bates, James R., et al. *ALSEP Termination Report.* Washington, D.C.: Government Printing Office, 1979.

A graphic look at the Apollo Lunar Surface Experiments Package (ALSEP) operations, from the placement of the first one on the Sea of Tranquility to the termination of data receipt on September 30, 1977. This is not an engineering book, but it does provide technical information on each of the experiments. The scope and purpose of each experiment are detailed, accompanied by an illustration. Annotated chronologies and performance details for each experiment are given. Each of the investigators has written a brief summary of the significant scientific results obtained from the ALSEP experiments. A bibliography leads the reader to more detailed works.

Bedini, Silvio A., Wernher von Braun, and Fred L. Whipple. *Moon: Man's Greatest Adventure.* New York: Harry N. Abrams, 1969.
Wernher von Braun, the "Father of the Moon Rocket," takes the reader through the history of the development of the Saturn family of launch vehicles. The book covers the efforts to place men on the Moon from the design phase through the first successful lunar landing. How does one design a launch vehicle to propel a manned spacecraft of unknown dimensions to the Moon for a project that does not exist? This was the task facing von Braun and his associates in 1961. What resulted was a vehicle six times larger and nearly one hundred times more powerful than the existing boosters.

Benson, Charles D., and William B. Faherty. *Moonport: A History of Apollo Launch Facilities and Operations.* Washington, D.C.: National Technical Information Service, 1978.
An unusual look at the Apollo program, in which the authors detail the growth and development of the facility and how it affected the lunar landing program. Some biographical data on a few of the more memorable personnel add a human touch to this tale of concrete and steel. One of the more interesting sections details the Apollo 204 accident and subsequent investigation. Important details of the accident and the attempts of ground support personnel to rescue the astronaut crew, left out of many books on the subject, are presented. The book is full of black-and-white photographs and illustrations and contains a highly detailed, annotated listing of sources.

Bilstein, Roger E. *Stages to Saturn: A Technological History of the Apollo/Saturn Launch Vehicles.* Washington, D.C.: Government Printing Office, 1980.
One title in the NASA History Series, this book chronicles the Apollo program literally from the ground up. Here is a look at the power behind the glory. The journeys to the Moon are shown from the perspective of the people who built and launched the Moon rockets. Details of each Saturn flight, from the first Saturn I in October, 1961, to the last Saturn V, which launched Skylab, are presented in chronological order. Fully illustrated and sporting an impressive forty-page bibliography, the book provides details on Apollo available nowhere else.

Booker, Peter, Gerald Frewer, and Geoffrey Pardoe. *Project Apollo: The Way to the Moon.* New York: American Elsevier, 1970.
The authors write about the efforts to place men on the Moon, as well as the Mercury and Gemini programs, which paved the way for Apollo. They look at the spacecraft, launch vehicles, flights, and astronauts involved. They also discuss the problems and accomplishments of each. Since the book is broad in coverage, there is very little detail on individual flights. The book is illustrated with black-and-white photographs and line drawings.

Borman, Frank, with Robert J. Sterling. *Countdown: An Autobiography.* New York: Silver Arrow Books, 1988, pp. 168-241.
Astronaut Borman writes of the Apollo 204 accident and the investigation which followed from an insider's point of view. He was one of the sleuths appointed by NASA to find the cause of the fire and a cure. He compares this inquiry with the one that followed the *Challenger* accident nineteen years later. As part of the Apollo spacecraft redesign team, Borman reveals some of the problems and infighting that occurred during the critical rebuilding stage. The portion of the book that is the most riveting is the chapter devoted to his Apollo 8 mission. What goes through one's mind when one is selected to be one of the first to go around the Moon? What does one do if lost in lunar orbit? Borman gives an insight into the human aspect of spaceflight.

Brooks, Courtney G., and Ivan D. Ertel. *The Apollo Spacecraft: A Chronology.* Vol. 3, *October 1, 1964-January 20, 1966.* Washington, D.C.: National Technical Information Service, 1976.
A complete, week-by-week (sometimes day-by-day) account of the Apollo program during the period when the emphasis was placed on the detailed engineering of the three spacecraft. Once the final version of the Saturn launch vehicles had been established, it was necessary to design and build the spacecraft to the weight limitations imposed by the size and strength of these vehicles. Programs were initiated to eliminate any item that was not absolutely necessary in order to minimize weight. Photographs and illustrations add to the text. Tables in the back summarize the organization of the Apollo program, the test flights, and the changes in the vehicles.

Brooks, Courtney G., James M. Grimwood, and Loyd S. Swenson, Jr. *Chariots for Apollo: A History of Manned Lunar Spacecraft.* Washington, D.C.: National Technical Information Service, 1979.
One of the titles in the NASA History Series, this book presents the "official" record of the United States' voyage to the Moon. There are dozens of black-and-white photographs of the manned, as well as unmanned, flights leading to the Apollo 11 lunar landing mission. Eight appendices present astronaut assignments, Apollo flights, funding, spacecraft component manufacturers, and the Apollo 11 experiments and lunar samples. One lists the procedures for selecting (in 1961) the site of the Manned Spacecraft Center. It was an important facility for the lunar landing program, and it may be more than coincidental that Houston was selected. Then Vice President Lyndon Johnson (for whom the center was later named) and the chairman of the House Independent Offices Appropriation Committee were both Texans. Detailed source notes and an extensively annotated bibliography provide a wealth of information for the researcher.

Chrysler Corporation. *Saturn IB Vehicle Handbook.* 4 vols. Washington, D.C.: National Technical Information Service, 1966.
If you ever wanted to build your own Saturn IB, this is the book for you. Hundreds of detailed drawings point out each part that went into making this launch vehicle. Volume 1 gives a general overview of the vehicle. The other volumes go into greater detail. These books were the manuals used by the technicians who worked on the Saturn IB. There is very little text, but no other work will answer as many questions about this second-generation booster.

Collins, Michael. *Carrying the Fire: An Astronaut's Journeys.* New York: Farrar, Straus & Giroux, 1983.
Everyone knows Neil Armstrong was the first to walk on the moon. Most remember that Buzz Aldrin went with him to the lunar surface. Few can tell you who waited in orbit while the other two "made history." Michael Collins was the only person who could not have watched the lunar landing as it happened. He was too busy in *Columbia* trying to locate the lunar module *Eagle* through his low-powered telescope and making sure Armstrong and Aldrin had a place to which they could return. Collins relays his feelings about the flight and what he would have done if *Eagle* and its crew were stranded on the Moon. This personal glimpse at the historic flight emphasizes the human element of the story, perhaps the most neglected aspect.

_____. *Liftoff: The Story of America's Adventure in Space.* New York: Grove Press, 1988.
Many books have been written about the Apollo program, most of them about Apollo 11. Few have provided an inside look at the delicate melding of man and machine. As part of this complete history of the United States' manned space programs, Collins devotes a large portion to Apollo. He sets the record straight about some of the misconceptions about astronauts and space machines. The book is illustrated with eighty-eight line drawings by James Dean, former NASA art director, which add stark realism to an otherwise unfamiliar world.

Columbia Broadcasting System. *10:56:20 P.M., EDT, 7/20/69: The Historic Conquest of the Moon as Reported to the American People by CBS News Over the CBS Television Network.* New York: Author, 1970.
"Oh, boy!" Those were the words Walter Cronkite used to echo the feelings of the entire world when man first landed on the Moon. The book, which contains the actual transcripts of the broadcasts, gives the reader the feeling of the moment. Only where necessary does a brief narration accompany the participants' words during the historic Apollo 11 mission. Most people who saw the landing and subsequent moonwalk on television watched Cronkite and astronaut Wally Schirra. Cronkite, the experienced reporter, and Schirra, the experienced space traveler, were as caught up in the excitement of the moment

as the television viewers. Photographs taken from the television monitors add to the behind-the-scenes look at how CBS broadcast one of the most historic events of the century.

Compton, William David. *Where No Man Has Gone Before: A History of Apollo Lunar Exploration Missions.* Washington, D.C.: Government Printing Office, 1989.
A decade and a half after Eugene Cernan placed the last footprints on the lunar surface, the debate continues as to whether the Apollo program was a scientific windfall or merely a political stunt. Compton's book, one of the titles in the NASA History Series, takes a look at Apollo's accomplishments and failures. It is still up to the reader to decide the answer. Illustrated with many black-and-white photographs and drawings, the work takes the reader inside NASA and the lunar landing program. A completely annotated source listing is almost as valuable as the text.

Cooper, Henry S. F., Jr. *Apollo on the Moon.* New York: Dial Press, 1969.
A look at the Apollo 11 lunar landing mission, including the tasks of the astronauts while on the Moon. The book discusses the training they underwent, their physical reaction to the lunar environment, and the samples of lunar soil they brought back with them. Although not greatly detailed, the work does give one the feel of being there, since it was written in the days immediately following the mission.

_____. *Thirteen: The Flight That Failed.* New York: Dial Press, 1973.
A fascinating look at the efforts to rescue three astronauts "lost in space" aboard the Apollo 13 command module. As they journeyed to the Moon, an explosion rocked their vessel, leaving them adrift in a lifeless spacecraft. Were it not for the lunar module, still attached to the front of the vehicle, and the engineers back on Earth, the crew members could have become just as lifeless. Although it reads like a novel, this work is based upon news reports and interviews with the participants and does not exploit the "newsworthiness" of the story.

Cortright, Edgar M., ed. *Apollo Expeditions to the Moon.* Washington, D.C.: National Technical Information Service, 1976.
A compilation of articles about the Apollo lunar landing program from the people who made it happen. Each of the later Apollo flights (Apollo 11 through 17) is discussed by the astronauts who flew the mission. Jim Lovell tells the tale of Apollo 13 from inside the crippled spacecraft. The crew, unaware of the media coverage their flight was getting, was surprised by the greeting they received upon their return to Earth. Christopher Kraft, who served as Director of Flight Operations for Apollo, tells what it was like to be in Mission Control

during the missions, and Wernher von Braun himself discusses the mighty launch vehicles of Apollo. Filled with color photographs and lengthy captions, the book truly captures the spirit of adventure that was Apollo.

_____. *Report of the Apollo 13 Review Board.* Washington, D.C.: Government Printing Office, 1970.
The official investigation of the Apollo 13 accident is presented in this work by the chairman of the Review Board. Four separate panels examined the mission events, manufacturing and testing of spacecraft components, spacecraft design, and project management. Although it was not written for the general audience, this report does present the data in an orderly, nontechnical way. Through thorough investigative techniques, the board concluded that the accident was preventable and caused in part by a lack of communications. A complete time line of events occurring during the flight is included in the appendix.

Cunningham, Walter. *The All-American Boys.* New York: Macmillan, 1977.
As part of the infamous "Wally, Walt, and Donn Show" from Apollo 7, Cunningham tells of his role in the mission and how the long-duration flight affected him, his crewmates, and their families. Eleven days in space can put a strain on any relationship, but working with an overloaded schedule and a head cold is enough to turn a sane man crazy. Fortunately, the astronauts selected for the crew were level-headed professional pilots and showed that man and machine could work together for long periods of time. Although not written for the researcher interested in statistics, this book does present a great deal of fact interwoven with the rhetoric.

Dooling, Dave. "Cape Canaveral and the Kennedy Space Center." In *Magill's Survey of Science: Space Exploration Series*, vol. 1, edited by Frank N. Magill. Pasadena, Calif.: Salem Press, 1989.
One of the essays on the history of space exploration in this five-volume set, which covers every aspect of the U.S. and Soviet manned and unmanned space programs, as well as those of nations newer to the space race. The essay looks at the two separate launch facilities: Cape Canaveral Air Force Station, located on Cape Canaveral, Florida, and the Kennedy Space Center, located on Merritt Island to the northwest. It traces the history of the sites and discusses their historical contributions to the United States' space programs. Includes an annotated bibliography and cross-references.

_____. "Johnson Space Center." In *Magill's Survey of Science: Space Exploration Series*, vol. 2, edited by Frank N. Magill. Pasadena, Calif.: Salem Press, 1989.

One of the essays on the history of space exploration in this five-volume set, which covers every aspect of the U.S. and Soviet manned and unmanned space programs, as well as those of nations newer to the space race. The Johnson Space Center, originally called the Manned Spacecraft Center, is located near Houston, Texas. It was first used as the mission control center for manned spaceflights during the Gemini program. This work discusses the center, its origins and its role in the Gemini, Apollo, Skylab, Apollo Soyuz, and Space Shuttle programs. Includes an annotated bibliography and cross-references.

Ertel, Ivan D., and Mary L. Morse. *The Apollo Spacecraft: A Chronology. Vol. 1, Through November 7, 1962.* Washington, D.C.: National Technical Information Service, 1969.
The beginnings of the Apollo program are chronicled here, along with the contributions of the Project Mercury and Gemini program flights. Comparisons are made between Apollo and its two predecessors. Apollo, like Mercury, had a well-defined objective. It also had the power that was Gemini's. This narrative of daily and weekly events during this period brings out some of the difficulties of planning a program to place men on the Moon and return them safely to Earth. Photographs and illustrations add to the text. Tables in the back summarize the funding of the Apollo program, its organization, the test flights, and the changes in the launch vehicles.

Ertel, Ivan D., and Roland W. Newkirk. *The Apollo Spacecraft: A Chronology. Vol. 4, January 21, 1966-July 13, 1974.* Washington, D.C.: National Technical Information Service, 1978.
The fourth and final volume of the chronology covers the last eight and one-half years of Apollo. It includes all flight tests of the Apollo spacecraft, as well as the last five Gemini flights, the Apollo 204 accident and its subsequent investigation, and the manned Apollo program. Chronicled are the day-to-day activities which brought all of the elements together to achieve the lunar landing goal. Photographs and illustrations add to the text. Tables in the back summarize the organization of the Apollo program, comparisons of the Block II versus the Block I command module, the flights and their objectives, the crews and their support teams, the Apollo experiments, and funding.

Farmer, Gene, and Dora Jane Hamblin. *First on the Moon.* Boston: Little, Brown, 1970.
The journey of Neil Armstrong, Buzz Aldrin, and Michael Collins to the Moon and back is told by the astronauts who made the trek. The book adds very little in the way of historical data about the flight, but it does make interesting reading. This is one of the first published accounts of the mission by the Apollo 11 crew and conveys their thoughts while relatively fresh in their

minds. A speculative epilogue by Arthur Clarke on the future of spaceflight concludes the book.

Furniss, Tim. *Manned Spaceflight Log.* London: Jane's, 1983, rev. ed. 1987.
This work covers the manned spaceflights of the Soviet Union and the United States from 1961 through 1986. A synopsis of each mission is given, along with pertinent data (date, crew, site, recovery, duration, spacecraft weight, and so forth) and several black-and-white photographs. The Mercury, Gemini, Apollo, Skylab, Apollo Soyuz, and Space Shuttle flights are listed chronologically. Included are the thirteen flights of the X-15 research aircraft which exceeded the fifty-mile altitude necessary to qualify its pilot as an astronaut under Air Force rules. There are astronaut photographs and, in the appendices, listings of space seniority and the current status of the astronaut and cosmonaut classes.

_____. *One Small Step.* Newbury Park, Calif.: Haynes, 1989.
Written to coincide with the twentieth anniversary of the first manned lunar landing, this book takes a look back at the origins of Apollo and updates the reader on the twelve men who walked on the Moon. In fact, one of the most interesting features of this work is the section (or rather, chapters) on each of them. Using titles which the author feels best describes each astronaut (for example, Buzz Aldrin is "The Second," Alan Bean, "The Painter"), he talks about their backgrounds, contributions to Apollo, and current status. A large portion of the manuscript details the ancestors of Apollo: Project Mercury and the Gemini program. The book is well written and contains a listing of references.

_____. *Space Flight: The Records.* London: Guiness Books, 1985.
Do you know the first manned spaceflight to be curtailed? It was Gemini V, which landed one orbit early to miss hurricane Betsy. Were you aware that the first spaceflight with more than one fifty-year-old person on board was that of STS 51-B/Spacelab 3, in April, 1985? These and dozens of other interesting and significant—or not so significant—facts are covered in this work. The first part of the book is a "diary" of manned spaceflight, listing each of the missions of the United States and Soviet Union. There is a chapter on manned spaceflight "firsts" and one on the manned space machines. Basic biographical information on each of the space travelers is given, accompanied by the person's photograph. The major information section is last and includes tables on manned spaceflight duration, space seniority, space experience, lunar spacemen, spacewalks, astroflights of the X-15, all known cosmonauts, NASA astronauts, Space Shuttle passengers, NASA flight crew selections, and the Space Shuttle schedule. There are hundreds of black-and-white photographs, a glossary of terms, and an index.

Goldstein, Norm, ed. *Moments in Space.* New York: Gallery Books, 1986, pp. 73-103.
Newspaper photographs from the Associated Press are the highlight of this book, which offers little text to accompany them. Much of the monograph is not to be relied on for accuracy, especially because the information included with the photographs has not been updated from what was known at the time of the event. Many of the photographs are grainy, but it is for their historical context that they should be viewed, not for their clarity.

Grissom, Betty, and Henry S. Still. *Starfall.* New York: Thomas Y. Crowell, 1974.
The widow of astronaut Gus Grissom, killed in the Apollo 204 launchpad fire, discusses her life before and after the event. She chronicles their lives during the Apollo era and raises some questions about the accident. The rigors of preparing for the first manned Apollo flight took their toll on both of them, as well as their children. After the accident, Betty Grissom was dissatisfied with the results of the investigation. She believed that the mishap was completely preventable and, at the time of the writing, had a suit filed against NASA. As intriguing as any book written by an astronaut, this work sheds new light on the making of an astronaut's spouse.

Grumman Corp. *Apollo Operations Handbook: Lunar Module LM 10 and Subsequent.* 2 vols. Washington, D.C.: Government Printing Office, 1971.
The most authoritative set of books on the vehicle that landed men on the Moon. Volume 1 contains drawings and diagrams of every system and subsystem in the lunar module. The function of each component is described in detail. Volume 2 gives the operational procedures for flying the spiderlike machine. Included are primary, backup, and contingency procedures for every phase of the lunar landing mission. The work was written by the engineers and scientists who designed the spacecraft.

Gurney, Gene. *Americans on the Moon: The Story of Project Apollo.* New York: Random House, 1970.
A review of the Apollo program from the first circumlunar flight through the first lunar landing. Although only four manned missions are discussed (Apollos 8 through 11), the goals of Apollo are explained, as well as the means used to accomplish them. Nontechnical in content, the discussion brings the technology of manned spaceflight down to Earth. The are a number of photographs, many of which are not presented in other works. A short preview of upcoming lunar exploration flights is included.

Hall, Al, ed. *Petersen's Book of Man in Space.* Vol. 3, *The Power and the Glory.* Los Angeles: Petersen, 1974.

A photographic chronology of the Apollo program's unmanned flights from Apollo 1 through Apollo 6. Photographs of the various components of Apollo's launch vehicles, from Little Joe II to the mighty Saturn V, fill the pages of this volume. Also detailed are the Cape Kennedy launch complexes and the astronaut training facilities. There is very little text; the pictures speak for themselves. The reader can see, for example, a Saturn V being built literally from the ground up. Perhaps the largest compilation of NASA and industry photographs.

_____. *Petersen's Book of Man in Space.* Vol. 4, *A Giant Leap for Mankind.* Los Angeles: Petersen, 1974.
This volume chronicles the flights of Apollo 7 through Apollo 11. Photographs show the preparation for each mission and the events of launch through splashdown. This work also shows the development of the lunar module, from its early stages right through to the final flights. One of the most overlooked aspects of the Apollo program is the need for a spacesuit that can withstand extremes of temperature and atmosphere, yet still be functional. A comparison of the early models of the spacesuit to the ones used on the Moon show what an accomplishment this was.

_____. *Petersen's Book of Man in Space.* Vol. 5, *Beyond the Threshold.* Los Angeles: Petersen, 1974.
The last volume in the five-part photographic essay of the U.S. space program covers the flights of Apollo 12 through Apollo 17. In addition, it looks at the scientific accomplishments of each mission. Hundreds of color and black-and-white photographs are the key to this set. This volume chronicles the Apollo Lunar Experiments Packages, Lunar Receiving Laboratory, the service module's Scientific Instrument Bay, and the Lunar Roving Vehicle. The probing question "Where's the bathroom?" is answered with photographs and drawings of the Urine Disposal Subsystem and Solid Waste Management System, the latter consisting mainly of adult-sized diapers and a germicide packet. The germicide was necessary, since gases produced during the decaying process could literally explode the sealed bags.

Hallion, Richard, and Tom O. Crouch, eds. *Ten Years Since Tranquility: Reflections upon Apollo 11.* Washington, D.C.: Smithsonian Institution Press, 1979.
The editors, now former curators at the National Air and Space Museum, have collected essays reviewing the social and political factors that led to the first lunar landing. Those who were involved wrote the essay about a particular aspect of the Apollo program. The technological developments, spin-offs, accomplishments in rocket science, and the scientific results of the lunar surface and orbital experiments are discussed. Illustrated with black-and-white photo-

graphs, the work is a concise view of the United States' journey to the Moon. A bibliography is included.

Irwin, James B., with William A. Emerson, Jr. *To Rule the Night: The Discovery Voyage of Astronaut Jim Irwin.* Nashville: A. J. Holman, 1973.
The flight of Apollo 15 is chronicled by its lunar module pilot, as he rediscovers his spiritual faith. Looking back at Earth from more than 200,000 miles has to make one feel the presence of God. Irwin parallels his scientific accomplishments with the renewal of his religious beliefs. Although written from a spiritual point of view, the book still provides a wealth of inside information about the flight. Black-and-white photographs help to illustrate the story, but the text alone is fascinating.

Irwin, Mary, with Madalene Harris. *The Moon Is Not Enough: An Astronaut's Wife Finds Peace with God and Herself.* Grand Rapids, Mich.: Sondervan, 1978.
Seven years after her husband rode the first "moon car" on the lunar surface, Mary Irwin tells her side of the story. It is the story of a partnership in which one gets to go on the adventure and the other has to stay home and worry. This is a charming look at the other side of Apollo 15, mostly from the point of view of the one who stayed home. Black-and-white photographs are included to enhance Mary Irwin's story. It is interesting to compare her view of the flight with that of her husband in his book (listed above).

Johnston, Richard S., Lawrence F. Dietlein, and Charles A. Berry, eds. *Biomedical Results of Apollo.* Washington, D.C.: National Technical Information Service, 1975.
Biomedical testing, under ideal conditions, is by its very nature an iffy proposition. Take your subjects 250,000 miles away from the laboratory and the chances of getting accurate data are next to none. These were the conditions under which scientists had to work during the Apollo program. The editors of this work have compiled a concise review of each experiment, including the theory behind the test, the means by which it was completed, and the results. The text is supplemented with photographs and drawings, as well as charts of the conclusions reached by each examiner. Every section of the book has its own reference listing, which will guide the researcher to more detailed works.

Kerrod, Robin. *Apollo.* London: Multimedia Books, 1989.
The story of the Apollo program is told in this concise, well-written work. The work begins with the early achievements of Project Mercury and the Gemini program. Mercury was man's first tentative step into the unknown region of the universe, only one hundred miles above. Gemini developed and perfected the rendezvous techniques so vital the success of the Moon missions. The story

would not be complete without mention of the "children" of Apollo: Skylab and the Apollo Soyuz Test Project. The work goes into detail about the development of the hardware for Apollo. In addition to the discussion of flight hardware, the author looks at the massive Launch Umbilical Towers, which were used to service the vehicle on the ground and which served as the launching pad. The spacecraft are detailed. Photographs, drawings, and a log of the Apollo missions add to the text.

Lattimer, Richard L. *All We Did Was Fly to the Moon.* History-Alive Series, vol. 1. Alachula, Fla.: Whispering Eagle Press, 1983, pp. 41-95.
In a very different look at the U.S. space program, Lattimer tells the tale of Apollo with many color and black-and-white photographs and reproductions of crew emblems and newspaper front pages. There is a synopsis of each flight, along with some very interesting trivia which the author gleaned from apparently a great number of sources. Unfortunately, a bibliography is not included. Perhaps the most entertaining tidbits are from the astronauts themselves. They tell how the crew emblems and spacecraft call signs were derived.

Lay, Bierne, Jr. *Earthbound Astronauts: The Builders of Apollo-Saturn.* Englewood Cliffs, N.J.: Prentice-Hall, 1971.
This is the story of the people who conceived, designed, and built the most powerful launch vehicle to ever be launched. The author looks at the difficulties in creating the vehicle that would send men to the Moon using technology that had not been invented. The biggest challenge, of course, was accomplishing the lunar landing mission before the end-of-decade deadline imposed by President John F. Kennedy. Of the twelve Saturn V's used during the Apollo program, none failed, an accomplishment unmatched by any other expendable launch vehicle. The story looks at the political, scientific, and economic obstacles faced by Wernher von Braun and his associates, some of which were more challenging than the engineering problems.

Lee, John B. "Earth-Landing Systems: Systems Applications." In *Manned Spacecraft: Engineering Design and Operation*, edited by Paul E. Purser, Maxime A. Faget, and Norman F. Smith. New York: Fairchild, 1964.
A compilation of essays based upon a series of lectures delivered at NASA's Manned Spacecraft Center, Louisiana State University, University of Houston, and William Marsh Rice University in 1963 and 1964. This paper discusses in some detail the systems designed to slow a spacecraft sufficiently to permit a safe landing. The parachute recovery systems used in the Mercury and Apollo spacecraft are compared. Also discussed is the paraglider designed for the Gemini program. The paraglider was to be used to allow the spacecraft to glide to a landing by means of a deployable, inflatable wing. The concept was

eventually dropped because of development problems. The essay is highlighted with black-and-white photographs and line drawings of the components, as well as a list of references.

Lewis, Richard S. *Appointment on the Moon.* New York: Ballantine Books, 1969, pp. 373-539.
This is one of the most complete accounts of the U.S. space program through the Apollo 11 lunar landing mission. The author takes the reader through the manned phase of Apollo, beginning with the Apollo 204 pad fire, which killed three astronauts. Unfortunately, he almost completely ignores the unmanned flights of the Saturn I and Saturn IB. He makes up for it, somewhat, by discussing the unmanned lunar probes which helped to make the Apollo 11 mission possible. There are several pages of black-and-white photographs and an excellent listing of reference material.

——————. "Man on the Moon." In *The Illustrated Encyclopedia of Space Technology: A Comprehensive History of Space Exploration,* by Kenneth Gatland et al. New York: Harmony Books, 1981.
This section in the book discusses the Apollo program and the United States' quest for the Moon. Each mission is described, along with the experiments. A map of the Moon is included, indicating where each Apollo landing site is located. There are color and black-and-white photographs, drawings, and charts. The major features of the program, including the spacecraft and launch vehicles, are discussed. There is a brief bibliography. The book includes a chronology of the major space events since Sputnik 1, a glossary of terms, and an index.

——————. *The Voyages of Apollo: The Exploration of the Moon.* New York: Quadrangle/New York Times, 1974.
This is the sequel to *Appointment on the Moon* (listed above) and covers in depth the seven manned Apollo flights to the Moon, beginning with Apollo 11. For some reason, the author chose to ignore Apollo 10, perhaps because it was not intended to land on the Moon. Of the seven, though, six did land and the other turned into the most dramatic rescue of the space age. Lewis views these journeys as "personal adventures, mass communication events and evolutionary episodes in our movement out of our earthly cradle."

Life magazine editors. *To the Moon and Back.* New York: Life Education Program, 1969.
A pictorial look at the United States' quest for the Moon as first published in the pages of *Life* magazine. In addition to presenting the Apollo 11 mission and biographical data on its crew, the work briefly describes all of the previous American manned flights of Project Mercury and the Gemini program, as well

as the Soviet manned missions. Biographies of the families of the Apollo 11 crew are included for the personal touch for which *Life* is famous. The photographs are the real value here, combining all aspects of the mission.

Logsdon, John M. *The Decision to Go to the Moon: Project Apollo and the National Interest*. Cambridge, Mass.: MIT Press, 1970.
Logsdon, a political scientist, looks at the political, social, and economical motivations that determined the course of the Apollo program. The author uses many NASA records and government documents, including presidential papers, to support his theories. It does not take a genius to realize that the challenge of President John F. Kennedy (and his subsequent assassination) influenced Congress and the general public to support Apollo. An evaluation of the spending prior to the first lunar landing of Apollo 11, compared to the budgeted amounts after, shows that this support dropped rapidly after the goal was met.

MacKinnon, Douglas, and Joseph Baldanza. *Footprints: The Twelve Men Who Walked on the Moon Reflect on Their Flights, Their Lives, and the Future*. Washington, D.C.: Acropolis Books, 1989.
Here is the Apollo lunar landing story as told by the twelve men who walked on the Moon. If you want to know what it was like to be part of Apollo program and take a stroll in the lunar sunlight, this is the book for you. The authors sat down with each of the astronauts and discussed the flights and their lives before the mission and since. Some of the tales of the behind-the-scenes activities are priceless. Only a few of the questions seemed out of place, but it should be left to the reader to decide which, if any, are. The book is illustrated with color paintings by astronaut-artist Alan Bean. He has annotated each painting with the ideas he had when he created them.

Magill, Frank N., ed. *Magill's Survey of Science: Space Exploration Series*. Vol. 1. Pasadena, Calif.: Salem Press, 1989, pp. 28-131.
This five-volume set covers every aspect of the U.S. and Soviet manned and unmanned space programs, as well as those of nations newer to the space race. The United States embarked on a challenge to place a man on the Moon and return him safely in early 1961. The answer to this challenge was Apollo. Each of the manned and unmanned flights of the program is detailed in this work, as are the spacecraft and launch vehicles. Each essay lists the pertinent data of the mission, launch vehicle, and spacecraft. One overview article chronicles the program from its beginnings to the completion of the final lunar landing mission, Apollo 17, and subsequent articles cover the Apollo missions individually in greater detail. Each article contains an annotated bibliography and cross-references.

Mailer, Norman. *Of a Fire on the Moon*. Boston: Little, Brown, 1970.
Mailer gives his impressions of the U.S. space program, in particular the flight of Apollo 11. He looks at the science that permitted the United States to accomplish more technologically in a nine-year period than it had in the previous six decades. He also discusses his own philosophy about the significance of the quest for the Moon and what the future will hold. The book is not one of the best from a researcher's point of view: It does contain many facts, but it presents very little in the way of new information. It does, however, provide an insight into the opinions of some members of the literary world about space exploration.

Mason, Robert Grant, ed. "Apollo to the Moon." In *Life in Space*. Alexandria, Va.: Time-Life Books, 1983.
The editors of *Life* magazine have sifted through hundreds of NASA's and their own photographs, taken during the first twenty-five years of the space age. What has resulted is a superb collection of photographs of each U.S. manned spaceflight, from Alan Shepard's suborbital hop in *Freedom 7* through the STS-6 Space Shuttle mission. Throughout the work are breathtaking color and startling black-and-white photographs. The photographs cover a range of topics, including the spacecraft, launch vehicles, and the Lunar Roving Vehicle. The focus of this segment is on the Apollo manned flights, with spectacular views of Earth, the Moon, the launches, splashdowns, and everything in between.

Masursky, Harold, G. W. Colton, and Farouk El-Baz, eds. *Apollo Over the Moon: A View from Orbit*. Washington, D.C.: National Technical Information Service, 1978.
Everyone who takes a trip to faraway places tries to capture some of the magic of the moment through photographs. The Apollo astronauts were no exception. Of course, much of their photography was done in the name of science, but that does not take away any of their beauty. There are dozens of black-and-white photographs, each one documented as to when and where it was taken. The stark beauty of the lunar landscape is enhanced by the black-and-white images. The most spectacular photographs are the stereographic pairs. Unfortunately, a stereographic viewer is not provided, but with a little work one can obtain fairly good stereo.

Mitchum, Ellen F. "Saturn Launch Vehicles." In *Magill's Survey of Science: Space Exploration Series*, vol. 3, edited by Frank N. Magill. Pasadena, Calif.: Salem Press, 1989.
One of the essays on the history of space exploration in this five-volume set, which covers every aspect of the U.S. and Soviet manned and unmanned space programs, as well as those of nations newer to the space race. Before the first satellite was placed in orbit, before there was a goal to put a man on the

Moon, there were the dreamers who thought big. Wernher von Braun and his fellow scientists believed that there would be a need for a very large launch vehicle in the United States' arsenal, not to hurl warheads at the enemy but to loft large payloads into Earth orbit and beyond. What developed was the Saturn family of vehicles: the Saturn I, Saturn IB, Saturn V, and a few others that never made it past the planning stage. This article delves into the roots of this family of giants and details their flights and their contribution to the Apollo program. Contains an annotated bibliography and cross-references.

Moreau, John. *First Men on the Moon: Historic Front Pages and Special Cartoon Portfolio.* Dayton, Ohio: Private printing, 1976.
This is an interesting collection of reproductions from many national newspapers celebrating the first manned landing on the Moon. In addition, there are editorial cartoons from some of the nation's finest artists. There is not a great deal of new data in these pages, but the collection does give the reader an awareness of public attitudes on the date of the first Moon landing. The assortment of cartoons ranges from images of national pride to nose-thumbing at the Soviets, whose Luna 15 was an attempt to upstage Apollo 11. It is also interesting to read some of the other articles which shared the headlines.

Morse, Mary L., and Jean K. Bays. *The Apollo Spacecraft: A Chronology.* Vol. 2, *November 8, 1962-September 30, 1964.* Washington, D.C.: National Technical Information Service, 1973.
According to the authors, this book covers the "teenage" years of the Apollo program. During this period, the program established most of its basic operational features, establishing that nominal Earth landing would be on the water, command/service module (CSM) to lunar module (LM) transposition and docking would be free-flying, the LM crew would operate from the standing position, and the LM would have four deployable landing legs instead of five. Initial testing of the major components was completed during this time. The day-to-day and week-by-week activities of the Apollo program are chronicled. Summaries of spacecraft weight by quarters, a list of major spacecraft component manufacturers, flight summary, organizational charts, and funding histories are included in appendices.

Murray, Charles, and Catherine Bly Cox. *Apollo: The Race to the Moon.* New York: Simon & Schuster, 1989.
An intriguing look at the people behind the accomplishment, this book details those whose unenviable task it was to translate a president's dream into reality. Much research has gone into this work. The reader gets a insight into the background of the Apollo program's team members, as well as a look at their extracurricular activities. They were, after all, only human; they simply had an inhuman goal to complete. The book is well written and contains an excel-

lent appendix of reference notes. Several black-and-white photographs give faces to the characters discussed in the book.

Otto, Dixon P., and Donald Andrew Gardner. *Moonrise: Apollo Plus Twenty.* Athens, Ohio: Main Stage, 1989.
A retrospective of the Apollo era through the completion of the Apollo 11 lunar landing mission. The first half of this work presents a chronology of the major events leading to Apollo 11. Although the entries are brief, they contain all of the pertinent data. The latter half provides a transcript (with commentary) of the flight of Apollo 11 as it was broadcast on television. The transcript covers every phase of the flight from liftoff to splashdown. There are many color and black-and-white photographs of the many Apollo missions, as well as a few of the other, related flights.

Pellegrino, Charles R., and Joshua Stoff. *Chariots for Apollo: The Making of the Lunar Module.* New York: Atheneum, 1985.
This is the story of the Grumman engineers and technicians who had the task of designing and building a spacecraft to land on the Moon. As research flights continued and the launch vehicles were developed, the Grumman people made appropriate changes to the lunar module (LM). The spiderlike spacecraft changed considerably during its early life. Mostly, it had to do a lot of dieting, trimming the weight that the Saturn V could not handle. Perhaps the most difficult feat these engineers accomplished was the unplanned use of the LM as a lifeboat to rescue Apollo 13. The book is full of historical data relating to the LM and the people who gave it life.

Pitts, John A. *The Human Factor: Biomedicine in the Manned Space Program to 1980.* Washington, D.C.: Government Printing Office, 1985.
One title in the NASA History Series, this book chronicles the life sciences programs of the U.S. manned spaceflights of the Mercury, Gemini, Apollo, and Skylab programs, and the Apollo Soyuz Test Project. There are dozens of black-and-white photographs, line drawings, tables, and charts about the tests and experiments used to test man's ability to live and work in the microgravity environment of orbital flight. An impressive appendix lists source notes and bibliographic references, and there is an index.

Pogue, William R. *How Do You Go to the Bathroom in Space?* New York: Tom Doherty Associates, 1985.
This and many other interesting questions about living in space are answered by former astronaut Pogue. He was one of three crew members who spent eighty-four days in orbit aboard Skylab. Actually, there are 156 questions which the author has gleaned from thousands that he and his fellow astronauts have received in a quarter century of manned spaceflight. Many of the ques-

tions lead to humorous answers, but most provide a great deal of firsthand information about matters of general interest. The questions touch on each of the U.S. manned space programs. Several appendices provide additional information, including a summary of the physiological effects of spaceflight, a list of Earth features recognizable from space, a guide to information and resources, and a bibliography.

Rabinowitch, Eugene, and Richard S. Lewis, eds. *Man on the Moon: The Impact on Science, Technology, and International Cooperation.* New York: Basic Books, 1969.
This illustrated work presents a collection of views as to the effects that lunar exploration and spaceflight in general have on life on Earth. The contributors write of the impact that the Apollo 11 lunar landing had on the Soviet Union. Although the opinions are dated and a bit overstated (primarily because of the relatively short period of time which had elapsed since the landing), they reflect the feeling that U.S. technology was the best in the world. Later studies would show that this technological advantage was quickly squandered.

Schirra, Walter M., Jr., with Richard N. Billings. *Schirra's Space.* Boston: Quinlan Press, 1988, pp. 177-210.
Wally Schirra knows spacecraft. As the only person to pilot the Mercury, Gemini, and Apollo spacecraft, Schirra knew what he wanted in his vehicle and in his mission. Interference from ground control was definitely not what his Apollo 7 crew wanted. In fact, they nearly staged the first mutiny in space when Mission Controllers wanted to cram more into their already overworked schedule. In the book Schirra tells about his contributions to Apollo and his feelings toward the entire program. Black-and-white photographs add to the text, which is a well-written look at the life of a "space jockey."

Simmons, Gene. *On the Moon with Apollo 15: A Guidebook to the Hadley-Appenine Region.* Washington, D.C.: National Technical Information Service, 1971.
This is a preflight guide to the Apollo 15 mission, with particular emphasis on the lunar activities. According to the author, it is intended to be used in conjunction with the coverage provided by the commercial television networks. Each of the lunar surface experiments is detailed, as is each moonwalk. The book, highlighted with black-and-white photographs and line drawings, is well written for the general reader. The researcher will find the tables very informative, containing among other things a time line of flight activities. It is interesting to compare the scheduled activities with the actual events. Most of the time, the astronauts were able to maintain the hectic pace. Includes a brief, annotated bibliography and a glossary of terms and acronyms.

_____. *On the Moon with Apollo 16: A Guidebook to the Descartes Region*. Washington, D.C.: Government Printing Office, 1972.
The second in a series of preflight guides for the last three Apollo lunar landings, this book provides the same wealth of information as the one described above. It covers the flight of Apollo 16.

_____. *On the Moon with Apollo 17: A Guidebook to the Taurus-Littrow Region*. Washington, D.C.: Government Printing Office, 1972.
This work covers the flight of Apollo 17, the last manned lunar landing of the Apollo program. Its scope is similar to the guides for the two previous missions, as described above.

Swann, G. A., et al. *Geology of the Apollo 14 Landing in the Fra Mauro Highlands*. Washington, D.C.: U.S. Geological Survey, 1977.
The book is written primarily for the geologist, but the general reader will find its contents interesting. It presents an in-depth report on the geological investigations performed during the Apollo 14 lunar landing mission. Dozens of black-and-white photographs taken during the two lunar walks document the samples returned by the astronauts. Each of the larger rock samples is displayed with pictures taken from all six sides, as well as data on the composition of the specimen. For comparison, the sample is shown oriented as it appears in the lunar surface documentation photograph. The book contains an extensive, annotated list of selected references. Large photographic maps of the region are provided separately to permit locating the position of the samples at the site. Also included are photographic panoramas taken on the lunar surface.

Ulrich, George E., et al., eds. *Geology of the Apollo 16 Area, Central Lunar Highlands*. Washington, D.C.: U.S. Geological Survey, 1981.
A comprehensive report on the geological investigations conducted during the Apollo 16 mission, this work provides a wealth of information. Hundreds of black-and-white photographs taken during the three lunar excursions document the samples returned by the astronauts. Each of the larger rock samples is displayed with pictures taken from all six sides, as well as data on the composition of the specimen. For comparison the sample is shown oriented as it appears in the lunar surface documentation photograph. The book contains an extensive, annotated list of selected references. Large photographic maps of the region are provided separately to permit locating the position of the samples at the site. Also included are photographic panoramas taken on the surface.

U.S. House of Representatives. *The Apollo 13 Accident: Hearings Before the Committee on Science and Astronautics*. Washington, D.C.: Government Printing Office, 1970.

This is the official report of the congressional committee that investigated the Apollo 13 accident. An oxygen tank in the service module ruptured, crippling the spacecraft and nearly costing the lives of its astronaut crew as they traveled to the Moon. The report supports NASA's own investigative conclusions as to the cause and remedy of the problem. There is a wealth of information about the mission and the inner workings of the Apollo command and service modules. There are several line drawings to complement the text. Although not an extremely large document, this report still contains political mumbo jumbo that must be mentally filtered out of the discussion. An appendix contains the entire report of the NASA Review Board.

_____. *Investigation into Apollo 204 Accident: Hearings Before the Subcommittee on NASA Oversight of the Committee on Science and Astronautics.* Washington, D.C.: Government Printing Office, 1967.
This is the comprehensive, multivolume report of the congressional committee that investigated the Apollo 1 accident. This work contains all of the testimony by witnesses, test results, and conclusions of the inquiry board established by NASA. Unlike the witch-hunts of the *Challenger* accident investigation, this report supports NASA's results. There are many photographic exhibits in the book, but because of the lack of quality reproduction, they provide very little additional information. It takes quite a while to wade through the mass of data, but a great deal of technical information is provided about the Block I Apollo spacecraft. The entire report of the NASA Review Board is included.

_____. *United States Civilian Space Programs 1958-1978.* Vol. 1. Washington, D.C.: Government Printing Office, 1981.
In a very concise report, the Committee on Space Science and Applications has compiled data on all U.S. space activity during its first two decades. After a brief introduction and summary chapter, the volume is divided into fourteen additional sections. The second chapter deals with the space-related issues under consideration by Congress. The remaining sections cover the history of NASA and its relationship to U.S. space policy, NASA facilities and tracking systems, launch vehicles and propulsion, manned spaceflight through 1975, the Space Transportation System, space life sciences, space science programs, materials processing in space, international cooperation in space, interagency and non-NASA governmental space activities, industrial and university support for NASA, space program benefits, and selected future space programs. Appendices contain Department of Defense manned spaceflight plans, NASA funding history, international space agreements, texts of President Jimmy Carter's space directives, documents relating to the legal aspects of the Space Shuttle, major U.S. space organizations, a master log of U.S. spaceflights, and a table of U.S. space orbital payloads by mission from 1957 through 1979.

U.S. National Aeronautics and Space Administration. *Analysis of Apollo 8 Photography and Visual Observations.* Washington, D.C.: National Technical Information Service, 1969.
Apollo 8 was the first manned mission to the Moon and, as such, was flown primarily to provide photographic coverage of the proposed manned lunar landing sites. Hundreds of black-and-white and color photographs were taken by the crew as they made ten orbits of the Moon. This work documents each of the photographs and presents an analysis of some of the most important ones. Tables in the appendices tell exactly when each photograph was shot, where the spacecraft was in relation to the Moon, what types of lenses and filters (if any) were used, the shutter settings, the Sun angle, and the availability of pictures of the same area shot from unmanned lunar probes. In addition to the text, the pictures offer an enormous amount of information about the surface of the Moon.

_____. *Analysis of Surveyor 3 Material and Photographs Returned by Apollo 12.* Washington, D.C.: National Technical Information Service, 1972.
Apollo 12 was the only flight to land near another spacecraft on the surface of the Moon. Surveyor 3 landed in the Ocean of Storms two years earlier to determine the feasibility of manned landings. The Apollo 12 astronauts, in addition to photographing the spacecraft, brought back Surveyor's trenching tool, camera, and several pieces of tubing and a cable. This book provides the researcher with information about what exposure to the lunar "atmosphere" does to man-made equipment. This information was useful in designing equipment for placement on the lunar surface by future crews. Copies of the black-and-white photographs taken by astronauts Conrad and Bean are included.

_____. *Apollo.* Washington, D.C.: Government Printing Office, 1974.
A large, full-color book that provides a brief overview of the Apollo program. The work is primarily a good source of photographs rather than data. It describes the manned and unmanned predecessors of Apollo, including Gemini and Mercury. There is a section on the Moon rocks which provides some unique color views of the crystalline structure of the samples.

_____. *Apollo Mission Report: Apollo 4 Through 17.* 14 vols. Washington, D.C.: National Technical Information Service, 1968-1973.
The official report on each of the flights in the Apollo program subsequent to the unmanned Saturn I and Saturn IB missions. Each volume was prepared by the Mission Evaluation Team and contains a wealth of data on the particular flight. There is a mission summary and sections which detail the flight, spacecraft, crew activities, orbital and surface experiments, in-flight demonstrations, biomedical evaluations, and mission ground support. An assessment of the mission objectives, as well as anomalies, is included. Tables summarize the

flight trajectory and activity time lines. Descriptions and drawings of the spacecraft, launch vehicles, and experiments packages are included. Considered to be the definitive study of each flight. Some volumes might have to be obtained directly from NASA.

_____. *Apollo 8: Man Around the Moon*. Washington, D.C.: Government Printing Office, 1968.
A brief, photographic report on the first manned flight to the Moon, this work discusses the flight and its objectives. Apollo 8 was the first manned mission to leave Earth orbit. It demonstrated that the Saturn V was capable of placing the Apollo spacecraft in lunar orbit. The booklet shows, through numerous color and black-and-white photographs, the astronauts' in-flight activities. Extensive coverage is given to the photographs taken of the Moon and of Earth from the vicinity of the Moon. There is very little written information, but the pictures do chronicle the mission.

_____. *Apollo 12: A New Vista for Lunar Science*. Washington, D.C.: Government Printing Office, 1970.
This work is a brief report on the accomplishments of the second manned lunar landing mission. Told mostly with color and black-and-white photographs, it presents a look at the mission. Apollo 12 proved that its predecessor was not a fluke, that astronauts could accurately land on the Moon and perform a variety of scientific tasks. One of its major accomplishments was the retrieval of parts from the Surveyor 3 spacecraft, an unmanned probe, which had landed in the Ocean of Storms two years earlier.

_____. *Apollo 13: "Houston, We've Got a Problem."* Washington, D.C.: Government Printing Office, 1970.
It was not the first in-flight accident to strike the U.S. space program, but Apollo 13 had the greatest chance for failure. While on a course for the Moon, the spacecraft was rocked by a small explosion. It was caused by an oxygen tank overheating in the service module attached at the rear of the conical command module (CM). When the tank blew, it took the second oxygen tank with it and nearly took the lives of the three crew members riding in the CM. Fortunately, the lunar module was still attached and served as a lifeboat for the crew. This book looks at the mission, mostly with color and black-and-white photographs.

_____. *Apollo 14: Science at Fra Mauro*. Washington, D.C.: Government Printing Office, 1971.
Another in the series of photographic studies of one of the manned Apollo missions, this work looks at Apollo 14. This mission included the first wheeled equipment transporter, which looked somewhat like a golf cart. This was

appropriate, since Mission Commander Alan Shepard became the first golfer on the Moon when he lofted one of those little white balls several hundred yards down the "green."

_____. *Apollo 15 at Hadley Base.* Washington, D.C.: Government Printing Office, 1972.
The first moon car, the Lunar Roving Vehicle, was driven during Apollo 15's three-day visit. It easily traversed the terrain and permitted the astronauts the opportunity to obtain geologic samples far from the landing site. The flight also featured the first use of a scientific instrument module in the service module for obtaining data and photographs from lunar orbit. This brief, photo-filled work tells about Apollo 15 with very little text.

_____. *Apollo 16 at Descartes.* Washington, D.C.: Government Printing Office, 1972.
A photographic essay on the Apollo 16 mission to the lunar surface. The mission placed two astronauts on the Moon for three days, during which they performed three moonwalks. Actually, they were more in the way of moon "rides," since this was the second flight to utilize the Lunar Roving Vehicle. Although some information about the mission is given, most of the work consists of photographs taken on the Moon or from orbit.

_____. *Apollo Operations Handbook: Block II Spacecraft.* Vol. 1, *Spacecraft Description.* Washington, D.C.: Government Printing Office, 1969.
This is the most complete technical reference written about the Apollo Block II command and service modules. The Block I spacecraft was designed to be used only in earth orbit, while the Block II was used to transport astronauts to and from the lunar environment. Every system and subsystem is detailed. There are line drawings of every component, as well as schematics of the electrical, hydraulic, and pneumatic networks. Complete operating instructions and tolerances for each item are given. Full-sized photographs of many of the components, switches, and dials amplify the text. It will probably be necessary to obtain a copy of this work directly from NASA.

_____. *Apollo Operations Handbook: Command and Service Module, Spacecraft 012.* Washington, D.C.: Government Printing Office, 1966.
This work is a complete technical reference to the Apollo Block I spacecraft. Specifically, it is about the systems and subsystem in the command and service modules used for the Apollo 204 mission. The command module and the astronaut crew were lost when a fire broke out inside the sealed cabin during a ground test. Every system and subsystem is detailed. There are line drawings of every component, as well as schematics of the electrical, hydraulic, and pneumatic networks. Complete operating instructions and tolerances for each

item are given. Full-sized photographs of many of the components, switches, and dials amplify the text. It will probably be necessary to obtain a copy of this directly from NASA, although a complete, reduced-size copy is included in the congressional accident investigation report.

_____. *Apollo Program Summary Report*. Washington, D.C.: National Technical Information Service, 1975.
Although not as thorough as the individual mission reports, this work discusses each of the manned and unmanned flights conducted during the Apollo program. Included are the mission objectives and results and a summary of the significant events which occurred during the Little Joe II, Saturn I, Saturn IB, and Saturn V flights. There are synopses of the lunar surface and orbital experiments, Earth resources photography, biomedical experiments, and in-flight demonstrations. A history of the development and performance of the spacecraft and launch vehicles is included, as well as a look at crew training and accomplishments. Appendices detail flight statistics, mission type designations, spacecraft weights, spaceflight records established, and flight anomalies. There are many photographs and line drawings to highlight the extensive text, as well as references for further research.

_____. *The First Lunar Landing: As Told by the Astronauts*. Washington, D.C.: Government Printing Office, 1970.
This is a transcript of the postflight press conference held on August 12, 1969. Astronauts Neil Armstrong, Michael Collins, and Edwin Aldrin, Jr., presented a forty-five-minute narration of mission photographs from their Apollo 11 flight. Following the presentation, questions were taken from the news media representatives. This is a fine booklet, which reflects the opinions of the crew about their historic flight. Most of the questions asked by the reporters cover topics of great interest to the general public: what the Moon looks like from orbit and on the surface, how it was to walk (or "hop") on the Moon, whether the astronauts were concerned about the lunar module's fuel supply, what their plans for the future were, and so on.

_____. *"In This Decade . . ."*: *Mission to the Moon*. Washington, D.C.: Government Printing Office, 1969.
This is a preflight look at the Apollo 11 lunar landing mission and the Mercury, Gemini, and Apollo flights which preceded it. The narration is very simple and adds little to the information available in larger works, but it provides a concise glimpse at these ancestral efforts. In addition, the booklet previews the first manned lunar landing attempt and future programs, including Skylab. At the time of the writing, Skylab was still called the Apollo Applications Program. Color and black-and-white photographs highlight the work.

_____. *Preliminary Science Report: Apollo 11 Through Apollo 17.* 6 vols. Washington, D.C.: Government Printing Office, 1969-1973.
Upon completion of each manned Apollo flight to the lunar surface, engineers, scientists from the various disciplines, and the astronauts who flew the mission wrote summaries of the expedition. Topics covered in these collections include landing site selection criteria; a description of the mission; and a summary of the scientific, photographic, and geologic results. There are dozens of color and black-and-white photographs, line drawings, and data tables. Each section has its own comprehensive reference list. Appendices contain glossaries, acronyms, and unit conversion tables. These books provide the researcher with enough facts and figures about the flights to write several books. Much of it has to be filtered, however, because it is filled with scientific terminology beyond the range of the average reader.

_____. *Saturn I Summary.* Washington, D.C.: National Technical Information Service, 1966.
This book was prepared by the engineers from NASA's George C. Marshall Spaceflight Center, where the Saturn I was designed and built. It outlines each of the ten unmanned flights and gives a brief history of the origins of the Saturn I. The Saturn booster program was initiated solely to develop the technology of large-thrust vehicles. By modifying existing hardware, a new rocket of desired thrust could be obtained. The Saturn I (and Saturn IB) first stage was composed of a central liquid-oxygen core tank surrounded by eight fuel and liquid oxygen tanks. The core was derived from the Jupiter missile, while the surrounding tanks came from the Redstone.

_____. *Scientific Results of Project Pegasus: Interim Report.* Washington, D.C.: National Technical Information Service, 1967.
The designers of the Saturn I were looking for "ballast" for the boilerplate Apollo spacecraft they would be launching atop the booster. What resulted was a large, winged structure called *Pegasus*. *Pegasus*, named for the flying horse of Greek mythology, was designed to collect data on micrometeoroid impacts during low-Earth-orbit flights. Three spacecraft were flown, one on each of the final Saturn I missions. This paper discusses the history of the project and the scientific results obtained. There are several charts and drawings and a list of references.

_____. *Surveyor III: A Preliminary Report.* Washington, D.C.: National Technical Information Service, 1967.
The object of the Surveyor program was to soft-land a series of spacecraft on the lunar surface to demonstrate that manned spacecraft could do the same. Surveyor 3 alighted in the Ocean of Storms on April 20, 1967. Its systems were shut down for the cold lunar night on May 3, and when it was time to

revive them, Surveyor failed to respond. During its short life, its television camera transmitted more than six thousand pictures and its surface-sampling scoop dug trenches. Two years later, Apollo 12 set down within six hundred feet of Surveyor. The astronauts photographed it and removed some of its equipment for analysis. This report details the results obtained during Surveyor's operation.

_____. *What Made Apollo a Success?* Washington, D.C.: National Technical Information Service, 1971.
NASA's rather self-indulgent look at the Apollo program and why it succeeded in landing the first men on the Moon and returning them safely to Earth. The work discusses the planning that went into the missions and how a team effort translated those plans into reality. It took the cooperation of many different government and scientific organizations to coordinate the activities of a flight. There is not a lot of detailed information contained in the essay, but it does give the reader an insight into the efforts necessary to pull off man's greatest exploration achievement.

U.S. Senate. *Apollo 13 Mission: Hearing Before the Committee on Aeronautical and Space Sciences.* Washington, D.C.: Government Printing Office, 1970.
This is the official report of the Senate committee hearings to determine the cause of the Apollo 13 accident. An oxygen tank in the service module ruptured, crippling the spacecraft and nearly costing the lives of its astronaut crew as they traveled to the Moon. The report supports NASA's own investigative conclusions as to the cause and remedy of the problem. This work is not as detailed as the House of Representatives' investigation report and provides little additional information.

Von Braun, Wernher, and Frederick I. Ordway III. *History of Rocketry and Space Travel.* 3d rev. ed. New York: Thomas Y. Crowell, 1975.
This is the story of the exploration of space from the earliest experiments with rocketry to the final flight of the Skylab program. Hundreds of experts on every aspect of this broad field contributed to the work. Most of the programs of the United States, the Soviet Union, and the rest of the nations engaged in space exploration at that time are detailed, both descriptively and with black-and-white and color photographs. It is one of the best references on the subject. The book also contains a large, chapter-by-chapter bibliography. The authors finish their discussion of the space programs with a look at the future, including the Space Transportation System.

Ward, Robinson J., Jr., comp. *A Funny Thing Happened on the Way to the Moon.* Greenwich, Conn.: Fawcett, 1969.

Although the exploration of space is a serious, often challenging business, there is still time for humor. Some of the humor presented in this book was unintentional, evolving from the frustrations and failures of the U.S. space program. The author has collected humorous events, jokes, and other tension-relieving anecdotes from the scientists, technicians, engineers, and astronauts involved in man's conquest of space. While it does not contain any pertinent data on the history of the space program, it does make these people seem a little more human.

Wilford, John Noble. *We Reach the Moon.* New York: W. W. Norton, 1969.
The author presents an account of the Apollo 11 lunar landing mission and a brief history of Apollo's predecessors. Most of the work concentrates on Apollo. The book is written in a journalistic style, and each flight is detailed in story. It is a well-written book, published within seventy-two hours of the completion of the Apollo 11 flight. The author admits his lack of scientific or engineering expertise, but the two years of research that went into the book's preparation are evident. Also evident is the amount of work that occurred during and immediately after the flight. There is a section of color photographs in the center of the book and there are a few line drawings throughout. A transcript of the major lunar surface activities is included in the back of the book. There is also a brief bibliography.

Wolfe, Edward W., et al. *The Geologic Investigation of the Taurus-Littrow Valley: Apollo 17 Landing Site.* Washington, D.C.: U.S. Geological Survey, 1981.
This is an extensive report on the geologic investigations performed during the Apollo 17 lunar landing mission. There are hundreds of black-and-white photographs and drawings taken during the three expeditions around the landing site to document the samples returned by the astronauts. Each of the larger rock samples is displayed with pictures taken from all six sides, as well as data on the composition of the specimen. For comparison the sample is shown oriented as it appears in the lunar surface documentation photograph. The book contains an extensive, annotated list of selected references. Large photographic maps of the region are provided separately to permit locating the position of the samples at the site. Also included are photographic panoramas taken on the surface.

Yenne, Bill. *The Encyclopedia of U.S. Spacecraft.* New York: Exeter Books, 1985.
A complete encyclopedia of U.S. spacecraft is presented in a book filled with color and black-and-white photographs. General information on the programs is provided in alphabetical order, with individual spacecraft, probes, or launch vehicles listed chronologically. Data on all of the manned spacecraft, including the Apollo command and service module, lunar module, Lunar Rover, and

Saturn launch vehicles, are furnished. Includes an appendix listing acronyms
and abbreviations, and an index.

_____. *The Pictorial History of World Spacecraft*. New York: Exeter
Books, 1988.

The history of the world's spacecraft and probes is told in chronological order
from Sputnik 1 through Cosmos 1870, spanning the first thirty years of the
space age. Included are all of the manned spacecraft and launch vehicles. Each
is detailed with charts, diagrams, illustrations, and color and black-and-white
photographs. Data on all of the manned spacecraft, including the Apollo
command and service module and the lunar module, are provided. An appendix
lists all of the spacecraft in service as of July, 1987, grouped according to the
countries or organizations responsible for them.

Skylab

Belew, Leland F., ed. *Skylab, Our First Space Station*. Washington, D.C.:
National Technical Information Service, 1977.

A colorful retrospective of the Skylab program and its four flights is presented
in this work. Technically speaking, the title is a misnomer, since Skylab was
not a "space station." By definition, a space station is a permanently manned
platform that can be completely resupplied. Astronauts replenished the food,
water, film, and a few other expendables, but Skylab's attitude control and
electrical and life support systems were not replenishable. The book is a good
reference, chronicling the program from its design and planning phases through
the completion of the third manned period. There are dozens of color photographs and drawings, including several spectacular pictures taken on orbit. A
mission summary table and an index are included. Belew was the manager of
the Skylab Program Office at the Marshall Space Flight Center, where Skylab
was built.

Belew, Leland F., and Ernst Stuhlinger. *Skylab: A Guidebook*. Washington, D.C.:
Government Printing Office, 1973.

This is a preflight guide to the Skylab program and provides in-depth, nontechnical information about the orbiting workshop and its components. Skylab, the
spacecraft, was built around the S-IVB third stage of the Saturn V launch
vehicle. The major components included the Orbital Workshop (OWS), Instrument Unit (IU), Airlock Module (AM), Multiple Docking Adapter (MDA), and
the Apollo Telescope Mount (ATM). As much of the spacecraft as possible
was made from existing hardware or with hardware requiring little modification. This guide describes the work of several thousand engineers and scientists
who conceived, designed, and built Skylab. Each of the experiments to be

performed during Skylab's stay in orbit are described, as well as the apparatus to conduct those experiments. Line drawings, black-and-white photographs, a glossary of terms and acronyms, an index, and a brief bibliography have been included.

Collins, Michael. "Life in Orbit." In *Liftoff: The Story of America's Adventure in Space.* New York: Grove Press, 1988.
Former astronaut Collins discusses the many aspects of living in space, with particular emphasis on the Skylab and Apollo Soyuz programs. He also talks about his two trips into space and the advantages that a large spacecraft, such as Skylab, has over the cramped quarters of the Apollo command module and, more so, the Gemini spacecraft. The book is illustrated with eighty-eight line drawings by James Dean, former NASA art director, which add stark realism to an otherwise unfamiliar world.

Compton, W. David, and Charles D. Benson. *Living and Working in Space: A History of Skylab.* Washington, D.C.: Government Printing Office, 1983.
One title in the NASA History Series, this book chronicles the Skylab program, from its conception during the early days of the Apollo program to the orbiting workshop's fiery plunge in 1979. There are dozens of black-and-white photographs of the three manned missions, as well as the launch of the unmanned workshop. Color photographs, taken from orbit, are in the back of the book. Line drawings show the inner workings of much of the equipment related to the missions. Includes an index and an impressive hundred-page appendix listing source notes and bibliographic references. Other appendices include a summary of the missions, astronaut biographies, in-flight experiments, Comet Kohoutek, and the International Aeronautical Federation world records set by Skylab.

Cooper, Henry S. F., Jr. *A House in Space.* New York: Holt, Rinehart and Winston, 1976.
This work is about the nine-month period from May 14, 1973, through February 8, 1974—the active life of the Skylab orbiting workshop. During this time, it was inhabited by three crews of astronauts for periods of twenty-eight, fifty-nine, and eighty-four days. The book was derived from articles written by Cooper, which appeared in *The New Yorker* magazine during this period. It looks more at the human aspect of the program than at its technical side, but still contains information useful to the researcher. There are many black-and-white photographs and color diagrams.

Eddy, John A. *A New Sun: The Solar Results from Skylab.* Washington, D.C.: National Technical Information Service, 1979.

Countless volumes of data about the biological and physiological effects of long-duration spaceflight on humans, plants, and animals were obtained during the Skylab program. In addition, the first space telescopes (combined in a structure called the Apollo Telescope Mount, or ATM) were used to study the Sun. The ATM derived its name from a study that was conducted to determine the feasibility of mounting a stable telescope on the Apollo service module. In actuality, the ATM was built around the lunar module descent stage. There is very little technical information, but the color and black-and-white photographs of the Sun alone make this book worthwhile.

Gatland, Kenneth. "The First Space Stations." In *The Illustrated Encyclopedia of Space Technology: A Comprehensive History of Space Exploration*, by Kenneth Gatland et al. New York: Harmony Books, 1981.
This section in the book discusses the early space stations of the United States and the Soviet Union. There is a fine four-page, full-color cutaway drawing of the Skylab workshop and the Soviet's Salyut space station. There are color and black-and-white photographs, drawings, and charts. The major features of the program, including the spacecraft and launch vehicle, are discussed. Includes a chronology of the major space events since Sputnik 1, a glossary of terms, and an index.

Goldstein, Norm, ed. *Moments in Space*. New York: Gallery Books, 1986, pp. 104-106.
Newspaper photographs from the Associated Press are the highlight of this book, which offers little text to accompany them. The Skylab missions are mostly overlooked, but there are a couple of clear photographs of the crew in orbit. Much of the monograph is not to be relied on for accuracy, especially because the information included with the photographs has not been updated from what was known at the time of the event. Many of the photographs are grainy, but it is for their historical context that they should be viewed, not for their clarity.

Johnston, Richard S., and Lawrence F. Dietlein, eds. *Biomedical Results from Skylab*. Washington, D.C.: National Technical Information Service, 1977.
Biomedical testing under the conditions of orbital flight was studied for relatively brief periods during the Mercury, Gemini, and Apollo programs. With Skylab, scientists would be able to conduct experiments on astronauts spending a month or more in space. The editors of this work have compiled a concise review of each experiment, including the theory behind the test, the means by which it was completed, and the results. The experiments were divided into four disciplines: neurophysiology; musculoskeletal function; biochemistry, hematology, and cytology; and cardiovascular and metabolic function. The text is supplemented with photographs and drawings, as well as charts of the

conclusions reached by each examiner. Every section of the book has its own reference listing, which will guide the researcher to more detailed works. Appendices detail the experimental support hardware and the operational life sciences support hardware.

Kerrod, Robin. *Apollo.* London: Multimedia Books, 1989.
The story of the Apollo program is told in this concise, well-written work. The book begins with the early achievements of Project Mercury and the Gemini program. Mercury was man's first tentative step into the unknown region of the universe only a hundred miles above. Gemini developed and perfected the rendezvous techniques so vital the success of the Moon missions. The story would not be complete without mention of the "children" of Apollo: Skylab and the Apollo Soyuz Test Project. The work goes into detail about the development of the hardware for Apollo. In addition to the discussion of flight hardware, the author looks at the massive Launch Umbilical Towers, which were used to service the vehicle on the ground and which served as the launching pad. The spacecraft are detailed. Photographs, drawings, and a log of the Apollo missions add to the text.

Lattimer, Richard L. *All We Did Was Fly to the Moon.* History-Alive Series, vol. 1. Alachula, Fla.: Whispering Eagle Press, 1983, pp. 98-113.
A brief look at the Skylab program is presented with minimal data and lots of photographs. In fact, color and black-and-white photographs, along with color reproductions of the crew emblems from each flight, are the highlight of the work. Lattimer wastes very little space on words, opting for a more graphic presentation. The story of how each emblem was designed is presented by one of the crew members. This book is mainly for trivia buffs, but the serious researcher will also enjoy reading it. The only major drawback to the book is the lack of a bibliography.

Lundquist, Charles A., ed. *Skylab's Astronomy and Space Sciences.* Washington, D.C.: Government Printing Office, 1979.
One of Skylab's main objectives was to perform experiments in the microgravity conditions of orbital flight over extended periods of time. Another was to look at the rest of the universe, especially the Sun, with the unblinking eye of the telescope. This study details these two aspects of the Skylab missions. Subjects covered in this work include stellar and galactic astronomy, interplanetary dust, Comet Kohoutek, energetic particles, Earth's atmosphere, and the orbital environment. Color photographs and art highlight this informative book.

Magill, Frank N., ed. *Magill's Survey of Science: Space Exploration Series.* Vol. 3. Pasadena, Calif.: Salem Press, 1989, pp. 1285-1308.

This five-volume set covers every aspect of the U.S. and Soviet manned and unmanned space programs, as well as those of nations newer to the space race. As an extension of the Apollo program, scientists and engineers studied ways of allowing astronauts to stay in Earth orbit for periods of up to three months. The result of these studies was Skylab, the United States' first attempt at a permanent manned presence in space. Three manned flight were accomplished, lasting twenty-eight, fifty-nine, and eighty-four days respectively. Each of the manned flights and the voyage of the unmanned orbiting workshop is detailed, as are the spacecraft and launch vehicles. There is an overview article that chronicles the program from its beginning, followed by articles that cover the missions individually. Each essay lists the pertinent data of the mission, launch vehicle, and spacecraft, and includes an annotated bibliography and cross-references.

Newkirk, Roland W., and Ivan D. Ertel, with Courtney G. Brooks. *Skylab: A Chronology.* Washington, D.C.: National Technical Information Service, 1977.
This is NASA's official record of the Skylab program, covering events on a day-to-day basis. At its inception the project was known as the Apollo Applications Program, since it was to use modified equipment from the lunar landing endeavor. Included in the coverage are the early space station designs, the development of the spacecraft and launch vehicles, astronaut training, and mission results. There are dozens of black-and-white photographs and line drawings of components. Appendices provide a summary of the Skylab flights: mission objectives, orbital activities, experiments, and extravehicular activity. Includes a glossary of abbreviations and acronyms and an index.

O'Leary, Brian. *Project Space Station.* Harrisburg, Pa.: Government Printing Office, 1983.
The author takes a look at the space station programs of the United States and the Soviet Union and discusses their practical applications and benefits. He traces the history of manned space platforms and, in the process, touches upon Skylab, Spacelab, and the Space Transportation System. The major systems of an orbiting space station, similar to the United States' *Freedom*, are described. Much of the emphasis of the book is on the political aspects of the program. Contains black-and-white photographs, a brief bibliography, and an index.

Pogue, William R. *How Do You Go to the Bathroom in Space?* New York: Tom Doherty Associates, 1985.
This and many other interesting questions about living in space are answered by former astronaut Pogue. He was one of three crew members who spent eighty-four days in orbit aboard Skylab. Actually, there are 156 questions which the author has gleaned from thousands that he and his fellow astronauts have received in a quarter century of manned spaceflight. Many of the ques-

tions lead to humorous answers, but most provide a great deal of firsthand information about matters of general interest. The questions touch on each of the U.S. manned space programs. Several appendices provide additional information, including a summary of the physiological effects of spaceflight, a list of Earth features recognizable from space, a guide to information and resources, and a bibliography.

Summerlin, Lee B., ed. *Skylab, Classroom in Space.* Washington, D.C.: Government Printing Office, 1977.

The Skylab Student Project was originated by NASA and the National Science Teachers Association as a means of involving schoolchildren, the next generation of scientists, in the study of space sciences. In 1972, twenty-five high school students from across the United States were selected to participate in the program. They were from among the more than four thousand students who had made proposals. This volume, filled with color and black-and-white photographs, details how and why the project was developed, describes the experiments flown aboard Skylab, and relates them to other scientific investigations carried out during the flights.

U.S. House of Representatives. *Skylab 1 Investigation Report: Hearing Before the Subcommittee on Manned Space Flight of the Committee on Science and Astronautics.* Washington, D.C.: National Technical Information Service, 1973.

In August, 1973, the subcommittee opened its investigation into the incident that occurred during the launch of the Skylab 1 spacecraft. At sixty-three seconds into the flight, there were indications that the workshop's micrometeoroid shield had deployed and that the workshop solar array wing 2 was no longer secured in its launch position. This, coupled with the failure of solar array wing 1 to deploy on orbit, should have terminated the mission. Fortunately, the first manned crew was able to free the stuck wing and install a shield over the sunside of the workshop. The workshop was usable. This report documents the accident, as best it could be reconstructed, and the procedures developed and implemented to recover from the effects of the incident. The are many black-and-white photographs and drawings to give the reader a great deal of technical information. Most of the contents are transcripts of the testimony of witnesses.

U.S. National Aeronautics and Space Administration. *"In This Decade . . ."*: *Mission to the Moon.* Washington, D.C.: Government Printing Office, 1969. This is a preflight look at the Apollo 11 lunar landing mission and the Mercury, Gemini, and Apollo flights that preceded it. The narration is very simple and adds little to the information available in larger works, but it provides a concise glimpse at these ancestral efforts. In addition, the booklet previews the first manned lunar landing attempt and future programs, including Skylab. At the time of the writing, Skylab was still called the Apollo Applications Program. Color and black-and-white photographs highlight the work.

_____. *MSFC Skylab Orbital Workshop Final Technical Report.* 5 vols. Washington, D.C.: National Technical Information Service, 1974.
The definitive technical reference on the Skylab orbiting workshop, this work covers all aspects of the program, including concepts, goals, design philosophy, hardware, and testing. The evolution of the workshop from a "wet" configuration (one flown as the fuel tank of the second stage of the Saturn IB into orbit, drained, purged, and then converted to a habitation area by the crew) to a "dry" structure (one launched completely outfitted in orbital configuration) is chronicled. The final configuration is discussed in detail, including structures, systems, and components. The testing program is reviewed, as well as the mission results and performance during launch and flight. Detailed line drawings, tables, and charts add to the text, as does a complete reference listing.

_____. *Skylab and the Sun.* Washington, D.C.: Government Printing Office, 1973.
The Apollo Telescope Mount (ATM) on the Skylab orbiting workshop was used to study the Sun in depth. This work was written to familiarize the reader with the Sun and what the Skylab program expected to gain by observing it. Scientists, astronauts, engineers, and other individuals closely associated with the ATM program wrote the articles. There is a brief overview of the program and the facts known about the Sun prior to Skylab. The studies proposed for the ATM, as well as the equipment designed to carry out the observations, are detailed. Appendices tell the reader where to obtain additional information about the program and the data to be received.

_____. *Skylab Experiments.* 7 vols. Washington, D.C.: Government Printing Office, 1973.
Prior to the beginning of the Skylab flights, NASA's Education Office, the Skylab Program Office, and the University of Colorado published a series of teaching guides to the experiments which were to be conducted in flight. These experiments were divided into four categories: physical sciences, biomedical sciences, Earth applications, and space applications. Each volume looks at the experiments' background, scientific objectives, description, data, crew activities, related curriculum studies, and suggested classroom demonstrations. Volume 1 covers physical science and solar astronomy; volume 2, remote sensing of Earth resources; volume 3, materials science; volume 4, life sciences; volume 5, astronomy and space physics; volume 6, mechanics; and volume 7, living and working in space. Each volume includes numerous line drawings and a glossary of terms.

_____. *Skylab Explores the Earth.* Washington, D.C.: National Technical Information Service, 1977.

Since the first flight of Project Mercury, one of NASA's primary goals of orbital space missions was the observation of Earth. There is no better vantage point than from above. Observation time for manned spacecraft is limited by life support supplies, and, prior to Skylab, the longest mission was the fourteen-day Gemini VII flight in 1965. This book studies the Earth observation experiments of Skylab during the 171 days it was occupied. It is filled with exciting color photographs of Earth, each of which is accompanied by a detailed caption. Several of the photographs are analyzed with the aid of a map of the region shown. Comparisons are made with color and black-and-white photographs taken of geologic sites and meteorologic phenomena during previous manned flights. Contains a glossary of terms and an index of the photographs used, alphabetized by geographic location.

_____. *Skylab Mission Report: Skylab 2 Through Skylab 4.*
3 vols. Washington, D.C.: National Technical Information Service, 1973-1974.

The official report on each of the manned flights in the Skylab program. Each volume was prepared by the Mission Evaluation Team and contains a wealth of data on the particular flight. There is a mission summary and sections which detail the flight, spacecraft, crew activities, orbital experiments, in-flight demonstrations, biomedical evaluations, and mission ground support. An assessment of the mission objectives, as well as anomalies, is included. Tables summarize the flight trajectory and activity time lines. Descriptions and drawings of the spacecraft, launch vehicles, and experiments packages are included. Includes a glossary of terms and a list of references.

_____. *Skylab Mission Report, Saturn Workshop.* Washington, D.C.: National Technical Information Service, 1974.

The official NASA report on the performance of the Skylab orbiting workshop from launch until the end of the last manned period. Included are summaries of the three manned periods and the intervals when the workshop was unmanned. Descriptions of the structural components and mechanisms are given, as well as their anomalies. A report is provided on each of the major systems and subsystems. Each of the experiments, involving solar physics, astrophysics, materials science and manufacturing, engineering and technology, student investigations, and science demonstrations, is detailed. Line drawings, black-and-white photographs, tables, charts, and an extensive reference listing add to the text.

Von Braun, Wernher, and Frederick I. Ordway III. *History of Rocketry and Space Travel.* 3d rev. ed. New York: Thomas Y. Crowell, 1975.

This is the story of the exploration of space from the earliest experiments with rocketry to the final flight of the Skylab program. Hundreds of experts on every aspect of this broad field contributed to the work. Most of the programs of the United States, the Soviet Union, and the rest of the nations engaged in space exploration at that time are detailed, both descriptively and with black-and-white and color photographs. It is one of the best references on the subject. The book contains a large, chapter-by-chapter bibliography. The authors finish their discussion of the space programs with a look at the future, including the Space Transportation System.

Yenne, Bill. *The Encyclopedia of U.S. Spacecraft.* New York: Exeter Books, 1985.
A complete encyclopedia of U.S. spacecraft is presented in a book filled with color and black-and-white photographs. General information on the programs is provided in alphabetical order, with individual spacecraft, probes, or launch vehicles listed chronologically. Data on all of the manned spacecraft, including the Apollo command and service module, the Skylab workshop, and the Saturn launch vehicles, are furnished. An appendix lists acronyms and abbreviations, and there is an index.

_____. *The Pictorial History of World Spacecraft.* New York: Exeter Books, 1988.
The history of the world's spacecraft and probes is told in chronological order from Sputnik 1 through Cosmos 1870, spanning the first thirty years of the space age. Included are all of the manned spacecraft and launch vehicles. Each is detailed with charts, diagrams, illustrations, and color and black-and-white photographs. Data on all of the manned spacecraft, including the Apollo command and service module and the Skylab workshop, are provided. An appendix lists all of the spacecraft in service as of July, 1987, grouped according to the countries or organizations responsible for them.

Apollo Soyuz

Belitzky, Boris. "Handshake in Orbit." In *The Illustrated Encyclopedia of Space Technology: A Comprehensive History of Space Exploration*, by Kenneth Gatland et al. New York: Harmony Books, 1981.
This section in the book discusses the joint U.S.-Soviet Apollo Soyuz Test Project. A brief history of the project is given, as are details of the two flights. There are dozens of color and black-and-white photographs, drawings, paintings, and charts. The major features of the program, including the spacecraft and launch vehicles, are discussed. Other chapters in the book discuss these

in greater detail. There is a brief bibliography. The book includes a chronology of the major space events since Sputnik 1, a glossary of terms, and an index.

Collins, Michael. "Life in Orbit." In *Liftoff: The Story of America's Adventure in Space*. New York: Grove Press, 1988.
Former astronaut Collins discusses the many aspects of living in space, with particular emphasis on the Skylab and Apollo Soyuz programs. He also talks about his two trips into space and the advantages that a large spacecraft, such as Skylab, has over the cramped quarters of the Apollo command module and, more so, the Gemini spacecraft. The book is illustrated with eighty-eight line drawings by James Dean, former NASA art director, which add stark realism to an otherwise unfamiliar world.

Ezell, Edward C., and Linda N. Ezell. *The Partnership: A History of the Apollo-Soyuz Test Project*. Washington, D.C.: Government Printing Office, 1978.
One title in the NASA History Series, this book chronicles the Apollo Soyuz Test Project, to date the only joint U.S.-Soviet manned spaceflight. The origins of the project, immediately following the successful completion of the Apollo 11 Moon landing mission, are traced. Also discussed are the political aspects of the venture. There are dozens of black-and-white photographs of the flight. Color photographs, taken from orbit, are in the back of the book. Line drawings show the inner workings of much of the equipment related to the mission. Includes an impressive seventy-page appendix listing source notes and bibliographic references, and an index. Other appendices include NASA organization charts, development of U.S. and Soviet manned spaceflight, a summary of the U.S./U.S.S.R. meetings, and descriptions of the ASTP launch vehicles.

Froehlich, Walter. *Apollo Soyuz*. Washington, D.C.: Government Printing Office, 1976.
This is an entertaining look at the Apollo Soyuz Test Project, the United States' last manned mission using expendable spacecraft and launch vehicles. It was designed to test a rescue method for astronauts or cosmonauts stranded in orbit and unable to be saved by their own country. The U.S. spacecraft, an Apollo command and service module and a docking module (stored in the adapter used to house the Apollo lunar module during launch), were boosted into orbit by a Saturn IB. The Soviets used their standard Soyuz spacecraft and A-2 booster. The book briefly looks at the mission's origin, the spacecraft, astronauts and cosmonauts, experiments, and results of the joint endeavor. There are numerous color photographs and appendices listing the times of major events, "firsts" achieved by Apollo Soyuz, major officials involved, scientific experiments, and principal Apollo contractors.

Kerrod, Robin. *Apollo.* London: Multimedia Books, 1989.
The story of the Apollo program is told in this concise, well-written work. The book begins with the early achievements of Project Mercury and the Gemini program. Mercury was man's first tentative step into the unknown region of the universe only a hundred miles above. Gemini developed and perfected the rendezvous techniques so vital to the success of the Moon missions. The story would not be complete without mention of the "children" of Apollo: Skylab and the Apollo Soyuz Test Project. The work goes into detail about the development of the hardware for Apollo. In addition to the discussion of flight hardware, the author looks at the massive Launch Umbilical Towers, which were used to service the vehicle on the ground and which served as the launching pad. The spacecraft are detailed. Photographs, drawings, and a log of the Apollo missions add to the text.

Lattimer, Richard L. *All We Did Was Fly to the Moon.* History-Alive Series, vol. 1. Alachula, Fla.: Whispering Eagle Press, 1983, pp. 114-117.
The book presents the history of the United States' pre-Shuttle space program in a brief but effective manner. Lattimer has interviewed twenty-nine astronauts and a host of others intimately involved with these programs. He has then condensed the information into a concise summary of each flight. The work features color reproductions of the crew emblems for every flight. One of the astronauts who flew the mission explains how the emblem was designed and how the spacecraft call signs were selected. Geared toward the trivia buff, this volume still provides a wealth of facts for the serious researcher.

Lee, Chester M., ed. *Apollo Soyuz Mission Report.* AAS Advances in the Astronautical Sciences, vol. 34. San Diego, Calif.: American Astronomical Society, 1975.
The official report on the Apollo Soyuz Test Project, prepared by the Mission Evaluation Team, contains a wealth of data on the flight of Apollo 18. Included are a mission summary and sections which detail the flight, spacecraft, crew activities, orbital experiments, in-flight demonstrations, biomedical evaluations, and mission ground support. An assessment of the mission objectives, as well as anomalies, is included. Tables summarize the flight trajectory and activity time lines. Appendices include descriptions and drawings of the spacecraft and launch vehicles, the as-flown ASTP flight plan, spacecraft history and mass properties, postflight testing, and a glossary of terms. There is also a summary of lightning activities by NASA for the mission.

Nicogossian, Arnauld E., comp. *The Apollo Soyuz Test Project Medical Report.* Washington, D.C.: National Technical Information Service, 1977.
This is a summary of the life sciences experiments performed during the nine-day Apollo 18 flight, the U.S. half of the joint U.S.-Soviet space mission

called the Apollo Soyuz Test Project. The researchers involved with each experiment write about their tests and the results. The experiments are divided into two groups: crew health and flight monitoring; and preflight, in-flight, and postflight medical testing. There are dozens of black-and-white photographs, charts, diagrams, and tables to enhance this technical work. The only disappointment is the lack of information about life sciences experiments conducted during the Soviet Soyuz 19 flight.

Page, Lou Williams, and Thorton Page. *Apollo Soyuz Experiments in Space.* 9 vols. Washington, D.C.: Government Printing Office, 1977.
This nine-part series of curriculum-related pamphlets for teachers and students of space science discusses the Apollo Soyuz mission. After the authors collected the data and assembled draft versions of the pamphlets, selected teachers from high schools and universities throughout the United States reviewed them and made suggestions. The result is a well-written, illustrated set. Each volume contains an introduction, discussion of the topic, questions and answers, a table of conversion units, a glossary of terms, and a briefly annotated bibliography. Topics covered are the flight, X rays and gamma rays, the Sun, stars and in between, the gravitational field, Earth from orbit, cosmic ray dosage, biology in zero gravity, zero-gravity technology, and general science.

Reynolds, Mike D. "The Apollo-Soyuz Test Project." In *Magill's Survey of Science: Space Exploration Series*, vol. 1, edited by Frank N. Magill. Pasadena, Calif.: Salem Press, 1989.
One of the essays on the history of space exploration in this five-volume set, which covers every aspect of the U.S. and Soviet manned and unmanned space programs, as well as those of nations newer to the space race. The essay on the Apollo Soyuz Test Project lists the pertinent data of the mission, providing a brief summary of the subject, the knowledge gained, its historical context, an annotated bibliography, and cross-references.

U.S. National Aeronautics and Space Administration. *Apollo Soyuz Test Project: Operations Handbook Command/Service/Docking Modules*. Vol. 1, *Spacecraft Description*. Washington, D.C.: National Technical Information Service, 1974.
This is the most complete technical reference written about the Apollo Block II command and service modules, as well as the docking module used to join the Apollo spacecraft with the Soyuz. Every system and subsystem is detailed. There are line drawings of every component, as well as schematics of the electrical, hydraulic, and pneumatic networks. Complete operating instructions and tolerances for each item are given. Full-size photographs of many of the components, switches, and dials amplify the text. It will probably be necessary to obtain a copy of this directly from NASA.

_____. *Apollo Soyuz Test Project: Summary Science Report.* 2 vols. Washington, D.C.: Government Printing Office, 1977.
Upon completion of the Apollo Soyuz flight, engineers, scientists from the various disciplines, and the astronauts who flew the mission wrote summaries of the venture. Topics covered in these two volumes include astronomy, Earth's atmosphere and gravity field, life sciences, materials processing, Earth observations, and photography. There are dozens of color and black-and-white photographs, line drawings, and data tables. Each section has its own comprehensive reference list. Appendices contain glossaries, acronyms, and unit conversion tables. These books provide the researcher with a bounty of facts and figures about the flight. Much of it has to be filtered, however, because it is filled with scientific terminology beyond the range of the general reader.

Von Braun, Wernher, and Frederick I. Ordway III. *History of Rocketry and Space Travel.* 3d rev. ed. New York: Thomas Y. Crowell, 1975.
This is the story of the exploration of space from the earliest experiments with rocketry to the final flight of the Skylab program. Hundreds of experts on every aspect of this broad field contributed to the work. Most of the programs of the United States, the Soviet Union, and the rest of the nations engaged in space exploration at that time are detailed, both descriptively and with black-and-white and color photographs. It is one of the best references on the subject. The book also contains a large, chapter-by-chapter bibliography. The authors finish their discussion of the space programs with a look at the future, including the Space Transportation System.

Yenne, Bill. *The Encyclopedia of U.S. Spacecraft.* New York: Exeter Books, 1985.
A complete encyclopedia of U.S. spacecraft is presented in a book filled with color and black-and-white photographs. General information on the programs is provided in alphabetical order, with individual spacecraft, probes, or launch vehicles listed chronologically. Data on all of the manned spacecraft, including the Apollo command and service module, the docking module, and the Saturn IB launch vehicle, are furnished. An appendix lists acronyms and abbreviations, and there is an index.

_____. *The Pictorial History of World Spacecraft.* New York: Exeter Books, 1988.
The history of the world's spacecraft and probes is told in chronological order from Sputnik 1 through Cosmos 1870, spanning the first thirty years of the space age. Included are all of the manned spacecraft and launch vehicles. Each is detailed with charts, diagrams, illustrations, and color and black-and-white photographs. Data on all of the manned spacecraft, including the Apollo

command and service module and docking module, are provided. An appendix lists all of the spacecraft in service as of July, 1987, grouped according to the countries or organizations responsible for them.

Space Transportation System

Allaway, Howard. *The Space Shuttle at Work.* Washington, D.C.: Government Printing Office, 1979.
This is a preview to the Space Shuttle program, written for NASA. Most of the information is accurate despite the changes made in the Shuttle after it began flying. There are many color and black-and-white photographs and line drawings. Colorful artists' renditions show how the first flight will be. The work discusses the orbiter and other components in detail and explains the purpose of the Space Transportation System. It concludes with an optimistic look at the future of spaceflight. Contains an index and a two-page, full-color cutaway drawing of the orbiter.

Allen, Joseph P., with Russell Martin. *Entering Space.* New York: Stewart, Tabori & Chang, 1984.
The story of an astronaut's journey in space, told in conjunction with a study of the U.S. exploration of space. This work is filled with colorful words and spectacular photographs of space travel from the ground up, and back again. There are hundreds of color photographs taken during the manned Gemini, Apollo, Skylab, Apollo Soyuz, and Space Shuttle programs, as well as those shots of our neighbors in the Solar System taken from unmanned probes. The spacecraft, launch vehicles, spacefarers, and their equipment are discussed in some detail, although primarily from the perspective of a single trip into orbit and back again. The is a very real sense of "being there" as Astronaut Allen describes his feelings during the various phases of flight. Contains a brief bibliography and an index.

Anderton, David A. *Space Station.* Washington, D.C.: Government Printing Office, 1985.
This NASA Educational Publication (EP-211) looks at the plans to build the United States' first permanently manned space station, *Freedom.* This work provides an overview of the program and the various design concepts developed by various NASA facilities and major aerospace contractors. At the time of the writing, the exact plans for constructing the space station were not finalized. Although this work does not provide any details, it does give some insight into the evolution of *Freedom.* There are many color photographs of the different design concepts.

Baker, David. *Space Shuttle.* New York: Crown, 1979.
The Space Shuttle orbiter is the world's first true aerospace plane, taking off vertically like a rocket and landing like an airplane. This work takes a good look at the early days of the Space Transportation System and how the Shuttle evolved into its present configuration. There are several artist's conceptions and photographs of models of the earlier versions. Most of the work deals with the Shuttle approach and landing tests, conducted during 1977. There is a preview of a flight of the Shuttle to orbit and how it will be used to carry cargo to space. For the modeler, there is a chapter on adapting an Airfix brand Shuttle kit to build several possible future versions of the vehicle. There are plenty of color and black-and-white photographs and a chronology of the Shuttle program from 1969 through 1979, with a forecast for the following decade.

Boeing Aerospace Co. *The Inertial Upper Stage User's Guide.* Seattle: Author, 1984.
The Inertial Upper Stage (IUS) is a high-altitude booster used in conjunction with either the Space Shuttle or the Titan launch vehicle. It was originally designed as a temporary stand-in for a reusable space tug and was called the "Interim" Upper Stage. When it became apparent that the space tug would not be developed in the foreseeable future, the Interim Upper Stage began its gradual evolution into the Inertial Upper Stage ("inertial" refers to its guidance technique). The IUS is built by Boeing for NASA and the Air Force. This book, filled with black-and-white photographs and line drawings, details this powerful booster and its associated hardware. It covers the vehicle's systems and subsystems, including its interfaces with the Shuttle and Titan. This book is a must for the person who wants to build an accurate model of the IUS.

Clark, Lenwood G., et al., eds. *Long Duration Exposure Facility (LDEF): Mission 1 Experiments.* Washington, D.C.: Government Printing Office, 1984.
The LDEF is a twelve-sided, open-grid reusable space platform that can be deployed from the Shuttle's cargo bay and later retrieved for return to Earth. It has been designed to provide a large number of economical opportunities for science and technology experiments that require modest electrical power and data processing while in space and that benefit from postflight laboratory investigations with the retrieved equipment hardware. The first LDEF was deployed from the Space Shuttle *Challenger* on April 7, 1984, for a one-year mission in Earth orbit. LDEF-1 carried fifty-seven science and technology experiments, including 12.5 million tomato seeds, packaged in kits, for later distribution to students from the upper elementary through university levels. Because of scheduling difficulties and the STS 51-L accident, the LDEF was not retrieved until January 12, 1990. This book discusses in great detail each of the experiments using black-and-white photographs and line drawings. The location of each experiment package on the LDEF is shown.

Collins, Michael. "Wings and Wheels at Last." In *Liftoff: The Story of America's Adventure in Space*. New York: Grove Press, 1988.
The Space Transportation System, with its faults and benefits, is discussed by Collins in his historical summary of the U.S. space program. After briefly reviewing the Space Shuttle program, Collins gives a report on the *Challenger* accident and his opinion as to the direction the program should take. He also discusses his feelings about carrying civilians into space on what has been shown to be a "research" spacecraft.

Cooper, Henry S. F., Jr. *Before Liftoff: The Making of a Space Shuttle Crew*. Baltimore: The Johns Hopkins University Press, 1987.
Space Shuttle Mission 41-G, with seven astronauts aboard *Challenger*, spent eight days in space. The crew included veteran Commander Robert Crippen and Mission Specialist Sally Ride, along with rookie Pilot Jon McBride, Mission Specialists Kathy Sullivan and David Leetsma, and Payload Specialists Paul Scully-Power and Canadian Marc Garneau. During the mission, the crew deployed the Earth Radiation Budget Satellite and conducted experiments. Two of the astronauts performed a spacewalk to demonstrate an on-orbit refueling system. Author Cooper made special arrangements with NASA to follow the crew from its formation through the completion of the mission. This is an engrossing look at the everyday life of an astronaut crew. The reader gets to sit in on briefings, join the crew for simulations, and even swim underwater for spacewalk practice. There are a few black-and-white photographs and an index.

David, Leonard. *Space Station Freedom: A Foothold on the Future*. Washington, D.C.: Government Printing Office, 1988.
This is a colorful booklet on the proposed space station *Freedom* and what it will mean to us in the future. There are dozens of color and black-and-white photographs and artist's conceptions to highlight the text. The history of the space station is chronicled from the early 1950's through the Skylab program. There are descriptions of the scientific missions and experiments conceived for *Freedom*. The individual components, and how they will be assembled in orbit, are described. The text is readable at all levels, and much information is packed into this work.

Elliot, James C. "Food and Diet for Space Travel." In *Magill's Survey of Science: Space Exploration Series*, vol. 1, edited by Frank N. Magill. Pasadena, Calif.: Salem Press, 1989.
One of the essays on the history of space exploration in this five-volume set, which covers every aspect of the U.S. and Soviet manned and unmanned space programs, as well as those of nations newer to the space race. This essay

260 America in Space

discusses the attempts to develop palatable food for spaceflight, which could be stored for long periods of time and retain all of its nutritional qualities. Although some of the early programs are mentioned, the main focus of the essay is on the Space Shuttle program. Provides an annotated bibliography and cross-references.

European Space Agency. *The International Solar Polar Mission: Its Scientific Investigations.* Washington, D.C.: Government Printing Office, 1983.
A series of essays written by some of the scientific investigators who have developed the Ulysses program. Ulysses, originally known as the International Solar Polar Mission, is designed to orbit the Sun from a unique vantage point. Its orbit will carry it over the Sun's polar regions. It will be launched from the payload bay of the Space Shuttle toward Jupiter. There it will use the giant planet's gravitational field to alter its trajectory in order for it to move out of the plane of the ecliptic. The essays discuss the mission of Ulysses and the equipment it will use in its study of the Sun.

Froehlich, Walter. *The New Space Network: The Tracking and Data Relay Satellite System.* Washington, D.C.: Government Printing Office, 1986.
This work looks at NASA's Tracking and Data Relay Satellite System (TDRSS), which permits continuous radio contact between Earth-orbiting spacecraft and ground stations. This system helps to eliminate costly ground-based tracking stations. It also permits radio communications with the Space Shuttle during reentry. Prior to TDRSS (pronounced "tea dress"), this was not possible, because of the communications blackout which occurred during the period when a returning spacecraft began to ionize the air around it. The booklet is filled with color photographs and artists' renditions of the TDRSS, as well as a description of the system's operations.

_____. *Spacelab: An International Short-Stay Orbiting Laboratory.* Washington, D.C.: Government Printing Office, 1983.
International cooperation is the status quo for the Spacelab program. Ten nations of the European Space Agency (ESA)— Austria, Belgium, Denmark, France, West Germany, Italy, The Netherlands, Spain, Switzerland, and the United Kingdom— have designed, built, and financed Spacelab. This Space Shuttle payload consists of interchangeable modules and pallets, which can be combined into a nearly unlimited mixture for a variety of scientific experimentation. This work looks at the Spacelab: what it does, how it came to be, and what its users expect from it. It is for the general audience and contains dozens of color photographs and artist's renditions. There is a very detailed cutaway drawing of the Spacelab 1 module and pallet.

Furniss, Tim. *Manned Spaceflight Log*. London: Jane's, 1983, rev. ed. 1987.
This work covers the manned spaceflights of the Soviet Union and the United States from 1961 through 1986. A synopsis of each mission is given, along with pertinent data (date, crew, site, recovery, duration, spacecraft weight, and so forth) and several black-and-white photographs. The Mercury, Gemini, Apollo, Skylab, Apollo Soyuz, and Space Shuttle flights are listed chronologically. Included are the thirteen flights of the X-15 research aircraft which exceeded the fifty-mile altitude necessary to qualify its pilot as an astronaut under Air Force rules. There are astronaut photographs and, in the appendices, listings of space seniority and the current status of the astronaut and cosmonaut classes.

_____. *Space Flight: The Records*. London: Guiness Books, 1985.
Do you know the first manned spaceflight to be curtailed? It was Gemini V, which landed one orbit early to miss hurricane Betsy. Were you aware that the first spaceflight with more than one fifty-year-old person on board was that of STS 51-B/Spacelab 3, in April, 1985? These and dozens of other interesting and significant—or not so significant— facts are covered in this work. The first part of the book is a "diary" of manned spaceflight, listing each of the missions of the United States and Soviet Union. There is a chapter on manned spaceflight "firsts" and one on the manned space machines. Basic biographical information on each of the space travelers is given, accompanied by the person's photograph. The major information section is last and includes tables on manned spaceflight duration, space seniority, space experience, lunar spacemen, spacewalks, astroflights of the X-15, all known cosmonauts, NASA astronauts, Space Shuttle passengers, NASA flight crew selections, and the Space Shuttle schedule. There are hundreds of black-and-white photographs, a glossary of terms, and an index.

_____. *Space Shuttle Log*. London: Jane's, 1986.
The first twenty-two flights of the Space Shuttle are chronicled in this concise work about the Space Transportation System. The first chapter traces the development and testing of the system, detailing the earlier designs of the vehicle and some of the research aircraft that paved the way for the orbiter. There is a section on the astronauts who fly the Shuttle, which includes photographs and brief biographical listings. Perhaps the most ironic segment is the listing of future flights, including the ill-fated STS 51-L mission. There are hundreds of black-and-white photographs and replicas of each of the individual crew emblems.

Ghitelman, David. *The Space Telescope*. New York: Gallery Books, 1987.
This work is a preview of the Hubble Space Telescope. It discusses Earth-based telescopes and their advantages and disadvantages. The author traces the

development of the Hubble Space Telescope and the problems of polishing the world's smoothest mirror: the 94-inch-diameter primary reflecting mirror. The design and construction of the Hubble Space Telescope are detailed, as are the plans for its deployment by the Space Shuttle. During its life, the telescope will be periodically serviced by the Shuttle and, if necessary, can be returned to Earth for refurbishment. A look at the expected increase in knowledge of the universe is included. There is a chapter about the life of the telescope's namesake, Dr. Edward Powell Hubble, the U.S. astronomer who, among other things, discovered that all galaxies are red-shifted (their motion away from us causes their light to shift toward the red end of the visible spectrum as a result of the phenomenon known as the Doppler effect). There are dozens of color and black-and-white photographs and paintings, an index, and a brief bibliography.

Goldstein, Norm, ed. *Moments in Space.* New York: Gallery Books, 1986, pp. 142-221.
The Shuttle program receives the greatest amount of coverage in this pictorial work, perhaps because of its contemporary nature or, more likely, because it was published shortly after the *Challenger* accident. Most of the photographs have been published elsewhere, and all of the ones in this book are in black and white, but that does not detract from the overall contribution of the work to the chronicling of the space program. There is very little text to accompany the photographs, and none of it has been updated to reflect current information about the missions. One glaring error is the caption for a photograph of Christa McAuliffe's family during the ill-fated STS 51-L launch. According to the caption, McAuliffe's sister and parents are tearfully reacting to the destruction of the space vehicle. Subsequent information has shown that they are reacting happily to the launch, moments before the accident.

Hall, Donald N. B., ed. *The Space Telescope Observatory.* Washington, D.C.: Government Printing Office, 1982.
This is a compendium of information about the Hubble Space Telescope, written by individuals or groups that have played a major role in the development of the first large-aperture, long-term optical and ultraviolet observatory to be launched into space. Most of the papers are highly technical and deal with the projected performance of the telescope. The dissertations represent an overview of the Hubble Space Telescope's scientific potential as perceived by the scientists involved in its development. Detailed line drawings and black-and-white photographs of the telescope's equipment are included. Each of the observatory's individual telescopes and cameras is detailed.

Hallion, Richard. *On the Frontier: Flight Research at Dryden, 1946-1981.* Washington, D.C.: Government Printing Office, 1984.

This is one of the titles in the NASA History Series, which provides an official look at the space agency, its programs and facilities. Just a bit northeast of Los Angeles lies a desert region just perfect for testing aircraft. In the southwest corner of the Mojave Desert is the Antelope Valley, a mecca for the aerospace industry. That is where the United States placed its Edwards Air Force Base, and that is where, in 1946, the National Advisory Committee for Aeronautics (NACA) sent a group of engineers and technicians to assist in a supersonic test program. The NACA High-Speed Flight Research Station became the NACA High-Speed Flight Station in 1954. With the coming of NASA, the station was redesignated the NASA Flight Research Center in 1959. In 1976, NASA renamed it the Hugh L. Dryden Flight Research Center. This is the story of the center and the flight testing that occurred there during its first thirty-five years. The information is presented in chronological order and covers such noted aerospace craft as the X-1, X-15, HL-10, X-24A, X-24B, and the Space Shuttle. Also detailed is the research that assisted the development of the Gemini and Apollo spacecraft. There are many black-and-white photographs and line drawings, an index, and an impressive bibliography. Appendices include program flight chronologies on the X-1, D-558, X-2, X-3, X-4, X-5, XF-92A, X-15, lifting bodies, XB-70A, and Space Shuttle approach and landing test program.

Jenkins, Dennis R. *Rockwell International Space Shuttle.* Arlington, Tex.: Aerofax, 1989.
This book, one of a series of so-called datagraphs, details the Space Shuttle orbiter. It begins with a discussion of the history and origins of the Space Transportation System. There are specifications and diagrams of these early designs and of several vehicles used to test the final version. The majority of the work is devoted to the finer details of the orbiter and its systems. There are hundreds of drawings and black-and-white photographs, plus a few bonus color ones. The orbiter is seen up close, from every possible angle. Cutaway drawings accompany the photographs, permitting an in-depth study of the components. This is a good research book, and it is a great book for the person who wishes to build an accurate scale model of the orbiter.

Kaplan, Marshall H. *Space Shuttle: America's Wings to the Future.* Fallbrook, Calif.: Aero, 1978.
The Space Shuttle was developed to replace expendable launch vehicles with a reusable one. This work studies the preparations for this new transportation system and then takes the reader through a "typical" Space Shuttle mission. The author discusses each of the components of the system— the orbiter, external tank, and solid rocket boosters. Payloads and spacewalks are also discussed. There are plenty of color and black-and-white photographs and line drawings to detail the components of the vehicle. Appendices cover companies

receiving contracts to build the Shuttle, Space Shuttle model information and specifications, astronaut candidate profiles, and a glossary of terms and acronyms. Most of the information and illustrations come directly from NASA and Rockwell International, the prime contractor for the orbiter. There are a few glaring errors, including the statement that Alan Shepard took the United States' first spaceflight on February 20, 1962. (Actually, he flew on May 5, 1961. John Glenn orbited the Earth on February 20.)

Kerrod, Robin. *Space Shuttle.* New York: Gallery Books, 1984.
A simplified look at the Space Transportation System geared toward the younger reader, this work contains many color photographs. There is not much in the way of technical information in this book, but even the researcher will enjoy looking at the pictures, which include some spectacular shots, especially those taken from orbit.

Lewis, Richard. "The Space Shuttle." In *The Illustrated Encyclopedia of Space Technology: A Comprehensive History of Space Exploration*, by Kenneth Gatland et al. New York: Harmony Books, 1981.
This section in the book takes a brief historical look at the Space Transportation System and the research aircraft which helped to develop the technology to make the Shuttle possible. Some of these early winged spacecraft and lifting bodies—the X-15, X-24A, X-24B, HL-10, M2F2, and M2F3—are pictured. There are color cutaway diagrams of the Space Shuttle's major systems: the orbiter, solid rocket boosters, and external tank. Some early designs of the Shuttle are included. There are also color and black-and-white photographs and drawings. The book includes a chronology of the major space events since Sputnik 1, a glossary of terms, and an index.

Lord, Douglas R. *Spacelab: An International Success Story.* Washington, D.C.: Government Printing Office, 1987.
One of the main purposes for building the Space Transportation System was to provide the capability of taking scientific work stations into orbit. What started as a plan for a space station developed into the Spacelab, an interchangeable set of modules and pallets which can be adapted for an unlimited number of experiment packages. This book, although not listed as part of the official NASA History Series, was written for NASA and provides a thorough look at the development and construction of Spacelab. There are discussions on the countries that helped build and pay for Spacelab, as well as a look at its first three missions. There are hundreds of color and black-and-white photographs and a summary of the program to date. Appendices present the Memorandum of Understanding, which provided for the implementation of the cooperative program to build Spacelab; the Joint Programme Plan; Programme

Requirements; and a list of key program participants. Like other NASA historical references, this one has an extensive bibliography.

McConnell, Malcolm. *Challenger: A Major Malfunction.* New York: Doubleday, 1987.
One of several "witch-hunt" books written in the wake of the *Challenger* accident of January, 1986. The resident space "expert" at *Reader's Digest*, McConnell levels his biased attacks at anyone and everyone within a hundred miles of the accident. He accuses then-NASA Administrator James Fletcher of having rigged the awarding of the solid rocket booster contract to Morton Thiokol. The joint between two of the lower segments of the right-hand booster is believed to be the culprit in the accident. McConnell attacks President Ronald Reagan for pressuring NASA to launch the first teacher in space in time for his State of the Union Address. The author claims to have sources no one else could find, yet he is unable to reveal one fact not found in the *Report of the Presidential Commission on the Space Shuttle Challenger Accident* (detailed below).

McMahan, Tracy, and Valerie Neal. *Repairing Solar Max: The Solar Maximum Repair Mission.* Washington, D.C.: Government Printing Office, 1984.
The Solar Maximum Satellite was launched on Valentine's Day, 1980, to study the Sun during one of its peak periods of activity. The satellite functioned for nearly a year before suffering what normally would be a fatal failure. NASA, however, would not let the patient die so easily. Once the Space Shuttle had become operational (more or less), the engineers who had built it hit upon a plan whereby astronauts from the Shuttle would zip over to Solar Max, grab it, lock it into their garage in the back of the orbiter's payload bay, fix the ailing satellite, and send it on its way. This effort was made because it cost about one-quarter of the price of a replacement satellite. This colorful booklet previews the rescue mission, the equipment needed to fix Max, and the astronauts who would attempt it.

McRoberts, Joseph J. *Space Telescope.* Washington, D.C.: Government Printing Office, 1982.
The Hubble Space Telescope will allow scientists to view the universe from a vantage point three hundred miles above Earth. There, unobstructed by the atmosphere, it will peer back into time, seven times farther than previously seen. It will be able to image the planets of the solar system at a resolution greater than before possible. Even a planet as far away as Saturn will be viewed with the clarity available from the Voyager spacecraft. This is a preview guide to the deployment mission. It uses a great number of color and black-and-white photographs, as well as drawings, to illustrate the telescope

and its mission. An excellent source of pre-launch information about this project.

Magill, Frank N., ed. *Magill's Survey of Science: Space Exploration Series.* Vol. 4. Pasadena, Calif.: Salem Press, 1989, pp. 1626-1827.
This five-volume set covers every aspect of the U.S. and Soviet manned and unmanned space programs, as well as those of nations newer to the space race. Reliance on expendable manned spacecraft and launch vehicles began to decline with the introduction of the Space Transportation System (STS). The main feature of STS was the reusable Space Shuttle orbiter. One article is devoted to an overview of the program, while a second discusses the test flights of *Enterprise.* The others list the pertinent data for each of the first twenty-six missions (STS-1 through STS-26). There is a brief summary of each flight, the knowledge gained, and the historical significance of each mission. Each article includes an annotated bibliography and cross-references. Aside from a few technical inaccuracies, the work is an excellent starting point for the researcher.

_____, ed. *Magill's Survey of Science: Space Exploration Series.* Vol. 4. Pasadena, Calif.: Salem Press, 1989, pp. 1884-1911.
As part of the "advertising" program for the development of the Space Shuttle, NASA began a program to provide scientists with facilities to study the micro-gravity environment while approximating the conditions of an earthbound laboratory. The result, a joint effort with the European Space Agency, is Spacelab. Using a combination of interchangeable modules and pallets, researchers can conduct an unlimited variety of experiments and studies. The first three Spacelab missions flown aboard the Space Shuttle are discussed in separate articles, as is the overall program. Each essay lists the pertinent data of the mission, the results of its investigations, an annotated bibliography, and cross-references.

Messerschmitt-Bölkow-Blohm. *First German SPACELAB: Mission D1.* Bremen, West Germany: MBB/ERNO, 1985.
The "Deutschland Spacelab Mission D1" was the first of a series of dedicated West German missions on the Space Shuttle. It flew aboard *Challenger* in October, 1985, the last successful mission of the orbiter. The modules contained equipment for seventy-six experiments in five disciplines: fluid physics, solidification, biology, medicine, and space-time interaction. This work details each of the experiments and the facilities used to run them. There are dozens of color photographs and drawings of the experiment packages. This publication, although published in West Germany, has been made available through NASA.

Neal, Valerie. *Renewing Solar Science: The Solar Maximum Mission.* Washington, D.C.: Government Printing Office, 1984.
A preview to the attempted Space Shuttle rescue of the Solar Maximum Satellite. It differs from the one above because its emphasis is on the satellite rather than on the rescue. There are numerous color photographs, including some that were transmitted from Solar Max before it developed problems. The scientific results returned by Max are highlighted and guide the reader to an understanding of the importance of repairing the satellite. There is a short preview of the repair mission and a fine drawing of the satellite, detailing its major components.

Nelson, Bill, with Jamie Buckingham. *Mission.* New York: Harcourt Brace Jovanovich, 1988.
The last successful flight of the Space Shuttle program, prior to the STS 51-L *Challenger* accident, included the second journey of a U.S. congressman. STS 61-C was launched on January 12, 1986, after numerous delays caused by bad weather and technical problems. This is the tale of this mission, as told by Congressman Bill Nelson, who acted as a payload specialist. There is not much technical information in this work, but there is a great deal about the inner workings of the Shuttle program. Nelson discusses his role on the flight, as well as those of his six crewmates.

Ogier, Divonna. "The Solar Maximum Mission." In *Magill's Survey of Science: Space Exploration Series*, vol. 3, edited by Frank N. Magill. Pasadena, Calif.: Salem Press, 1989.
One of the essays on the history of space exploration in this five-volume set, which covers every aspect of the U.S. and Soviet manned and unmanned space programs, as well as those of nations newer to the space race. Every eleven years or so, the Sun begins a period of dynamic activity. Scientists have attempted to study this activity from the vantage point of orbit. The Solar Maximum Satellite (commonly known as "Solar Max") was launched in 1980 to study the Sun during that cycle's peak year. For ten months, Max gathered valuable data, then suddenly suffered a major malfunction. Scientists determined that it would be possible to repair the satellite on orbit. This was accomplished on the eleventh Space Shuttle mission (STS 41-C). This article discusses the Solar Max Satellite and its mission, as well as the successful rescue. Contains an annotated bibliography and cross-references.

O'Leary, Brian. *Project Space Station.* Harrisburg, Pa.: Government Printing Office, 1983.
The author takes a look at the space station programs of the United States and the Soviet Union and discusses their practical applications and benefits. He traces the history of manned space platforms and, in the process, touches upon

Skylab, Spacelab, and the Space Transportation System. The major systems of an orbiting space station, similar to the United States' *Freedom*, are described. Much of the emphasis of the book is on the political aspects of the program. Includes black-and-white photographs, a brief bibliography, and an index.

Otto, Dixon P. *On Orbit: Bringing on the Space Shuttle.* Athens, Ohio: Main Stage, 1986.
This book, by the publisher of *Countdown* magazine, is a concise look at what the author calls "The First Space Shuttle Era." It chronicles the Space Transportation System from its inception through the *Challenger* accident. The first part of the work discusses the early design concepts for the Shuttle and some of the factors that influenced its evolution. There is also a brief description of a typical Shuttle mission. The highlight of the book is the coverage of each of the first twenty-five missions. Each is presented with the particulars of the flight, including crew, launch and landing times, duration, orbits, and payload. There are several black-and-white photographs from each flight and a portfolio of color pictures in the center section.

Pogue, William R. *How Do You Go to the Bathroom in Space?* New York: Tom Doherty Associates, 1985.
This and many other interesting questions about living in space are answered by former astronaut Pogue. He was one of three crew members who spent eighty-four days in orbit aboard Skylab. Actually, there are 156 questions which the author has gleaned from thousands that he and his fellow astronauts have received in a quarter century of manned spaceflight. Many of the questions lead to humorous answers, but most provide a great deal of firsthand information about matters of general interest. The questions touch on each of the U.S. manned space programs. Several appendices provide additional information, including a summary of the physiological effects of spaceflight, a list of Earth features recognizable from space, a guide to information and resources, and a bibliography.

Rayman, Marc D. "Space Shuttle Mission 14." In *Magill's Survey of Science: Space Exploration Series*, vol. 4, edited by Frank N. Magill. Pasadena, Calif.: Salem Press, 1989.
One of the goals set for the Space Shuttle program at its inception was the capability to service and retrieve disabled satellites. The first demonstration of this capability came during the STS 51-A mission. In February, 1984, the Space Shuttle *Challenger* successfully deployed two communications satellites. Unfortunately, their solid rocket motors failed to perform properly, leaving the satellites in useless elliptical orbits rather than in their desired geosynchronous orbit. NASA and the contractors (and their insurance companies) decided that it would be cheaper to retrieve the satellites, refit them with new motors, and

relaunch them either aboard another Shuttle mission or atop a Delta launch vehicle. This article details the event-filled mission, which, in addition to the rescue of the two satellites, deployed two satellites and conducted numerous experiments. The particulars of the mission are presented in a concise format with important data given and technical jargon eliminated. There is a brief annotated bibliography. As a footnote to the story, the two rescued satellites were successfully relaunched in April, 1990.

Ride, Sally K., with Susan Okie. *To Space and Back*. New York: Lothrop, Lee & Shepard Books, 1986.
Former astronaut Ride tells about her two trips into space (aboard *Challenger* on STS-7 and STS 41-G). This work was written mainly for children, but it provides the first look at space travel from a woman's perspective. There are dozens of color photographs from her flights and from the other Space Shuttle missions. She talks about each phase of a typical mission and her reactions to the events which occurred during her flights. Contains a glossary of terms and an index.

Ridenoure, Rex. "The Get-Away Special Experiments." In *Magill's Survey of Science: Space Exploration Series*, vol. 2, edited by Frank N. Magill. Pasadena, Calif.: Salem Press, 1989.
One of the essays on the history of space exploration in this five-volume set, which covers every aspect of the U.S. and Soviet manned and unmanned space programs, as well as those of nations newer to the space race. The Get-Away Special (GAS) program was developed as a means for scientists, engineers, and students to launch payloads into orbit aboard the Space Shuttle. It was designed to meet the needs of the "small" space experimenter. This essay discusses the program, its components, and some of the experiments carried into space. Provides an annotated bibliography and cross-references.

Rogers, William, et al. *Report of the Presidential Commission on the Space Shuttle Challenger Accident*. 5 vols. Washington, D.C.: Government Printing Office, 1986.
On January 28, 1986, seven astronauts flew the Space Shuttle *Challenger* on its last mission. Seventy-three seconds after lifting off from the Kennedy Space Center, the giant external tank attached to the orbiter disintegrated. This is the official report of the commission appointed by President Ronald Reagan to investigate the accident. The fourteen-person commission included such notable persons as former Secretary of State William P. Rogers (chairman), former astronauts Neil Armstrong (vice chairman) and Sally K. Ride, and former test pilot Charles (Chuck) Yeager. The report, along with its four-volume set of appendices and hearings transcripts, indicates that the most probable cause of the accident was a failure in the joint between the lower two segments of the

right solid rocket motor. The work details the flight and the subsequent investigation. There are dozens of color and black-and-white photographs and line drawings for emphasis. Many of the photographs have not been made available in any other document. The reader who wants to know the truth (as best it can be known) should favor this work over those tabloid-style books that tried to cash in on the accident.

Shayler, David J. *Shuttle Challenger: Aviation Fact File*. London: Salamander Books, 1987.
The life and times of the Space Shuttle *Challenger* are revealed in words and pictures. The comprehensive text, written in the wake of the STS 51-L accident, discusses this orbiter only. It looks at *Challenger*'s humble beginnings as a Static Test Article and follows its career through nine missions and the final one. Information on each flight includes preflight and postflight activities, in addition to those during the flight. This is a large-format book with numerous color and black-and-white photographs.

Smith, Mervyn. *An Illustrated History of Space Shuttle: U.S. Winged Spacecraft, X-15 to Orbiter*. Newbury Park, Calif.: Haynes, 1985.
This work traces the history of the Space Shuttle orbiter and the research aircraft from which it was derived. Each of these ancestors contributed in some way or another to the final design of the orbiter. Included in the discussions are the X-1 series, X-2, X-3, X-20, X-24A, X-24B, HL-10, D-558-I, D-558-II, M2F2, M2F3, and the X-15. There are hundreds of color and black-and-white photographs of these pioneers, as well as the pioneers who flew them. Seven appendices chronicle the flight programs of the X-15, M2F2, HL-10, X-24A, M2F3, X-24B, and the Space Shuttle (through STS 51-C). This is one of the best collections of information on the early research aircraft and lifting bodies.

Steinberg, Florence S. *Aboard the Space Shuttle*. Washington, D.C.: Government Printing Office, 1980.
A preview of the Space Transportation System is provided for a general audience. The major features of the Space Shuttle orbiter are described, accompanied by line drawings and color photographs of its crew compartment. All of the conveniences of home are provided to the astronaut crew. There is a sleeping area, an eating area, and, of course, a space "potty." The extravehicular mobility unit (spacesuit), for taking expeditions outside the orbiter, is also discussed, as is the remote manipulator system arm for payload deployment and retrieval. There is not much technical information, but there are plenty of pictures.

Taylor, L. B., Jr. *For All Mankind: America's Space Programs of the 1970s and Beyond*. New York: E. P. Dutton, 1974.

The author discusses the benefits of the United States' space programs of the early 1970's, especially the multiple benefits derived from communications satellites and Earth resources satellites. He describes these programs as well as the Space Transportation System, which was in the later stages of planning and development. The book discusses the full range of possibilities for the Space Shuttle and some of its payloads. Much is to be gained by comparing the goals of the system in 1974 and its accomplishments through the next decade and a half. There are black-and-white photographs and an index.

_____. *Space Shuttle.* New York: Thomas Y. Crowell, 1979.
This is a preview of the Space Transportation System and the plans for making it the main means of taking U.S. (and some foreign) payloads into space. It also discusses the Space Shuttle's potential for the industrialization and colonization of space. The author details the development and testing of the system, how other nations are involved in the program, and the criticisms and benefits of a reusable spacecraft. There are black-and-white photographs and line drawings and a bibliography.

Tobias, Russell R. "Space Shuttle Mission 12." In *Magill's Survey of Science: Space Exploration Series*, vol. 4, edited by Frank N. Magill. Pasadena, Calif.: Salem Press, 1989.
It is usually considered to be in poor taste to review one's own work, so I will not tell you what I think about this particular chapter in the five-volume set. However, as author of this annotated bibliography, I am fortunate to be able to point out a gross error without fear of retribution from its maker. In fact, if someone else had noted the error, I would let them take the credit for having noticed it. This chapter deals with the STS 41-D mission, which deployed three communications satellites and conducted a variety of experiments in 1984. Due to a pad abort involving the shutdown of the Space Shuttle's main engines prior to ignition of the solid rocket motors, the mission had to be rescheduled. In doing so, NASA combined the payloads from the original STS 41-D with the upcoming STS 41-F mission. The STS 41-F crew was reassigned to another flight. In the published version of the work, the combined mission is listed as STS 41D/F. NASA, however, never gave this designation to the revised flight and this author never included the designation in his original work. Somewhere between the final draft and the published work, someone decided to change it. This one malefaction should not dissuade the researcher from using this otherwise fine publication. I am, nevertheless, relieved that this blight on my reputation has been removed.

Trento, Joseph J. *Prescription for Disaster.* New York: Crown, 1987.
One of several "witch-hunt" books written in the wake of the *Challenger* accident of January, 1986. According to the publishers, Trento was an "investi-

gative reporter" for Cable News Network. However, very little investigation of the book reveals its obvious bias and attempt to exploit the "newsworthiness" of the subject. If you want facts about the accident, read the *Report of the Presidential Commission on the Space Shuttle Challenger Accident* (detailed above).

U.S. General Accounting Office. *Space Exploration: Cost, Schedule, and Performance of NASA's Galileo Mission to Jupiter.* Washington, D.C.: Government Printing Office, 1988.
The chairman of the Senate Committee on Commerce, Science, and Transportation asked the GAO to assess the cost, schedule, and performance of several NASA projects. This work is the report of their findings on the Galileo mission to Jupiter. Galileo was launched from the Space Shuttle *Atlantis* in October, 1989. The report provides a general overview of the program, including its objectives, scope, and methodology. There are spacecraft configuration drawings and information relating to cost, schedule, and performance. A chronology of the project, through the date of the report, is presented. There is a glossary of terms used. This is a look at the program from a financial point of view.

_____. *Space Exploration: Cost, Schedule, and Performance of NASA's Magellan Mission to Venus.* Washington, D.C.: Government Printing Office, 1988.
This work is the report of the GAO's findings on the Magellan mission to Venus, which was launched from the Space Shuttle *Atlantis* in May, 1989. The report provides a general overview of the program, including its objectives, scope, and methodology. There are spacecraft configuration drawings and information relating to cost, schedule, and performance. A chronology of the project, through the date of the report, is presented. There is a glossary of terms used.

_____. *Space Exploration: Cost, Schedule, and Performance of NASA's Ulysses Mission to the Sun.* Washington, D.C.: Government Printing Office, 1988.
This work is the report of the GAO's findings on the Ulysses mission to the Sun, scheduled to be deployed from the Shuttle *Discovery* in October, 1990. The report provides a general overview of the program, including its objectives, scope, and methodology. There are spacecraft configuration drawings and information relating to cost, schedule, and performance. A chronology of the project, through the date of the report, is presented. There is a glossary of terms used.

_____. *Space Exploration: NASA's Deep Space Missions Are Experiencing Long Delays.* Washington, D.C.: Government Printing Office, 1988.

This work is the report of the GAO's findings on four of NASA's proposed deep space missions. The report covers the Galileo mission to Jupiter, the Ulysses mission to the Sun, the Magellan mission to Venus, and the Mars Observer mission. The report provides a general overview of the program, including its objectives, scope, and methodology. There are spacecraft configuration drawings and information relating to cost, schedule, and performance. A chronology of the project, through the date of the report, is presented. There is a glossary of terms used.

_____. *Space Science: Status of the Hubble Space Telescope Program.* Washington, D.C.: Government Printing Office, 1988.
This work is the report of the GAO's findings on the Hubble Space Telescope, launched from the Space Shuttle *Discovery* in April, 1990. The report provides a general overview of the program, including its objectives, scope, and methodology. There are spacecraft configuration drawings and information relating to cost, schedule, and performance. A chronology of the project, through the date of the report, is presented. There is a glossary of terms used.

_____. *Space Station: NASA Efforts to Establish a Design-to-Life-Cycle Cost Process.* Washington, D.C.: Government Printing Office, 1988.
In 1985, the Senate Committee on Commerce, Science, and Transportation directed NASA to outline its plans for the space station *Freedom* to ensure that it did not overlook future operations costs during the station's definition, design, and development phases. NASA responded that it would control operations costs by using a design-to-life-cycle cost approach, which establishes the projected total life-cycle cost of a system as a design requirement equal in importance to performance and schedule concerns, and which establishes cost elements as management goals. This is the GAO's report on this approach. Appendices include a system design tradeoff model and comments from NASA on the report.

U.S. House of Representatives. *Investigation of the Challenger Accident: Report of Committee on Science and Technology.* Washington, D.C.: Government Printing Office, 1986.
Not content to let the Presidential Commission get all of the "press" for the investigation of the *Challenger* accident, this committee of the House of Representatives conducted its own hearings. The Committee held ten formal hearings involving sixty witnesses, made an extensive review of the report of the Rogers Commission, and held numerous briefings and interviews with NASA officials, contractor personnel, outside experts, and other interested parties. They concluded that NASA's drive to achieve its launch schedule created pressure throughout the agency that directly contributed to unsafe launch conditions. What they failed to point out was the lack of congressional support

for the original Space Transportation System concept, which did not need to rely on "unsafe" solid rocket motors. They also overlooked the fact that prior to STS 51-L, they considered the Shuttle safe enough to carry a senator and a house representative into space. There are a lot of black-and-white photographs and line drawings; the quality of these illustrations, however, leaves much to be desired.

_____. *The Need for an Increased Space Shuttle Orbiter Fleet*. Washington, D.C.: Government Printing Office, 1982.
This is an earlier record of the lack of foresight on the part of Congress. After holding a hearing with officials from NASA, the Air Force, contractor representatives, and other interested parties (most of whom stated a need for a fifth orbiter), the Committee on Science and Technology concluded that a fifth orbiter would be necessary. This would be especially true if, according to the testimony of NASA Associate Deputy Administrator Phillip Culbertson, "the four orbiter fleet were reduced to three orbiters in 1986 due to the loss of an orbiter. . . ." Congress decided that, on the whole, it would be financially impractical to provide the funds for this fifth orbiter. Hindsight is usually 20-20, but some of the forecasts presented are eerie in light of the *Challenger* accident.

_____. *Space Shuttle Status Report for the Committee on Science and Technology, 1977-1980*. 4 vols. Washington, D.C.: Government Printing Office, 1976-1979.
The purpose of these status reports was to provide the members of the Subcommittee on Space Science and Applications with source material addressing the issues associated with cost, performance, and schedule of the Space Shuttle program prior to the hearings to fix NASA's operating budget. Each report gives a synopsis of the Space Transportation System and its activities for the previous fiscal year. Some of the issues addressed by the committee were the report of the Aerospace Safety Advisory Panel, the economics of the Space Shuttle, performance and weight margins, scheduling, and critical technical areas. The reports are filled with charts, tables, line drawings and black-and-white photographs. Each of the issues is discussed at length, including the testimony of witnesses, and the committee's conclusions are presented.

_____. *United States Civilian Space Programs 1958-1978*. Vol. 1. Washington, D.C.: Government Printing Office, 1981.
In a very concise report, the Subcommittee on Space Science and Applications has compiled data on all U.S. space activity during its first two decades. After a brief introduction and summary chapter, the volume is divided into fourteen additional sections. The second chapter deals with the space-related issues under consideration by Congress. The remaining sections cover the history of NASA

and its relationship to U.S. space policy, NASA facilities and tracking systems, launch vehicles and propulsion, manned spaceflight through 1975, the Space Transportation System, space life sciences, space science programs, materials processing in space, international cooperation in space, interagency and non-NASA governmental space activities, industrial and university support for NASA, space program benefits, and selected future space programs. Appendices contain Department of Defense manned spaceflight plans, NASA funding history, international space agreements, texts of President Jimmy Carter's space directives, documents relating to the legal aspects of the Space Shuttle, major U.S. space organizations, a master log of U.S. spaceflights, and a table of U.S. space orbital payloads by mission from 1957 through 1979.

U.S. National Aeronautics and Space Administration. *EASE/ACCESS: Framework for the Future.* Washington, D.C.: Government Printing Office, 1985.
In preparation for permanent space construction, NASA's Marshall Space Flight Center in Huntsville, Alabama, developed two experiments to demonstrate the ability of astronauts to build large structures in space. The experiments were flown aboard the Space Shuttle *Atlantis* on mission STS 61-B in November, 1985. The first of the experiments is the Experimental Assembly of Structures in Extravehicular Activity (EASE). EASE consists of six aluminum beams, each 12 feet long, which form a tetrahedral cell when pieced together. The Assembly Concept for Construction of Erectable Space Structures (ACCESS) consists of mastlike, 4.5-foot assembly fixtures. These are raised to a vertical position, and the fixture's three guide rails unfold like an umbrella. When fully erected, the structure is 45 feet tall. This booklet is filled with color photographs and discusses the experiments in detail.

_____. *Galileo to Jupiter.* Washington, D.C.: Government Printing Office, 1979.
A brief preflight guide to the Galileo spacecraft, which will orbit Jupiter and send a probe to explore its atmosphere. Although the mission described in this booklet is not the one that was flown, it does give the researcher an insight into the spacecraft. The mission depicted would have been launched from the Space Shuttle in 1982 and would have used an Inertial Upper Stage (IUS) to boost it to Jupiter. Unlike the two-stage IUS used in 1989 during its actual deployment, the IUS for this mission was to have three stages. It would propel Galileo toward Mars, where the spacecraft would get a gravity assist from the red planet. Development problems with the three-stage IUS forced NASA to switch to the more powerful, liquid- propellant Centaur upper stage. The *Challenger* accident forced NASA to drop plans for Centaur and switch to the already proven two-stage IUS. There are a number of color drawings of the spacecraft and its mission, as well as color photographs taken by the Voyager 1 spacecraft.

_____. *Get Away Special (GAS) Small Self-Contained Payloads: Experimenter Handbook.* Washington, D.C.: Government Printing Office, 1984.
The purpose of NASA's Get Away Special (GAS) program is to encourage the use of space by all researchers, foster enthusiasm in the younger generation, increase knowledge of space, be alert to possible growth of GAS investigation into a prime experiment, and generate new activities unique to space. The GAS payloads are self-contained and are not permitted to draw upon any Shuttle services beyond three on-off controls that are operated by an astronaut. The experimenter is required to provide any electrical power, heating, data-handling, and other facilities within the GAS container. This document provides the experimenter with all the information necessary to develop a payload for one or more of these containers. Specifications for each of the available containers, as well as safety requirements, are included. There are tips for the experimenter and a brief, annotated bibliography to guide the investigator to books that might be useful in the design of the experiment.

_____. *Magellan: The Unveiling of Venus.* Pasadena, Calif.: Jet Propulsion Laboratory, 1989.
This is a preflight guide to the Magellan spacecraft deployed from the Space Shuttle *Atlantis* on May 4, 1989, as part of the STS-30 mission. Magellan's primary goal is to make radar studies of the surface of Venus while in orbit around the cloud-covered planet. The spacecraft was built mostly of spare parts from other planetary projects, most notably Voyager and Galileo. The booklet is filled with color and black-and-white photographs, line drawings, and artists' renditions. The project is detailed, as are the spacecraft and its one main scientific instrument, the synthetic aperture radar (SAR). SAR uses the Doppler shift to create a three-dimensional image of the surface. It will greatly enhance our knowledge of Venus.

_____. *National Space Transportation System Reference.* 2 vols. Washington, D.C.: Government Printing Office, 1988.
This is the most complete technical reference about the Space Transportation System written in nontechnical terminology. It is an enlarged and updated version of the *Press Information* books published by Rockwell International, maker of the Space Shuttle orbiter. The last Rockwell version was printed in 1984, but because of budget reductions instituted at Rockwell in 1985, their Media Relations Office could not update and reprint it. NASA, however, wanted a new edition when the Shuttle resumed operations after the *Challenger* accident. They contracted with Rockwell to provide the text and artwork. Volume 1 details the systems and facilities, while the second volume covers NASA centers and management. There are hundreds of line drawings and black-and-white photographs. Each system and subsystem is presented in great detail. Emphasis, of course, has been placed on the orbiter systems, but there

is still a great deal of information about the solid rocket boosters and the external tank. Also detailed are the crew equipment and escape systems, NASA centers and responsibilities, and payloads. Includes a summary of mission events, a chronology of the Space Shuttle program, a list of contractors, and a glossary of acronyms and abbreviations.

_____. *Office of Space Sciences-1 Experiment Investigation Descriptions.* Washington, D.C.: Government Printing Office, 1982.
The OSS-1 experiments package was flown onboard the Space Shuttle *Columbia* in March, 1982, during the third flight of the Space Transportation System program. The investigations studied space plasma physics, the orbiter environment, solar physics, life sciences, space technology, and astronomy. This booklet discusses each of the experiments in detail and provides a technical description of the equipment. Line drawings and a detailed bibliography are included.

_____. *On the Wings of a Dream: The Space Shuttle.* Washington, D.C.: Government Printing Office, 1989.
This is an uplifting look at the Space Shuttle program, written in the early days of the post-*Challenger* recovery period. The Space Transportation System is briefly discussed, as is the daily life of astronauts aboard the orbiter. Some of the routines of space life, including eating, sleeping, dressing, and going to the bathroom, are presented. Extravehicular activity and the Spacelab are also discussed. Contains a table of the first twenty-six flights and plenty of color photographs. This is not a book for the researcher as much as it is for the general reader.

_____. *OSTA-1 Experiments.* Washington, D.C.: Government Printing Office, 1981.
On its second flight, the Space Shuttle *Columbia* carried the first science and applications payload scheduled by the Space Transportation System. This payload, called OSTA-1, was developed by NASA's Office of Space and Terrestrial Applications (OSTA) to provide an early demonstration of the Shuttle's research capabilities. The payload consisted of the Shuttle Imaging Radar-A, Shuttle Multispectral Infrared Radiometer, Feature Identification and Location Experiment, Measurement of Air Pollution from Satellites, Ocean Color Experiment, Night/Day Optical Survey of Lightning, and Heflex Bioengineering Test. The booklet previews the flight of STS-2 and discusses the OSTA-1 experiments in great detail. There are black-and-white photographs and line drawings and a bibliography.

_____. *OSTA-2 Payload.* Washington, D.C.: Government Printing Office, 1982.

The OSTA-2 payload was carried into orbit during the second flight of *Challenger*, STS-7, in June, 1983. The experiments package consisted of two facilities that operated automatically. These were the Materials Experiment Assembly, sponsored by NASA, and the Materialwissenschaftliche Autonome Experimente unter Schwerelosigkeit, sponsored by the German Ministry for Research and Technology. The booklet discusses the two experiment packages and their Mission Peculiar Support Structure in great detail. There are several line drawings to show the inner workings of the equipment.

_____. *OSTA-3 Experiments*. Washington, D.C.: Government Printing Office, 1984.
The OSTA-3 experiments were carried aboard *Challenger* during the STS 41-G mission, which was flown in October, 1984. It was the second generation of the first science and applications payload carried by the Space Shuttle. Three of the OSTA-1 experiments were reflown in modified form: the Shuttle Imaging Radar, Feature Identification and Location Experiment, and the Measurement of Air Pollution from Satellites. In addition, the Large Format Camera was designed to take stereoscopic, wide-angle, high-resolution metric photographs of Earth. The booklet describes the experiments and uses black-and-white photographs and line drawings to detail the experiment equipment.

_____. *Report to the President: Actions to Implement the Recommendations of the Presidential Commission on the Space Shuttle Challenger Accident*. Washington, D.C.: Government Printing Office, 1986.
On June 6, 1986, the Rogers Commission presented the report of its findings and recommendations to President Ronald Reagan. After reviewing the report, the president instructed NASA Administrator James C. Fletcher to undertake a program to implement these recommendations. On July 14, 1986, Fletcher delivered NASA's plans to comply with the order. This report addresses the nine recommendations of the commission and presents a detailed plan for the implementation of each.

_____. *Science in Orbit: The Shuttle and Spacelab Experience, 1981-1986*. Washington, D.C.: Government Printing Office, 1988.
The opportunity to conduct large-scale experiments in Earth orbit escaped the U.S. space program for nearly a decade, from the end of the last Skylab mission in February, 1974, to the first Spacelab mission aboard *Columbia* in November, 1983. Now the United States has the capability to obtain the necessary data to launch a permanently manned space station. This book studies the Space Transportation System and the Spacelab research laboratory. It chronicles the two programs and looks at the science gained from the first twenty-four Shuttle flights. Disciplines detailed include life sciences, materials science, solar physics, space plasma physics, atmospheric science, Earth

observation, astronomy, and astrophysics. In addition, experiments conducted to test the technology needed to build the space station *Freedom* are presented. There are dozens of color and black-and-white photographs.

_____. *Shuttle Flight Operations Manual.* 30 vols. Washington, D.C.: Government Printing Office, 1978-1989.
This is the complete technical reference on the Space Shuttle orbiter and its associated payloads. Detailed is each of the orbiter's major systems: caution and warning; electrical power; environmental control and life support; communications and instrumentation; data processing; guidance, navigation, and control; applications software; propulsion; auxiliary power units; structures and mechanics; crew systems; displays and controls; extravehicular activity equipment; payload deployment and retrieval; upper stages; and Spacelab support. There are hundreds of drawings and diagrams to accompany the explicit text. This set is a must for the researcher who wants to know everything about the orbiter.

_____. *Space Shuttle.* Washington, D.C.: Government Printing Office, 1975.
A very early look at the Space Transportation System, this book discusses the major components and a typical Shuttle flight. The systems and subsystems of the orbiter, external tank, and solid rocket boosters are detailed using black-and-white photographs and line drawings to amplify the text. The earthly benefits of the Shuttle program are also discussed, as is its economic impact on society. An appendix lists the major contractors and subcontractors of the vehicle.

_____. *Space Shuttle.* Washington, D.C.: Government Printing Office, 1976.
This is an updated, colorful version of the above-listed book on the Space Transportation System. It has been compiled from official NASA and contractor press information. The Shuttle's major components are discussed using words, color and black-and-white photographs, line drawings, and artist's concepts. A typical mission is profiled, along with a discussion of some of the future payloads. The earthly benefits derived from the system and the economic impact of the Shuttle are discussed. Some of the benefits discussed are in the areas of Earth resources, astronomy, communications, environment, and life sciences.

_____. *The Space Station: A Description of the Configuration Established at the Systems Requirements Review (SRR).* Washington, D.C.: Government Printing Office, 1986.

This work takes a brief yet in-depth look at the planned space station *Freedom*. In response to President Ronald Reagan's 1984 commitment to develop a permanently manned space station within a decade, NASA undertook an examination of the many missions that a space station might carry out and of the many ways in which the station might be configured. This effort reached a major milestone in 1986, called the systems requirements review (SRR). SRR decisions established the "baseline" configuration for *Freedom*. The report details this configuration, as well as the process which derived it. There are many pages of black-and-white photographs and line drawings. Includes a chart depicting the assembly sequence for *Freedom*, as well as a brief history of the space station concept.

_____. *Space Station Development Plan Submitted to the Committee on Science, Space, and Technology, U.S. House of Representatives.* Washington, D.C.: Government Printing Office, 1987.
This plan for the development of a permanently manned space station was submitted by NASA in response to a request by the committee. The plan submitted was based on internal planning and budgetary considerations. Included in the plan are program objectives and requirements, development strategy, management approach, and program schedule. The work reads like most government documents, but the reader can get an idea of the work involved in getting a program of this magnitude off the ground. There are numerous line drawings and charts, a list of reference documents, and a glossary of acronyms and abbreviations. One large appendix details the space station's components and the auxiliary equipment necessary to run it.

_____. *Space Station Reference Configuration Description.* Washington, D.C.: Government Printing Office, 1984.
In order for potential contractors to bid on a particular project, they must have some information about the item on which they will be bidding. This document presents such a guideline for the space station *Freedom*. The information was generated to provide a focal point for the definition and assessment of program requirements, establish a basis for estimating program cost, and define a reference configuration in sufficient detail to allow its inclusion in the definition phase of the program. This is the first official look at how the space station will appear in orbit during each phase of construction. It details the manned core, unmanned platforms, payload accommodations, crew accommodations, and related subsystems. There are dozens of line drawings, a bibliography, and an evaluation of the assembly operations crew time lines.

_____. *Space Transportation System and Associated Payloads: Glossary, Acronyms, and Abbreviations.* Washington, D.C.: National Technical Information Service, 1985.

In the fast-paced world of space travel, it has become necessary to develop a large set of new words and abbreviations. At the moment that the solid rocket boosters (SRBs) expend their fuel and are jettisoned, a lot can happen and it can happen rapidly. Since the Space Shuttle is traveling at about five times the speed of sound when this occurs, it is important to say things in a swift, compact, and clearly understood manner. Instead of the flight controllers reporting, "Everything looks fine right now and your solid rocket boosters are being separated at this point in the flight," they say, "Go at SRB sep." This book, which NASA tries to update regularly (although these updates are not published very often), contains an alphabetical listing of these special words. The glossary contains definitions of some of the terms commonly used in conjunction with the Shuttle and its payloads. It is a very good reference, especially when read in conjunction with some of the more technical documents.

_____. *Spacelab 1*. Washington, D.C.: Government Printing Office, 1983.
This is a preview of the first Spacelab mission flown aboard the Space Shuttle. The work discusses the need for a reusable orbital research facility and the history of Spacelab's development. The experiments to be conducted during the mission are detailed, and brief biographies of the two payload specialists, their backups, and the two mission specialists for the flight are provided. Color and black-and-white photographs and drawings accentuate the text. This is for general audiences, although the researcher will find a great deal of detail about Spacelab's experiments.

_____. *Spacelab 1 Experiments*. Washington, D.C.: Government Printing Office, 1983.
Spacelab 1 was launched aboard the Space Shuttle *Columbia* in November, 1983. It was the inaugural mission of the versatile, reusable research facility funded, developed, and built by the European Space Agency. This work, using black-and-white photographs and drawings, details each of the seventy different experiments in five research disciplines: astronomy and solar physics, space plasma physics, atmospheric physics and Earth observations, life sciences, and materials sciences. The summaries include the purpose, importance, and method of each experiment. The identification number, sponsor, and principal investigator's name and affiliation are provided for each experiment.

_____. *Spacelab 2*. Washington, D.C.: Government Printing Office, 1985.
Spacelab 2 was actually the third mission flown by this scientific research facility. Delays in the development of some of its equipment caused its flight to be switched with the Spacelab 3 mission. Spacelab 2, the first pallet-only mission, was carried into orbit aboard *Challenger* in July, 1985. It consisted of thirteen experiments in six scientific disciplines: solar physics, atmospheric

physics, plasma physics, high-energy astrophysics, technology research, and life sciences. This work previews the flight, with emphasis on the experiments. Each is detailed, including the identification number, sponsor, and principal investigator's name and affiliation, and is accompanied by color photographs and drawings.

_____. *Spacelab Mission 2 Experiment Descriptions.* 2d ed. Washington, D.C.: Government Printing Office, 1982.
NASA's official guide to the experiments carried aboard Spacelab 2 contains very detailed information about each experiment. In addition to the discussion of the test, the experimental apparatus is detailed, including a diagram of the equipment and its physical dimensions and characteristics. There is a line drawing of Spacelab as it is seen in the Space Shuttle's payload bay. The location of each of the experiments is included.

_____. *Spacelab 3.* Washington, D.C.: Government Printing Office, 1984.
Spacelab 3 was carried into orbit aboard the Space Shuttle *Challenger* in April, 1985. It consisted of a long module and Mission Peculiar Equipment Support Structure (MPESS), which carried the fifteen investigations in five scientific disciplines: materials sciences, life sciences, fluid mechanics, atmospheric science, and astronomy. This booklet discusses the mission and its flight crew, including the two payload specialists and their backups. Each of the experiments is detailed, including the identification number, sponsor, and principal investigator's name and affiliation, and is accompanied by color photographs and drawings.

_____. *Spacelab Mission 3 Experiment Descriptions.* Washington, D.C.: Government Printing Office, 1982.
NASA's official guide to the experiments carried aboard Spacelab 3 contains very detailed information about each experiment. In addition to the discussion of the test, the experimental apparatus is detailed, including a diagram of the equipment and its physical dimensions and characteristics. There is a line drawing of Spacelab as it is seen in the Space Shuttle's payload bay. The location of each of the experiments is included.

_____. *Spartan: Science with Efficiency and Simplicity.* Washington, D.C.: Government Printing Office, 1984.
This is a preflight look at the Shuttle Pointed Autonomous Research Tool for Astronomy (Spartan), a retrievable free- flying platform for high-energy astrophysics, solar physics, and ultraviolet astronomy studies. Spartan is carried to orbit inside the payload bay of the Space Shuttle, where it is deployed by the orbiter's remote manipulator system arm. It can then operate independent of the Shuttle for periods up to forty hours. After completing its mission, it

is recaptured by the manipulator arm and placed back in the stowed position for return to Earth. This brief work has several color photographs and color renditions of Spartan in flight. Despite its simplicity, the work provides much information about this unique satellite.

_____. *STS-1 Orbiter Final Mission Report.* Washington, D.C.: Government Printing Office, 1981.
This is the official record of the first Space Shuttle mission, on April 12, 1981. Since this was a test flight, a great deal of information was collected on all of the Shuttle's systems. This report details each of the tests and measurements made during and after the flight. Nearly every minute of the two-day mission is chronicled. There is a report by the crew as to the effectiveness of preflight training and the handling of *Columbia.* There is a complete biomedical, trajectory, and flight control evaluation. A complete anomaly summary, with the corrective action taken, is included. There are a number of black-and-white photographs, line drawings, charts, and tables.

_____. *STS Orbiter Mission Report: STS-2 Through STS-4.* 3 vols. Washington, D.C.: Government Printing Office, 1981-1982.
These are the official reports for the final three missions of *Columbia* during the Orbiter Flight Test (OFT) program. As with the report on the first flight (see *STS-1 Orbiter Final Mission Report,* listed above), the performance of each of the vehicle's main systems—orbiter, solid rocket motors, and external tank—is detailed. In addition, the orbiter's major subsystems are discussed. There is a report by the individual crews as to the effectiveness of preflight training and the handling of the vehicle. There is a complete biomedical, trajectory, and flight control evaluation. A complete anomaly summary, with the corrective action taken, is included. There are a number of black-and-white photographs, line drawings, charts, and tables.

_____. *STS Space Shuttle Program Mission Report: STS-5 Through STS-7.* 3 vols. Washington, D.C.: Government Printing Office, 1982-1983.
Beginning with *Columbia*'s first operational flight (STS-5) and continuing through *Challenger*'s first two missions (STS-6 and STS-7), mission reports contained much less information. Fewer tests on orbiter subsystems were being conducted, and, since commercial and scientific payloads were now being carried, much of the emphasis switched to the cargo and its support equipment. A list of mission objectives and a summary of the flight are given. There is an evaluation of the major Shuttle components, as well as a crew equipment assessment. There are very few black-and-white photographs, line drawings, tables, and charts.

_____. *STS National Space Transportation Systems Program Mission Report: STS-8 Through STS-35.* 31 vols. Washington, D.C.: Government Printing Office, 1983-1991.

As Space Shuttle flights became more and more routine, fewer mission objectives relating to the measurement of subsystem performance were necessary. Eventually, these mission reports were reduced to a summary of the flight, sequence of events, vehicle assessment, remote manipulator system operations, payloads and experiments, detailed test objectives, detailed secondary objectives, and anomalies. Line drawings and black-and-white photographs became scarcer, and there were only a few necessary tables and charts. These reports do detail the mission and provide valuable information about each flight.

_____. *STS-41D (14) Launch Attempt Report.* Washington, D.C.: Government Printing Office, 1984.

The Shuttle program had flown thirteen successful missions without an incident which might have proven disastrous, until STS 41-D. The terminal countdown (which extends from the T-minus-20-minute mark through solid rocket booster ignition) for the second launch attempt of the mission on June 26, 1984, proceeded normally until it was time to fire the Shuttle's main engines. The three engines ignite sequentially at T minus 6.6 seconds (in a staggered start mode, with engine 3, engine 2, engine 1 igniting at 120-millisecond intervals). Engine 3 ignited, followed by number 2, but then number 3 shut down as a result of an indication of improper opening of the main fuel valve. Since the number 3 engine quit, *Discovery*'s onboard computers shut down engine number 2. This report details the apparent cause of the aborted launch and the sequence of events that led to it. STS 41-D was successfully launched on August 30, 1984.

_____. *STS-51F Launch Attempt Report.* Washington, D.C.: Government Printing Office, 1985.

The second aborted launch of the Space Shuttle program occurred during the first attempted launch of the Spacelab 3 mission on July 12, 1985. As with the abort on STS 41-D, this one came during the Space Shuttle main engine (SSME) ignition sequence. SSME number 3 ignited on time, followed by numbers 2 and 1. The abort was automatically executed by *Challenger*'s computers when the engine chamber coolant valve on SSME-2 was slow in closing from 100 percent open to 70 percent open, as required for startup. This report discusses the launch attempt and the causes for the malfunction. STS 51-F was successfully launched on July 29, 1985. At 5 minutes and 43 seconds after liftoff, both temperature readings for the SSME-1 high-pressure turbopump indicated above acceptable limits, resulting in a premature shutdown of SSME-1 and the declaration of an abort-to-orbit (ATO) condition.

_____. *STS 51-L Data and Design Analysis Task Force Historical Summary.* Washington, D.C.: Government Printing Office, 1986.

Immediately following the STS 51-L *Challenger* accident, NASA formed an Interim Mishap Investigation Board, which was replaced by the 51-L Data and Design Analysis Task Force. This replacement (in name only) was necessary to coincide with the official investigation of the Rogers Commission. The task force was to determine, review, and analyze the facts surrounding the launch of *Challenger*; review all factors relating to the accident determined to be relevant; examine all other factors which could relate to the accident; utilize the full required technical and scientific expertise and resources available within NASA; document task force findings and determinations and conclusions; and provide this information to the Presidential Commission. This report is the historical summary of the official NASA investigation into the accident. It includes a chronology of the flight and subsequent events through the presentation of the commission's report to the president.

_____. *Tracking and Data Relay Satellite System (TDRSS) Users' Guide.* Washington, D.C.: Government Printing Office, 1984.

Although most people will not have a direct need to use NASA's Tracking and Data Relay Satellite System, many will find this book to be quite informative. The TDRS'S (pronounced "tea dress") is a network of three geosynchronous satellites used to communicate with and track other spacecraft. One of the two operational TDRSes is located over the equator at 41 degrees west longitude, while the second is at 171 degrees west. The third, an on-orbit spare, is at 62 degrees west longitude. The operational satellites are spaced 130 degrees apart to permit the use of only one ground tracking station, which is located at White Sands, New Mexico. Each satellite is carried into low Earth orbit by the Space Shuttle and propelled to its operational position by the Inertial Upper Stage. This document was written to assist in user planning activities, but it provides the researcher with a great deal of technical information available nowhere else. Numerous line drawings, schematic diagrams, and charts augment the text.

U.S. National Aeronautics and Space Administration and U.S. Air Force. *STS Inertial Upper Stage (IUS) Systems Handbook, Basic,* Rev., G. Washington, D.C.: Government Printing Office, 1988.

The Inertial Upper Stage (IUS) is a high-altitude booster that is used in conjunction with either the Space Shuttle or the Titan launch vehicle. It was originally designed as a temporary stand-in for a reusable space tug and was called the "Interim" Upper Stage. When it became apparent that the space tug would not be developed in the foreseeable future, the Interim Upper Stage began its gradual evolution into the Inertial Upper Stage ("inertial" refers to its guidance technique). This volume is the official handbook on the IUS used by everyone associated with its development, construction, deployment, and use. It contains hundreds of detailed drawings and schematics. Although much of it is highly technical, the illustrations make it easy to understand.

U.S. Senate. *Space Shuttle and Galileo Mission.* Washington, D.C.: Government Printing Office, 1980.
The main reason for including this document in this bibliography is to permit a review of the early days of the Galileo mission to Jupiter. However, it serves a dual purpose by providing Senator William Proxmire's own words on the subject of the project, the Space Transportation System, and the U.S. space program. In his opening statement he says, "[The Galileo] program is a program that has great merit and very, very substantial support in the country and the Congress, but it is also a program, as you know, that is very expensive and involves a great deal of money." The report also presents a discussion of the safety and reliability of the Space Shuttle. It is not a very large work, but it does present some insight into the behind-the-scenes struggles to get the Shuttle and some of its most important payloads off the ground.

Von Braun, Wernher, and Frederick I. Ordway III. *History of Rocketry and Space Travel.* 3d rev. ed. New York: Thomas Y. Crowell, 1975.
This is the story of the exploration of space from the earliest experiments with rocketry to the final flight of the Skylab program. Hundreds of experts on every aspect of this broad field contributed to the work. Most of the programs of the United States, the Soviet Union, and the rest of the nations engaged in space exploration at that time are detailed, both descriptively and with black-and-white and color photographs. It is one of the best references on the subject. The book contains chapter-by-chapter bibliographies. The authors finish their discussion of the space programs with a look at the future, including the Space Transportation System.

Wilson, Andrew. *Space Shuttle Story.* New York: Hamlyn, 1986.
Written for a general audience, this book is filled with color photographs. It traces the history of the Space Transportation System from the early design concepts through the twenty-fifth launch. Information is provided on each of the flights, although there is very little detail. There are a few technical errors, so one cannot rely on its information as the sole source. Many of the facts about the astronauts who flew the Shuttle during the period are presented.

Yenne, Bill. *The Encyclopedia of U.S. Spacecraft.* New York: Exeter Books, 1985.
A complete encyclopedia of U.S. spacecraft is presented in a book filled with color and black-and-white photographs. General information on the programs is provided in alphabetical order, with individual spacecraft, probes, or launch vehicles listed chronologically. Data on all of the manned and unmanned

spacecraft, including the Space Shuttle and its unmanned payloads, are furnished. An appendix lists acronyms and abbreviations, and there is an index.

_____. *The Pictorial History of World Spacecraft*. New York: Exeter Books, 1988.

The history of the world's spacecraft and probes is told in chronological order from Sputnik 1 through Cosmos 1870, spanning the first thirty years of the space age. Included are all of the manned spacecraft and launch vehicles. Each is detailed with charts, diagrams, illustrations, and color and black-and-white photographs. Data on all of the manned spacecraft, including the Space Shuttle and its unmanned payloads, are provided. An appendix lists all the spacecraft in service as of July, 1987, grouped according to the country or organization responsible.

THE FUTURE

General Studies

Baker, David. *The Rocket: The History and Development of Rocket and Missile Technology.* New York: Crown, 1978.
This large, "coffee-table" book covers the technological and political development of manned and unmanned missiles and rockets. It provides a complete history of solid and liquid propulsion systems from fire-sticks to Moon rockets. Propulsion systems are examined for their advantages and faults, and how they influence the design of the overall vehicle. The ancestry of U.S. and Soviet launch vehicles is traced to the war machines from which they were derived, all the way back to their common grandparent, the German *Vergeltungswaffe Zwei*, or V-2. The author concludes the work with a forecast about future vehicles, including reusable, atomic-powered, and interplanetary launch vehicles. A compendium of launch vehicles and ballistic missiles and of rocket-powered aircraft is provided. Each vehicle is detailed with information about its origin, configuration, development and flight history, and descendants. There is a silhouette of the vehicle, scaled for comparison with the others in the compendium. Hundreds of color and black-and-white photographs and illustrations enhance the comprehensive text. There are tables of data on space launch vehicles; research rockets; strategic and tactical ballistic missiles; and antiballistic, air-to-ground, surface-to-air, air-to-air, antiship, antisubmarine, and anti-armor missiles. Contains an index and a bibliography.

Gatland, Kenneth, et al. *The Illustrated Encyclopedia of Space Technology: A Comprehensive History of Space Exploration.* New York: Harmony Books, 1981.
"Illustrated" should be underscored in the title of this work, because it is the color and black-and-white photographs, drawings, paintings, and charts that are the highlight of this work. Several chapters are devoted to programs that are still in the planning stage, including man on Mars, space factories, bases on the Moon, space cities, and starships. This futuristic view is presented by some of the finest science writers, and it is interesting to note how many of their predictions have come to pass in the decade following publication of the book. Includes a chronology of the major space events since Sputnik 1, a glossary of terms, and an index. Each chapter has its own list of references.

Ley, Willy. *Satellites, Rockets and Outer Space.* New York: New American Library of World Literature, 1956, rev. ed. 1962.
This pocketbook is a fascinating look at the U.S. space programs to put satellites into orbit. The author discusses these early satellites and some of the

feuding that went on between the Army and the Navy over who would be the first to launch a satellite. Some of the earliest space launch vehicles are described. Nontechnical physics lessons are presented in a discussion of propulsion and orbital mechanics. There is a section devoted to the solar system, with emphasis on the third planet. In the final chapter there is a discussion of some future plans, including Moon cars and men on Mars. This last chapter is perhaps the most interesting, especially in the light of events that occurred during the subsequent quarter century. There are several line drawings and a few color photographs.

Ride, Sally K. *Leadership and America's Future in Space.* Washington, D.C.: Government Printing Office, 1987.
In response to growing concern in both Congress and the Administration over the long-term direction of the U.S. civilian space program, NASA Administrator Dr. James Fletcher formed a task group to define potential U.S. space initiatives. This is the report of the group, which identified four candidate initiatives for study and evaluation: Mission to Planet Earth, Exploration of the Solar System, Outpost on the Moon, and Humans to Mars. Each of the four fields is discussed in terms of background; strategy and scenario; technology, transportation, and orbital facilities; and summary of the project. The "leadership in space" status of the United States has dropped considerably since the Apollo program, and Dr. Ride addresses the reasons for this. There a drawings, tables, charts, color photographs, a reference list, and a list of the additional studies which went into the creation of the report.

Sagan, Carl. *Cosmos.* New York: Random House, 1980.
In 1980, the Public Broadcasting Service aired the series *Cosmos*, which tells the story of our discovery of the universe. This book is based upon that series. It presents, in a very interesting way, how man is exploring with modern ground- and space-based instruments the solar system and beyond. The history of the universe, as understood in 1980, is chronicled. The book is filled with color and black-and-white photographs, paintings, and etchings of the universe and its examiners—both human and mechanical. The author describes the probabilities of galactic civilizations and our search for them, as well as plans to go calling on them. Contains an extensive bibliography and an index.

Taylor, L. B., Jr. *For All Mankind: America's Space Programs of the 1970s and Beyond.* New York: E. P. Dutton, 1974.
The author discusses the benefits of the United States' space programs of the early 1970's, especially the multiple benefits derived from communications satellites and Earth resources satellites. He describes these programs as well as the Space Transportation System, which was in the later stages of planning and development. The book discusses the full range of possibilities for the

Space Shuttle and some of its payloads. Much is to be gained by comparing the goals of the system in 1974 and its accomplishments through the next decade and a half. There are black-and-white photographs and an index.

U.S. House of Representatives. *United States Civilian Space Programs 1958-1978.* Vol. 1. Washington, D.C.: Government Printing Office, 1981.
In a very concise report, the Committee on Space Science and Applications has compiled data on all U.S. space activity during its first two decades. After a brief introduction and summary chapter, the volume is divided into fourteen additional sections. The second chapter deals with the space-related issues under consideration by Congress. The remaining sections cover the history of NASA and its relationship to U.S. space policy, NASA facilities and tracking systems, launch vehicles and propulsion, manned spaceflight through 1975, the Space Transportation System, space life sciences, space science programs, materials processing in space, international cooperation in space, interagency and non-NASA governmental space activities, industrial and university support for NASA, space program benefits, and selected future space programs. Appendices contain Department of Defense manned spaceflight plans, NASA funding history, international space agreements, texts of President Jimmy Carter's space directives, documents relating to the legal aspects of the Space Shuttle, major U.S. space organizations, a master log of U.S. spaceflights, and a table of U.S. space orbital payloads by mission from 1957 through 1979.

U.S. National Commission on Space. *Pioneering the Space Frontier.* New York: Bantam Books, 1986.
The challenge to predicting the future is that there will be so many more people around to say you were wrong. The National Commission on Space was given such a formidable task by Congress and President Ronald Reagan. They listened to the testimony of experts and other concerned parties, then voted on which ideas they thought were most likely to succeed. This report presents their views on such topics as civilian space goals for twenty-first century America, low-cost access to the solar system, opening the space frontier during the next twenty years, and the next fifty years of U.S. leadership on the space frontier. There are many color renditions of some of these proposed activities and a glossary of terms used. There is also a comprehensive bibliography.

Von Braun, Wernher, and Frederick I. Ordway III. *History of Rocketry and Space Travel.* 3d rev. ed. New York: Thomas Y. Crowell, 1975.
This is the story of the exploration of space from the earliest experiments with rocketry to the final flight of the Skylab program. Hundreds of experts on every aspect of this broad field contributed to the work. Most of the programs of the United States, the Soviet Union, and the rest of the nations engaged in space exploration at that time are detailed, both descriptively and with black-

and-white and color photographs. It is one of the best references on the subject. The book also contains a large, chapter-by-chapter bibliography. The authors finish their discussion of the space programs with a look at the future, including the Space Transportation System.

Current Plans

Manned Planetary Exploration

Ride, Sally K. *Leadership and America's Future in Space.* Washington, D.C.: Government Printing Office, 1987.
In response to growing concern in both Congress and the Administration over the long-term direction of the U.S. civilian space program, NASA Administrator Dr. James Fletcher formed a task group to define potential U.S. space initiatives. This is the report of the group, which identified four candidate initiatives for study and evaluation: Mission to Planet Earth, Exploration of the Solar System, Outpost on the Moon, and Humans to Mars. Each of the four fields is discussed in terms of background; strategy and scenario; technology, transportation, and orbital facilities; and summary of the project. The "leadership in space" status of the United States has dropped considerably since the Apollo program, and Dr. Ride addresses the reasons for this. There a drawings, tables, charts, color photographs, a reference list, and a list of the additional studies that went into the creation of the report.

National Aero Space Plane

U.S. General Accounting Office. *A Technology Development and Demonstration Program to Build the X-30.* Washington, D.C.: Government Printing Office, 1988.
The chairman of the Senate Committee on Commerce, Science, and Transportation asked the GAO to assess the cost, schedule, and performance of several NASA projects. This work is the report of their findings on the National Aero Space Plane program is a technology development and demonstration program to build and test the X-30 experimental flight vehicle. The X-30 is designed to take off horizontally from a conventional runway, reach hypersonic speeds up to twenty-five times the speed of sound, attain low Earth orbit, and return to land on a conventional runway. The report provides a general overview of the program, including its objectives, scope, and methodology. There are spacecraft configuration drawings and information relating to cost, schedule, and performance. A chronology of the project, through the date of the report,

is presented. There is a glossary of terms used. This is a look at the program from a purely financial point of view.

Space Stations

Anderton, David A. *Space Station*. Washington, D.C.: Government Printing Office, 1985.
This NASA Educational Publication (EP-211) looks at the plans to build the United States' first permanently manned space station, *Freedom*. This work provides an overview of the program and the various design concepts developed by various NASA facilities and major aerospace contractors. At the time of the writing, the exact plans for constructing the space station were not finalized. Although this work does not provide any details, it does give some insight into the evolution of *Freedom*. There are many color photographs of the different design concepts.

Belew, Leland F., ed. *Skylab, Our First Space Station*. Washington, D.C.: National Technical Information Service, 1977.
A colorful retrospective of the Skylab program and its four flights is presented in this work. Technically speaking, the title is a misnomer, since Skylab was not a "space station." By definition, a space station is a permanently manned platform that can be completely resupplied. Astronauts replenished the food, water, film, and a few other expendables, but Skylab's attitude control and electrical and life support systems were not replenishable. The book is a good reference, chronicling the program from its design and planning phases through the completion of the third manned period. There are dozens of color photographs and drawings, including several spectacular pictures taken on orbit. A mission summary table and an index are included. Belew was the manager of the Skylab Program Office at the Marshall Space Flight Center, where Skylab was built.

Belew, Leland F., and Ernst Stuhlinger. *Skylab: A Guidebook*. Washington, D.C.: Government Printing Office, 1973.
This is a preflight guide to the Skylab program and provides in-depth, nontechnical information about the orbiting workshop and its components. Skylab, the spacecraft, was built around the S-IVB third stage of the Saturn V launch vehicle. The major components included the Orbital Workshop (OWS), the Instrument Unit (IU), the Airlock Module (AM), the Multiple Docking Adapter (MDA), and the Apollo Telescope Mount (ATM). As much of the spacecraft as possible was made from existing hardware or with hardware requiring little modification. This guide describes the work of several thousand engineers and scientists who conceived, designed, and built Skylab. Each of the experiments

to be performed during Skylab's stay in orbit is described, as well as the apparatus to conduct it. Line drawings, black-and-white photographs, a glossary of terms and acronyms, an index, and a brief bibliography are included.

Compton, W. David, and Charles D. Benson. *Living and Working in Space: A History of Skylab.* Washington, D.C.: Government Printing Office, 1983.

One title in the NASA History Series, this book chronicles the Skylab program, from its conception during the early days of the Apollo program to the orbiting workshop's fiery plunge in 1979. There are dozens of black-and-white photographs of the three manned missions, as well as the launch of the unmanned workshop. Color photographs, taken from orbit, are in the back of the book. Line drawings show the inner workings of much of the equipment related to the missions. Includes an index and an impressive hundred-page appendix listing source notes and bibliographic references. Other appendices include a summary of the missions, astronaut biographies, in-flight experiments, Comet Kohoutek, and the International Aeronautical Federation world records set by Skylab.

Cooper, Henry S. F., Jr. *A House in Space.* New York: Holt, Rinehart and Winston, 1976.

This work is about the nine-month period from May 14, 1973, through February 8, 1974—the active life of the Skylab orbiting workshop. During this time it was inhabited by three crews of astronauts for periods of twenty-eight, fifty-nine, and eighty-four days. The book was derived from articles written by Cooper, which appeared in *The New Yorker* magazine during this period. It looks more at the human aspect of the program than at its technical side, but still contains information useful to the researcher. There are many black-and-white photographs and color diagrams.

David, Leonard. *Space Station Freedom: A Foothold on the Future.* Washington, D.C.: Government Printing Office, 1988.

This is a colorful booklet on the proposed space station *Freedom* and what it will mean in the future. There are dozens of color and black-and-white photographs and artist's conceptions to highlight the text. The history of the space station is chronicled from the early 1950's through the Skylab program. There are descriptions of the scientific missions and experiments conceived for *Freedom*. The individual components, and how they will be assembled in orbit, are described. The text is readable at all levels of understanding, and much information is packed into this work.

Eddy, John A. *The New Sun: The Solar Results from Skylab.* Washington, D.C.: National Technical Information Service, 1979.

Countless volumes of data about the biological and physiological effects of long-duration spaceflight on humans, plants, and animals were obtained during the Skylab program. In addition, the first space telescopes (combined in a structure called the Apollo Telescope Mount, or ATM) were used to study the Sun. The ATM derived its name from a study that was conducted to determine the feasibility of mounting a stable telescope on the Apollo service module. In actuality, the ATM was built around the lunar module descent stage. There is very little technical information, but the color and black-and-white photographs of the Sun alone make this book worthwhile.

Gatland, Kenneth. "The First Space Stations." In *The Illustrated Encyclopedia of Space Technology: A Comprehensive History of Space Exploration*, by Kenneth Gatland et al. New York: Harmony Books, 1981.
This section in the book discusses the early space stations of the United States and the Soviet Union. There is a fine four-page, full-color cutaway drawing of the Skylab workshop and the Soviets' Salyut space station. There are color and black-and-white photographs, drawings, and charts. The major features of the program, including the spacecraft and launch vehicle, are discussed. Includes a chronology of the major space events since Sputnik 1, a glossary of terms, and an index.

Johnston, Richard S., and Lawrence F. Dietlein, eds. *Biomedical Results from Skylab*. Washington, D.C.: National Technical Information Service, 1977.
Biomedical testing under the conditions of orbital flight was studied for relatively brief periods during the Mercury, Gemini, and Apollo programs. With Skylab, scientists would be able to conduct experiments on astronauts spending a month or more in space. The editors of this work have compiled a concise review of each experiment, including the theory behind the test, the means by which is was completed, and the results. The experiments were divided into four disciplines: neurophysiology; musculoskeletal function; biochemistry, hematology, and cytology; and cardiovascular and metabolic function. The text is supplemented with photographs and drawings, as well as charts of the conclusions reached by each examiner. Every section of the book has its own reference listing, which will guide the researcher to more detailed works. Appendices detail the experimental support hardware and the operational life sciences support hardware.

Lundquist, Charles A., ed. *Skylab's Astronomy and Space Sciences*. Washington, D.C.: Government Printing Office, 1979.
One of Skylab's main objectives was to perform experiments in the microgravity conditions of orbital flight over extended periods of time. Another was to look at the rest of the universe, especially the Sun, with the unblinking eye of the telescope. This study details these two aspects of the Skylab missions.

Subjects covered in this work include stellar and galactic astronomy, interplanetary dust, Comet Kohoutek, energetic particles, Earth's atmosphere, and the orbital environment. Color photographs and art highlight this informative book.

Magill, Frank N., ed. *Magill's Survey of Science: Space Exploration Series.* Vol. 5. Pasadena, Calif.: Salem Press, 1989, pp. 1828-1863.
This five-volume set covers every aspect of the U.S. and Soviet manned and unmanned space programs, as well as those of nations newer to the space race. Since 1971, the Soviet Union has had a permanently manned space station in orbit. The United States had Skylab for nine months in 1973-1974, but that was not a "real" space station. By the end of this century, the United States plans to have the space station *Freedom* in orbit. Five articles in this reference work are devoted to the design and uses of *Freedom*, its development, international contributions to *Freedom*, the modules and nodes from which it will be constructed, and what it will be like working and living aboard it. Each article includes an annotated bibliography and cross-references.

Newkirk, Roland W., and Ivan D. Ertel, with Courtney G. Brooks. *Skylab: A Chronology.* Washington, D.C.: National Technical Information Service, 1977.
This is NASA's official record of the Skylab program, covering events on a day-to-day basis. At its inception the project was known as the Apollo Applications Program, since it was to use modified equipment from the lunar landing endeavor. Included in the coverage are the early space station designs, the development of the spacecraft and launch vehicles, astronaut training, and mission results. There are dozens of black-and-white photographs and line drawings of components. Appendices provide a summary of the Skylab flights: mission objectives, orbital activities, experiments, and extravehicular activity. Includes a glossary of abbreviations and acronyms and an index.

O'Leary, Brian. *Project Space Station.* Harrisburg, Pa.: Government Printing Office, 1983.
The author takes a look at the space station programs of the United States and the Soviet Union and discusses their practical applications and benefits. He traces the history of manned space platforms and, in the process, touches upon Skylab, Spacelab, and the Space Transportation System. The major systems of an orbiting space station, similar to the United States' *Freedom*, are described. Much of the emphasis is on the political aspects of the program. Contains black-and-white photographs, a brief bibliography, and an index.

Summerlin, Lee B., ed. *Skylab, Classroom in Space.* Washington, D.C.: Government Printing Office, 1977.
The Skylab Student Project was originated by NASA and the National Science Teachers Association as a means of involving schoolchildren, the next genera-

tion of scientists, in the study of space sciences. In 1972, twenty-five high school students from across the United States were selected to participate in the program. They were chosen from among the more than four thousand students who had made proposals. This volume, filled with color and black-and-white photographs, details how and why the project was developed, describes the experiments flown aboard Skylab, and relates them to other scientific investigations carried out during the flights.

U.S. General Accounting Office. *Space Station: NASA Efforts to Establish a Design-to-Life-Cycle Cost Process.* Washington, D.C.: Government Printing Office, 1988.
In 1985, the Senate Committee on Commerce, Science, and Transportation directed NASA to outline its plans for the space station *Freedom* to ensure that it did not overlook future operations costs during the station's definition, design, and development phases. NASA responded that it would control operations costs by using a design-to-life-cycle cost approach, which establishes the projected total life-cycle cost of a system as a design requirement equal in importance to performance and schedule concerns, and which establishes cost elements as management goals. This is the GAO's report on this approach. Appendices include a system design tradeoff model and comments from NASA on the report.

U.S. House of Representatives. *Skylab 1 Investigation Report: Hearing Before the Subcommittee on Manned Space Flight of the Committee on Science and Astronautics.* Washington, D.C.: National Technical Information Service, 1973.
In August, 1973, the subcommittee opened its investigation into an incident that occurred during the launch of the Skylab 1 spacecraft. At sixty-three seconds into the flight, there were indications that the workshop's micrometeoroid shield had deployed and that the workshop solar array wing 2 was no longer secured in its launch position. This, coupled with the failure of solar array wing 1 to deploy on orbit, should have terminated the mission. Fortunately, the first manned crew was able to free the stuck wing and install a shield over the sunside of the workshop. The workshop was usable. This report documents the accident, as best it could be reconstructed, and the procedures developed and implemented to recover from the effects of the incident. There are many black-and-white photographs and drawings to give the reader a great deal of technical information. Most of the contents are transcripts of the testimony of witnesses.

U.S. National Aeronautics and Space Administration. *EASE/ACCESS: Framework for the Future.* Washington, D.C.: Government Printing Office, 1985.
In preparation for permanent space construction, NASA's Marshall Space Flight Center in Huntsville, Alabama, developed two experiments to demonstrate the ability of astronauts to build large structures in space. The experiments were

flown aboard the Space Shuttle *Atlantis* on mission STS 61-B in November, 1985. The first of the experiments is the Experimental Assembly of Structures in Extravehicular Activity (EASE). EASE consists of six aluminum beams, each 12 feet long, which form a tetrahedral cell when pieced together. The Assembly Concept for Construction of Erectable Space Structures (ACCESS) consists of mastlike, 4.5-foot assembly fixtures. These are raised to a vertical position, and the fixture's three guide rails unfold like an umbrella. When fully erected, the structure is 45 feet tall. This booklet is filled with color photographs and discusses the experiments in detail.

_____. *MSFC Skylab Orbital Workshop Final Technical Report.* 5 vols. Washington, D.C.: National Technical Information Service, 1974.
The definitive technical reference on the Skylab orbiting workshop, this work covers all aspects of the program, including concepts, goals, design philosophy, hardware, and testing. The evolution of the workshop from a "wet" configuration (one flown as the fuel tank of the second stage of the Saturn IB into orbit, drained, purged, and then converted to a habitation area by the crew) into a "dry" structure (one launched completely outfitted in orbital configuration) is chronicled. The final configuration is discussed in detail, including structures, systems, and components. The testing program is reviewed, as well as the mission results and performance during launch and flight. Detailed line drawings, tables, and charts add to the text, as does a complete reference listing.

_____. *Science in Orbit: The Shuttle and Spacelab Experience: 1981-1986.* Washington, D.C.: Government Printing Office, 1988.
The opportunity to conduct large-scale experiments in Earth orbit escaped the U.S. space program for nearly a decade, from the end of the last Skylab mission in February, 1974, to the first Spacelab mission aboard *Columbia* in November, 1983. Now the United States has the capability to obtain the necessary data to launch a permanently manned space station. This book studies the Space Transportation System and the Spacelab research laboratory. It chronicles the two programs and looks at the science gained from the first twenty-four Shuttle flights. Disciplines detailed include life sciences, materials science, solar physics, space plasma physics, atmospheric science, Earth observation, astronomy, and astrophysics. In addition, experiments conducted to test the technology needed to build the space station *Freedom* are presented. There are dozens of color and black-and-white photographs.

_____. *Skylab and the Sun.* Washington, D.C.: Government Printing Office, 1973.
The Apollo Telescope Mount (ATM) on the Skylab orbiting workshop was used to study the Sun in depth. This work was written to familiarize the reader with the Sun and what the Skylab program expected to gain by observing it. Scien-

tists, astronauts, engineers, and other individuals closely associated with the ATM program wrote the articles. There is a brief overview of the program and the facts known about the Sun prior to Skylab. The studies proposed for the ATM, as well as the equipment designed to carry out the observations, are detailed. Appendices tell the reader where to obtain additional information about the program and the data to be received.

_____. *Skylab Experiments*. 7 vols. Washington, D.C.: Government Printing Office, 1973.
Prior to the beginning of the Skylab flights, NASA's Education Office, the Skylab Program Office, and the University of Colorado published a series of teaching guides to the experiments that were to be conducted in flight. These experiments were divided into four categories: physical sciences, biomedical sciences, Earth applications, and space applications. Each volume looks at the experiments' background, scientific objectives, description, data, crew activities, related curriculum studies, and suggested classroom demonstrations. Volume 1 covers physical science and solar astronomy; volume 2, remote sensing of Earth resources; volume 3, materials science; volume 4, life sciences; volume 5, astronomy and space physics; volume 6, mechanics; and volume 7, living and working in space. Each volume includes numerous line drawings and a glossary of terms.

_____. *Skylab Explores the Earth*. Washington, D.C.: National Technical Information Service, 1977.
Since the first flight of Project Mercury, one of NASA's primary goals for orbital space missions was the observation of the Earth. There is no better vantage point than from above. Observation time for manned spacecraft is limited by life support supplies, and, prior to Skylab, the longest mission was the fourteen-day Gemini VII flight in 1965. This book studies the Earth observation experiments of Skylab during the 171 days it was occupied. It is filled with exciting color photographs of Earth, each of which is accompanied by a detailed caption. Several of the photographs are analyzed with the aid of a map of the region shown. Comparisons are made with color and black-and-white photographs taken of geologic sites and meteorologic phenomena during previous manned flights. Contains a glossary of terms and an index of the photographs used, alphabetized by geographic location.

_____. *Skylab Mission Report: Skylab 2 Through Skylab 4*. 3 vols. Washington, D.C.: National Technical Information Service, 1973-1974.
The official report on each of the manned flights in the Skylab program. Each volume was prepared by the Mission Evaluation Team and contains a wealth of data on the particular flight. There is a mission summary and sections which detail the flight, spacecraft, crew activities, orbital experiments, in-flight

demonstrations, biomedical evaluations, and mission ground support. An assessment of the mission objectives, as well as anomalies, is included. Tables summarize the flight trajectory and activity time lines. Descriptions and drawings of the spacecraft, launch vehicles, and experiments packages are included. Contains a glossary of terms and a list of references.

_____. *Skylab Mission Report, Saturn Workshop.* Washington, D.C.: National Technical Information Service, 1974.
The official NASA report on the performance of the Skylab orbiting workshop, from launch until the end of the last manned period. Included are summaries of the three manned periods and the intervals when the workshop was unmanned. Descriptions of the structural components and mechanisms are given, as well as their anomalies. A report is provided on each of the major systems and subsystems. Each of the experiments, involving solar physics, astrophysics, materials science and manufacturing, engineering and technology, student investigations, and science demonstrations, is detailed. Line drawings, black-and-white photographs, tables, charts, and an extensive reference listing add to the text.

_____. *The Space Station: A Description of the Configuration Established at the Systems Requirements Review (SRR).* Washington, D.C.: Government Printing Office, 1986.
This work takes a brief yet in-depth look at the planned space station *Freedom*. In response to President Ronald Reagan's 1984 commitment to develop a permanently manned space station within a decade, NASA undertook an examination of the many missions that a space station might carry out, and of the many ways in which the station might be configured. This effort reached a major milestone in 1986, called the systems requirements review (SRR). SRR decisions established the "baseline" configuration for *Freedom*. The report details this configuration, as well as the process from which it was derived. There are many pages of black-and-white photographs and line drawings, as well as a chart depicting the assembly sequence for *Freedom*. There is also a brief history of the space station concept.

_____. *Space Station Development Plan Submitted to the Committee on Science, Space, and Technology, U.S. House of Representatives.* Washington, D.C.: Government Printing Office, 1987.
This plan for the development of a permanently manned space station was submitted by NASA in response to a request by the committee. The plan submitted was based on internal planning and budgetary considerations. Included in the plan are program objectives and requirements, development strategy, management approach, and program schedule. The work reads like most government documents, but the reader can get an idea of the work

involved in getting a program of this magnitude off the ground. There are numerous line drawings and charts, a list of reference documents, and a glossary of acronyms and abbreviations. One large appendix details the space station's components and the auxiliary equipment necessary to run it.

_____. *Space Station Reference Configuration Description*. Washington, D.C.: Government Printing Office, 1984.
In order for potential contractors to bid on a particular project, they must have some information about the item on which they will be bidding. This document presents such a guideline for the space station *Freedom*. The information was generated to provide a focal point for the definition and assessment of program requirements, establish a basis for estimating program cost, and define a reference configuration in sufficient detail to allow its inclusion in the definition phase of the program. This is the first official look at how the space station will appear in orbit during each phase of construction. It details the manned core, unmanned platforms, payload accommodations, crew accommodations, and related subsystems. There are dozens of line drawings, a bibliography, and an evaluation of the assembly operations crew time lines.

Unmanned Planetary Exploration

U.S. General Accounting Office. *Space Exploration: Cost, Schedule, and Performance of NASA's Mars Observer Mission*. Washington, D.C.: Government Printing Office, 1988.
The chairman of the Senate Committee on Commerce, Science, and Transportation asked the GAO to assess the cost, schedule, and performance of several NASA projects. This work is the report of their findings on the Mars Observer mission to Mars. The mission began as the Mars Geoscience Climatory Orbiter in 1984 and was later renamed the Mars Geoscience Climatory Observer and subsequently shortened to Mars Observer. Its primary purpose is to explore the geology, topography, and climatology of Mars from a low-altitude polar orbit. The report provides a general overview of the program, including its objectives, scope, and methodology. There are spacecraft configuration drawings and information relating to cost, schedule, and performance. A chronology of the project, through the date of the report, is presented, as well as a glossary of terms used. This is a look at the program from a purely financial point of view.

_____. *Space Exploration: NASA's Deep Space Missions Are Experiencing Long Delays*. Washington, D.C.: Government Printing Office, 1988.
This work is the report of the GAO's findings on the Galileo mission to Jupiter. Galileo was launched from the Space Shuttle *Atlantis* in October, 1989.

The report provides a general overview of the program, including its objectives, scope, and methodology. There are spacecraft configuration drawings and information relating to cost, schedule, and performance. A chronology of the project, through the date of the report, is presented, as well as a glossary of terms used. This is a look at the program from a purely financial point of view.

IMPACT OF SPACE EXPLORATION

General Studies

Logsdon, John M. *The Decision to Go to the Moon: Project Apollo and the National Interest.* Cambridge, Mass.: MIT Press, 1970.
As a political scientist, Logsdon takes a look at the political, social, and economic influences that shaped the Apollo program. Using many NASA records and government documents, including presidential papers, to support his theories, he has written an authoritative work. It would not have been called the "Race for the Moon" had the political ramifications not outweighed the scientific potential. This is best demonstrated by comparing the congressional and public support for the space program before and after the Apollo 11 lunar landing. This is a very interesting study whose thesis still holds true today.

Rabinowitch, Eugene, and Richard S. Lewis, eds. *Man on the Moon: The Impact on Science, Technology, and International Cooperation.* New York: Basic Books, 1969.
A collection of opinions by noted scholars and scientists regarding the effect the U.S. space program had on the rest of the world, this work shows its age. Some of the topics included are the impact of the Apollo 11 lunar landing on the Soviet Union, international cooperation, and joint exploration. The report also discusses the influence of the space program on the aerospace industry.

Sheffield, Charles, and Carol Rosin. *Space Careers.* New York: William Morrow, 1984.
This is a bit outdated, but the work does provide some information about NASA and a career with this organization. Chapters discuss the history of the various programs of NASA and what a person interested in working for NASA on one of these programs should do to prepare for the job. This career planning begins in high school; the authors discuss choices that the reader would have to make in order to secure the position desired. A look at some of the opportunities in the space programs of other countries is included, and the future of the aerospace industry is considered. There are a number of lists in the book, including suggested readings, colleges and universities, aerospace careers, and space organizations.

U.S. House of Representatives. *United States Civilian Space Programs 1958-1978.* Vol. 1. Washington, D.C.: Government Printing Office, 1981.

In a very concise report, the Committee on Space Science and Applications has compiled data on all U.S. space activity during its first two decades. After a brief introduction and summary chapter, the volume is divided into fourteen additional sections. The second chapter deals with the space-related issues under consideration by Congress. The remaining sections cover the history of NASA and its relationship to U.S. space policy, NASA facilities and tracking systems, launch vehicles and propulsion, manned spaceflight through 1975, the Space Transportation System, space life sciences, space science programs, materials processing in space, international cooperation in space, interagency and non-NASA governmental space activities, industrial and university support for NASA, space program benefits, and selected future space programs. Appendices contain Department of Defense manned spaceflight plans, NASA funding history, international space agreements, texts of President Jimmy Carter's space directives, documents relating to the legal aspects of the Space Shuttle, major U.S. space organizations, a master log of U.S. spaceflights, and a table of U.S. space orbital payloads by mission from 1957 through 1979.

Impact on Society

Gomery, Douglas. "Military Meteorological Satellites." In *Magill's Survey of Science: Space Exploration Series*, vol. 3, edited by Frank N. Magill. Pasadena, Calif.: Salem Press, 1989.
One of the essays on the history of space exploration in this five-volume set, which covers every aspect of the U.S. and Soviet manned and unmanned space programs, as well as those of nations newer to the space race. These satellites provide weather data, which are used for a variety of military purposes, including the scheduling of reconnaissance satellite launchings and the planning of other military operations. Although very little unclassified information is available, this work does discuss some of the better known satellites. Includes an annotated bibliography and cross-references.

Hussain, Farooq, and Curtis Peebles. "Military Space Systems." In *The Illustrated Encyclopedia of Space Technology: A Comprehensive History of Space Exploration*, by Kenneth Gatland et al. New York: Harmony Books, 1981.
This section in the book discusses many of the so-called spy satellites of the United States and the Soviet Union. Some of the earlier U.S. projects, such as the Discovery series of satellites and the proposed Manned Orbiting Laboratory, are described. There are color and black-and-white photographs, drawings, charts, and a brief bibliography. The book contains a chronology of the major space events since Sputnik 1, a glossary of terms, and an index.

Newman, John. "Spy Satellites." In *Magill's Survey of Science: Space Exploration Series*, vol. 5, edited by Frank N. Magill. Pasadena, Calif.: Salem Press, 1989.
Spies have been around since the first cave man grew leery of his neighbor. It is only natural that when man first journeyed into space, he would investigate the use of a "spy in the sky." This chapter sneaks a peek at the spy satellites of the major space powers and gives a brief overview of what is known about them. Since they are supposed to be a secret (despite what one reads in *Aviation Week and Space Technology*), very little has been written about them. This work gives the reader a rough idea about what is up there, looking down at us. Includes an annotated bibliography and cross-references.

Peebles, Curtis. "Electronic Intelligence Satellites." In *Magill's Survey of Science: Space Exploration Series*, vol. 1, edited by Frank N. Magill. Pasadena, Calif.: Salem Press, 1989.
The electronic eavesdropper satellites of the United States, Soviet Union, and Great Britain are discussed in this essay. Very little information is provided, given the classified nature of the subject. Contains an annotated bibliography and cross-references.

Streeter, Lulynne. "The Commercial Use of Space Program Innovations." In *Magill's Survey of Science: Space Exploration Series*, vol. 1, edited by Frank N. Magill. Pasadena, Calif.: Salem Press, 1989.
One of the essays on the history of space exploration in this five-volume set, which covers every aspect of the U.S. and Soviet manned and unmanned space programs, as well as those of nations newer to the space race. According to the author, NASA's Technical Utilization program has resulted in more than thirty thousand secondary applications of aerospace technology and data in the public and private sectors over the past thirty years. The essay looks at the issue and discusses how NASA disseminates these data. Contains an annotated bibliography and cross-references.

U.S. National Aeronautics and Space Administration. *Space Shuttle*. Washington, D.C.: Government Printing Office, 1976.
This is an updated, colorful version of the above-listed book on the Space Transportation System. It has been compiled from official NASA and contractor press information. The Shuttle's major components are discussed using words, color and black-and-white photographs, line drawings, and artist's concepts. A typical mission is profiled, along with a discussion of some of the future payloads. The earthly benefits derived from the system and the economic impact of the Shuttle are discussed. Some of the benefits discussed include those in the areas of Earth resources, astronomy, communications, environment, and life sciences.

_____. *Spinoffs*. Washington, D.C.: Government Printing Office, annual. Ever wonder where we get all those fabulous space-age products? We get them from the space program. Few people realize that items such as Teflon, polarized sunglasses, fiber optics, personal computers, pudding-in-a-can, and lightweight ski outfits came from the needs of the space program. As a means for getting Americans to realize that they are directly benefiting from the tax dollars spent, NASA publishes an annual booklet of these "spinoffs." More than thirty thousand of these spinoffs have emerged from the secondary application of aerospace technology. Although readily available from the Government Printing Office, few copies of this annual publication reach the average citizen. Copies can be requested from any NASA facility.

Yearley, Clifton K., and Kerrie L. MacPherson. "U.S. Private Industry and Space Exploration." In *Magill's Survey of Science: Space Exploration Series*, vol. 3, edited by Frank N. Magill. Pasadena, Calif.: Salem Press, 1989.
One of the essays on the history of space exploration in this five-volume set, which covers every aspect of the U.S. and Soviet manned and unmanned space programs, as well as those of nations newer to the space race. The United States' system of free enterprise has always encouraged those in the private sector to get involved financially with government projects. NASA has relied on nongovernment industry to provide the materials and manpower to accomplish its goals. Although NASA has been the primary source for a way into space, more and more of its activities are being turned over to private businesses. This work discusses the relationships between the government agencies and the private sector. Contains an annotated bibliography and cross-references.

Space Law and Politics

Christol, Carl Quimby. *The Modern International Law of Outer Space*. Elmsford, N.Y.: Pergamon Press, 1982.
This is one of the better books on the United Nations Outer Space Treaty and its impact on the exploration of space by manned and unmanned spacecraft, both military and civilian. The entire treaty is discussed authoritatively and completely. Most of the legal jargon has been translated into understandable English, and the book makes an excellent reference material for the researcher.

Giberson, Karl, and Todd Crofford. "The Outer Space Treaty." In *Magill's Survey of Science: Space Exploration Series*, vol. 3, edited by Frank N. Magill. Pasadena, Calif.: Salem Press, 1989.
One of the essays on the history of space exploration in this five-volume set, which covers every aspect of the U.S. and Soviet manned and unmanned space programs, as well as those of nations newer to the space race. The United

Nations Outer Space Treaty was signed in 1967 and is the foundation of the modern system of international space law. This work discusses the treaty and its effect of the military and civilian space programs of the United States, Soviet Union, and other space-capable nations. Its shortcomings are also discussed. Includes an annotated bibliography and cross-references.

Magill, Frank N., ed. *Magill's Survey of Science: Space Exploration Series.* Vol. 3. Pasadena, Calif.: Salem Press, 1989, pp. 1606-1617.
This five-volume set covers every aspect of the U.S. and Soviet manned and unmanned space programs, as well as those of nations newer to the space race. When the United States and the Soviet Union began to explore space, lawmakers from around the world saw the need for a set of rules governing this unchartered region. The Outer Space Treaty of 1967, the first of many such laws, was drafted by the United Nations and covered such things as the rescue of astronauts, liability of launching states, registration of space objects, and the exploration of celestial bodies. These articles discuss the pros and cons of these laws, how enforceable they are, and what effect they have had on the development of space technology. Each article includes an annotated bibliography and cross-references.

EARTHBOUND SUPPORT

General Studies

Allen, Jon L. *Aviation and Space Museums of America*. New York: Arco, 1975. Although this work is a bit outdated, there are a lot of interesting facts about a lot of equally fascinating museums. Most of these museums are still operating and would provide the aerospace enthusiast a great opportunity to be among the history makers. There are more than fifty museums discussed in individual chapters. The chapters are arranged geographically by region of the United States. Each museum is detailed with facts about its history, location, and the artifacts it possesses. There are numerous black-and-white photographs and an index. An appendix lists aerospace organizations, and another gives the addresses of aerospace publications.

Anderson, Fred. *Northrop: An Aeronautical History*. Los Angeles: Northrop Corp., 1976. This book relates the story of Northrop Corporation from 1939 through 1976. This giant of aircraft design and construction was created in a leased Hawthorne, California, hotel in August, 1939, by engineer John K. Northrop. The author leads us through Northrop's illustrative history from pre-World War II N-3PB patrol bombers to the F-18 Navy air combat fighter of today. Each craft is detailed in configuration and contribution to aviation history. There are numerous black-and-white photographs. Research aircraft, the forerunners of the Space Shuttle, are discussed. These include the X-4, and the M2F2, M2F3, and HL-10 lifting bodies. Northrop also makes the F-5 fighter and its derivative, the T-38 Talon, used as a training aircraft by astronauts.

Bryan, C. D. B. *The National Air and Space Museum*. New York: Bantam Books, 1982. Step inside one of the most fascinating museums in the world of aerospace and you will find it filled with aircraft, spacecraft, mockups, and launch vehicles. This is the Smithsonian Institution's National Air and Space Museum in Washington, D.C. There are hundreds of aircraft, from the Wright Flyer and the *Spirit of St. Louis* to the Bell X-1 and the Douglas A-4C *Skyhawk*. There are almost as many spacecraft and launch vehicles, including *Freedom 7*, the Apollo 11 command module, a replica of the Apollo 11 lunar module, Skylab, and an F-1 engine from the Apollo Saturn V. This book is divided into two sections: "Air" and "Space." Each discusses the vehicle's history and what significant contribution it made to warrant its inclusion. There are dozens of color and black-and-white photographs of the vehicles as they appear in the museum and as they looked before they were retired to this place of honor.

While the museum has added many more attractions to its collection since the publication of this book, it will give the researcher and traveler a hint of what to expect when he or she arrives.

DeWaard, E. John, and Nancy DeWaard. *History of NASA: America's Voyage to the Stars.* New York: Exeter Books, 1984.
This is a brief, photo-filled look at NASA's programs more than it is a look at NASA itself. Each of the manned and unmanned programs, including Mercury, Gemini, Apollo, Skylab, the Space Shuttle, Voyager, and Viking, is discussed in general. There is very little "new" information provided, but there are dozens of color and black-and-white photographs which, in themselves, make the book worthwhile. An index is included.

Kerrod, Robin. *The Illustrated History of NASA.* New York: Gallery Books, 1986.
One of the better books about the manned and unmanned space programs undertaken by NASA, this work was written shortly after the *Challenger* accident. Although it mainly discusses the programs of NASA, there is one chapter devoted to NASA and its facilities throughout the United States. There are hundreds of color and black-and-white photographs. An appendix lists some of the highlights of NASA's first quarter century in chronological order. Contains an index and an epilogue devoted to the STS 51-L mission.

Lay, Bierne, Jr. *Earthbound Astronauts: The Builders of Apollo-Saturn.* Englewood Cliffs, N.J.: Prentice-Hall, 1971.
The focus of most manned spaceflights is usually the astronauts on board. About the only time you read about the scientists and engineers who built the components is when something goes awry. The book takes a look at the Apollo Saturn V lunar launch vehicle and the scientific, economic, and political hurdles which had to be overcome before it would fly. This is not just the story of a vehicle, it is the story of people. The work gives the reader a chance to meet them and to understand their drive to meet the challenge of putting a man on the Moon by the end of the 1960's.

Magill, Frank N., ed. *Magill's Survey of Science: Space Exploration Series.* 5 vols. Pasadena, Calif.: Salem Press, 1989.
This five-volume set covers every aspect of the U.S. and Soviet manned and unmanned space programs, as well as those of nations newer to the space race. In order for the United States to accomplish its missions in space, a variety of support was needed. Most of this support came from the research centers across the United States and the tracking network around the world. Articles in this work cover most of NASA's facilities: Ames Research Center, Cape Canaveral and the Kennedy Space Center, Goddard Space Flight Center, the Jet Propulsion Laboratory, Johnson Space Center, Langley Research Center,

Lewis Research Center, Marshall Space Flight Center, and Vandenberg Air Force Base. The Deep Space Network and the Spaceflight Tracking and Data Network are also discussed. Each essay details the facility and its contribution and includes an annotated bibliography and cross-references.

Murray, Charles, and Catherine Bly Cox. *Apollo: The Race to the Moon.* New York: Simon & Schuster, 1989.
It took a large number of innovative people to take the political aspirations of a president and turn them into the greatest accomplishment in the history of exploration. This work looks at the human side of the achievement. In order to "establish their territory," they established their own community with their own unique language. Engineers, scientists, technicians, and visionaries—they created a technology and overcame enormous odds. Sometimes their lives were adversely affected, but they stuck together as a family. The book is well written and contains an excellent appendix of reference notes. Several black-and-white photographs give faces to the characters discussed in the book.

Newell, Homer. *Beyond the Atmosphere: Early Years of Space Science.* Washington, D.C.: Government Printing Office, 1980.
This is one of the volumes in the NASA History Series, the official history of the U.S. space programs. This book covers the scientific investigations made possible by sounding rockets, satellites, and space probes. The author begins with a look at the early pioneers of rocketry and some of the first space scientists. The National Aeronautics and Space Administration was created in response to the launch of Sputnik 1 and the desire to release the military from its role in space exploration. NASA's design and organization are discussed, along with its interaction with other agencies, the military, and universities. Particular attention is given to the California Institute of Technology's Jet Propulsion Laboratory. There are dozens of black-and-white photographs, line drawings, tables, and charts. An impressive appendix lists source notes and bibliographic references, and there is an index.

Ordway, Frederick I., III, and Mitchell R. Sharpe. *The Rocket Team.* Foreword by Wernher von Braun. New York: Thomas Y. Crowell, 1979.
The men responsible for the launch vehicles that put humans on the Moon also were responsible for the missiles of World War II that brought destruction from the sky. This is the story of the group of German scientists and engineers, headed by von Braun, who developed the science of rocketry from the early 1930's through the Saturn family of launch vehicles. Much of the information about their days at Pennemünde was classified until this book was written. This is fascinating reading about scientists, dedicated to the betterment of mankind, being forced to develop war machines. There are black-and-white photographs, a bibliography, and an index.

Pellegrino, Charles R., and Joshua Stoff. *Chariots for Apollo: The Making of the Lunar Module.* New York: Atheneum, 1985.
This is the story of the Grumman engineers and technicians who had the task of designing and building a spacecraft to land on the Moon. As research flights continued and the launch vehicles were developed, the Grumman people made appropriate changes to the lunar module (LM). The spiderlike spacecraft changed considerably during its early life. Mostly, it had to do a lot of dieting, trimming the weight that the Saturn V could not handle. Perhaps the most difficult feat the engineers accomplished was the unplanned use of the LM as a lifeboat to rescue Apollo 13. The book is full of historical data relating to the LM and the people who gave it life.

U.S. House of Representatives. *United States Civilian Space Programs 1958-1978, Volume I.* Washington, D.C.: Government Printing Office, 1981.
In a very concise report, the Committee on Space Science and Applications has compiled data on all U.S. space activity during its first two decades. After a brief introduction and summary chapter, the volume is divided into fourteen additional sections. The second chapter deals with the space-related issues under consideration by Congress. The remaining sections cover the history of NASA and its relationship to U.S. space policy, NASA facilities and tracking systems, launch vehicles and propulsion, manned spaceflight through 1975, the Space Transportation System, space life sciences, space science programs, materials processing in space, international cooperation in space, interagency and non-NASA governmental space activities, industrial and university support for NASA, space program benefits, and selected future space programs. Appendices contain Department of Defense manned spaceflight plans, NASA funding history, international space agreements, texts of President Jimmy Carter's space directives, documents relating to the legal aspects of the Space Shuttle, major U.S. space organizations, a master log of U.S. spaceflights, and a table of U.S. space orbital payloads by mission from 1957 through 1979.

U.S. National Aeronautics and Space Administration. *Apollo Mission Report: Apollo 4 Through 17.* 14 vols. Washington, D.C.: National Technical Information Service, 1968-1973.
The official report on each of the flights in the Apollo program subsequent to the unmanned Saturn I and Saturn IB missions. Each volume was prepared by the Mission Evaluation Team and contains a wealth of data on the particular flight. There is a mission summary and sections that detail the flight, spacecraft, crew activities, orbital and surface experiments, in-flight demonstrations, biomedical evaluations, and mission ground support. An assessment of the mission objectives, as well as anomalies, is included. Tables summarize the flight trajectory and activity time lines. Descriptions and drawings of the spacecraft, launch vehicles, and experiments packages are included. Considered

to be the definitive study of each flight. Some volumes might have to be obtained directly from NASA.

_____. *Apollo Program Summary Report*. Washington, D.C.: National Technical Information Service, 1975.
Several chapters in this work discuss the role ground-based technicians, scientists, equipment, and facilities played in the successful achievements of the Apollo program. Topics include launch facilities, equipment, and prelaunch activities; the Eastern Test Range and Kennedy Space Center; the Lunar Receiving Laboratory; the Lunar Quarantine facilities; tracking stations; and recovery forces. The book summarizes the effectiveness of the support personnel and equipment. Black-and-white photographs and line drawings add to extensive text, as well as reference listings for further research.

Von Braun, Wernher, and Frederick I. Ordway III. *History of Rocketry and Space Travel*. 3d rev. ed. New York: Thomas Y. Crowell, 1975.
This is the story of the exploration of space from the earliest experiments with rocketry to the final flight of the Skylab program. Hundreds of experts on every aspect of this broad field contributed to the work. Most of the programs of the United States, the Soviet Union, and the rest of the nations engaged in space exploration at that time are detailed, both descriptively and with black-and-white and color photographs. This is one of the best references on the subject. The book also contains a large, chapter-by-chapter bibliography. The authors finish their discussion of the space programs with a look at the future, including the Space Transportation System.

Wells, Helen T., Susan Whiteley, and Carrie E. Karegeannes. "NASA Installations." In *Origins of NASA Names*. Washington, D.C.: National Technical Information Service, 1976.
Ever wonder how a particular spacecraft, launch vehicle, or program derived its name? Although this work is dated, it provides a great number of answers regarding these names. This is one of the volumes in the NASA History Series, and it is a wonderful book for trivia buffs. It discusses the major NASA projects, launch vehicles, satellites, space probes, sounding rockets, and manned spacecraft. This chapter discusses the names of NASA installations. Appendices list abbreviations, acronyms, and terms; international designation of spacecraft; NASA major launch records, 1958-1974; and NASA naming committees. There are black-and-white photographs, an index, and an in-depth bibliography.

Space Centers

Alexander, George. *Moonport, U.S.A.* Los Angeles: W. P. Bronnell, Jr., 1977.
A brief but thorough guide to the Kennedy Space Center, which provides the

reader with a compact encyclopedia of the United States' space program. In addition to chronicling every aspect of the U.S. venture into space, Alexander gives detailed descriptions of the launch vehicles and spacecraft used to accomplish the deeds. There are hundreds of photographs and illustrations to add to the concise text. A glossary of terms relating to the space technology, not otherwise covered in the work, is included. It provides a wealth of information to the high school student as well as the engineer.

Baker, David. *The Rocket: The History and Development of Rocket and Missile Technology.* New York: Crown, 1978.
This large, "coffee-table" book covers the technological and political development of manned and unmanned missiles and rockets. It provides a complete history of solid and liquid propulsion systems from fire-sticks to Moon rockets. Propulsion systems are examined for their advantages and faults and how they influence the design of the overall vehicle. The ancestry of U.S. and Soviet launch vehicles is traced to the war machines from which they were derived, all the way back to their common grandparent, the German *Vergeltungswaffe Zwei*, or V-2. The author concludes the work with a forecast about future vehicles, including reusable, atomic-powered, and interplanetary launch vehicles. A compendium of launch vehicles and ballistic missiles and of rocket-powered aircraft is provided. Each vehicle is detailed with information about its origin, configuration, development and flight history, and descendants. There is a silhouette of the vehicle, scaled for comparison with the others in the compendium. Hundreds of color and black-and-white photographs and illustrations enhance the comprehensive text. The launch facilities and tracking stations used by the United States and Soviet Union are discussed in association with the vehicles launched from them. Includes an index and a bibliography.

Benson, Charles D., and William B. Faherty. *Moonport: A History of Apollo Launch Facilities and Operations.* Washington, D.C.: National Technical Information Service, 1978.
NASA's official history of the Kennedy Space Center, chronicling the growth and development of the U.S. spaceport. The book also shows how the space center impacted life along Florida's coast. Appendices give details on each component of Launch Complex 39, as well as a breakdown of the persons and equipment used for each Apollo mission. In addition, a copy of the Apollo 14 countdown is included and depicts the intricacies of getting a mission off the ground. The book is full of black-and-white photographs and illustrations and contains a highly detailed, annotated listing of sources.

Bilstein, Roger E. *Orders of Magnitude: A History of the NACA and NASA, 1915-1990.* Washington, D.C.: Government Printing Office, 1989.

This is the third edition of the concise history of the National Advisory Committee for Aeronautics (NACA) and its successor agency, the National Aeronautics and Space Administration (NASA). This edition was published to coincide with the twentieth-anniversary celebration of the flight of Apollo 11. The author traces the history of NACA and NASA in concise chapters divided into chronological eras. This is an interesting look at these aerospace pioneers and some of the programs they developed to study air and space phenomena. There are dozens of black-and-white photographs and an index.

Dooling, Dave. "Cape Canaveral and the Kennedy Space Center." In *Magill's Survey of Science: Space Exploration Series*, vol. 1, edited by Frank N. Magill. Pasadena, Calif.: Salem Press, 1989.
One of the essays on the history of space exploration in this five-volume set, which covers every aspect of the U.S. and Soviet manned and unmanned space programs, as well as those of nations newer to the space race. The essay looks at the two separate launch facilities: Cape Canaveral Air Force Station, located on Cape Canaveral, Florida, and the Kennedy Space Center, located on Merritt Island to the northwest. It traces the history of the sites and discusses their historical contributions to the United States' space programs. Contains an annotated bibliography and cross-references.

_____. "Johnson Space Center." In *Magill's Survey of Science: Space Exploration Series*, vol. 2, edited by Frank N. Magill. Pasadena, Calif.: Salem Press, 1989.
One of the essays on the history of space exploration in this five-volume set, which covers every aspect of the U.S. and Soviet manned and unmanned space programs, as well as those of nations newer to the space race. The Johnson Space Center, originally called the Manned Spacecraft Center, is located near Houston, Texas. It was first used as the mission control center for manned spaceflights during the Gemini program. This work discusses the center, its origins, and its role in the Gemini, Apollo, Skylab, Apollo Soyuz, and Space Shuttle programs. Includes an annotated bibliography and cross-references.

Elliot, James C. "Space Centers and Launch Sites in the United States." In *Magill's Survey of Science: Space Exploration Series*, vol. 4, edited by Frank N. Magill. Pasadena, Calif.: Salem Press, 1989.
One of the essays on the history of space exploration in this five-volume set, which covers every aspect of the U.S. and Soviet manned and unmanned space programs, as well as those of nations newer to the space race. There is a brief summary of the facilities, their historical context, an annotated bibliography, and cross-references. The essay is not extensive enough to provide details on all facilities, but it does give a great deal of history about each. Contains an annotated bibliography and cross-references.

314 *America in Space*

Hallion, Richard. *On the Frontier: Flight Research at Dryden, 1946-1981.* Washington, D.C.: Government Printing Office, 1984.
This is one of the titles in the NASA History Series, which provides an official look at the space agency, its programs and facilities. Just a bit northeast of Los Angeles lies a desert region just perfect for testing aircraft. In the southwest corner of the Mojave Desert is the Antelope Valley, a mecca for the aerospace industry. That is where the United States placed its Edwards Air Force Base, and that is where, in 1946, the National Advisory Committee for Aeronautics (NACA) sent a group of engineers and technicians to assist in a supersonic test program. The NACA High-Speed Flight Research Station became the NACA High-Speed Flight Station in 1954. With the coming of NASA, the station was redesignated the NASA Flight Research Center in 1959. In 1976, NASA renamed it the Hugh L. Dryden Flight Research Center. This is the story of the center and the flight testing that occurred there during its first thirty-five years. The information is presented in chronological order and covers such noted aerospace craft as the X-1, X-15, HL-10, X-24A, X-24B, and the Space Shuttle. Also detailed is the research that assisted the development of the Gemini and Apollo spacecraft. There are many black-and-white photographs and line drawings, an index, and an impressive bibliography. Appendices include program flight chronologies on the X-1, D-558, X-2, X-3, X-4, X-5, XF-92A, X-15, lifting bodies, XB-70A, and Space Shuttle approach and landing test program.

Hartman, Edwin P. *Adventures in Research: A History of Ames Research Center, 1940-1965.* Washington, D.C.: National Technical Information Service, 1970.
This is one of the titles in the NASA History Series. It discusses the Ames Research Center, located near San Francisco, California. Ames was established at its present location in 1940, because of ready electric power availability, a climate ideal for flight research (when the fog lifts), a nearby university community, and an urgent need to increase the United States' aeronautical research capability. It is named for the late Dr. Joseph S. Ames, chairman of NASA's predecessor organization, the National Advisory Committee for Aeronautics. The facility is best known for its many wind tunnels, but it also houses laboratory facilities for research and technology development in aeronautics, space science, life science, spacecraft missions, and applications of new science and technology from the space program to contemporary national needs. There are numerous black-and-white photographs, an index, and an impressive bibliography of resources.

Kaplan, Judith, and Robert Muniz. *Space Patches from Mercury to the Space Shuttle.* New York: Sterling, 1986, rev. ed. 1988.
This work, written and published by one of the manufacturers and distributors of cloth patches and vinyl decals, discusses the emblems' design by the astro-

naut crews and other participants in space programs. Overall, the work has been well researched and contains many interesting facts about the origins of these patches. Few people realize how the practice of designing crew patches began. The authors discuss Gemini V's "covered wagon" patch, the first ever flown, and the story behind the hidden "8 Days or Bust." The only major error concerns the Apollo 1 patch. It is an error that did not originate with this book, but is perpetuated by reference to the story of the patch's design. The crew of Apollo 1, officially known as Apollo 204, were killed in a fire that swept through their command module during a ground test. According to the authors, the crew patch has a black overlock border "as a sign of mourning for the lost crew." The patch does have this black border, but if one looks carefully at color photographs or films of the crew, the black border can be seen on the patch. Unless someone went back and airbrushed black borders on these prints, the crew must have been wearing the black-bordered patches before the accident. The book is filled with color photographs of the patches from various manned and unmanned missions, as well as space centers and other miscellaneous events. Contains an appendix listing the U.S. manned flights and an index.

Lolich, Clarice. "The Jet Propulsion Laboratory." In *Magill's Survey of Science: Space Exploration Series*, vol. 2, edited by Frank N. Magill. Pasadena, Calif.: Salem Press, 1989.
One of the essays on the history of space exploration in this five-volume set, which covers every aspect of the U.S. and Soviet manned and unmanned space programs, as well as those of nations newer to the space race. The Jet Propulsion Laboratory (JPL), part of the California Institute of Technology, is primarily responsible for the exploration of the solar system with unmanned spacecraft. This essay details the origin of JPL and its contributions to the space program. Emphasis is placed on JPL's role in the lunar and planetary unmanned programs. Includes an annotated bibliography and cross-references.

Lutz, Reinhart. "Vandenberg Air Force Base." In *Magill's Survey of Science: Space Exploration Series*, vol. 1, edited by Frank N. Magill. Pasadena, Calif.: Salem Press, 1989.
One of the essays on the history of space exploration in this five-volume set, which covers every aspect of the U.S. and Soviet manned and unmanned space programs, as well as those of nations newer to the space race. The essay discusses the launch facility used to place payloads in a polar orbit, unattainable from the Cape Canaveral facility. It tells of the origins of the base and the selection of its location. Contains cross-references and an annotated bibliography.

Muenger, Elizabeth A. *Searching the Horizon: A History of Ames Research Center, 1940-1976.* Washington, D.C.: Government Printing Office, 1985.
This is one of the titles in the NASA History Series. It discusses the Ames Research Center, located near San Francisco, California. This work essentially updates the information found in *Adventures in Research: A History of Ames Research Center, 1940-1965*, by Edwin P. Hartman, which is discussed above. There are numerous black-and-white photographs, an index, and an impressive bibliography of resources.

Rosenthal, A. *Venture into Space: Early Years of Goddard Space Flight Center.* Washington, D.C.: National Technical Information Service, 1968.
This is one of the volumes in the NASA History Series, the official history of the U.S. space programs. This book covers the history of NASA's Goddard Space Flight Center through 1963. The center, named for rocket pioneer Robert H. Goddard, was established on May 1, 1959, as NASA's first major scientific laboratory devoted entirely to the exploration of space. The modern, campuslike complex is located in Greenbelt, Maryland, only thirteen miles northeast of the nation's capital. During the early days (like today), the center was responsible for collecting and housing all the data from every U.S. spaceflight. Its scientists and engineers have developed spacecraft and launch vehicles, including the highly successful Delta. There are dozens of black-and-white photographs, line drawings, tables, and charts. An impressive appendix lists source notes and bibliographic references, and there is an index.

Shortal, Joseph A. *A New Dimension—Wallops Island Flight Test Range: The First Fifteen Years.* Washington, D.C.: National Technical Information Service, 1978.
The Wallops Station, located on Wallops Island, Virginia, was established by the National Advisory Committee for Aeronautics in 1945 to gather information about Earth's atmosphere and its near-space environment. During its first fifteen years, the facility launched more than six thousand research vehicles. Consisting of from one to seven stages, these vehicles were used to gather scientific information on the flight characteristics of airplanes, launch vehicles, and spacecraft and to increase our understanding of the upper atmosphere and space environment. This large volume details the history of the facility, including its role in the development of wartime aircraft and missiles, ramjets, supersonic bodies, hypersonic vehicles, high-temperature research, ballistic missile nose cones, guided missiles, sounding rockets, and Project Mercury. There are numerous black-and-white photographs and drawings and an index. Appendices detail rocket motors used at Wallops, program identification, flight operations, preflight jet operations, and rocket propulsion systems developed at Wallops.

Skinner, David, et al. "The Space Centres." In *The Illustrated Encyclopedia of Space Technology: A Comprehensive History of Space Exploration*, by Kenneth Gatland et al. New York: Harmony Books, 1981.

This section in the book discusses the facilities around the world from which satellites and probes are launched. Each is briefly discussed, accompanied by a map of the area in which the launch site is located. Most of the discussion about each center revolves around the launch vehicles which are launched there. There are two four-page, full-color drawings of the major launch vehicles. Each is drawn to scale for comparison. There are color and black-and-white photographs, drawings, and charts. The book contains a chronology of the major space events since Sputnik 1, a glossary of terms, and an index.

U.S. National Aeronautics and Space Administration. *National Space Transportation System Reference.* 2 vols. Washington, D.C.: Government Printing Office, 1988.

This is the most complete technical reference about the Space Transportation System written in nontechnical terminology. It is an enlarged and updated version of the *Press Information* books published by Rockwell International, maker of the Space Shuttle orbiter. The last Rockwell version was printed in 1984, but because of budget reductions instituted at Rockwell in 1985, their Media Relations Office could not update and reprint it. NASA, however, wanted a new edition when the Shuttle resumed operations after the *Challenger* accident. They contracted with Rockwell to provide the text and artwork. Volume 1 details the systems and facilities, while the second volume covers NASA centers and management. There are hundreds of line drawings and black-and-white photographs. Each system and subsystem is presented in great detail. Emphasis has been placed on the orbiter systems, but there is still a great deal of information about the solid rocket boosters and the external tank. Also detailed are the crew equipment and escape systems, NASA centers and responsibilities, and payloads. There is a summary of mission events, a chronology of the Space Shuttle program, a list of contractors, and a glossary of acronyms and abbreviations.

Van Nimmen, Jane, and Leonard C. Bruno, with Robert L. Rosholt. *NASA Historical Data Book 1958-1968.* Vol. 1, *NASA Resources*. Washington, D.C.: National Technical Information Service, 1976.

This is the first in what was intended to be a series of volumes providing a comprehensive statistical summary of the first decade of the National Aeronautics and Space Administration, from its post-Sputnik creation until the Apollo 8 astronauts became the first men to circle the Moon. This volume measures dollars, people, and things and is designed to provide a reference source for a variety of purposes. The summary documents the immense growth and eventual leveling off of the agency's programs. It covers NASA's budget and financial history, its scattered installations, its manpower resources, and a statistical summary of its contractual history. This work is ideal for the "number cruncher," but it is difficult for the common researcher to wade through its 547 pages. There is no table of contents or index, and one is forced to find things by the "hunt and peck" method. However, it does provide a great deal of information about how the mighty dollar influences the decisions of the NASA. There are scores of tables and charts.

Wells, Helen T., Susan Whiteley, and Carrie E. Karegeannes. "NASA Installations." In *Origins of NASA Names*. Washington, D.C.: National Technical Information Service, 1976.
Ever wonder how a particular spacecraft, launch vehicle, or program derived its name? Although this work is dated, it provides a great number of answers regarding these names. This is one of the volumes in the NASA History Series, and it is a wonderful book for trivia buffs. It discusses the major NASA projects, launch vehicles, satellites, space probes, sounding rockets, and manned spacecraft. This chapter discusses the names of NASA installations. Appendices list abbreviations, acronyms, and terms; international designation of spacecraft; NASA major launch records, 1958-1974; and NASA naming committees. Includes dozens of black-and-white photographs and index and an in-depth bibliography.

Tracking Stations

Christensen, Eric. "The Spaceflight Tracking and Data Network." In *Magill's Survey of Science: Space Exploration Series*, vol. 4, edited by Frank N. Magill. Pasadena, Calif.: Salem Press, 1989.
One of the essays on the history of space exploration in this five-volume set, which covers every aspect of the U.S. and Soviet manned and unmanned space programs, as well as those of nations newer to the space race. The essay gives a summary of the organization of NASA's worldwide network of tracking stations and identifies their significance in the context of history.

Froehlich, Walter. *The New Space Network: The Tracking and Data Relay Satellite System*. Washington, D.C.: Government Printing Office, 1986.
This work looks at NASA's Tracking and Data Relay Satellite System (TDRSS), which permits continuous radio contact between Earth-orbiting spacecraft and ground stations. This system helps to eliminate costly ground-based tracking stations. It also permits radio communications with the Space Shuttle during reentry. Prior to TDRSS (pronounced "tea dress"), this was not possible because of the communications blackout that occurred during the period when a returning spacecraft began to ionize the air around it. The

booklet is filled with color photographs and artists' renditions of the TDRSS, as well as a description of the system's operations.

U.S. General Accounting Office. *Space Exploration: NASA's Deep Space Missions Are Experiencing Long Delays.* Washington, D.C.: Government Printing Office, 1988.
This work is the report of the GAO's findings on four of NASA's proposed deep space missions. The report covers the Galileo mission to Jupiter, the Ulysses mission to the Sun, the Magellan mission to Venus, and the Mars Observer mission. The report provides a general overview of the program, including its objectives, scope, and methodology. There are spacecraft configuration drawings and information relating to cost, schedule, and performance. A chronology of the project, through the date of the report, is presented. There is a glossary of terms used.

U.S. National Aeronautics and Space Administration. *Tracking and Data Relay Satellite System (TDRSS) Users' Guide.* Washington, D.C.: Government Printing Office, 1984.
Although most of us will not have a direct need to use NASA's Tracking and Data Relay Satellite System, many will find this book to be quite informative. The TDRS'S (pronounced "tea dress") is a network of three geosynchronous satellites used to communicate with and track other spacecraft. One of the two operational TDRSes is located over the equator at 41 degrees west longitude, while the second is at 171 degrees west. The third, an on-orbit spare, is at 62 degrees west longitude. The operational satellites are spaced 130 degrees apart to permit the use of only one ground tracking station, which is located at White Sands, New Mexico. Each satellite is carried into low Earth orbit by the Space Shuttle and propelled to its operational position by the Inertial Upper Stage. This document was written to assist in user planning activities, but it provides the researcher with a great deal of technical information available nowhere else. There are numerous line drawings, schematic diagrams, and charts to augment the text.

Van Nimmen, Jane, and Leonard C. Bruno, with Robert L. Rosholt. *NASA Historical Data Book 1958-1968.* Vol. 1, *NASA Resources.* Washington, D.C.: National Technical Information Service, 1976.
This is the first in what was intended to be a series of volumes providing a comprehensive statistical summary of the first decade of the National Aeronautics and Space Administration, from its post-Sputnik creation until the Apollo 8 astronauts became the first men to circle the Moon. This volume measures dollars, people, and things and is designed to provide a reference source for a variety of purposes. The summary documents the immense growth and eventual leveling off of the agency's programs. It covers NASA's budget and

financial history, its scattered installations, its manpower resources, and a statistical summary of its contractual history. This work is ideal for the "number cruncher," but it is difficult for the common researcher to wade through its 547 pages. There is no table of contents or index, and one is forced to find things by the "hunt and peck" method. However, it does provide a great deal of information about how the mighty dollar influences the decisions of the NASA. There are scores of tables and charts.

AMERICA
IN
SPACE

INDEX